D1615259

BARNAVE

BARNAVE

The Revolutionary Who Lost His Head for Marie-Antoinette

John Hardman

YALE UNIVERSITY PRESS
NEW HAVEN AND LONDON

Published with assistance from the Annie Burr Lewis Fund.

For information about this and other Yale University Press publications, please contact:
U.S. Office: sales.press@yale.edu yalebooks.com
Europe Office: sales@yaleup.co.uk yalebooks.co.uk

Set in Minion Pro by IDSUK (DataConnection) Ltd
Printed in Great Britain by TJ Books, Padstow, Cornwall

Library of Congress Control Number: 2022950312

ISBN 978-0-300-27084-6

A catalogue record for this book is available from the British Library.

10 9 8 7 6 5 4 3 2 1

To my brother Richard Hardman, a dedicated doctor
To his wife, Jane Hardman

CONTENTS

List of Illustrations viii
List of Principal Characters x
Acknowledgements xiv

Introduction 1
1 Reluctant Lawyer 6
2 The Origins of the French Revolution According to Barnave 31
3 Political Awakening: Barnave in the Pre-Revolution, 1787–9 41
4 The Assemblies at Romans: The Last Estates of Dauphiné 68
5 From Estates-General to National Assembly 85
6 The Decisive Phase, 14 July–6 October 1789 113
7 The Year 1790 159
8 Barnave's Private Life 188
9 Barnave and the Court Before the Flight to Varennes 203
10 Barnave on the Defensive 220
11 Varennes and Its Repercussions 229
12 The Revision of the Constitution 256
13 Governing in Secret 275
14 The Return of the Native: January–August 1792 302
15 A Long Incarceration 316
16 Trial and Death 336
Conclusion 349

Endnotes 356
Bibliography 380
Index 387

ILLUSTRATIONS

1. Maison Barnave. © Le Dauphiné Libéré.
2. *Louis XV, King of France*, by John Chapman, 1805. © National Portrait Gallery, London.
3. Barnave miniature, by Louis-Marie Sicardi with lock of hair ad verso, 1785. Courtesy of Gallery Jaegy-Theoleyre.
4. *Assemblée des notables*, by unknown artist, 1787. Musée Carnavalet, Histoire de Paris (G.43256) CC0 Paris Musées / Musée Carnavalet – Histoire de Paris.
5. *Charles-Alexandre de Calonne*, by Élisabeth Louise Vigée le Brun, 1784. © Royal Collection Trust / His Majesty King Charles III 2022.
6. *Barnave with Janus head*, by anonymous artist, 1791. © Musée Carnavalet, Histoire de Paris (G.26362), CC0 Paris Musées / Musée Carnavalet – Histoire de Paris.
7. *La France reçoit des trois ordres les voeux de toute la Nation et les présente à Louis XVI et M. Jacques Necker*, by Louis Dubois, *c.* 1791. Musée Carnavalet, Histoire de Paris (P696/3) CC0 Paris Musées / Musée Carnavalet – Histoire de Paris.
8. *Le Serment du Jeu de paume*, by Jacques-Louis David, 1791–92. © Photo 12 / Alamy.
9. *The severed heads of the royal officials murdered in July 1789*, by Anne-Louis Girodet. Bibliothèque nationale (IFN-8410751) / Stanford University Libraries.
10. *Baronne Anne Louise Germaine de Staël as Corinne on Cape Misenum*, by Élisabeth Louise Vigée le Brun, 1807. © Heritage Image Partnership / Alamy.
11. *Déclaration des droits de l'homme et du citoyen*, by Jean-Jacques-François Le Barbier, *c.* 1789. Musée Carnavalet, Histoire de

Paris (P809) CC0 Paris Musées / Musée Carnavalet – Histoire de Paris.

12. Terracotta bust of Barnave, by Jean Houdon, *c.* 1790. Musée des Beaux-Arts Grenoble.
13. Barnave's passport aged thirty. Archives Nationale de France (A.N.W. 13).
14. *Adrien Duport*, by unknown artist, *c.* 1790. © The Picture Art Collection / Alamy.
15. *Assignat* of 200 livres. DEA / G. Dagli Orti / Getty Images.
16. *Portrait de Mirabeau dans son cabinet de travail*, by Laurent Dabos, 1791. Musée Carnavalet, Histoire de Paris, P108, CC0 Paris Musées / Musée Carnavalet – Histoire de Paris.
17. *Louis XVI stopt in his flight at Varennes*, after Domenico Pellegrini, 1796. Bibliothèque nationale de France (FOL-QB-201 (125)).
18. *Portrait de Georges Danton*, by Constance Marie Charpentier, *c.* 1790. Musée Carnavalet, Histoire de Paris (P714) CC0 Paris Musées / Musée Carnavalet – Histoire de Paris.
19. *Les deux ne font qu'un*, by anonymous artist, 1791. Library of Congress Prints and Photographs Division Washington, D.C. (20540 USA, LC-USZC2–3603).
20. *Duportdu Tertre*, by anonymous artist, 1868. Musée Carnavalet, Histoire de Paris (G.42268) CC0 Paris Musées / Musée Carnavalet.
21. *Axel von Fersen*, by Niclas Lafrensen, 1784. © Heritage Images / Getty Images.
22. *Le Roi Janus, ou l'homme à deux visages*, by anonymous artist, after 1791. Musée Carnavalet, Histoire de Paris (G.25643), CC0 Paris Musées / Musée Carnavalet – Histoire de Paris.
23. *The storming of the Tuileries 10 August 1792*, by Jacques Bertaux, 1793. © The Picture Art Collection / Alamy.
24. *Exécution de Louis XVI, le 21 Janvier 1793*, by Charles Benazech, *c.* 1793. © The Picture Art Collection / Alamy.
25. *The execution of the famous Brissot and his accomplices*, 1793. © Classic Image / Alamy.
26. *Barnave in the Conciergerie prison*, nineteenth-century engraving.
27. 'Postmortem', by Barnave. Archives Nationale de France (A.N.W 13).
28. *Exécution de Robespierre et de ses complices conspirateurs contre la liberté et l'égalité*, by anonymous artist, 1794. Bibliothèque nationale de France (QB-370 (48)-FT 4).

⚜

PRINCIPAL CHARACTERS

BARNAVE'S FAMILY

Barnave, Antoine-Pierre-Joseph-Marie, 1761–93.

Barnave, Jean-Pierre, father, 1712–89, avocat au Parlement de Grenoble.

Barnave, Marie-Louise née de Pré de Seigle de Presle, mother, 1735–1804.

Barnave, Jean-Pierre-César du Gua, brother, 1763–83.

Barnave, Marie-Françoise-Adélaide, sister, 1764–1828.

Barnave, Julie, sister, afterwards Mme Saint-Germain, 1766–1845, recipient of Barnave's last letter; she commissioned the publication of his papers.

Barnave, Antoine, paternal uncle, d. 1788, owner of a château at Vercheny where Barnave spent his youthful summers and which he inherited in 1789.

De Presle, Marie-Anne née André, maternal grandmother, through whom Barnave was related to Necker and d'André, q.v. Their common ancestor made and lost a fortune in the Mississippi bubble.

Necker, Jacques, 1732–1804. Though very distant the Barnave family were aware of the relationship.

Staël, Germaine, Madame de, 1766–1814, daughter of Necker, lover of Narbonne, q.v., intermediary between Barnave and Necker.

THE ROYAL FAMILY

Louis XVI, 1754–93, king 1774–92.

Louis-Charles, the 'second dauphin', 1785–95, sometimes called Louis XVII, 1793–5. Barnave was captivated by the boy who sat on his knee in the carriage returning from Varennes.

Leopold II, 1747–92, Holy Roman Emperor 1790–2, brother of Marie-Antoinette. Barnave hoped he would obtain international recognition for the French Revolution.

Marie-Antoinette, 1755–93, she and Barnave ruled France through a secret correspondence in 1792.

MINISTERS

Brienne, Loménie de Brienne, Étienne-Charles de, 1727–94, archbishop of Toulouse, prime minister 1787–8. Barnave called him and Lamoignon 'the devil ministers'.

Calonne, Charles-Alexandre de, 1734–1802, finance minister 1783–7. Barnave called him the 'artful author' of all royal policies in the pre-Revolution and wrote an extended refutation of his *Lettre au roi*.

Lamoignon, Chrétien-François de, justice minister 1787–8.

Montmorin, Armand Marc, comte de, 1745–92, foreign secretary 1787–91.

Narbonne, Louis comte de, minister of war 1791–2. Lover of Madame de Staël, placed through Barnave's influence, his advocacy of war destroyed Barnave's system.

Necker, Jacques, 1732–1894, finance minister 1776–81, de facto prime minister 1788–9. Barnave came to regard his cousin a 'charlatan'.

Tertre, Marguerite-Louis-François Duport du, 1754–93, minister of justice 1790–2. The conduit for the implementation of Marie-Antoinette and Barnave's policy in 1791.

BARNAVE'S ALLIES

D'Aiguillon, Armand-Désiré Vignerot-Duplessis-Richelieu, duc de, 1761–1800, deputy, one of the richest men in France.

Danton, Georges-Jacques, 1759–94, president of the Cordelier Club, later minister of justice. Barnave's link to the popular movement.

Desmoulins, Camille, 1760–94, journalist and Cordelier, initially close to Barnave.

Dumas, Mathieu, 1753–1837, deputy in the Legislative Assembly. He gave up his seat in the berline so that Barnave could sit next to the king and queen.

Duport du Tertre, see above.

Duport, Adrien, 1759–98, *parlementaire* then deputy in the Constituent Assembly. Formed the 'triumvirate' with Barnave and Alexandre de Lameth, q.v.

Girardin, Stanislas, comte de, 1762–1827. Barnave thought he was one of only a handful who showed any spine in the Legislative Assembly.

Jarjayes, François-Augustin Regnier de, 1745–1822, the go-between in the Barnave–Marie-Antoinette correspondence, which is in his handwriting.

Laborde de Méréville, François-Louis-Jean-Joseph, 1761–1801, deputy. Son of a fabulously rich court banker.

Lameth, Alexandre, chevalier de, 1760–1829, courtier then deputy in the Constituent Assembly. Barnave was his best friend.

Lameth, Charles-Malo-François, comte de, 1757–1832. Barnave lodged in his Paris *hôtel* 1789–92.

Lameth, Théodore, 1756–1829, deputy in the Legislative Assembly.

Le Chapelier, Isaac-René-Guy, 1754–94, Breton deputy, co-founder with Barnave of the Jacobin Club.

Menou, Jacques-François, baron de, 1756–1820, deputy.

Mirabeau, Honoré Gabriel, comte de, 1749–91, deputy in the Constituent Assembly, secret adviser to Marie-Antoinette. Barnave was designated to be the number two in his complicated grand project and was in a sense his heir.

Mounier, Jean Joseph, 1758–1806, deputy in the Constituent Assembly. Barnave was his deputy in the Dauphiné revolt in 1788 but in 1789 thought that 'he did not realise there had been a revolution'. Seceded from the National Assembly in protest at the October Days.

Thouret, Jacques-Guillaume, 1746–94, Barnave's staunchest supporter over the revision of the constitution.

Of these, Alexandre and Charles de Lameth, d'Aiguillon, Méréville and Menou formed an inner circle.

BARNAVE'S ENEMIES

Brissot, Jean-Pierre, 1754–92, editor of the *Patriot français* and deputy in the Legislative Assembly. Barnave's most determined opponent, first of his colonial policy and second of his wish to avoid war with Austria.

Cazalès, Jacques-Antoine-Marie de, 1758–1805, leader of the right wing in the Assembly, badly wounded by Barnave in a duel.

Chépy, Pierre, an obscure employee in the foreign office who played a role in getting Barnave sent before the Revolutionary Tribunal.

Dubois-Crancé, Edmond-Louis-Alexis, 1747–1814, deputy, penned scathing attacks on Barnave.

Duquesnoy, Adrien-Cyprien, 1759–1808. Hated Barnave as a bumptious provincial avocat, attacking him both in his private journal and in his *L'Ami des Patriotes*.

Fersen, Axel von, 1755–1810, lover of Marie-Antoinette, tried to push her in a reactionary direction.

Pétion, Jérôme, 1756–94, deputy, mayor of Paris, led the resistance to the revision of the constitution.

Robespierre, Maximilien, 1758–94, deputy, opposed Barnave's colonial policy and restriction of the franchise.

OTHER POLITICIANS

André, Antoine-Balthazar-Joseph d', 1759–1825, influential centrist deputy, Mirabeau's parliamentary manager.

David, Jacques-Louis, 1748–1825, painter, deputy, member of the Committee of General Security.

Lafayette, Gilles, marquis de, 1757–1834, commander of the Parisian National Guard. Barnave disliked him but thought he was the only man who could save the monarchy in 1792.

Malouet, Pierre-Victoire, 1750–1814, right-centre deputy in the Constituent Assembly, attacked by Barnave but helped him in the revision of the constitution.

Orléans, Louis-Philippe-Joseph, duc d', 1747–93, first Prince of the Blood, wrongly suspected of financing Barnave.

Pompignan, Jean-Georges Lefranc de, 1715–90, archbishop of Vienne, deputy, the subject of Barnave's wittiest satire, he later preserved the fragile unity of the Estates of Dauphiné.

THE REVOLUTIONARY TRIBUNAL

Fouquier-Tinville, Antoine Quentin, 1746–95, public prosecutor of the Revolutionary Tribunal that condemned Barnave to death.

Herman, Armand-Joseph, 1759–95, president of the tribunal.

ACKNOWLEDGEMENTS

First I want to thank the two anonymous academic readers of my typescript for their enthusiasm for the book and for helping me to dodge the snares of the culture wars. One of the readers gave such a detailed and expert close reading of the script that the task of the copy editor must have been greatly lightened. Nevertheless that copy editor, Elizabeth Stone, performed her task with great skill and tact – knowing just when to step in and when to stay her hand. I so wholeheartedly agreed with her suggestions that a process which in the past has taken weeks was accomplished in days. Finally, Rachael Lonsdale ironed out any remaining obscurities.

Much of the material I used consisted of Barnave's hastily scrawled jottings which can be hard to read. I am indebted to Joy Jones and Munro Price for helping decipher some of these. I also wish to thank Alan Peachment for alerting me to a holograph document of Barnave's on eBay in which he predicted the rise and disintegration of a united Europe.

This is the fourth book I have published with Yale University Press and I wish to thank Heather McCallum for keeping faith with me over the years and in particular for sorting out some knotty problems concerned with present one. I also wish to thank Katie Urquhart for her help with sourcing the illustrations and Meg Pettit for adding the final polish.

I am always in need of technical assistance and have relied on such stalwart friends as Alan Peachment and Harry Procter. I also want to thank Nigel Leather of Level-1, Northwich, for assistance over the years. Once he formatted ten CD-ROMs from the Archives Nationales for me which were otherwise unusable in this country.

Finally, I owe a very special debt to Emmanuelle Lize who during a chink in the lockdowns managed to film the voluminous Barnave archive in the Archives Nationales. It is so jumbled that even Fouquier-Tinville's goons made little headway in classifying it and only managed to mark the documents of 'special interest' for possible use at Barnave's trial. It would, therefore, have taken me many months to go through the archive in situ even had Covid restrictions allowed.

This is my lockdown book, speeded by forced restrictions, enlivened only by spells of work in my private wood aided by my volunteer friends Rod Fishburne, Mike Barnes and Graham Shaw.

INTRODUCTION

How does one write the life of a man who died at thirty-two, was known for only three of his years but left as well as his published works some 10,000 pages of manuscript dealing with everything under the sun: political theory, foreign policy (his forte), maxims in the La Rochefoucauld mould, nostrums for a long life? A man of contradictions extending far beyond the trope that he was 'a man of the people' and 'a man of the court'. A didactic man of austere morals who dressed as an English dandy, running up considerable tailor's bills. A man who on the same page as meditations in Latin and French on total annihilation after death drew a profile sketch of a naked woman from neck to knee with prominent nipples.

He was a misogynist if we are to judge him by his private aphorisms, and though he had good relations with women at the easy social level, his letters to those about whom he cared deeply – his mother, his would-be lovers and Marie-Antoinette – are full of complaints and tension. A man with a bourgeois father and a noble mother who fought for the rights of his bourgeois 'caste' (his word) yet despised the manners of his colleagues at the Grenoble bar – and at the height of his fame associated almost exclusively with the court aristocracy. An urbanite in a largely agricultural country. An advocate of the sanctity and power of property who privately thought the unemployed should be supported by the state – but not have the vote. A man who thought that slavery was 'absurd' and that 'all is lost through injustice' but considered both slavery and its ancillary trade a necessary evil for the foreseeable future. A man proud of the Revolution and the country that gave it birth who yet thought that without protection France could not survive competition with Britain and the United States – a mercantilist who bought and devoured Adam Smith's *The Wealth of Nations*.

Barnave's life is of interest on three levels: (1) as a parliamentary orator in the first phase of the French Revolution, the Constituent Assembly (1789–91); (2) as a historian and theoretician of the Revolution who is regarded, rightly or wrongly, as a precursor of Marxian dialectical materialism; and (3) for directing the government of France through a secret correspondence with Marie-Antoinette during the last half of 1791.

Barnave also enjoyed a posthumous life as a romantic hero. Possessed of physical beauty and blessed with an early death, he was the model for Julien, the hero of Stendhal's *Le Rouge et le Noir*, in which the author introduces four of his chapters with quotations from 'the immortal Barnave'. The quotations reveal a romantic man. Stendhal's Chapter 19, 'To Think Is To Suffer', has a Barnave epigraph: 'The curiously comical aspect of everyday events conceals from us the very real suffering caused by our passions.' Chapter 24, 'A Provincial Capital' – Grenoble? – is headed by: 'What noise, what a number of busy people! What plans for the future in a twenty-year-old head! What entertainment to divert the mind from love!' And Chapter 31, 'Make Her Afraid', has: 'So this is the wondrous miracle of your civilization! You have turned love into a humdrum affair.'[1]

This romantic image, however, was not the one Barnave presented to his contemporaries, who regarded him as clinical, cool, even callous. His infamous comment on the murder of the king's officials after the storming of the Bastille was considered by many as typical of the man: 'Is the blood that has been shed all that pure?' It has been said that 'never in his writings did the influence of women penetrate his frigidity' and that 'a cord was missing' in Barnave's makeup.[2] Nothing could be further from the truth. He was 'burning inside', and I have discovered four letters of a passionate and despairing intensity which date from his Paris period. These bear out the Stendhal version.

No previous book has even attempted to cover all the aspects of this remarkable man. The best biography to date is in English not French: Eliza Bradby's *Life of Barnave* was published in two volumes in 1915. However, by rejecting as a forgery the series of forty-four letters apiece exchanged by Barnave and Marie-Antoinette in the second half of 1791 she debarred herself from considering the third major aspect of Barnave's work, as does that fine scholar Georges Michon, the historian of Barnave's friend and colleague Adrien Duport.[3] I argue that this correspondence enabled the two to govern France by letter after Barnave's career had officially ended with that of the Constituent Assembly in September 1791.

However, if one allows for the biographer's bias in favour of him, Bradby gives the definitive account of Barnave's parliamentary career; and that is what Barnave was famous for in his lifetime, though I feel his oratory is somewhat overrated. Barnave spoke ad lib from skeletal notes, and I have often used these in preference to the delivered version as being fresher and closer to what he actually thought. In fact, much of Barnave's archive consists of fragmentary drafts, many with crossed-out sections. This poses a philosophical question: what is more characteristic – first or final thoughts; inner or public ones? I see this as an opportunity rather than a problem.

Barnave had a highly original mind, but it was displayed before and after rather than during the time of the Constituent Assembly, when his most original creation lay outside of Parliament in the Jacobin Club, with its nationwide network of affiliated societies. The club is usually associated with Robespierre: he took it over in 1791, but Barnave with Le Chapelier had founded it in the autumn of 1789 and he drew up its regulations. I have found evidence that he planned something like this from July or even February 1789.[4] The club exerted pressure on the National Assembly as well as the king, as did the popular movement through Danton whose many links with Barnave I have uncovered.

Barnave's authorial originality is to be found not in the six pamphlets he published in 1788–9 but rather in the allocution which as a novice barrister he was privileged to make to the Parlement of Grenoble in 1783 which contains his theory of history almost full-blown, with its emphasis on 'the force of things', rather than 'circumstances', as the dynamic of change.[5] His lecture can be summarised as follows: in early 'hunter gatherer' society there is 'primitive equality' (which Barnave claims women 'have entirely forgotten') because no one owns the land. In the next stage the king has the largest share of the land but less than the feudal aristocracy collectively so he is no more than first among equals. The development of towns creates a bourgeoisie (from 'bourg', a town) and these create industrial and commercial wealth, represented by money, which they give the king to form a standing army to protect them from feudal predators. This standing army lies outside the economic framework. If it becomes predatory, it can even be self-financing with its own fiscal agents – in particular tax farmers. These things come about through 'the force of things', not individuals.

These ideas were expanded to incorporate the outbreak (but not the course) of the Revolution when he returned to Grenoble in 1792. He had not predicted the resumption of the struggle between the king and the aristocracy in 1787. The aristocracy defeated the king in the 'noble revolt' but were not to enjoy the chestnuts they had snatched from the fire: 'clothed with an appearance of power they flattered themselves that they could dispense with the monarch but real power eluded them; education, the tide of public opinion was on the side of the commons and power bypassed the aristocracy, as it were, to go straight to the people'.[6] He summarised his theory: 'A new distribution of wealth prepares a new distribution of power. Just as the possession of landed estates elevated the aristocracy, so industrial property elevates the power of the people.'[7]

But, and here he goes beyond Marx's later theory, it is not just brute economic clout which elevates the people but the education and good manners which wealth enables.

Though his historical manuscripts were published in 1843 by Bérenger de la Drôme, at the behest of Barnave's surviving sister, they were ignored both by Marx and de Tocqueville and their importance was brought to the fore only by Jaurès's *Histoire socialiste* (1901–7). Bérenger supplied a title to Barnave's best-known historical work: *Introduction à la Révolution française*. But in 1988 Patrice Gueniffey published a critical edition of the work and gave it a new title: *De la Révolution et de la Constitution*.[8] Gueniffey had discovered among Barnave's papers, confiscated for use at his trial, a single sheet with that title, together with an outline of three chapters.

He assumed that had Barnave lived to publish the work he would have stuck to the three chapters. Apart from the inherent unlikelihood of anyone publishing a book (as opposed to a play) in such a restricted way, Gueniffey overlooked the words written in a miniscule script above his new title: '*commerce et industrie – militaire – hommes et places*' (patronage). Apart from 'commerce et industries', these do not figure much in the *Introduction à la Révolution française*, whose title I retain.

We do not know whether Barnave planned to publish this work, whatever its title. He did, however, intend to publish the much larger opus which he entitled *Réflexions sur la Révolution française* because twice he refers to 'my readers'.[9] Both this work and his *Introduction à la Révolution française* have a strange combination of theory and his own experience in the Revolution. The *Réflexions* also have extensive sections on foreign policy, past and present. He also planned to write another book, a sort of manual on how to organise a free government in France – 'this', he wrote, 'is my enterprise' and he thought that 'the moment was propitious to jot down one's thoughts'. He sketches out an 'Introduction' and then the headings of only seven 'chapters': (1) 'Maxims of a free government'; (2) 'Of liberty in a monarchy'; (3) 'Of the national polity; unity of the National Assembly [*corps national*] in a monarchy', that is, one legislative chamber; (4) 'Of the administration of justice'; (5) 'Of the military force'; (6) 'Of the Administration'; and (7) 'Of public morality'.

His 'Introduction' to this runs:

> Need to found institutions on a basis of principles – of the spirit which should guide them – need for institutions appropriate to a free government to perpetuate the spirit of freedom. That is my enterprise.
>
> Spirit of free governments. Liberty is compatible with monarchy. Its maxims.
>
> Disposition of the French to be free under a king.[10]

This is his credo.

Barnave never – even in his later writings – integrates the actual course of the Revolution beyond 1789 within his general theory. Perhaps for him the defeat of the aristocracy by his class marked the end of history. It is this lack of integration which leads me to doubt whether what is regarded as Barnave's masterpiece, whatever title one chooses to give it, was as important to Barnave as it has become to his readers. It is perhaps significant that two modern editions of the work publish only the first, theoretical, part.[11]

— ONE —

RELUCTANT LAWYER

On trial for his life before the Revolutionary Tribunal in 1793, Antoine Barnave alluded to an 'infamous caricature', a popular engraving of him dressed as a svelte, handsome English dandy but with two profile heads.[1] In 1791 an English visitor saw a realisation of this cartoon 'at the waxworks in the Palais Royal'. Nor would this visitor have needed to travel so far for already 'the caricature was entertaining all the taverns in London'.[2] The Janus figure was a common Revolutionary trope for ambivalence (Louis XVI was thus presented). The Roman god who gave his name to January looks left to the departing year and right to the coming one, glancing back as it were to the *ancien régime* and forwards to the French Revolution. In the cartoon Barnave's left-facing Janus head is captioned 'the man of the people'; the right, 'the man of the court'. The former radical is now Marie-Antoinette's secret adviser, though concrete evidence of this did not emerge until 1913.[3]

Barnave claimed that there was no contradiction. In fact, this duality was present throughout his life and can even be traced back beyond his birth to his parentage: his father was a rich bourgeois lawyer, his mother a noblewoman, which symbolises the explosive mixture which when detonated by a financial crisis would create the French Revolution. An extra catalyst was provided by Barnave's Protestant faith at a time when his co-religionists, though no longer persecuted, lacked 'civil status', something not rectified until 1788.

Sources vary as to Barnave's paternal ancestry. There was the usual conjectural remote ancestor, Latinised as Gononus de Barnava on the electoral list for officers for the tiny town of Saillans in Dauphiné in 1415. We then jump to Barnave's great-grandfather François-Michel Barnave

(1619–98), whose brother, Jean, was a cavalry captain. Jean gave himself the aristocratic addition 'de la Comtériche' from a property he owned, but this did not disguise the fact that he was a *roturier* (non-noble) and as such could not progress beyond the rank of captain. Another source has François-Michel himself as the captain. Either way, his career symbolised the roads blocked even to the upper bourgeoisie, something which was to form a big part of Barnave's (and many others') revolutionary development. Barnave's younger brother was a sub-lieutenant in the artillery, in which Carnot, the 'organiser of victory' for the armies of the Republic, had been trapped as a captain before the Revolution. It has been said that if a natural conservative such as Carnot turned against the *ancien régime*, it was indeed doomed.[4]

François-Michel had a son, Michel (b. 1644), who owned a silk mill. His son, Antoine (one of nine children), a captain in the Maubourg regiment, was himself the father of five, including Jean-Pierre, Barnave's father.[5] Antoine had married a Protestant, Jeanne Grivet, from Orange, and although he himself never converted – indeed leaving money to two Catholic orders – the children were brought up in their mother's faith. She died in 1755 and, having refused the Catholic last rites, was denied a burial in hallowed ground.[6] Antoine Barnave, by a will of 1735, left a total of 4,120 livres (about £170), including 2,000 livres to each of his two sons and 30 livres, plus their dowries, to each of his two daughters. He asked to be buried inside the parish church of Vercheny – a mark of status if granted and of aspiration in any case.

Jean-Pierre (1712–89) studied law at the University of Orange and in 1737, aged twenty-five, bought the office of procureur (solicitor), whose task was to present cases before the Parlement of Dauphiné at Grenoble. The Parlement was one of thirteen 'sovereign courts' in France. They were appeal courts, but they had also acquired a political role through registering royal legislation, which they increasingly dared to modify or even reject. They exercised this role in the abeyance of the Estates-General, the nearest equivalent to the English Parliament, which had not met since 1614. Their re-emergence in 1789 marked the beginning of the French Revolution and of Barnave's meteoric career. The Parlement was easily the biggest employer in Grenoble, a town of some 20,000 surrounded by the mountains from which Barnave's family had come.

Jean-Pierre was an austere man who worked hard, socialised little and married late. He soon built up an impressive business, employing several clerks. He was also a cultured man, to judge from his surviving library. Volumes ranged from the obligatory Rousseau to Pliny, a 1693 history of the Edict of Nantes, whose abolition in 1685 had led to the persecution and exile of Protestants, and works on chemistry and the cultivation of silkworms, which he also pursued. Naturally, Barnave himself had access to the library and two books in particular may be said to have had an influence on him: a book on diplomacy (1774) – by Mably? – and a *Histoire des revolutions l'Angleterre* (1723), which would have prepared him for his favourite modern author, David Hume, and in particular his account of the English Civil War. There was also a work on geography, another of Barnave's interests. Barnave himself would become something of a bibliophile. Jean-Pierre's success enabled him to purchase a small country estate 4 miles to the north of Grenoble in a hamlet called Saint-Robert in the village of Saint-Egrève. The park stretched down to the Isère and the farm was let out to a tenant on a share-cropping basis.

It was definitely a gentleman's residence and one of his clients, Lacoste de Maucune, a judge (*conseiller*) in the Parlement, reading the way his mind was travelling, decided to fix M. Barnave up with a noble wife. In any case, at forty-eight it was time he married, unless he was determined to remain a bachelor like his elder and only surviving sibling, Antoine. It must be said at the outset, and it was a distinction on which Barnave would himself expatiate, that the French noblesse had little or nothing in common with the English nobility. There were about 250,000 nobles in France, some of them as poor as church mice. In England there were only some eighty nobles, peers of the realm who had a seat in the House of Lords. The French noblesse had nowhere like that to sit. They were without an institutional basis of power. But they were privileged in ways the English aristocracy were not. They were exempt from the main direct tax, the *taille*, and, as mentioned, the higher ranks of the army were reserved to them. So their privileges were a nuisance both to Louis XVI (who needed to tax them to pay for naval rearmament) and to the *bonne bourgeoisie* (such as the Barnaves) who were richer and better educated than most nobles and yet saw their careers blocked.

But if you could not beat them, you joined them. For 25,000 livres (£10,000) you could buy the office of king's secretary, which conferred hereditary nobility with the same privileges as a duke. And many did. But these *annobli* posed a dilemma both for the king and Barnave. The king received his £10,000 but the future tax base was thereby reduced. But, as Barnave would write, 'if *annoblissement* was banned, this irrevocable limitation', by turning the nobility into a caste, 'would increase the antipathy between the classes and the humiliation of the lower one'. If, on the other hand, ennoblement continued, the haute bourgeoisie's pool of talent would be drained because all those with 'money and education would rush to be ennobled and the nation would continue to consist of a defenceless multitude'.[7] The merchant, having made his pile of money, is corrupted by it, or rather, 'though he himself remains true to his tastes and habits, he conceives of other ones for his children and gives them a different education'. If there is a king and a nobility in a state, it is inevitable that 'the merchant will make immense sacrifices only to obtain an ambiguous place for his children among the courtiers and noblemen'.[8]

There was a halfway house: 'personal [lifetime] nobility'. The family of Jean-Pierre's intended objected that he was only a lowly solicitor and thought that he should at least join the ranks of the barristers (*avocats*). He had resisted partly because (unlike his famous son) he was no orator and may have had a slight speech impediment. But, under pressure, he took the plunge and soon progressed to being one of the 'consistorial advocates' – an elite of forty men who ruled over the 400 advocates who pleaded before the Parlement of Grenoble. On certain occasions they were invited to sit with the judges themselves.[9] The consistorial advocates enjoyed personal nobility which could not be passed on to their children.

Nobility could not be transmitted by a noble mother either. Lacoste de Maucune was friendly with the widow of an army major with five unmarried daughters on her hands. She was a Protestant and had three properties, including a Paris town house, but they did not yield much income. She rejoiced in the name Marie-Anne de Pré de Seigle de Presle, and her eldest daughter, Marie-Louise, was selected. She was only twenty-four and as Jean-Pierre was approaching fifty her mother wanted money to maintain her in case of his early death. Maucune was scandalised – such contracts should not be made unless the bridegroom was at least 100! – and Marie-Louise herself apologised to Jean-Pierre for her mother's behaviour. Perhaps Maucune thought she was not quite a lady: her grandfather was plain Jean André, who had made a fortune in John Law's Mississippi Bubble and bought nobility the usual way through the office of king's secretary. He engaged one of his daughters to a court nobleman, to the scandal of Saint-Simon. An André ancestor had emigrated to Switzerland after the revocation of the Edict of Nantes and from him descended Suzanne Curchod, the wife of Jacques Necker, finance minister 1776–81 and 1788–90, with whom Antoine Barnave would have important dealings.

Marie-Louise, a 'blonde beauty' with a 'dazzling complexion', was, to judge by her correspondence with her eldest son, Antoine, an intelligent woman. But to judge from her erratic orthography, she had had little education, perhaps because her religion barred her from the Catholic schools and the family could not afford a private tutor such as the young Barnave would enjoy.

Relations between Barnave senior and his mother-in-law rapidly improved when he enrolled as an avocat and when, by the end of the year, she was told she would be a grandmother. She was full of motherly solicitude in letters addressed to 'Madame de Barnave' – the noble apostrophe 'd' often signalled aspiration rather than reality. Robespierre called himself 'de Robespierre' and Danton 'd'Anton' before the Revolution. Jean-Pierre's elder brother, Antoine, the chatelain of Barry and Vercheny, bequeathed his property to '*noble* Jean-Pierre-François Barnave' and in his default to '*noble* Antoine-Pierre-Joseph-Marie Barnave', the subject of this biography. He also, and with no more title, sported a coat of arms: 'or on a crescent argent' (with other details).[10] The Robespierre family also sported a coat of arms, equally without sanction. Significantly, when writing to her son, Marie-Louise signed herself 'de Presle-Barnave'.[11]

Barnave senior, who was a champion of his co-religionists, had in that very year, 1760, won some relaxation of the 1749 decree on Protestant marriages. But to make sure that their children were regarded as legitimate, the couple decided on a Catholic ceremony. But as Madame de Presle explained to Jean-Pierre, a certain amount of obfuscation was needed to get a bishop's licence:

> I do hope you get a favourable response from My Lord Bishop and that you get a prompt response on the reading of the ban and dispensation from needing another. There is no need to say that my daughter is not a Catholic; she is, and we all are in our sense of the word but they will interpret it differently. Try not to explain yourself further. I am persuaded that provided you stick to this line all will proceed without a hitch for [the marriage at] Lyon provided that nothing gets out so we must keep a profound silence.

They chose Lyon because it was 77 miles from Grenoble, and they told no one where they were going. Madame de Presle pretended she was going to Bordeaux to prevent any ill-wishers from Grenoble informing the Lyon authorities.[12]

The marriage took place at St Peter's, Lyon, on 9 September 1760, between 'Noble Pierre-François Barnave, avocat au Parlement de Grenoble, elder [*sic* for 'younger'] son of le sieur Antoine Barnave, former captain of the Maubourg Regiment, and demoiselle Marie-Louise de Pré de Seigle de Presle, eldest daughter of the late Jean de Pré de Seigle Sieur de Presle, Major de la Citadel of Montélimar'.[13] Jean-Pierre was styled 'noble' though he had not yet obtained his personal nobility, but his father is only 'le sieur', which was often used in a condescending way.

This arranged marriage between a couple from different classes and generations was nevertheless seemingly a happy one. Marie-Louise tempered her husband's austerity and brought him into the social round with visits to the theatre and the salons of the haute bourgeoisie. The nobility tended to shun her because, in their eyes, she had married beneath her. In Grenoble the nobility consisted mainly of military officers – Grenoble, on the border with Savoy, was a garrison town – and judges in the local Parlement. Originally, the judges had been bourgeois, but now they were *noblesse de robe* (the lawyer's gown). Nevertheless, it was a judge in the Parlement who had arranged Jean-Pierre's marriage with a noblewoman. And to compensate for imagined sleights, Madame Barnave made herself *plus bourgeoise que les bourgeois*, just as Jean-Pierre and his brother started styling themselves noble.

She drew a line, however, between the haute bourgeoisie and what we would call the lower middle class. That at any rate emerges from an incident in 1765. Madame Barnave had organised a grand reception at her house. Her husband's clerks were included but as the dining room was too small to take everyone, they were put in the offices. However, one clerk who was related to the hostess was allowed in the dining room. The other clerks were so insulted that they left without touching their food and all the lawyers' clerks in Grenoble met in July 1765 to declare their solidarity with their slighted brethren.

The incident caused such a stir that a song in the local patois commemorated it. Its main butt was less the arrogance of Madame Barnave than the jumped-up pretensions of her husband, whose ancestors had come down from the mountains wearing homespun and hobnailed boots. No amount of 'fine bread and raiment could disguise their lack of breeding'. Another song, this time in standard French, attacks Madame Barnave near the bone: 'The estimable wife of this hero / Thinking him at least a knight / Too jealous of her nobility, at derogating takes fright.' Another ditty mocked her for claiming that her husband was as great as Jean de Cambolas, a celebrated lawyer from Toulouse.[14] Brun-Durand notes that 'Mme Barnave was not popular', while Gallier talks of 'the irritability of this vainglorious family', whose 'pretensions to nobility cut little ice'.

By the time of this incident, Marie-Louise had already borne her husband four children. The future politician was the eldest, born on 21 September 1761, and baptised Antoine-Pierre-Joseph-Marie in a Catholic church so as not to prejudice his future career. In 1763, when his mother became pregnant again, he was sent to a wet nurse near Montélimar, of which her brother was now commandant. Shortly after the birth of Marie-Louise's second son, Barnave was brought back to Grenoble. The second boy was named Jean-Pierre-César. But in the family, he was always known as Dugua (du Gua) after a Barnave property called Gua (meaning 'ford').

Now that Marie-Louise had a growing family, her mother gave her advice on household economy – and economy is the operative word. She would give her daughter her servant 'little . . . Grillette'. 'Marion would have liked you to take another kitchen girl so that she could look after the little one. But that would mean you have three servants for the kitchen at high wages which would not do. Domestics like to be paid a lot for little work. Grillette will be plenty for you and it will suffice to give her eight écus (£2) for her first year. She irons a little and doesn't cook badly.'[15]

Soon the boys had a sister, Marie-Françoise-Adélaide (14 July 1764–2 March 1828). Adélaide, as she was known, inherited her mother's beauty and complexion. Julie, the youngest of the siblings, was born on 26 September 1766. She was little and frail, a brunette, studious, with black eyes and small feet which affected her gait. Widowed in 1817, she died in 1845, having prepared her brother Antoine's manuscripts for publication in 1843.

Three years after Julie's birth there occurred another of these comedies of manners which symbolised the Barnaves' social position *entre deux mers*, though they were not as poor as the wine of that name. On 26 January 1769, M. and Madame Barnave, accompanied by their nine-year-old son Antoine, attended a performance of the tragedy *Beverley et le Joueur*, a French version of Edward Moore's *The Gamester*, later set to music by Hector Berlioz. M. Barnave sat in the stalls with the other men, as was the custom, while Madame Barnave with her young son went to the dress circle. Every seat was taken – but there was an empty box. It was locked and had a small notice to the effect that it was reserved for a military commissar serving under the commandant of Dauphiné, the duc de Clermont-Tonnerre. Nothing deterred, Mme Barnave entered the box via an adjoining one, climbing over a balustrade, which necessitated at one point raising a leg indelicately in the air. The manager asked her to leave but she refused; he then summoned the duc de Clermont, who was attending the play in another box, and he sent in 'four Swiss Guards, bayonets at the ready'. M. Barnave persuaded his wife to yield but shouted out, 'Gentlemen, my wife is leaving on the orders of the governor.'[16] The nobles in the audience clapped to see Madame Barnave's discomfiture, whether because they thought she was a bourgeois or because she had derogated by marrying one.

The bourgeoisie, however, stormed out in sympathy and accompanied the Barnaves home, and this 'sort of procession of the prettiest and best dressed ladies of the town' prompted a contemporary to write, 'there is no doubt that our ladies of what is called the haute bourgeoisie are superior in many respects to those who claim to be women of breeding [*condition*] and event to those who really are of noble birth.'[17] Madame Barnave improvised a party followed by a 'ball and collation' and all 'the notable personages of the town attended'. Next day the Parlement assembled to question whether the policing of the theatre should devolve to the local police rather than the military. Clermont wrote to the secretary of state with responsibility for the province, describing the events as 'a sort of riot'. But he was not upheld, and the policing of the theatre was transferred to the civil authorities.

'This took place in 1770', under the relatively liberal or Parlement-friendly rule of the duc de Choiseul, 'but already', as Barnave's editor Bérenger notes, 'it displayed the agitation which would later turn its attention to more serious matters'. Bérenger probably refers to the French Revolution, but he may have been referring to another event which was also called a revolution at the time: the coup d'état of Louis XV and his chancellor Maupeou against the Parlements which occurred in January 1771. Madame Barnave boycotted the theatre, as did the bourgeoisie in sympathy. After a year she yielded to the plea of the authorities that the boycott 'was threatening the survival of an enterprise on which several families relied for their livelihood'.[18]

One can imagine incidents similar to this occurring all over France in the years before the Revolution, with the same sensibilities stirred, the same questions asked. Why should theatres be policed at all, whether by the army or the local constabulary? Why should the noblesse look down on the haute bourgeoisie, who were 'superior in many respects' to them? However, the first provincial manifestations of the Revolution occurred in Dauphiné and one of its two joint leaders, Barnave, had been at the centre of this grotesque comedy of manners. And not just at the theatre, for the little boy was allowed to stay up long beyond his bedtime for the impromptu festivities at his home. It has been justly said that 'there is no doubt that the insult to his mother, who was his first teacher, influenced the later conduct of Barnave'.[19]

There was another incident involving Madame Barnave, recorded on 21 November 1771 by a local diarist with good connections, which can be regarded 'as a continuation of the same affair'. The duc de Clermont-Tonnerre happened to be visiting Madame Dupérier, a neighbour of Madame Barnave's at Saint-Robert. Since the two ladies were 'close friends and relatives', Madame Barnave was there, too, sitting in a chimney nook. Another guest, hoping to ingratiate himself with Clermont, asked her to make way for one of Clermont's friends so they could set up a card table. Madame Barnave had already arranged to join Madame Dupérier's table, but she was so insulted at having been asked to make way for a friend of the governor (just as in the theatre incident) that 'despite Madame Dupérier's attempts to detain her, she stormed off back to her own house'.[20]

The local historian de Beylié thought it was not fanciful to say that Barnave's jottings on 'the grand seigneur' and 'the courtier' were inspired by the behaviour of Clermont-Tonnerre towards his mother. The grand seigneur 'commands with cool authority and brooks no resistance'. However, such men were a dying breed now that 'French vanity and the mingling of the orders in society have permitted a large number to copy them with success'. The courtier 'from his youth upwards has lived in the pure idiom of politesse'. He was subject to 'subtle censure' at court but 'he can scarcely imagine that the bourgeoisie are capable of judging him'.[21] So for the youthful Barnave, though equality of conditions had arrived, the respect which should go with it still lagged behind. And although talent was recognised, not all careers were open to it.

The Barnaves were a close-knit family. Later Madame Roland, a political enemy, would call Antoine 'cold'. He could display the reserve said to be characteristic of his province but his correspondence with the three female members of his family is warm and full of gentle badinage. Bérenger, probably relying on Julie for his information, tells us that the father's busy career 'did not allow him much time for his children', though he did unbutton when regaling them with stories of the great men in French history. Then, 'his cold face became animated, he spoke, he depicted with passion . . . and his son retained every one of these talks'. A distant father, then, for whom Barnave felt 'deep respect'. It was his mother who was the object of 'his tender love and confidences', as he was of hers. She had 'all the sparkle (*éclat*) that goes with a combination of the most amiable gifts of mind, figure and heart'. It has been said that the pride Barnave was to display in the National Assembly but which we can detect also in his earlier career 'came from his mother, the daughter of a chevalier de Saint-Louis, constrained by poverty to marry [plain] M. Barnave . . . a woman as haughty as she was intelligent, for whom the domination of her household was insufficient compensation for the rumples caused by what was considered in those times a mésalliance'.[22]

Madame Barnave seems to have acted as an intermediary between her children and her austere, even severe, husband if we can judge by the start of a long and over-quoted letter Antoine wrote to his father in 1780, when he was nineteen. Barnave, who was assisting his father in his legal practice, had mislaid some document. Since his father was uncommunicative, Barnave was reduced to writing to him, 'having learned from my mother why you have been angry with me'.[23]

Although the Barnaves had used the Catholic rite for marriage and baptisms as a necessary formality, sending the children to a Catholic school would have required a sustained pretence beyond their capacity. So, while Madame Barnave taught the children the rudiments of the Protestant religion, a tutor was hired to teach everything else. The abbé Laurent was chosen – a Catholic but one with catholic tastes. Laurent taught him 'Latin, a little mathematics and later English and Italian. He also cultivated the leisure arts, above all painting'. Barnave specialised in drawing and watercolours, and to judge from his surviving works, especially a self-portrait, was at least competent, though his doodle of a naked woman in profile is barely that.[24] Later, 'philosophy, public law and history, absorbed him' and he would skip from one to the other as relaxation.[25]

It has been observed that having a private tutor, instead of mixing with other boys at school, had its disadvantages, to go with the compensating advantage of 'maintaining the [Protestant] traditions of his family'. For he missed 'rubbing shoulders with men which from an early age teaches tolerance and keeps within salutary limits an exaggerated opinion of oneself'. This is a fair comment: Barnave was arrogant and could be intolerant; and he acknowledges his imperfections only as bars to an attainable perfection of mind and character. The same critic also observes that private tuition gave him the opportunity 'to range over a wide number of disciplines but necessarily gave him a superficial knowledge of philosophy, history and constitutional law'.[26] Barnave, in short, had all the merits and vices of the autodidact – his was a mind unregulated by correction.

'He familiarised himself with English writers and carried his predilection for this nation so far as to imitate their customs and manners with a sort of affectation which, coupled with his social success, hid his character and his talents under a veneer of frivolity.' He loved clothes of an English cut, especially overcoats, of which an enemy said he had dozens. Well-built and 5'4" tall – an average height for the times – with striking, large blue eyes, his swept-back 'blond hair in buckles harmoniously framed a large and high forehead', a proud chin and a slightly retroussé nose. He had a large voluptuous mouth and a smile of disdain played on his lips, revealing dazzling white teeth. His passport description, aged thirty, is more prosaic: 'dark blond hair and eyebrows, blue eyes, medium mouth, large forehead, thin features'.[27] A contemporary thought he looked like 'a young fury'.[28]

He was attractive to women but his attitude to them was ambivalent. He drew a sketch and made notes for a poem on women's breasts: 'I will sing of them like the troubadours, but I will never attain the warmth of the Provencal language' – despite his purchase of a dictionary of the langue d'oc. But he also wrote: 'the study of women is the rock on which all lofty thoughts founder. Too often it is the tomb of scruples. You approach women when you are . . . excitable, changeable. Such a constitution leads to feebleness and a wandering imagination.' 'To please women . . . you have to share their interests. . . . And so men become women.' In 1780, when he was nineteen and meant to be studying for the law, his father discovered and read a cache of letters he had written to women. Instead of rebuking his parent for spying on him, Barnave just wrote that he was 'astonished' that his father should take such a 'serious' view of 'the frivolous products of his spare time'. 'You know what the passions are like at my age' – did his father? – but he was too aware of 'the dangers of libertinage' ever to do anything to damage his 'public reputation and his own self esteem'. This consciousness of what he owed to himself, his 'gloire', would remain with him to his dying day.

Barnave would spend his vacations either at his uncle's property at Vercheny, or on the estate at Saint-Robert, where his passion was for riding. He delighted in riding down to the river at Saint-Robert via the steep, wooded escarpments. On one occasion before setting out for Vercheny, he gave his mother strict written instructions on how the horse he left behind should be treated. To make sure he wrote to Julie: 'Just give my mother a gentle reminder to pay great attention to the care of my horse. I hope she has not lost the piece of paper I gave her – every point in it is of importance. She must not let David [his father's tenant] or even my father get her to make any changes. My Saint-Egrève horse likes to have special treatment.'[29]

DUGUA

Barnave was very protective of his siblings, good-humouredly chiding his sisters with somewhat laboured badinage on their childish flirtations. With his younger brother Dugua, this protectiveness went to extreme lengths. When he was sixteen, he challenged a man who had insulted his brother, then fourteen, to a duel. It was a swordfight and Barnave was wounded, not deeply but inches from his heart. In Paris he would fight a duel with two noble deputies, one of whom he badly wounded. Duelling was normally the preserve of the nobility; and that is perhaps a clue to his actions.

Dugua was a brilliant mathematician, and it was decided to send him to the artillery academy, the École militaire de Génie, which had been founded at Mézières (Ardennes) to train artillery officers. This was one of the first military academies and artillery would play a major part in Napoleon's victories. Dugua passed out top of his class and the abbé Bossu, the chief examiner, said he had never met a candidate who knew more.[30] In December 1783 he was garrisoned in Paris as a sub-lieutenant when he fell ill. We do not know the complaint, but it must have been serious because Barnave, without telling his parents, borrowed money and galloped on his well-tended horse the 358 miles to Paris. There he tended his brother for three months but to no avail: Dugua died in his arms on 17 March 1783 and, a rare distinction, was buried inside the church of Saint-Laurence.[31]

Reading Barnave's appreciation of his brother feels like eavesdropping on a confessional. In 1855 Saint-Beuve reviewed Bérenger's edition of Barnave's works, recording his surprise that they had not had more impact. He considered that 'he lamented his brother in heart-felt sentiments altogether in the antique style'. Barnave wrote:

> You are one of those whom I plucked from the world to place next to my heart. Alas! You are no more than a memory, a fleeting thought, no more palpable than a leaf in the wind or an insubstantial shadow. But my heart and senses can still embrace you; and for your brother your beloved image will never be extinguished, never become a mere phantom. Always in my thoughts, you will come to brighten my solitude. In life you were ever the companion of my

pursuits. We spent those sweet early years together. We grew up side by side and the bonds of love grew with our strength. You outshone your years, and your excellent qualities exceeded your parents' expectations. Then when you were far away [at Mézières] I took pride in singing your praises.

Oh! Dear companion. You still are and I hope you always will be with me. When a gentle thought comes to me, I will associate you in my happiness. I will summon you especially when I am contemplating some noble deed and take a sweeter pleasure in it from contemplating your smiling face. Often you hover over my thoughts as I drift off to sleep. I do not hide from you, but it is true that when I dwell on my shortcomings, I do not try so hard to summon you up. Then I no longer see you smile. Oh! Your beautiful face is a truer guide than men's morality.[32]

Barnave also wrote a remarkable critical appreciation of his brother's cast of mind – as remarkable for its psychological insight as for the mind described:

He liked literature but his extreme youth, the attraction of pleasure, the long and relentless study of mathematics and the mental laziness which turns to literature for pleasure rather than consolation and instruction, left him little time for reading. However, he read rapidly and lost nothing. He had a retentive memory not only for things but also words. So, he had a passable knowledge of French and Italian literature. Bad taste was impossible, given his exquisite sensibility, cool head and broad intellect. And familiarity with abstractions taught him to discern nuances that the multitude missed. But I think he was too headstrong to be a good judge and his verdict was based on feelings. He couldn't get outside of himself to put himself in the place of a century, a people or a class of men. His heart ruled his head. He looked for the man in the writer and his affection for the author judged the work. With him the alignment of a book with his passions and his principles was always the primary consideration. He could certainly have distanced himself from his prejudices, but he didn't want to and that too was part of his character. For he had no pretensions, no curiosity; but rather a supreme indifference to what others thought of his mind.[33]

Barnave returned home to comfort his family. Naturally his mother was devastated and remained so for a long time. Barnave wrote an account of a day in her life that autumn. Although deeply felt it too is a literary exercise and none the worse for that. He entitles it: '*Sur ma mère*':

> She had got up feeling ill; we all went down to lunch; after a bit she joined us, but she didn't touch the food. This upset us all.
>
> Since she had a stomach ache, I suggested coffee. She drank some. For the rest of the day, she felt better but we found her melancholy. She was so delicate and tender that the smallest thing awakened deep emotions.
>
> The mistral was blowing. All day it rattled the trees against the windows and brought down the last leaves of the year. In the evening as the day drew to a close, our mother, Adélaide and I went for a walk. On our way we sang tender, sad songs [probably from Gluck's *Armeda* because afterwards] we spoke of the talents of Madame Saint-Huberti [who had created the role of Mélisse and toured the Midi with it].
>
> In the evening the wind, the clouds and the swirling leaves sang a sad song. We were moved and gradually silence replaced our tender conversation. 'This wind makes me sad' . . . [our mother] said. A moment later I spoke, and she said nothing more. She was oppressed. She remained so for some time despite our words and caresses, to which she was unable to respond. Finally, the display of our affection calmed the violence of her agitation. We managed to get through to her . . . with an effort she was able to pronounce my brother's name, allowing herself to rest on my shoulder. Her overworked nerves relaxed; she sobbed; tears gave her relief. Our sympathy evoked hers; I portrayed a Dugua happier than we were, happy if he could see all the traces of him that he had left behind in our hearts. We promised to strive all our lives to console each other for our loss. Her tears flowed more freely. She became calmer; but for the rest of the walk, we remained silent, and the cause of her suffering stayed with us all.[34]

⚜

It was Barnave's habit to write a retrospective of his personal development at the end of each year, noting where he had done well, where he could do better – the sort of school report children nowadays write themselves. A young man's exhortation. That for 1784 does not directly mention Dugua's death that March but it is not fanciful to attribute to it the kind of epiphany it records, a moving up a gear, a heightened or, as he put it, 'exquisite sensibility'. He writes: 'The summer of this year and the preceding spring was a time when my thoughts were more exalted, my ideas were nobler, my feelings were grander and raised to another level; and these things were accompanied with a more active, livelier turn of mind, an exquisite sensibility and perfect execution I had not known hitherto.'

But there was also a new restlessness, a disquiet, less balance between work and play. 'I noticed things more keenly and had more new ideas but also developed them less, less constancy, less concentration. . . . My esteem for men and things followed somewhat the same course as my ideas; my feelings for them have deepened but my life has become more dissipated in consequence, more practical, less theoretical [*plus éloigné du cabinet*].' 'A great defect of mine' was to 'criticise' my earlier writings instead of improving them and 'following up on riches already acquired'.

He attributes this malaise, this 'weakness, uncertainty and laziness of my mind and character' 'more than anything else to lack of encouragement, of emulation and immediate goal'. 'Yes, my situation offers some resources' but it 'lacks immediate prospects and everything that stabilises, encourages and strengthens'. The 'lack of encouragement' obviously refers to his father, who blamed him for his extravagance, dissipation and, as we have seen, his dealings with women. In that letter he had said explicitly, 'If one thing has damaged me – and I say this with bitterness – it is your lack of confidence in me.'[35]

One wonders also what effect his three-month sojourn in the capital had had on him. It has been suggested 'that it was certainly at this time that he received instructions to develop the Neckerist following in Dauphiné'. A well-informed enemy wrote: 'From the very beginning Barnave was Necker's sworn ally and his agent in Dauphiné during the first disturbances in that province.'[36] He was doubly if distantly related to the once and future minister through the connection with Necker's wife mentioned above and also through that wife's cousin, née d'André, who had married Necker's brother. There was certainly a strong Neckerite network in Dauphiné, a province whose nascent industry had received financial support from the minister. The Dauphiné banker Claude Périer was in regular contact with Necker's bank. Périer was to help bankroll Barnave's lifestyle when he represented Dauphiné in the National Assembly.[37]

While in Paris Barnave would have noticed the beginnings of the short-lived economic boom resulting from the end of the American war in 1783 and the 'pump priming' of the economy by the new finance minister, Necker's rival Calonne. He would have heard of the financial crisis which brought Calonne to power. He would have seen new buildings going up on all sides – evidence of the luxury he deplored, but also of what Talleyrand famously called 'the sweetness of living' in this Indian summer of the *ancien régime*. And could it have been his visit to Paris that made him think there was more to life than riding his horse, fencing, looking after his sisters, visiting provincial compeers and dutifully ploughing on with his legal practice? For this was now his main but not his only activity.

For three years Barnave had been a practising barrister pleading before the Parlement of Grenoble. When he was seventeen his father, now sixty-nine, had indicated that he wanted his eldest son to take over the family practice. Barnave consented, 'though the profession you wanted me to follow was little to my taste, given the headlong decline in its status that I have and continue to witness'. This must have been hurtful to a father at the top of that profession. In his private meditations, Barnave is more explicit, saying that he will bring to the profession 'my own probity and nobility, marvellously burnished by youth, by the advantages of wealth and by the elegant manners which are so foreign to the bar'. He also tells his father that he only expects to achieve a 'middling' position at the bar because his temperament is not suited to acquiring the 'long and hard-won erudition' requisite for success.[38]

'However, the lack of opportunities in and the uncertainty of all the other careers available' gave him no choice. For what else could he do without a revolution? He could follow several ancestors and his own younger brother into the army, but their example showed that as a *roturier* he would be unlikely to progress beyond the rank of captain. He could be a judge in a lesser court like Mounier, his Dauphiné comradein-arms in 1788/89, or like his father combine several posts as judge in a manorial court. An obvious ambition would be to be a judge (*conseiller*) in the Parlement. After all, his father as *avocat consistorial* was an associate *conseiller*. And the political aspect of a *parlementaire*'s role would have attracted him: 'a strong attraction concentrated all my attention to works on public [constitutional] law'. However, this was well-nigh impossible given his religion and the 1762 ruling restricting admission to the Parlement to those with four degrees of nobility in the male line or relatives of sitting members.

So, a barrister it had to be for the time being; but he did not intend to remain one: 'Whatever public career I wish to follow, for now I must opt for the bar.' At least having a job would give him 'domestic independence'. Until he took up his seat in the Estates-General at Versailles when he was twenty-seven, Barnave lived at home – dividing his time between three of them: the town flat his father rented in Grenoble near the Parlement, Saint-Robert and Vercheny. He had complained that, while his father was occupied with his business, his mother and uncle managed the estate without reference to him, even though he, like Dugua, had matured more quickly than most boys. Maybe now he was not reliant on pocket money he would be listened to.

But he was determined that although he would pursue his legal career conscientiously, he would not let it 'hold back the development of my taste, my ideas or my character and morals. This can be done (1) by the way I exercise the profession' – that of a gentleman? – and (2) by time given to other occupations, in particular in acquiring 'the necessary skills for my future occupation'. And he must be careful not to 'unlearn' the culture he had acquired, especially history and philosophy, which would be necessary for his 'future employment'. But he gives no indication as to what that future employment might be, nor can we imagine one for him without the fortuitous arrival of the French Revolution.

To practise as an advocate Barnave needed a degree. There were two universities in Dauphiné, one at Valence and one at Orange. Both were of poor quality and a government commission in 1738 had recommended closing them both and setting up a unitary university for the province at Grenoble, which had one briefly in the fourteenth century. Naturally, the proposal was backed by the local Parlement but a new government, preoccupied with the War of the Austrian Succession, shelved the idea.[39] So Barnave, like his father, got his formal qualifications at the University of Orange. Formal is the operative word: the candidates were given not just the questions but the answers in advance and of these they only had to mouth the first words. The residence requirement was waived for a fee. Graduates were mocked as 'the asses from Orange'.

Barnave's actual instruction would have come from one of the three law professors in Grenoble who gave private tuition and presumably from his father. Barnave travelled to Orange on 25 September 1779 and on 27 September received the degree of Bachelor of Law. He presented himself at 6 a.m. It would have been logical to have done the whole thing on the 26th but the regulations stipulated that he must spend at least twenty-four hours in Orange to give custom to the local hostelries. He was not required to subscribe to the tenets of the Catholic faith but he was required to sign, as Antoine-Joseph Barnave de Grenoble, a declaration that he subscribed to the bull of Innocent X (1653) and his successor Alexander VII (1656) condemning the works of Cornelius Jansen as heretical.[40] Since Barnave was a Protestant, this did not pose any difficulty – except perhaps one of keeping a straight face. He continued his studies for a further year at Grenoble before returning to Orange to obtain his licence to practice. The formalities were the same, 'with this sole difference that the honoraria were more abundant, and the compliments exchanged between the professors and the candidate were more fulsome'.

Barnave was a conscientious barrister even though the career did not claim his heart or entire attention. Two of his cases were his first published works. One concerned twenty-nine members of two extended and much intermarried families, the Bouillanne and the de Richaud, living in the remote Quint Valley. They claimed that as nobles they were exempt from certain taxes, but their nobility was challenged by the fisc and by their neighbours. The neighbours had a vested interest in making them pay because the taxes in question were *solidaire*, that is, the village was responsible for a fixed amount and would have to make up for the exemption of the claimants.

There was no doubt that the nobility of both families went back a long way. Tradition had it that their two ancestors, then butchers, had rescued the future Louis XI (1461–83), then the dauphin ruling Dauphiné, from the clutches of a large bear with their cleavers. When he became king, Louis, known as the spider because of his web of spies, ennobled both butchers. Certainly, a bearskin featured on their coat of arms. Barnave spoiled a rather good story by dating their nobility back further to the fourteenth century. The question was not whether they had been ennobled but whether they had forfeited their nobility by their lifestyle and were liable to the taxes in question. They were peasants in every other respect than their birth – driving their plough but wearing a rusty sword as their neighbours spitefully jested. The family were so poor that no other noble family would marry into it and so proud that they would not marry beneath them. So, they intermarried for four centuries. Technically, you could forfeit or 'derogate from' your nobility by engaging in trade, practising the Protestant religion or generally failing to 'live nobly'.

Barnave argued that several royal ordinances permitted or condoned nobles trading and that the rationale behind the ban was not one of honour but the practical one that if all the nobles became merchants, the fisc would suffer. Just because you replace a dead sheep, it does not make you a trader; nor does amusing yourself making a pair of shoes make you a cobbler, he argued, like Aristotle. Barnave regaled the judges with many more such sallies. Whether his witticisms and at times specious arguments succeeded we do not know. In a sense it did not matter. The case was heard in 1787 and three years later nobility itself was abolished. But when in 1794 punitive measures were introduced against nobles, one imagines that the Bouillanne and de Richaud family endured them not just stoically but proudly as confirmation of their status. One imagines also that their spiteful neighbours were as ready to denounce them to the agents of the Committee of Public Safety as they had been to those of the fisc.[41]

⚜

Given his views on the social and intellectual inferiority of his new colleagues at the bar, it may seem surprising that they should have chosen him to deliver the annual address to the Parlement on behalf of the advocates at the closing ceremony of the judicial year in July 1783.

In choosing Barnave to give the address, his colleagues must have known that his real interest was constitutional law and so would have wanted him to deliver a thinly veiled political speech. This was his break. In his autobiography he writes, 'in 1783 I gave a lecture to the Parlement of Grenoble on the necessity for the separation of powers [legislative, executive and judicial] in the body politic'. He was well prepared: 'I had already read and analysed the majority of French works then existing on political laws before I acquired a smattering of the elements of civil law.'[42] Political law in 1783 was the relationship between the crown and the Parlements.

Barnave's central argument is that 'the combination of military command and the unrestrained ability to raise taxation always gives the possessor a superiority which destroys the balance between [executive, legislative and judiciary] powers' famously extolled by Montesquieu in his 1748 *De l'esprit des lois*, based on a misunderstanding of the English constitution. This balance Barnave implies should be guaranteed by a written constitution instead of the ill-defined Fundamental laws of the kingdom: 'My hypothesis requires . . . a complete and precise body of laws to define the constitution.' For 'general legislation cannot be exclusively exercised by a single power without either its increasing without bounds or resulting in the subversion of the state'. This ran counter to the central tenet of absolute monarchy famously asserted by Louis XV in the *séance de flagellation* of 1766, written by the young crown lawyer Charles-Alexandre de Calonne, that 'legislative power belongs to me unfettered and undivided'.

Barnave considers first the 'boundless increase' in royal power in Europe from the feudal period and then the 'subversion of the state', culminating in a phantasmagorical portrayal of a decadent France at the end of Louis XV's reign. The early princes started by using the mystique of the Catholic Church to enhance their authority and 'enslave the nation'. But no sooner had the prince achieved that than he used the nation (which hated the clergy as much as the king did) to muzzle the Church.

Then 'he will be able to arm the people against the feudal magnates [the king and the Third Estate, Barnave's perennial dream] because the people hate their superiors and fail to realise that equality between the subjects is *a common servitude* [another leitmotif]'. But no sooner has the prince broken the magnates than 'he raises them up again to play them off against the people, having turned independent rivals into servile associates who have emanated from his power and cherish his grandeur as the source of their éclat' (Louis XIV). But this association in itself dilutes the prince's power because 'having created enough for himself, he has to create more for them [his new partisans]'; 'no matter how large his court, his power must continue to expand in order to satisfy all the courtiers', who are 'the children and defenders of arbitrary government'. Men take the place of laws.

All this is made possible by the growth of regular armies. At first the people who have been 'softened up' welcome this alternative to irregular armies, which create havoc when they are disbanded. They are proud of an army which protects them and are happy to pay for it. But they have to pay more and more because the king needs more and more 'gold' to placate those whose real power he has undermined with the help of the people, that is, 'the magnates who with great credit and honours have only a small amount of property' and 'the clergy because he had deprived them of their empire but still needs their endorsement'.

However, the bulk of the money goes to the tax collectors who need to be compensated for their public execration: 'to recruit them one has to compensate them'. He had in mind particularly the farmers of the indirect taxes – a group he also lacerates in one of his court cases and who would be guillotined en masse in 1794. 'Soon a state within a state arises. The tax farmer now a prince himself will have his own tribunals and army. His soldiers will be paid more than those of the monarch and his rigorous orders will be enforced with more bloodshed than is required for the policing and defence of the realm.' What Barnave could not have realised was that even as he was delivering his speech (July 1783), Louis XVI, with some misgiving because he regarded them as 'columns of the state', was planning to abolish the syndicate of tax farmers. It led to a crisis from which Barnave's bête noire, Calonne, would emerge as finance minister.

Barnave now drifts into lurid reverie: 'A time comes', and here he is surely thinking of the end of Louis XV's reign after the 1771 coup against the Parlements, 'when this corruption of the body politic, this insane despotism hurtles towards its destruction'. 'All virtues, especially patriotic virtues, have been forgotten. The love of gold, luxury, frivolity is in the saddle.' People spend instead of earning. 'The government preserves the outward trappings of strength, but this is very deceptive.' 'No one loves the constitution' and most people, taxed out of existence in order to put wealth into fewer and fewer hands, emigrate to find gainful employment where they can. The stupefied and enslaved remnant are kept down only by the army. But with profitable labour abandoned the prince can no longer afford to pay it. 'At the fatal hour the soldier wakes up and debates whether he should be a satellite or a master. He pronounces. At a given signal, prince, empire, government, all evaporate and the place occupied by the state is given over to a marauding and predatory band.' But, he writes with dramatic irony, 'To say that equilibrium once upset can only be restored by a violent revolution would, I think, be to underestimate human inconstancy and vicissitudes.' Frenchmen do not have the perseverance to see a revolution through.

⚜

Barnave's analysis of the rise and fall of regimes adumbrates many of the ideas which he would develop in the *Introduction à la Révolution française*. What he omits – because it had not yet occurred and he did not predict it – is the resumption of the struggle between the king and the aristocracy (1787–8), resulting in their mutual exhaustion and leading to a new development: the Third Estate, the commons, seizing power from both in 1789. But he does realise that the apparent strength of the great nobility is illusory because 'the size of their property is mediocre' and they are entirely dependent on 'gold' from the king. And to obtain this 'gold' the king is forced to overtax the land – which many consider the fundamental vice of Calonne's reform package, which sparked off the Revolution.

Barnave would criticise Calonne for introducing 'excessive equality' into his devolved administrations. This criticism is foreshadowed in the 1783 lecture: the prince 'can arm the people against the magnates because the people hate their superiors and fail to realise that equality among subjects *is a common servitude* [Barnave's emphasis]; but scarcely have the magnates been abased than he raises them up again to oppose them to the people, having exchanged independent rivals for docile associates emanating from his own power'.

This argument would explain why the king turned from opposing the nobility in 1787–8 to defending them in 1789. Perhaps the key word is 'subjects': equality is inappropriate for 'subjects' in a despotism but desirable for 'citizens' in a democracy. Earlier in his lecture, Barnave treats of the origin of power. In a time of primitive equality, there is 'the sovereignty of the people or the entire disposal of power'. Authority is exercised by several and is but 'a commission from the people'. But soon 'nature and the arts create personal inequality among men'; and 'sooner or later so many inequalities create political inequalities'. But come the Revolution, Barnave would insist that both king and National Assembly were delegates of the people, where true sovereignty resided; that is, they had received 'a commission from the people'.

In Barnave's papers there is what I take to be a draft for this speech. It contains a critique of the *parlementaires* which he would have been unwise to deliver in their presence. The *parlementaires*, he argues, were annoyed at being excluded from a system they had helped to create. So they allied with the other group that had helped the king to power – the Third Estate, which had lost the right to consent to taxation. Their resistance to royal policies was 'badly conceived' based as it was on a combination of 'old ideas which were no longer applicable' and 'new ideas inconsistent with their actual conduct'. The new ideas were that the Parlements were the true representatives of the people but they undermined this claim by 'the self-interested cowardice of a portion of its members' – by which he meant that their resistance was merely to raise their price to the king, who bought them off with pensions so that the pensioners formed a '*parti ministériel*' within the Parlements. This as often as not led to 'base compliance'. 'As I propose', Barnave planned to tell his auditors, 'to develop in some depth [my theories on] the essence, the interests and the conduct [of the Parlements] I will say no more for the present.'[43]

⚜

We have seen how Barnave's private position in society and his career were determined and felt as friction between the haute bourgeoisie, to which his father belonged, and the nobility, from which his mother stemmed. His career options were limited by the 1762 *règlement* in the

Parlement of Grenoble, which restricted entry to those with four generations of nobility in the male line, and the Ségur Ordinance of 1781, which imposed the same restrictions on commissioned entry into the army. His social relations were symbolised by the theatre incident. But in the crisis of the regime which began in 1787 the private and the political were about to merge with the realisation that political change could happen and that only this could resolve the social issues. When he looked back on these developments near the end of his life his analysis was not very different even with the benefit of hindsight.

— TWO —

THE ORIGINS OF THE FRENCH REVOLUTION ACCORDING TO BARNAVE

The point at which it dawned on Barnave and many others that the earth was shifting was the convocation of the Assembly of Notables, which met on 22 February 1787. Barnave is explicit: 'From the convocation of the Notables [31 December 1786] my whole attention was directed to political matters . . . [which] stirred all my mental and spiritual faculties.'[1] Louis XVI, on the advice of Calonne, his finance minister (1783–7), assembled the Notables, a consultative body, to obtain backing for a comprehensive reform package, which encountered objections from all sides, not least Barnave. To see how this situation arose we can do worse than follow Barnave's own 1792/3 analysis of the origins of the French Revolution up to the meeting of the Notables. The general lines of his analysis had already been adumbrated in his 1783 address: the link between taxation and a standing army; the king using the Third Estate to subdue the magnates and Church and then giving them wealth instead of power in order to keep the Third Estate in check. This replaced the ideal alliance between king and the Third Estate.

Though he ranges over antiquity, Asia and even Africa 'to understand the place we [in the French Revolution] occupy in a more extended system', Barnave quickly homes in on Europe: 'It is in contemplating the general trend which from feudalism to our days has led the European governments successively to change their shape that we may clearly see the point at which we have arrived and the general causes which have led us there.'[2] He uses the three Aristotelian categories of government: aristocracy, monarchy and democracy (which includes constitutional monarchy, his preferred form). The basis of aristocratic rule is 'landed property', that of monarchy is 'public force' and that of democracy is 'moveable wealth', the product of commerce and industry.[3]

In the Middle Ages, when towns were few and tiny, 'moveable wealth' scarcely existed. 'The rule of the aristocracy endured as long as an agrarian people were ignorant of or neglected the [mechanical] arts', which 'the barbarians' had destroyed together with the Roman Empire.[4] When land was the basis of power, though the kings had the largest individual holding, the magnates collectively had more. So, the king was merely *primus inter pares* (first among equals). By the seventeenth century, however, Louis XIV was able to boast on his inscriptions that he was *nec pluribus impar* (not unequal to many).

For, gradually, 'those great factories which are called towns' developed and 'through their union were able to offer an efficacious resistance to the power of the great landed magnates'. The great feudatories represented a centrifugal or 'federative tendency' – always a bugbear for Barnave – the towns a centripetal or unitary one. Steadily the town (bourg) dwellers (literally, the 'bourgeois') amassed enough wealth to buy up portions of the land of an aristocracy whose wealth was being drained by an increasing love of luxury and empty display.

A transitional stage was reached. 'The people, having acquired some wealth through the development of industry, consented to give a portion of it to the prince to obtain his protection against the magnates . . . and he saw his power emerge from a long tutelage.' 'With the product of taxation, he paid for the judges and for the whole machinery of government, but he did something more important . . . which made for a governmental revolution': he created a standing army. 'When aristocratic and democratic forces are equally balanced . . . royal power manages to subjugate them both by playing them off against each other.' But after using the people to subjugate the aristocracy, the ruler uses the aristocracy to restrain the further advance of the people. He does this by utilising the prestige of the aristocracy, which has survived the elimination of its real power, and by letting it staff a centralised army – the 'noble spirit has degenerated into a militarised servility'.

But there was a weakness in the royal position – at least there was in France: the Parlements. Just as they 'had been the principal agents of the aggrandisement of royal power [extending the king's writ over the whole kingdom as new provinces were acquired], so they were of its decadence'. The kings in their reluctance to assemble the Estates-General (the nearest equivalent to the English Parliament) had used the endorsement of the Parlements to 'sell' their legislation and especially their unpopular taxation and loans to the people. Furthermore, 'in their desperate search for money they sold offices and the magistracy', which could not now be dismissed as they owned their posts, 'was independent. It had been bourgeois and royalist; it became noble, feudal and refractory. There resulted a combination extremely unfavourable to power, having the judiciary against it; because then it had to combat the very force which was meant to support it.'[5]

This meant that paradoxically the English king in Parliament – a polity which had resulted from a civil war which was worth the bloodshed – 'secured a greater level of obedience than the *ancien régime* government of France, which was almost despotic but in which the judicial bodies were directed by a principle of volition contrary to that of royal power.'[6] The prime example of this paradox related to taxation. 'Despotism . . . pillages private property but so far from increasing the yield from taxation, it never dares to seize as much as a people represented [in Parliament] freely grants. It has to conciliate (depending on the form of government) either the magnates or the people.' It also tends to rely on indirect rather than direct taxation because 'the former is easier to disguise as to its nature or yield while the latter is always transparent.'[7]

This has brought us to the reign of Louis XV (1715–74), where Barnave's countdown to the Revolution becomes more dense, more specific, more personal. It is the reign in which is sited Montesquieu's *De l'esprit des lois* (1748), which Barnave critiques: 'M. de Montesquieu seems to me to be describing a form of government which is in fact only a precarious state and a transition between two more defined forms of government.' The French polity could either develop into despotism – Barnave thinks it did at the end of Louis XV's reign – or a democratic state. The aristocracy had been defeated by Richelieu and Louis XIV but 'respect and honours which only arise from power, also survive it for some time. A chivalric nobility can continue to reign for some time after the real basis of its power has gone.' Montesquieu failed to realise that what he is describing 'could not endure because it was based on a fund of prestige whose basis no longer existed and that soon the monarchy would need other limits and other supports.' Montesquieu's monarchy was heading either towards a military despotism or an 'organised' (constitutional) monarchy. Montesquieu had argued that 'intermediary bodies', like the aristocratic Parlements, protected the people from the king and the king from the people. Barnave argues that the people themselves provide the king both a 'limit' and a 'support'.

Barnave had no love of the Catholic Church either. He considered that in the feudal period, the Catholic Church had acquired 'an absurd and excessive power' exercised at the expense of king, nobles and people alike. But as people congregated in towns the power of the Church as well as that of the magnates diminished for 'it seems that a strong spirit arose from the fermentation in a large assemblage of men'. Luther acted 'as a spark on combustible material' because 'when the moment marked by the nature of things for its decadence has arrived, despite its apparent grandeur, a single man becomes a major threat to it'.[8] Here Barnave prefigures later analysis of 'structures and conjunctures' or triggers and causes.

The Catholic Church was now under attack from the *philosophes* as well, led by the sceptical Voltaire with his famous motto *écraser l'infame* ('crush the rascals' – the Catholic Church). Not that Barnave liked the *philosophes* much better – in the Revolution he was taxed with this dislike by his enemy Brissot. Barnave thought that the king allowed the *philosophes* to attack the Church provided that it left him alone. But 'since the government would not permit the *philosophes* to discuss it during the *ancien régime*, they devoured religious superstition instead. When the moment to attack the government arrived, half the battle had already been won because, the altar having already been destroyed in men's mind, the *philosophes* could direct their whole attention against the superstitious respect for monarchy.'[9]

In the 1750s and 1760s the Parlements not only attacked the Church and the Jesuits but challenged the king's attempts to increase taxation (and end tax evasion) to pay for overseas and continental wars. The taxes were particularly unpopular because the wars went badly. The Peace of Aix-la-Chapelle (1748) was called 'the mad peace' because France relinquished substantial gains in Belgium to get back lesser losses to England in what was becoming a struggle for empire. In the next war (the Seven Years War, 1756–63) that struggle was lost when France surrendered some valuable sugar islands in the Caribbean,

Canada and (most important of all) her dominant position in India, whose economy exceeded in size all of Europe put together.

The losses were blamed on France's new ally, Austria, sealed by the marriage of the heir to the French throne, the dauphin, though he never visited Dauphiné, the future Louis XVI, to the woman with whom Barnave would govern the country in 1791, the Archduchess Maria-Antonia. He thought that the 1756 alliance with Austria was contrary to 'the nature of things' – a key phrase with Barnave – and was rather 'the product of the circumstances of the moment and personal combinations' – his key antithesis – for France's natural allies were Turkey and Prussia. They, however, were the natural enemies of Austria: Turkey had been at the gates of Vienna in 1683 and Prussia had 'raped' Silesia from Austria in 1740. But a rider to Barnave's central thesis is that an unnatural situation can subsist for some time and so it was with the Austrian alliance.

The Austrian alliance 'maintained France in an apparently stable but actually retrograde state'. She concluded alliances with minor states such as Spain and Savoy but 'her power was lost'. France, whose primacy in Europe 'had hitherto been uncontested, saw three powers [Russia, Prussia and Austria] rise to its level'. The peace 'could be qualified as a shameful inaction which gave rise to great scandals, introduced serious incompetence into the government, sapped the mainsprings of royal power and paved the way to great events'.

The long peace had a corrosive effect. Malesherbes wrote an essay on the topic: 'What Can the Nobility Do in Time of Peace?' And one of Barnave's themes is that external wars such as the Crusades are a necessary outlet for surplus wealth and energy, which would otherwise be directed internally as civil wars. He writes: 'In France the Revolution was accomplished when the esprit of the army changed whether by the natural progress of things or the influence of a long peace or of a war for liberty' – France's participation (1778–83) in the American War of Independence.[10] Unemployed in peace time the common soldier lost his martial esprit de corps, fraternising with the citizens where he was billeted. The noble officers resumed their saecular struggle with the monarchy.

Louis XV's 'softness and scandalous life' – skulking in his private brothel, the Parc-aux-Cerfs in the grounds of Versailles, instead of dying at Rossbach – did not at first lead to collapse. Louis did not say '*après moi le déluge*' but he said words to the effect that he was managing the situation cleverly but that his successor would have to look to it. And Barnave conceded that he was 'not without skill'. 'And power was still new': the power perfected by Louis XIV. But 'whereas Louis XIV developed his power in order to enslave a nation which was still proud and generous . . . [Louis XV] debased the nation in order to subject it to a power which was already degraded'. Barnave had a sneaking admiration for Louis XIV until he fell into the hands of priests during his 'decrepitude'. Under him, 'despotism achieved its perfect development' and Frenchmen were content 'that their constitutional rights were subordinated to the gloire of the king'.[11] But whereas Louis XIV 'esteemed' his people, Louis XV hated them. 'His agents smashed every obstacle, prostituted morals, and seemed to want to dry up the very founts of self-respect and honour, prizing riches above birth, creating a thousand shameful ways to achieve riches. They were moving towards that kind of equality which gives despotic governments security.' There is always a strand in Barnave's thinking akin to the *thèse aristocratique* which sees distinctions of birth and education as a bar to tyranny, whether monarchical or republican.

'Even literature and the arts', he continues, 'took their colour from current morality.' 'In the previous century there had been a vigour, an imagination a sort of constructive tension (*ces frictions brillantes*) which had kept the national spirit alive despite Louis XIV's tyranny.' But now the *philosophes* were tame: they were given free vent against religious 'superstition provided they agreed to respect the throne. They were even seen to prostrate themselves before it.' Barnave probably has in mind Voltaire, whose *Eloge de Maupeou* praised Louis XV's chancellor, this 'charlatan . . . wearing the mask of royalism' who implemented Louis XV's attack on the Parlements which Barnave, in company with many, considered the final transformation of the monarchy into a despotism.[12]

Until the mid-century the crown and the thirteen appeal courts who registered his legislation had had a cosy relationship. It was in both their interests to prevent the Estates-General from meeting, as the Estates-General would diminish the authority of crown and appeal courts, as they did when they finally met in 1789. As Barnave explains:

'When the princes, arrogating the legislative power, stopped convoking the Estates-General . . . they affected to consult the Parlement on major matters and on new laws because the assent of this respected body inspired more confidence and docility in the people – hence the registration of edicts', but this grew from a 'convenience' to an obligation.[13]

When the crown and Parlement system was working well, the Parlement would register royal legislation after having made constructive 'remonstrances'. Though there were disputes over religious matters, the Parlements did not starve the king of money. But the need to fight wars both on land and at sea (and navies were more expensive than armies because of the capital outlay on ships) led to strains within the system. The result was that in the 1750s the king struggled with and in the 1760s capitulated to the Parlements.

Finally, in 1771 an exasperated if lazy Louis XV, exhausted through excess at the age of sixty and with an heir only fifteen (the boy's father, the 'old' dauphin, having died in 1764), decided on one last throw of the dice to assert his authority while there was still time. As Barnave said, the Montesquiean system was only a transitional state: it must resolve itself either into despotism or democracy. Louis XV, Barnave considered, took the former course when his chancellor, Maupeou, replaced the Parlement of Paris with a rival conciliar body, the Grand Conseil, and reduced the Parlement's vast jurisdiction by creating six less prestigious *conseils supérieurs*. Provincial Parlements also suffered and the Parlement of Dauphiné, which had been obstreperous or brave (depending on one's point of view), was lucky to escape with only remodelling: a reduction in the number of its judges to forty-three. Barnave's father was a senior barrister working in the Parlement and the family lived nearby. Symbolically, the measures against the Parlement coincided with the introduction in 1771 of a new head of the king on the coinage. For forty years the king's youthful bust on the coins had been preserved unchanged. But now, as in *The Picture of Dorian Gray*, the image of a handsome young man was replaced by that of a grim old tyrant, every vice etched into his skin.

This is how Barnave describes the final scene:

> In the end such was the success of the systematic degradation of the nation that it no longer cared for anything but the love of gold, the

> delights of pleasure and the most frivolous vanity; and when it was finally put to the test by the violent acts which marked the end of the reign it combined such obedience with such contempt for its master that it seemed ready to suffer everything.

But it was the king himself who had to 'suffer everything', dying in agony in 1774 from a virulent form of black smallpox, his settlement still in the balance. His successor undid his work by recalling the Parlement. Louis XV's body was so infected and putrid that there was no lying-in state – he was rushed to the royal burying place in the Cathedral of Saint-Denis and bricked up in his tomb lest the infection spread. The lurid corruption of his physical body must have seemed to Barnave to symbolise the putrefaction of the body politic he left behind – a putrefaction of the king's two bodies.

For the body politic, too, was tainted by a mortal illness. The nation had been obedient, 'but the existing government had nonetheless reached the period of its maturity. Deprived of the ties of respect and affection it ruled as it were only by mechanical means.' However, 'the two privileged orders who still staffed the machinery of government were ruined by their luxurious lifestyle and degraded by their morals' at a time when the fundamental strength of the commoners, the Third Estate, was increasing all the while.

For 'one can attribute the French Revolution solely to the progress of civilisation, enlightenment and industry; because it is this cause which by elevating the Third Estate increased its comfort, its education and its pride and made a democratic revolution inevitable. It is this which gave a great power to public opinion.' 'Where public opinion is a great force, must it not resolve into a representative assembly?' he asks rhetorically.[14] But why and how does it so resolve itself, like some sediment left from boiling off liquid? What was the transmission mechanism?

A clue may be given by insights of Barnave's later taken up by de Tocqueville and Marx: 'Everything obeys the dominant force until a small portion of that force, passing to the other side, is sufficient to turn the balance the other way'; and: 'Insurrection against power is always begun by those who are closest to it. To attempt an insurrection, a habit of ambition is needed and a foretaste of power.'[15] That is why the kings never let an ex-minister return to power and when Louis XVI recalled Necker (twice), he lived to regret it. In other words, what is needed to storm the citadel is a Trojan horse – men at the centre of government responsive to public opinion.

Necker, Barnave argues, had 'two [power] bases': (1) 'opinion' and (2) the money he could raise by loans – essential if you were fighting a war without increasing taxation which, to be fair to him, was the king's remit. 'Necker was the first in France in our time to enjoy what is called 'popularity.'[16] 'It was the reputation and popularity he had acquired by his *Compte rendu*, by his morals, by his writings, by his wife's hospital work [and, one should add, her salon], finally by the ostentation of all these virtues so new in a French statesman . . . whose effect is blunted in countries which have often witnessed hypocrisy but infallible in a country where a minister affects it for the first time.'

In 1781 Necker published his *Compte rendu au roi* (actually *au peuple*) in an attempt to bolster credit both national and personal. The *Compte* purported to prove that despite three years fighting in the American war without an increase in taxation government revenues enjoyed a surplus of 10 million livres on the 'ordinary account'. In fact, there was a deficit of over 50 million. Necker had simply omitted the cost of the war because it was not an 'ordinary' occurrence. Nevertheless, the Parlement of Grenoble thanked Necker for 'lifting the veil which enveloped [royal] finances in mystery'.[17]

Necker's 'positive, material and immediate power base was credit out of which he wanted to create a state necessity and which he sought to associate ostensibly with his person as a tribute paid to confidence in his virtue, but which was secretly based on his links with a multitude of Swiss and Genevan bankers, whom he nailed to his ministerial mast by profits as enormous as they were assured'. Barnave considered that there were two kinds of 'charlatan minister': those who flattered the people and those who flattered the king.[18] In the latter category there were, under Louis XV, 'd'Aiguillon [foreign secretary], Terray [finance minister] and Maupeou'. Under Louis XVI, it was Calonne who flattered the king and he certainly did. Calonne, as we shall see, comes in for Barnave's especial criticism, but he argues here that those like Necker who flatter the people are the more dangerous.

Necker resigned in 1781 because he felt the king was not fully supporting him over pamphlet attacks on the veracity of the *Comte rendu*. His *Compte* had made it impossible for his successors to plead poverty. And yet the crown was poor: half its revenue went on servicing the debt and raising taxes was difficult for the reason Barnave gave. Under Necker radical surgery on the body politic had been delayed for too long. His two successors, Joly de Fleury and d'Ormesson, did plan major reforms but fell before they could implement them. D'Ormesson even gave the king a date for their implementation: 1787, when a key tax and also the tax farmer's contract both expired. It was left to his successor Charles-Alexandre de Calonne, appointed in 1783, to try to implement them.

— THREE —

POLITICAL AWAKENING

BARNAVE IN THE PRE-REVOLUTION, 1787–9

In 1783, the year in which Barnave delivered his speech on the separation of powers and the year he rode to Paris to tend to Dugua, the new finance minister, d'Ormesson, told the king that in 1787 a key tax and the contract with the syndicate which 'farmed' the indirect taxes in return for an advance would both expire. But this would be the opportunity to abolish tax farming and make the main universal tax, the *vingtième*, genuinely universal by making all classes and all regions pay their fair share. Fair taxation would mean increased taxation, as Barnave would observe. D'Ormesson fell in November but his successor, Calonne, faced the same problem and offered the same solution with the same timescale.

D'Ormesson had relatives in the Parlement – his cousin would become its last *premier président* in 1788; he may have hoped to get his measures registered there. Calonne, however, had personally quarrelled with the Parlement through his association with Louis XV's disputes with that body, so he resurrected what the king called 'the unwonted apparatus' of an Assembly of Notables, such as had last met in 1626. These assemblies were not elected but nominated by the king from fixed categories – the dukes, lesser nobility, bishops, representatives of the provincial estates and, an introduction reflecting the growth of the towns, mayors, a few of whom were non-noble and many of whom had been recently ennobled. He had to steer a course between the Scylla of independent-minded members and the Charybdis of a puppet Assembly whose endorsement would not sway the Parlement when it came to register the new edicts.

The king's announcement on 31 December 1786 that he was convoking an Assembly of Notables for the following year was for Barnave the moment when his political dreams seemed attainable:

> Ideas which had exercised me when they were still the object of idle curiosity absorbed me totally when public events began to clothe them with some hope. From the convocation of the Notables my whole attention was directed to political matters. The thought of seeing my country freed from its chains and the caste to which I belonged raised from the state of humiliation to which an insane government seemed to be increasingly condemning it [for example, the Ségur Ordinance] stirred all my mental and spiritual faculties.[1]

Everyone scrambled to learn about the 'unwonted apparatus'. Loménie de Brienne, archbishop of Toulouse, who would act as 'leader of the opposition' in the Assembly, dug out the papers of his ancestor who had been a secretary of state during the 1626 Assembly. Barnave was not so fortunate, but on 3 January he bought the procès-verbal of the 1626 Assembly, for which the local printer/bookseller charged him 1 livre 4 sols.[2] As we have seen Barnave was used to books – both from his father's library and from those he purchased for self-improvement and for his legal career. But his political reawakening led to a spate of purchases, so that in the space of two years he ran up a bill of 698 livres with M. Girond, the local printer and bookseller, of which 386 was still owing on 1 February 1789. These mostly related to the developing political situation, but there were many others. The Assembly of Notables was meant to be held in camera, the king receiving private advice and, he hoped, public endorsement, though there were inevitable leaks. So Barnave's first purchase relating to the Assembly was on 13 April, the *Mémoires* [proposals] *présentées* a *l'Assemblée des Notables* [by Calonne] – an official publication designed to stem the rising tide of opposition – it cost 1 livre 16 sols.

Of course, Barnave would have been able to read leaked accounts in the press but meanwhile he had to content himself with a wide variety of unrelated matter, including *L'art de prolonger la vie*,[3] for which he paid 6 livres. The dramatic irony will not be lost on the reader. He kept up his riding skills with baron d'Eisenberg's *L'Art de monter à cheval, ou*

Description du manège moderne dans sa perfection, expliqué par des leçons nécessaires... (6 livres) and *École de la Cavalerie.* He also bought Fanny Burney's novels *Evelina* (two volumes) and *Cecilia* (four volumes) and paid the printer 3 livres to have them bound. Barnave, who was something of a bibliophile, liked to have his books bound privately because commercial bindings 'ruined the margins' and where illustrations were featured he preferred early editions with first state engravings.[4] His Burney purchases were French-language editions and he later bought French editions of Adam Smith's *Wealth of Nations* and Blackstone's *Commentaries* – at this stage he thought a modified version of the English political system might suit France.

His tutor, Laurent, had given him lessons in English and Italian but, unlike Louis XVI, he did not read English fluently. Both men were heavily influenced by David Hume's *History of England* but Louis probably read it in the original, Barnave in translation. He did, however, take his Italian studies further, buying an Italian dictionary, a grammar and the 1787 edition of G. Trissino's sixteenth-century epic verse *L'Italia liberata* – about Justinian's lieutenant Count Belisarius, later the subject of an opera by Donizetti and a novel by Robert Graves. Barnave also bought a dictionary of his native langue d'oc. The Revolutionary authorities would try to stamp out local languages.

There was no need to try out his Italian on Salieri's *Tamare*, which Barnave purchased for 1 livre 4 sols in June for it was the last of Salieri's four French operas. The libretto was by Beaumarchais and, like the *Marriage of Figaro*, was irreverent towards authority, depicting as it does a popular revolt against a tyrannical sultan. But its timing was more sensitive than Figaro's: by the time it received its Paris premiere on 8 June the Notables and Parlements were in almost open revolt. Barnave bought the score on the 20th.

Beaumarchais was a quintessential figure of the late *ancien régime*: financier, subversive playwright, polemicist, forger, habitué of the ministerial antechamber and inner sancta. The informal procedures of the regime enabled him to slip between the cogs of the political machine, while his protean activities enabled him to play a significant part in the early stages of France's involvement in the American war. Barnave's interest in him in 1787 centred on his role in the Kornmann affaire – a cause célèbre second only to the Diamond Necklace affair, which had ended in the previous year, discrediting Marie-Antoinette and most of the institutions of the regime.

Kornmann, a failing banker, had married a Swiss woman who brought him a large fortune and bore him two children. She then ran off with one Daudet de Jossan, who was protected by the war minister Montbarey. When Montbarey fell in 1780, Kornmann was able to obtain a *lettre de cachet* from the police minister Lenoir imprisoning his wife in an institution for prostitutes. She soon obtained her release and hired Beaumarchais to advance her case for legal separation and division of assets – divorce was permitted only in special cases. Barnave bought two sets of Beaumarchais's memoranda: a pamphlet criticising him and his reply. He also bought Madame Kornmann's memorandum and that of her lover, his last purchase devoted to the case on 8 September – the grand total was 10 livres 15 sous. Barnave was not exempt from the popular delight in cases involving the salacious and the political – here, arbitrary imprisonment, connections with ministers and the right to divorce. Madame Kornmann obtained hers in 1793 in accordance with the law of 20 September 1792.

On 11 June 1790 Barnave had not settled his account though the bookseller had asked an attorney 'a long time ago' to remind him. 'Doubtless', M. Giroud's son charitably assumed, the attorney had 'forgotten the commission'. Now Giroud was 'pressed for money'; he was no longer operating as a bookseller or printer; he had tried to sell a house to meet his creditors but no one wanted it 'even at a knock down price'. Would Barnave give him 'at least 100 écus' [600 livres] given that the outstanding debt was at least 700 livres'?[5] On 1 February he repaid 192 l 1s, leaving a balance of 369 livres 9 sous, but we do not have details of subsequent purchases from Giroud totalling some 350 livres. After these he would have bought from Paris booksellers.

These were substantial purchases and Barnave put some thought into his choice of them. We know this because in March 1788 he wrote a piece celebrating choice as the guiding light of instruction. As he wrote:

> Instruction is a prize of infinite price and richness for the intelligent man. But here more than anywhere else choice is necessary. Varied, frivolous, meticulous, badly directed methods of study overload and

> confuse the mind and are a waste of time and effort. They impair originality and one's natural faculties. Oh! Happy principle of choice. It is the guiding light which simplifies everything . . . and enables the limited faculties of man to embrace an immense space of matter and sensations.[6]

The centrepiece of Calonne's proposals was an *impôt territoriale* ('land tax') which would replace the *vingtièmes* and be payable by all landowners, including the clergy, without exception or evasion, thus yielding more than the three *vingtièmes* put together and answering the king's imperative that the poor should not pay any extra. Land was to be divided into four categories on the basis of its rental value. This classification was to be carried out, in the provinces that had not retained their estates, by a three-tier system of assembly, at parish, district and provincial levels. Calonne felt that if the provincial assemblies were composed of the three orders (clergy, nobility and commons) sitting distinctly, as in the provincial estates, they would be dominated by the clergy and the nobility, who would rig the assessment. This, he told the king, was a weakness in Necker's provincial administrations, which in addition were presided over by a bishop.

Therefore, in the proposed assemblies the sole criterion for membership would be the possession of land. The president of the provincial assembly would not be the man with the highest social rank but the delegate of the district which contributed the most taxation. In earlier drafts, half the seats were to be reserved for the clergy and nobility; in the memorandum presented to the Assembly of Notables, this concession was omitted. In the Third Estate, which included many prosperous non-noble landowners – merchants, lawyers, men such as Barnave – Calonne saw a vast untapped source of support for royal authority. He told the king in November: 'If there is a clamour from vested interests, it will be drowned by the voice of the people which must necessarily prevail, particularly when, by the creation of the assemblies . . . the government has acquired the support of that national interest which at the moment is powerless and which, well-directed, can smooth over all difficulties.'[7] Calonne (like Necker) envisaged that the provincial assemblies would gradually take over the political and administrative role of the Parlements.

One wonders how Barnave would have reacted had he read Calonne's letter to the 'poet laureate', Pons-Denis Echouchard Lebrun, outlining the themes he wanted mentioned in the poet's ode on the forthcoming Assembly of Notables. Previous poets, Calonne told him, had sung the praises of the 'bloody exploits of the conquerors of the earth' but Lebrun's task was to sing 'the useful virtues of a benevolent king'. Nor should his muse be kings who, however benevolent, ruled alone. Patriotism only exists where a king rules in conjunction with 'a nation'. The Assembly would be 'formed by a more enlightened choice' and would therefore better represent the nation than had the old Estates-General. Whereas Louis XIV's 'fatal ambition' had led to the despotism of Louis XV, Louis XVI 'would give back to the nation its existence. The 'odious empire of arbitrary government' would end. Unequal taxation would be ended, as would exemptions and exceptions.[8]

Having seen Barnave's views on representation, growth of the towns and equal taxation, one might have expected him to welcome Calonne's proposals, including as they did an alliance between king and the Third Estate against the aristocracy; a role for people of his class in the provincial assemblies; and fairer taxation. That he did not helps to explain why Calonne did not receive the support he expected. Barnave scribbled down in note form his instant reaction to Calonne's measures under the heading 'Concerning possible revolutions in France'. Lest we think Barnave too prescient, it will be recalled that before 1789 'revolution' signified just a turnabout – for example, his enemies called Maupeou's 1771 coup d'état a 'revolution'.

Barnave opened his reflections by condemning 'the stubborn false sense of security of the Prince in attacking all the orders [clergy, nobility and Third Estate] at once'.[9] One might have thought he meant that Calonne should not have jeopardised his excellent measures by alienating too many vested interests at the same time, given that the king had warned his minister that the reforms would cause 'an insurrection of the clergy, the great landed proprietors and all those who have a vested interest in opposing them'. But that was not Barnave's view then or even as late as March 1789 when, perversely for a radical, Barnave blamed Calonne for introducing 'excessive equality' in the composition of his proposed provincial assemblies by 'establishing no distinctions of orders or rank and determining precedence and even the presidency in the Assembly solely in virtue of age'.[10]

Barnave seems to have been influenced by one of the first books out of the block, abbé Baudeau's *Idées d'un citoyen presque sexaganaire sur l'état actuel du royame de France*,[11] which criticised Calonne for making wealth the sole criterion for membership of his assemblies: this 'singular' provision 'collapsed the distinctions and prerogatives of the nobility, the clergy and the upper bourgeoisie who performed roles in magistracy, jurisprudence, medicine, surgery, pharmacy, science and the fine arts but which did not square with his principles of . . . republican equality'. These groups were sacrificed for the sake of 'stupid bourgeois vanity'. The context makes it clear that Baudeau is talking about *lower* bourgeois vanity.[12] Barnave was always explicit that it was the upper bourgeoisie that should have political power and Baudeau conveniently enumerates the kind of people Barnave has in mind. Baudeau surprisingly thinks that Calonne was inspired by Rousseau's *Du contrat social* (1762) and that the provincial assemblies would form little republics. The idea of a federation of republics was to become a bogey for Barnave.

For the present what concerned him was the link between an 'excessive equality' based solely on landed wealth and despotism. Barnave, then, thought Calonne was preparing for despotism by weakening the Montesquieuan 'intermediary powers' – the corporate organisation of the Church, the residual powers of the nobility and the Parlements. Barnave was saying that if Calonne had succeeded (and Talleyrand believed that if the king had toughed it out, he would have done), then France would not have developed into the constitutional monarchy he desired. And there is something in it for if Calonne's measures were revolutionary, it was the Revolution of Napoleon rather than of the Rights of Man. Indeed, Mirabeau, Calonne's once and Barnave's future collaborator, told Marie-Antoinette that if the king played his cards right, the levelling policies of the National Assembly might produce the same result.

Barnave took a cynical and rather convoluted view of Calonne's motives. The Third Estate, he explained, and the Parlements who had delivered the monarchy from servitude to the feudal aristocracy were subsequently betrayed by the 'baleful operations of Richelieu' and made to pay the greatest burden of taxation. But Calonne, 'the artful author of all the plans which are [still] followed today [1788]', realised that a disaffected Third Estate would be an obstacle to his plans for total despotism. So he sought to neutralise their opposition by 'a system of seduction which promised in future an equal assessment of taxes between the orders'. Calonne reckoned that if taxation was made fairer, there would be less resistance to increasing it. Henceforth, Barnave continued, the only privileges left to the nobility and clergy would be honorific ones. But these would merely serve 'to burden the Third Estate with new humiliations'.

Barnave argued that the king by 'attacking all the orders at once, through the drunkenness of blind despotism and financial necessity resulting from unbridled expenditure could bring about a general state of insurrection'.[13] But insurrection was 'the last and worst of all resorts'.[14]

The Notables' attack on Calonne's measures centred on the size and origins of the annual deficit and the king's right to raise additional taxation to fund it. The dispute on the deficit goes back to Necker's 1781 *Compte rendu*. If, as he claimed, there was an annual surplus of 10 million livres after three years of war, how could there be an annual deficit of 112 million livres now, as Calonne claimed? As Nicolaï, the head of the Chambre de Comptes, said in a printed speech bought by Barnave, how could there be a deficit after six years of peace and increased taxation?[15] How, he implied, without government extravagance and/or malfeasance? Calonne could not defend his accounting without impugning Necker's, and Necker had many supporters in the Assembly. Indeed, though he was not a member, Necker, rather than Brienne, became the real leader of the opposition, albeit in absentia. Necker and Calonne conducted their controversy not through pamphlets but whole books – and Barnave bought the lot.[16]

But neither man convinced the other or their adherents. And for clarification of an issue which dominated the Assembly and has divided scholars ever since, we turn again to the abbé. Baudeau explained that every year the finance minister – all finance ministers – 'anticipated', that is, borrowed against the following year's revenue, the exact amount needed to balance the books. Necker inherited a real deficit of 60 million and had to anticipate a larger amount each year, so that Joly de Fleuy (finance minister 1781–3) had to 'anticipate' 100 million in

1782. Therefore Calonne is saying that in order to balance the books for 1787, he will have to 'anticipate' 112 livres of the future revenue for 1788. By definition there will always be a balance. Necker got to his surplus by bringing out his book in January but including the income from a loan of 10 million to be raised in March. So, Baudeau says, both men were right and both men were wrong. 'Q.E.D.' he proclaims. How much of this Barnave accepted we do not know but, as we have seen, he came to regard both men as 'charlatans'. Necker was also attacked by a man with whom Barnave would be much associated: Gabriel-Honoré Riquetti, better known as the comte de Mirabeau. Barnave bought the *Lettres de M. de Mirabeau sur l'administration de M. Necker* (1787) for 1 livre 16 sous.

Mirabeau had collaborated with Calonne on his measures and was suspected of working to have him recalled to office during the Revolution, but he was disappointed at not being made secretary to the Assembly. In revenge, or perhaps to raise his price, Mirabeau condemned the steps Calonne took to support the stock market during the crisis developing round the Assembly of Notables. This asset purchase policy, commonplace today, Mirabeau denounced as '*agiotage*' (speculation) and Barnave bought his production for 1 livre 4 sous.[17]

Even assuming that Calonne was right about the size of the deficit – and the king, rightly fearful of leaks, was reluctant to furnish the Notables with all the evidence – some of the Notables queried the right of the king to raise the additional taxation needed to fund it without some form of consent. Contrary to widespread belief, Calonne had no intention of making the endorsement of the Assembly a substitute for registration by the Parlements. Rather, he wanted their endorsement to smooth the way for registration of his measures by *lit de justice* simultaneously throughout the kingdom. But some Notables – most famously, the grandstanding and self-proclaimed hero of the American war, Lafayette – said that endorsement by the Parlements was not sufficient: the nation must give its consent through the Estates-General.

Lafayette first bruited this idea in his bureau, one of seven working committees into which the Assembly was divided. He observed that the second *vingtième* was due to expire in 1791 and added: 'It strikes me that we ought to beseech His Majesty to determine here and now on the convocation of a truly National Assembly for that time.' Artois, the king's brother, who was president of the bureau, blunt but displaying far more intelligence in the Assembly than he did when he became king in 1824, having to battle long hours, often single-handedly, for Calonne's measures, stepped in and 'asked whether ... it was the convocation of the Estates-General he was requesting. He [Lafayette] replied that this was precisely the object of his request.'[18] Lafayette subsequently published his ideas and Barnave bought the printed version on 30 April.

Barnave next took up his pen on 8 August 1787 and noted 'the events which have occurred since I wrote the foregoing have taken the most favourable turn'. Barnave had been right to talk of the king's 'false sense of security in attacking all the orders at once'. They combined and 'fell on ... [Calonne] like a prey they wanted to devour'.[19] As a last desperate throw of the dice Calonne appealed from the Notables to the people by publishing his proposals together with a detachable preface, the *Avertissement*,[20] which Barnave bought for 1 livre 16 sous. He also bought the Notables' riposte, their *Observations*, for 3 livres in June. On Palm Sunday, 1 April, the *Avertissement* was read out from the pulpit by all the curés in Paris and distributed in large numbers in the provinces. This maddened the attack dogs still further and enabled Marie-Antoinette and the justice minister, Miromesnil, to persuade the king to dismiss Calonne (8 April). Miromesnil, whom Calonne brought down with him, was the father-in-law of Albert de Bérulle, the young *premier président* of the Parlement of Grenoble, and himself a Notable. Bérulle was a leader of the provincial *parlementaire* opposition in the Notables and would oppose the government when he returned home.[21]

Calonne was succeeded by his collaborator, the *conseiller d'état* Bouvard de Fourqueux, who during his brief ministry (9 April–1 May) sought to continue his policies. Bouvard was brought down by a run on the stock exchange and by manoeuvring by Marie-Antoinette and her protégé, the 'leader of the opposition' Loménie de Brienne, archbishop of Toulouse, who together with the justice minister, Lamoignon, ruled as a duumvirate for the next eighteen months.

Calonne had inserted Lamoignon into the ministry just before his fall and there is some justification in Barnave's claim that the duumvirate's policies were the continuation of Calonne's by other means. But they did answer Barnave's criticisms of the composition of the provincial assemblies: half the seats and the presidency were reserved for the nobility and clergy. Voting was still by head rather than by order – a fact little noticed at the time. Despite some modifications to Calonne's programme – the land tax would now be limited in amount and duration rather than open-ended and granted for a specific need – the Parlement rejected it and confessed that it was incompetent to grant taxation which could only be done by the Estates-General. Nicolaï in the speech mentioned went further: the Parlements 'had never had the right to consent to taxation'.

This was the 'favourable turn' to which Barnave alludes:

> The Parlement supported by the peers [who had honorary seats there] demands the Estates-General and refuses to register any taxes. The prince, feeble and badly advised, is imprisoned in his frigid tone and wooden conduct. His wife [Marie-Antoinette] and his brother [the comte d'Artois] continue to do him a disservice with the people. I think that some extraordinary outcome is probable but, as I said above, I ask myself whether we have enough gumption to work for the future.[22]

This is Barnave's first reference to Marie-Antoinette.

Barnave did not just see the Estates-General as a way of restraining the king but one of liberating the Third Estate and, with it, himself: 'Provincial Assemblies *with influence* would raise the Third Estate but the Estates-General would make it a reality' (my emphasis). Indeed, 'as the lot of this order is raised at home and abroad and in public life there would almost be no reason why sensible roturiers should still want to be ennobled'. For, 'personal merit would reclaim its lustre; the art of thinking and speaking would be a title to influence in public affairs. The superior man would take his rightful place. Lofty spirits could have legitimate ambitions.' And – lest there be any doubt that Barnave had himself in mind – 'The man of genius could . . . play a role in public affairs without the petty constraints which disgust him with the professions.'

It is perhaps not fanciful to see in this sentence Barnave's intention to leave the legal profession in order to have himself elected as a deputy to the Estates-General. And to this end he would cease his private scribbling and build on the reputation won with his 1783 lecture by publishing a series of pamphlets on the evolving political situation.

Stendhal writes, 'I believe that the mother of the immortal Barnave who was worried that he was neglecting his legal practice for Montesquieu and Mably was reassured by my grandfather' – Dr Gagnon, who was the Barnaves' family doctor.[23]

On 12 June the Parlement of Grenoble sent a delegation to Versailles asking for the restoration of the old Estates of Dauphiné, with double representation for the Third Estate and voting by head, but with the stipulation that all its proposals would require registration in the Parlement. The government refused and offered a provincial assembly instead. In July 1787 the Parlement of Grenoble registered the edict setting up a provincial assembly in Dauphiné with its seat at Grenoble. The majority was narrow and on 11 August the Parlement registered restrictions which would have negated the government's purpose: the new Assembly must not assess any tax or consent to any loan which had not been registered in the Parlement. As the *règlement* of 4 September creating the Dauphiné Assembly ignored these provisos, the Parlement declared it to be illegal. Nevertheless, it was opened by the Intendant Caze de la Bove on 1 October. But on the 6th the Parlement's standing committee, chaired by a man whom Egret dubbed 'the incarnation of intransigent aristocratic opposition', stopped proceedings in the provincial assembly. On 15 December the Parlement renewed its interdict by 28 votes to 8, and two of its members were summoned to Versailles for a reprimand.[24]

Barnave's attitude to the provincial assembly seems to have followed the same trajectory as that of the Parlement. We have seen that on 8 August he had given a guarded welcome to the new institution: so Barnave's marginal note on the comte de Virieu's pamphlet praising the new Assembly for Dauphiné may not have been as ironic as Fonvrielle suggests. When Virieu claimed that the new Assembly would allow talent to rise, Barnave commented: 'a fine exercise in developing genius'. (Barnave employed few commas or full stops, let alone the exclamation mark, which would have settled the question.) But when Virieu claimed that the Parlements had for centuries usurped the role of representing the nation, Barnave commented that their 'knowledge and force' conferred a 'kind of representation'.[25] His view was that in the absence of the Estates-General, the Parlements fulfilled a necessary role.

A year later Barnave's criticisms were stronger: the proposed provincial assemblies would be both expensive (300,000 livres a year) and harmful.[26] The only good they could achieve would be in relation to public works. Since the members knew each other there was danger of parish pump corruption in the tax assessments. The job would be better done by the intendant, who would not have local favourites and had his reputation to consider. This view is unconventional for the reputation of intendants was at rock bottom in 1787–9 and the institution was about to disappear, but Barnave considered that the *ancien régime*'s superb administrative machine had kept it going after its ideological basis had crumbled.[27] Caze de la Bove was popular in Dauphiné and had taken steps to improve the economy of the province.[28] Barnave thought that 'all bodies tend to increase their power' and over time the new assemblies would be bound to gain influence at the expense of the Parlements, but would be less able to resist the crown.[29]

The Parlements were still necessary given that the promise to convene the Estates-General was 'purely illusory'. This was especially so since the main function, whether of Parlements or of provincial assemblies, was the grant of taxation. And if membership of the new assemblies became elective, they would be more popular than the Parlements. But since they had no regular place in the constitution, the government could replace them with the intendant at will. Meanwhile, 'they would perfectly answer the genius of the fisc: to despoil without noise or resistance' – Colbert's dream of plucking the goose without making it hiss. Such an interpretation was not a million miles from the justification Calonne gave a sceptical king for creating provincial assemblies.[30]

The impasse between crown and Parlement was resolved (or so it was hoped) by the coup d'état against the Parlement of Paris of 8 May 1788, followed by similar measures against its provincial brethren. The coup conferred the political functions of the Parlements on a new body: the *Cour plénière* – Maupeou had merely changed the personnel of the Parlement. In a letter to her brother Joseph II of 24 April, Marie-Antoinette defined the central objective of the coup: 'The thinking is to confine the Parlements to the function of judges and to form another Assembly which will have the right of registering taxes and general laws for the whole kingdom' – rather than see the twelve local Parlements try to modify them in accordance with the local constitutions.[31] Not only would the Parlement be confined to their judicial functions but even these would be reduced since the vast jurisdiction of the Parlement of

Paris – nearly half of France – would be carved up and distributed among intermediate courts (*grand bailliages*) which would make justice more accessible. It would also be cheaper since the *épices*, or the gratuities that the litigants were obliged to give the judges, were abolished.

Immediately after the coup Barnave jotted down some reflections on the central point which the queen had defined. They may have simply been a gut reaction to the coup but the heading suggests that these may have been notes for a chapter: 'Of making the law uniform throughout the kingdom' ('*de la loi rendue uniforme dans tout le royaume*'). While recognising the benefits, he considered that such a matter 'touching the very constitution required national consent'. Without this, it constituted 'a violent innovation'. 'Effected by the arbitrary audacity' of the government, it would be disastrous, but even operated by the 'sovereign nation', there were dangers and if it were done too 'rapidly, there would be dangerous discontent' because 'precedents' were different in each jurisdiction. Furthermore, there would be problems with cases already in the system. This 'and other inconveniences would destroy all the advantages for the first generation'. He was unconsciously predicting the teething pains of the Revolutionary upheaval to come. But though Barnave, like Malesherbes, thought that Calonne and Lamoignon were making a mistake in trying to rush everything through at once, that was in fact the only way it could be done – and was, on 4 August 1789.

Barnave also thought that the *Cour plénière* would 'tend to move cases of final appeal to the king's council.[32] Within months, however, he had come to share one of Marie-Antoinette's conclusions: 'Reduce the Parlements to the functions of judges.'[33]

There follows an obscure passage which Barnave heads with 'Quid?' – what 'if the court does not undertake to rid itself of the Parlements but turns the nation against them by giving it some momentary satisfaction. . . . Some temporary and hardly dangerous ways of representing itself.' He seems to be thinking that the king could set up a puppet Estates-General – even an unreconstructed one would probably do the job. He starts a new paragraph: 'The particular force on which the Parlements pride themselves is a puerile illusion.' For, as the keeper of the seals Miromesnil had said, Louis XV's fear of the Parlement had been 'puerile': 'How can one fear three or four thousand unarmed men in black robes?'[34]

Barnave accepts the *thèse parlementaire* that the Parlement was descended from the Frankish gatherings which represented the nation but now its 'essence has changed': the Parlements of Paris and Toulouse had been hived off from the original and the other Parlements 'made to match', so that now 'it was no longer the Assembly of the representatives of the nation'.[35]

Lamoignon's reform of criminal procedure represented the work of a lifetime. He abolished the *question préalable* by which a condemned man was tortured to reveal his accomplices and the execution of the death sentence would be delayed for a month to allow appeals. He virtually abolished seigneurial justice by insisting that a manorial court be equipped with a strong prison and a graduate judge.[36] Barnave's father, a pluralist seigneurial judge, was a graduate, but whether the manors he serviced each boasted a strong prison is not known. Lamoignon sought to diminish the Parlements' hold over the people by confining the cases they dealt with to the rare civil cases involving sums of over 20,000 livres, criminal charges against nobles and a few specialised cases. But at a time when the government was trying to win over the Third Estate, the measure served to alienate them: there was one court for nobles and another for roturiers. The socially sensitive Barnave felt this keenly, writing: 'The honour and life of all the citizens will no longer be decided by the same tribunals. Every citizen who is neither noble nor privileged will be delivered up to punishment by lower tribunals as vagabonds used to be.'[37]

⚜

Clermont-Tonnerre, the military commandant, and Caze de la Bove received their copies of the edicts in thirteen sealed and numbered packets. They were to be registered 'militarily' in the Grenoble Parlement on 10 May in strict numerical sequence. A coup d'état by numbers, then, and one effected by automata. Except that many of the officers in the Vieille-Marine Regiment on duty had close links with Brittany, a province even more rebellious than Dauphiné. After the enforced registration of the decrees, the concierge was instructed to lock the venerable doors. The previous day, the Parlement, knowing what was coming, passed a resolution proclaiming (among other things) that anyone accepting office in one of the new jurisdictions was 'a traitor to king and country'. Such language, wrote Augustin Périer, employed by those who were meant to uphold 'what was called the constitution', demonstrated that '*the force of things* necessitated major changes to which the ancient rules must absolutely bend' (my emphasis).[38] He must have got Barnave's phrase 'the force of things' from a study of his manuscripts.

On 25 May the municipal officers of Grenoble petitioned the king, saying that since Grenoble had little commerce or industry, the livelihoods of the inhabitants were entirely dependent on the Parlement. The barristers of Grenoble inaugurated a 'strike fund' and Barnave drew up an agenda for their deliberations which echoed the Parlement's anathema against 'scabs' and stipulated that new judicial offices were illegal unless they had been registered by the Parlements or Estates-General (*Assemblée nationale*).[39] These anathema had their effect, some appointees to the *grand baillages* refusing their preferment from fear of *parlementaire* reprisals.

But others accepted, including those at Valence, where one judge published a satirical pamphlet against *parlementaire* pretensions. There was intense rivalry between Grenoble and Valence: when the province of Dauphiné was abolished in 1790, two of the new départements were carved out of it: Isère in the south, with Grenoble as its capital, and Drôme in the north, under Valence. The Parlement of Grenoble had tried to poach Valence's university. Grenoble had a Parlement but it was now suspended, while Valence now had its *grand baillage*. These divisions would later play a part in Barnave's story.

THREE BARNAVE PAMPHLETS AND A RIPOSTE

The May Edicts, as they were known, prompted the first of a series of pamphlets published by Barnave: *Esprit des édits registrés militairement au Parlement de Grenoble le 10 Mai 1788* – perhaps an ironic echo of Montesquieu's *De l'esprit des lois*, the handbook of the resistance. It was circulated clandestinely on 7 June and over the following days. The first edition featured on the frontispiece a small engraving of winged Fame blowing his (and Barnave's own) trumpet. Overblown, hysterical and formulaic, it was not Barnave's finest work and to those who had listened to his 1783 lecture there was little new. Tocqueville seems to concur when he feels bound to mention it not as being groundbreaking but as 'depicting the physiognomy of the moment' *et praeterea nihil*.[40]

Barnave argued that the reason for the coup d'état was less the Parlement's refusal to register the new taxation than its 'abandonment of its long-held pretensions' to sanction royal legislation in favour of the 'ancient rights of the Estates-General' – a specious claim as the government had already promised to convoke the Estates-General for 1792.[41] Barnave, however, believed that it planned to have made itself self-sufficient by that date so that the estates, without the power of the purse, would be 'useless', 'dishonoured' and 'permanently discredited'. A letter of Marie-Antoinette to her brother Joseph II on 23 November suggests that such may have been the government's calculation: 'What causes me much distress is that the king has announced that he will hold the Estates-General five years from now. There was such a general clamour for this that it was thought better for the king to anticipate a direct demand and that by taking the necessary precautions and controlling the timing he could avoid the problems associated with these assemblies.'[42]

Barnave also argued that for them to be useful, the government must be 'forced' to convoke the estates and to achieve this the people should refuse the new taxes.[43] Barnave further thought, echoing his 1783 lecture, that even if the estates won the right to grant taxation, it would not be enough to secure royal compliance because the bureaux of the finance ministry were expert at devising expedients to raise money without consent, such as the sale of offices or 'taxes disguised as loans'.[44] That was indeed how the *ancien régime* had kept itself afloat but also why, without consent, it was perpetually short of money.

And it was this shortage that had destroyed the 'reputation abroad, of a France already considered as a ruined nation'. She had allowed Prussia and England to invade 'an allied Republic', Holland, in 1787. The naval minister, Castries, had wanted to send an expeditionary force but Brienne had overruled him for lack of funds.[45] 'The Orient [Turkey] which we had protected appealed to us in vain' for help against the Austrian and Russian invasion 'and seems itself to set us an example of courage'. To cap it all, 'a rival nation devours our substance with impunity, thanks to a treaty negotiated from a weak position' – the Eden commercial treaty with England in 1786.[46] Cheaper English textiles threatened the silk industry for which the Barnaves provided cocoons from their worms. The national humiliation of abandoning two allies played a part in the outbreak of the Revolution, as did resentment from the losers from the commercial treaty (always more vocal in such cases than the winners).

The pamphlet went through several editions and was circulated nationwide. Egret called it 'the leading *parlementaire* pamphlet'.[47] But its message did not go unchallenged. On 19 July the newly created *grand baillage* of Bourg-en-Bresse ordered the pamphlet be suppressed and made some telling criticisms of it on the way. Barnave's histrionic prose was ridiculed: 'one would have thought the republic was in danger and Caesar about to cross the Rubicon'. His historical accuracy was also questioned: 'when one reads on page one that "the Third Estate and the Parlements formed the only opposition to a power they themselves created" he is advancing an erroneous principle: the Magistrature never created power in France. Our kings predate the law courts.'

Barnave was also attacked for employing the old trope of the 'king's religion being surprised'. 'The ministers are deceiving the prince and the people', Barnave claimed. But, the *grand baillage* countered, 'such a rash conclusion has ever been the device employed when one wants to censure the king's decisions and nullify their effect. His real bitterness is directed against the prince. Does he not participate in the discussion in his council? Is he ignorant of his own orders? Do not his words come out of his own mouth?'[48]

In fact – but did he know it? – Barnave's assertions were not far from the mark. After the defeat of his reform programme by the Notables, the king sank into a depressive apathy. According to the account of Malesherbes, a minister without portfolio, the council merely rubber-stamped decisions already taken by the duumvirate of Brienne and Lamoignon and, he might have added, by Marie-Antoinette, who attended these cabinet committees.[49]

Even so, as the *grand baillage* justly remarked, 'is not allowing oneself to impugn the honour of a large number of loyal subjects for obeying the king to impugn that of the king himself? . . . Should the civil existence and reputation of honourable men depend on their having the same opinions as others of their fellow citizens?' Here it is not fanciful to see a trend towards the Robespierrean orthodoxy of 1793/4.

In a passage which must have embarrassed Barnave because it was near the bone, the *grand baillage* attacked him for his snobbery towards the members of the new tribunal. Snobbery is the only word and here we may recall both his mother's treatment of her husband's clerks and, especially, Barnave's contempt for the manners of his colleagues at the bar. Barnave was chided for saying that 'local judges stewing in the ignorance and personal animosities which ferment in little towns, judges who are weak because of their slender means will abuse the despotic powers put in their hands'.

The *baillage* thundered:

> From what moral code has this author and those who think like him, plucked the notion that those who are born in a mediocre station are more vicious than those to whom an accident of birth has given titles or riches. Do these dangerous gifts of fortune guarantee virtue and talent? Can honour and intelligence not be found among ordinary citizens? Happily, deprived of the wherewithal for the dissipation which so often leads youth astray, they can concentrate on their studies. They receive the same public education . . . as the rich and powerful and mediocrity is often the preserver of morality and promises useful citizens for the *patrie*.

And, the *grand baillage* continued, why should nobles complain of being judged by the *roturiers* in the new tribunals? 'Has the *roturier* not always been judged by the noble, the serf by his *seigneur*, the poor by the rich, the weak by the strong? Why find difficulties in the new order for introducing a measure of equality when none was found in the old?' The *grand baillage* highlights the central paradox of the pre-Revolution: the Third Estate castigating the king for introducing more equality. Barnave was an extreme exponent of this stance.

The *grand baillage* also refers to the virtual abolition of seigneurial justice, which Barnave, on behalf of his father, had a vested interest in defending. Finally, Barnave is chastised for lamenting the lack of a supreme court in France and failing to find one in the Plenary Court which would unite the nation with general legislation.

Copies of the Bourg-en-Bresse, ruling from 'deep in an isolated province, far from the court, far from the Parlements',[50] are more readily available today than Barnave's pamphlet.[51] It must have struck a chord with those 'loyal subjects' it defends. Their voice would soon be lost, for there is no losers' history. The *grand baillage* presents an idealised picture of a reformed *ancien régime* that might have been. The whole nation would be linked by 'a valuable chain' stretching upwards from parish to provincial assemblies and from estates to the Estates-General and the king himself – a similar image had been presented to the king by Calonne when proposing his reforms.[52]

Barnave, like the *baillage*, seeks to involve the whole nation in his enterprise. But where the *baillage* presents a hierarchy of institutional links leading from parish assembly to the king in his council, a two-way chain of command, Barnave presents a flat number of categories, presently suffering under 'the criminal passions of two men', Brienne and Lamoignon, but who would soon have nothing between them and a reinvigorated Estates-General. There are office holders, landowners, merchants and 'state creditors who have suffered state defaults' and will find security by being backed by the nation. All should refuse to obey the new laws and let 'universal infamy and public insult be the reward of those cowards [like the *grand baillage*] who sit in the seats of the [real] magistrates'.

To reinforce his appeal to all sections of society, in one of his pamphlets, *Avis aux campagnes du Dauphiné*, Barnave poses as a peasant and in another a soldier, two groups tangential to the political process but which would act as *dei ex machina* at critical stages of the French Revolution. The peasant addresses a *subdélégué* and the soldier a military council. Barnave's peasant, speaking in patois, says he would rather discharge his *corvée* (forced labour on the royal highway) as 'a few days' work' than the tax proposed by the government; and asks why the nobles and clergy should be exempt when they 'clog up the roads far more'. 'The *Cour plénière* is stuffed with grand *seigneurs*, cronies of the ministers, who haven't even heard of us. As for your confounded *grand baillages* . . . surely the king does not want the people to be judged by bandits who rob Peter to pay Paul and most like will send me to the galleys for objecting to their caressing my wife.' 'My advice is that all the village communes should ask the king to restore the Parlement and bring back that big Assembly . . . the one they call the, what's it? Estates-General to give him a good idea of what is needed to make his people happy.'[53]

Barnave's soldier is more sophisticated than his peasant, and older too, one imagines. He has divided loyalties: one to the 'King-General', the other to the 'King-Sovereign'.[54] But 'why hesitate . . . the king has been betrayed . . . by the criminal passions of two men', Brienne and Lamoignon. They, through Guibert's army reforms – a response to defeat by Prussia – 'have sought to turn the French soldier into a Prussian automaton', 'a machine' designed to crush liberty. But 'if the Despot of Berlin debases human nature and commands machines', the French king 'still reigns over human beings'.

Moreover, the 'Prussian' innovations – and here Barnave speaks from family experience – block all hope of advancement for the long-serving officer. The Prussian officer class was rigidly aristocratic and the Ségur Ordinance and Guibert's reforms reflected this by enabling well-born young nobles to jump the ranks: 'long – service is humiliated . . . all the honours are given to Johnny-come-latelies, humiliating barriers [to promotion] are erected to dash any hope of emulation and hold several classes in the same position'.

THE DAY OF TILES

Our *grand baillage* brought its condemnation of Barnave to this climax: 'Can one adequately deplore the errors of a writer who so far from groaning at the events he has perhaps witnessed . . . is not afraid to spur the people on to excesses which always harm it?' The pamphlet provided a footnote after 'witnessed' – 'Sedition de Grenoble' – implying that Barnave had participated in the riots which culminated in the population hurling tiles against the soldiers from the rooftops. This is what Barnave later wrote: 'I did not hesitate to throw myself first into the breach: I wrote my *Esprit des lois* and circulated it in the streets of Grenoble on the very day when in my natal town the first blood was shed in France for the Revolution.'[55] There is no evidence that Barnave did participate in the riot but as Clermont reported to Brienne on 9 June: 'this brochure called "*Esprit des lois*" was widely distributed on the night of the 7th and yesterday'. He noted that it was spreading throughout the province like wildfire: apparently peasant women could not get enough of it and it was feared that the curés would read extracts from the pulpit.[56]

After the forced registration of the May Edicts, the duc de Tonnerre (son of the man who had crossed Madame Barnave) and the intendant had been ordered to issue the members of the Parlement with *lettres de cachet* exiling them from Grenoble. But they had chosen to disobey orders for fear of provoking a riot. The *parlementaires* were due to retire to their country estates for the vacation in any case. But on 20 May they returned to the city for the start of the new judicial year. Finding the Parlement building locked, they repaired to the town house of Président de Bérulle and passed an inflammatory ruling which accused the *Cour plénière* of being 'totally subservient to the government'. This was too much for Brienne and on 6 June orders reached Tonnerre reiterating the command to exile the Parlement.

On the 7th he proceeded to execute his orders. At 8 a.m. *lettres de cachet* were delivered to the *parlementaires* ordering them to go back to their country estates. When word of this got out, a riot broke out. With the Breton contingent of his troops unreliable, and fearing a bloodbath, Clermont ordered the Parlement to hold a token session. They were embarrassed to be the beneficiaries of a riot and afterwards crept back to their country estates under cover of darkness to await developments.

That was not Barnave's way. In the absence of the Parlement, the representation of Grenoble devolved on the town council. But Barnave thought that its authority should be bolstered by 'a contingent of nobles and other citizens'. Such is the expression of Imbert de Granges, who on 12 June met with Barnave, Mounier and the baron de Gilliers to discuss tactics.

Mounier was the guiding spirit of the Dauphiné resistance, Barnave his first lieutenant. Slightly older than Barnave, Joseph Mounier was the son of a merchant draper of Grenoble. He married young and his father gave him about £1,000 to set up home. He wanted to leave the trade and even join the army but his father, like Barnave's, persuaded him to become an advocate. Soon, however, he bought the office of *juge royale* in a lesser court in Grenoble, working alternate years with an episcopal judge. This left him time to verse himself in the same fields as Barnave: constitutional law and the English political system. He had become friends with an Englishman in Grenoble, who continued the correspondence after he had left for Paris. It would seem that Mounier and Barnave were close collaborators rather than close friends. Forceful, even dogmatic, Barnave calls Mounier 'imperious'.

Protest meetings were held at the town hall on 14 June and 2 July. The minutes were drawn up by Mounier but bore a close resemblance to a pamphlet Barnave drafted for the occasion: *Respectueuse supplications que présentent au roi les notables citoyens de la Ville de Grenoble*.[57] Mounier's text was given to Clermont and the intendant to pass on to the king, whose response was to summon the mayor and his deputy to Versailles for a reprimand and to forbid the town council to meet except for routine business.

In his pamphlet, Barnave tells the king that but for the intervention of the *parlementaires* and 'ourselves', 'the blood of millions of men would have been shed' – the total population of Dauphiné was 660,000. 'Everyone from the commander-in-chief of your troops to the least of those whom the people is accustomed to respect, everyone oblivious of disdain and social distinctions exposed themselves to insult and death to save the lives of the unfortunate.' How far down the social scale did one need to proceed to reach 'the least of those whom the people is accustomed to respect'? To notaries, perhaps. No matter, Barnave introduces a new distinction to replace the old society of orders – social respect – and a new criterion: that of restraining the common people. Barnave also puts the rights and privileges of the province of Dauphiné in context: 'though we are prepared to sacrifice these privileges for the good of the nation in a general assembly [of the Estates-General], we will not allow them to be taken away without our consent'.

On 21 July the town meetings were expanded to a 'General Assembly of the Municipalities' of the province, which met at the magnificent château of Vizille, provided by the rich industrialist Claude Périer, who had already provided funds for the rebels' propaganda machine. 'At daybreak the fine walnut-shaded avenue leading from Grenoble to Vizille was covered by the deputies of the three orders followed by crowds of onlookers.'[58] The ownership of land assessed at 50 livres' tax was set as the requirement for Third Estate delegates to the Assembly. In order to qualify, Barnave, who was still living at home, purchased the house of Chabrier in the Temple quarter of Vercheny from his uncle Antoine Barnave, the captain-chatelain of the village.[59]

⚜

Much more research is needed to establish the degree and areas of resistance to the May Edicts countrywide. A systematic examination could be made of the correspondence between the military commandants and intendants with Brienne and in particular with the secretary of state with responsibility for a province – in the case of Dauphiné, a border province where troops were stationed, it was the war secretary, the comte de Brienne, the premier's brother. Common sense would suggest that the towns dependent on a Parlement were the focal points of resistance both because the edicts were directed against those bodies and because in many of these towns the economy depended on them to a large extent. Grenoble was totally dependent, as we have seen. But those towns which gained a *grand baillage* could be expected to support the edicts, though some would be scared of *parlementaire* reprisals should the king lose. Valence, the second city of Dauphiné, is a good example of this. One of its aldermen wrote just after the 8 May coup d'état that Grenoble 'had wanted to rob Valence of its university . . . if Valence could take its revenge by acquiring a *grand baillage* it would'. And it did. The inhabitants 'lived in the delicious hope that the *grand baillage* established at Valence would bring them a fortune which would be built on the ruins of Grenoble'.[60]

Grenoble invited the other towns and villages of the province to organise meetings similar to theirs but only 194 out of 1,212 parishes responded. And where they did, it was only the upper clergy (not the parish priests), the nobility and upper bourgeoisie who joined in. As Mounier put it, 'the lowest classes awaited the result of our deliberations in calm expectation'.[61] Perhaps they were just not interested. As the diplomat Bombelles put it, 'it is not the people who are in revolt. . . . They are well aware that they are not being stirred up for the defence of their hearths and the scraps of comfort remaining to them. All the hostility comes from the *seigneurs* and the *parlementaires* who in a new regime would have (by a fairer distribution of taxation) to pay the money they have always refused to give to the public treasury'.[62]

As a pamphlet inspired by the intendant put it: 'If the Third Estate rejected the reforms, it is that they have allowed themselves to be strangely mistaken as to where their real interests lie by a blind loyalty to a Parlement which claims to represent them after having had the ridiculous pretension of excluding them from their ranks' – a point Barnave also made.[63]

Apart from Valence, the other big town which resisted Grenoble's blandishments was Vienne. Its archbishop, Georges Lefranc de Pompignan, aged seventy-two, was an ally of Brienne's and president of the aborted Provincial Assembly of Dauphiné. Many pro-government pamphlets competed with Barnave's productions and none were more extreme than Pompignan's own.

Brienne had sent a letter to the archbishop outlining the king's case. The archbishop enclosed a copy with a circular letter of his own dated 15 July enjoining the curés of his diocese 'to take every favourable opportunity to expound its principles to those of their parishioners in need of enlightenment'.[64] The use of the parish priest for propaganda was common practice: we have seen Calonne enjoin the curés to read his *Avertissement* from the pulpit, and many did.

On 8 August Barnave took up the challenge with his most brilliant pamphlet: *Lettre de M. Blanchard, magister du village du Moivieux à Monseigneur Georges Lefranc de Pompignan, L'archevêque de Vienne*. Over the summer, Barnave's authorial anonymity had enabled him to play several parts. Previously he had donned a peasant's smock and a soldier's uniform. The same message is conveyed to widely differing audiences in different registers: the Plenary Court is stuffed with courtier yes-men; the judges in the *grand baillages* are incompetent, dishonoured and plebeian; the good king is betrayed by traitorous ministers; only the Estates-General can grant taxation, and so on. But in this, his most sparkling effort, Barnave took up a village schoolmaster's cane with which to beat the archbishop, punning ironically on his surname, Le Franc (meaning 'free, honest'). The fictional schoolmaster has a fictional wife, Madeleine, and comes from a fictional village, Moivieux.

The archbishop concluded his circular to the curés with the routine exhortation that they must all shout its message 'from the rooftops'. But out of this commonplace phrase Barnave spins an extended jeu d'esprit based on the devil's temptation of Jesus. He tells Pompignan to pull up his cassock and climb to the rooftops where he will see spread out before him 'all the different provinces of France where the demons of the court want to set up *grand baillages*'.

> You will offer the post of *premier président* to whoever will bow down and worship them [the devil ministers]. Standing on the rooftops, together with the chimney sweeps who run the *grand baillage* of Rennes, you will chant, you will exalt Brienne and Lamoignon and their famous edicts. From Rennes let your eye travel down to Lyon and Valence and hasten to give your holy blessing to those poor tribunals which can never grow and prosper in an atmosphere of opprobrium and ignominy.

And Pompignan, himself the recipient of gifts from the demon ministers, was only arguing their case 'because the Parlement would have no truck with your provincial assembly of which you were the magnificent president'. Barnave scoffs at the archbishop's repetition of the old trope that 'kings hold their power from God alone'. The divine right of kings is 'against the nature of things' since 'the bishopric is anterior to the bishop, the cure to the curé . . . and peoples to kings'. Barnave usually employs the phrase 'the nature of things' to show that power ultimately reflects material wealth, but here he means that the divine right of kings is against reason and natural law. The archbishop, however, argues that obedience to the king had a higher, biblical sanction than mere human laws and adduces the stock argument based on Jesus' reply to the priests: 'Render unto Caesar the things that are Caesar's.' Barnave replies that the priests had presented Jesus with a trick question and that in any case his reply was ambiguous.

He then compared the tribute penny with a coin bearing the inscription of 'our good king' and argued that the state of the taxpayer under Louis XVI was less favourable than that of the Jews under Augustus, given that the French were asked to pay 'two *vingtièmes* collected rigorously [that is, without tax evasion], even though one should have ended after the war'. Pompignan also employed that other stock biblical saying of St. Paul's: 'there is no power but from God; they that resist shall receive to themselves damnation'. The schoolmaster's wife thought that

Paul was 'talking through his hat when he said that women should obey their husbands' but that aside, 'it is the LAW that is the power. Law is reason and it is reason which comes from God.'

'The spread of enlightenment, genuine in some particulars', the archbishop concedes, 'but exaggerated in others, has marched side by side with the spread of irreligion' and 'the birth and propagation of anarchical maxims' can be attributed to the wildfire spread of 'impious books'. In evidence of this he quotes (without irony, though Brienne was a notorious atheist and friend of *philosophes*) a resolution passed by the General Assembly of the Clergy in 1765, 'through the mouth of the prelate subsequently elevated to the position of principal minister', that 'the same mentality which has dared to interrogate God . . . soon moved on to questioning the rights . . . of the terrestrial masters'. We have seen Barnave put it somewhat differently: because the king had allowed the *philosophes* to attack the Church, when they turned their fire on the king himself the divine sanction for his rule was eroded.

Though, as we shall see, Barnave was an atheist, this open letter shows that he had lost none of his mother's teachings and must have supplemented them with further study. His schoolmaster is a man of learning – he calls himself a '*magister*'. Like Barnave, he knows his Roman law and no doubt his canon law too. In addition to trading exegetical blows with the archbishop, he supplies him with another text to consider: Ecclesiasticus 21.1. And though Barnave as a Protestant would have been familiar with a French-language bible, for the benefit of the archbishop he supplies the verse in the Latin Vulgate with which Pompignan was familiar. It translates as: 'My son has thou sinned? Do so no more but ask pardon for thy former sins.'

— FOUR —

THE ASSEMBLIES AT ROMANS

THE LAST ESTATES OF DAUPHINÉ

The Vizille Assembly had prorogued its session 'until such time as the new edicts shall have been withdrawn and the [legitimate] tribunals restored to their functions'. A date of 1 September was indicated. Before that date, however, the national situation had been transformed. On 25 August Brienne resigned, handsomely compensated with pensions for himself and family and a diamond-encrusted gold snuff box from the queen, and Necker, considered a champion of Dauphiné, was recalled as finance minister but also de facto prime minister. Marie-Antoinette had tried to persuade Necker, regarded as the only man who could restore the government's financial credit, to work under Brienne. When he refused, she was instrumental in Necker's recall. Barnave did not know of the queen's role. Few did. Barnave would tell her in 1791 that she needed to work on her propaganda. The news arrived in Dauphiné on 29 August and Barnave withdrew his latest pamphlet, *Avis aux campagnards*, from circulation. Four hundred copies had been printed at a cost to Barnave of 13 livres 10 sols.[1]

To understand these changes, we have to look at the situation at Versailles. A clue may be given by Barnave's insight: 'Everything obeys the dominant force until a small portion of that force, passing to the other side, is sufficient to turn the balance the other way.'[2] The regime was divided at the top, both within the ministry and within the royal family itself. Although Brienne was Marie-Antoinette's nominee, her favourite, Madame de Polignac, had been a strong supporter of Calonne. So had the king's younger brother, the comte d'Artois. In alliance they aimed to bring Brienne down; so, when on 8 August Barnave wrote that 'the king's wife [Marie-Antoinette] and his brother [Artois] continue to do him a disservice with the people', he did not know the inside picture. They were at odds.

He would, however, have known that the minister for the household and Paris, the baron de Breteuil, had refused to sign the *lettres de cachet* committing twelve noble deputies of the Breton estates to the Bastille and had resigned on 25 July. The Breton deputation had been sent to Versailles to protest against the May Edicts. So the regime crumbled from within. And Necker was waiting in the wings: 'Insurrection against power is always begun by those who are closest to it. To attempt an insurrection, a habit of ambition is needed and a foretaste of power.'[3] Necker had tasted power and was consumed by ambition. And Barnave knew it.

The government agreed to the restoration of the Estates of Dauphiné but there was haggling about where and when organisational issues should be decided. The government preferred the town of Romans, some 20 miles north-east of Valence in more government-friendly territory, and insisted that its discussions were restricted to the organisation of the future Estates of Dauphiné. The terms were accepted but to save face there would be a token meeting on 1 September. The Assembly, however, would be immediately prorogued until 5 September at Romans. Barnave must have been behind the choice of his home hamlet of Saint-Robert and he arranged with the Benedictine monks to have the use of their church for the assembly. The meeting consisted of little more than a roll call and the adjournment. It was over by 11 o'clock and one imagines that afterwards they all repaired to the Barnaves' for refreshment.

The response of the Third Estate (as opposed to that of the nobility) to the invitation to meet on 1 September was mixed. As Egret observes, 'a large proportion of the bourgeoisie of Dauphiné remained indifferent to the propaganda of the Grenoble barristers and abstained from attending the gatherings at Vizille and Saint-Robert'.[4] Indeed, out of 1,009 communes, 490 obeyed the government's decree of 2 August and 'bypassing the Saint-Robert assembly, on 31 August they elected delegates to the officially sanctioned assembly at Romans'. This gives a useful count of the degree of opposition to the May Edicts. If Dauphiné (with Brittany the most rebellious province) was evenly divided, what does that say for the rest of France? The government's appeal to the Third

Estate had likely made some impression, which is logical since they were the beneficiaries, and that opposition came mainly from the nobility, who were the losers, and the *basoche*, who were dependent on the other losers, the Parlement. Perhaps Egret was also right in saying that Brienne was only brought down by a banal 'treasury crisis'[5].

THE NECKER MINISTRY AND THE RESTORATION OF THE PARLEMENT

Against Brienne's parting advice, the Parlement was reinstated without conditions and to general rejoicing. This, however, turned to dismay and anger when on 25 September, in registering the edict convoking the Estates-General, it added the infamous rider, 'and that according to the forms observed in 1614', which implied not only that the number of deputies of the Third Estate should not be doubled and voting be by order but also that the old electoral unit of the *baillage* should be retained. It represented a riposte to the Declaration of 5 July inviting a public discussion on the organisation of the Estates and an attempt to foil the king's attempts to modernise the Estates by having the provincial assemblies elect to the Estates-General without distinction of order at all.

The Parlement's ruling was a recipe for paralysis at best. Its mailed hand which had been cleverly masked in a patriotic glove was now revealed: they wanted either to paralyse the Estates-General or dominate them as individual nobles with the most experience of public affairs. Why did Barnave ever support them? He explains: 'The aristocracy of *commissaires* [those with a revocable commission such as the intendants] is more transitory but more violent than the aristocracy of *officiers*' – those who had bought their job such as the *parlementaires*. Violent episodes such as the Maupeou coup d'état were followed by the restored Parlements and with them the somnolent repression of the Third Estate. He prefaces this reflection with a riposte to those who supported Calonne's egalitarian tendencies: 'You prefer despotism to aristocracy but aristocracy always accompanies despotism.'[6] Barnave believed that despots always had to buy off the aristocracy with privileges at the expense of the Third Estate. In any case, Barnave's open letter asking the king to restore the Parlement was sent before news of these events reached Romans. In the coming years Barnave would exact his revenge on all the Parlements for this cynical betrayal. All that wasted ink attacking the *grand baillages*!

For the moment he scribbled, 'carried away by my subject I am throwing down some disjointed ideas on the parlementaire body':

> They want to sit in judgement on the three orders but do not want to be recruited from them all [– a point we have seen that had been made by a ministerial pamphlet].
>
> They want to be powerful but cannot be without the assistance of the Third Estate, the only one that is detached from the court, the only one that is attached to the law, the only one that is republican [*sic*, meaning 'public spirited'] – and they abjure the Third Estate!
>
> Their dominant mentality is an isolated and reactive esprit de corps, the remains of an aristocratic mindset, guided by the same principles ... but such a mentality [which is] entirely inimical, entirely at variance with opinion, mores and current reality [*l'état des chose*] has the additional vice of not being supported by any effective force.

In 1912 Henri Carré made the point that some two-thirds of the Third Estate deputies belonged to the *basoche*, who worked under the judges in the Parlements. They had been the inferiors of the *parlementaires* both in the judicial and the social hierarchies. In 1788 they had defended them but now they were legislators themselves, they considered that they were their successors.[7] Barnave realised before the *parlementaires* that their gamble of dominating the Estates-General for which they had suicidally clamoured would not pay off. In 1788 he wrote: 'The restored Estates-General . . . would reduce the Parlement to the function of judges.'[8] In fact they went further. On 3 November 1789 Barnave's ally Alexandre de Lameth proposed 'prolong[ing] the vacations indefinitely' or, as he candidly put it, 'bury[ing] the Parlements alive'. The motion passed easily.[9]

On 15 October 1790, Lafayette, as commander of the new National Guard, closed down the Palais de Justice. The day before the *chambre des vacations* signed a solemn protest and affirmation of principles.[10] Président Rosambo placed the protestation in an envelope and gave his wife instructions that if he should die, it should be given to the next doyen and so on – a sad tontine to the number of seven. A domestic servant informed the authorities of the existence of the protestation and the letter and all seventeen concerned were guillotined on 1 Floréal in Year II of the Republic.

The Parlement's ruling on the composition of the Estates-General acted as an alarm for the Third Estate, which had slept through Calonne's appeal. Only in Dauphiné, which Barnave called 'the consultant advocate' of France, had the bourgeoisie fully participated in the revolt and formed an alliance with the nobility, which Barnave had realised was likely to be temporary. Mounier and Barnave had become national figures, celebrities even. But now other figures emerged in print and in action. One of them was Barnave's distant cousin (through d'André) and future colleague Adrien Duport. He led a ginger group later known as the 'Society of Thirty' (actually it numbered over fifty) who, though mostly noble, argued the Third Estate's case.[11]

Necker, however, for all his boasted sensitivity to the public mood, failed to read it now. He failed to realise that the Parlement was a busted flush whose gratuitous advice could safely be ignored. Instead, he panicked and postponed the meeting of the Estates-General, which he had advanced to 1 January, back again to 1 May to allow himself time to consult a reconvened Assembly of Notables.

SETTING UP THE DAUPHINÉ ESTATES, ROMANS 5–28 SEPTEMBER AND 1–8 NOVEMBER

Barnave in a letter to his uncle at Vercheny, who died shortly afterwards on 26 October, describes how three twelve-man committees were set up to 'prepare the work of the Assembly', each comprising two clerics, four nobles and six members of the Third Estate. The first was to organise future meetings of the Estates, the third to keep the minutes, the second was for 'general matters, letters and everything to do with general welfare'. 'It met in my apartments because they were the most commodious' and its members were dubbed 'the committee of the *enragés*' because of their forward stance. The first committee was nicknamed 'the pacifists' and the third 'the newly converted' – those who had responded to the government's ruling. Barnave's committee sent the General Assembly the resolution taken at Vizille that the replacement tax for the *corvée* should be paid by all three orders. This was adopted by the General Assembly on 15 September.

One of the Assembly's first acts was to send complimentary letters to Necker and the king, with composite drafts by Mounier and Barnave.[12] Necker's letter 'complimented him [on his return to office] and [urged him] to look to the interests of the province'. But we know what Barnave really thought of Necker, not just from what we have seen from his later works, but from something he had written in the summer of 1788:

> The profound despotism of Necker led him to set up the pernicious institution of the provincial assemblies [*sic* for 'Administrations'] in order to stifle liberty at birth. This man hides the need to dominate and a total ignorance of the principles of government behind [the illusion of?] great talents. He reduces everything to administration. He bases the foundation of states on the ease with which loans can be floated and on the chance of having a virtuous prince and administrator at the helm.[13]

We have already seen how Barnave considered that Necker aimed to make the nation dependent on credit and credit on himself. Barnave now thought that virtuous institutions, especially a virtuous constitution, were a better guarantee than relying on the personal credit of a minister or the biological accident of a good king.

The preparatory work for the meeting of the estates reveals dissensions between the orders. The nobles feared that if the representation of the Third Estate was doubled and voting was by head, the nobility would always be outvoted because of Trojan horses in its midst, especially the *annoblis*, 'who', the Chevalier du Bouchage complained, 'having only just emerged from the Third Estate and still having relatives, friends, and all the bonds of social relations there, are bound to retain its ethos and defend its interests at the expense of those of the nobility'. The marquis de Viennois, descended from an illegitimate son of the last dauphin, Humbert II, warned of those nobles who 'infected by a spirit of modern philosophy' were becoming 'echoes of a few of their friends in the Third Estate'.[14]

The curés, often only one generation from the soil, were also suspect. The Third Estate 'wanted to admit the greatest number of curés possible at the expense of the higher clergy'. Yet the Third Estate did not want Trojan horses in its midst. They argued that the tenants of great landowners or those who 'farmed' their feudal dues should not represent the Third Estate because they lacked independence. But the nobility wanted roturiers with a vested interest in the maintenance of the feudal regime to have influence. For the abolition of the regime, which had already been undermined by the monarchy,[15] was the great underlying fear of the nobility.

The friction is clear from two letters Barnave wrote to his mother and uncle at this juncture. The first session of the Assembly had seen altercations, probably over the payment of the *corvée* tax, Barnave told his mother; but she urged 'prudence and moderation'.[16] Barnave replied, 'I'll heed the warnings contained in your letter. Breaking with the first two orders is not the best way to help the third, since we would thereby completely lose the means of making them see reason.' His letter to his uncle was more specific and prophetic:

> We are very calm, working hard and all goes well. But it is impossible to go quickly given the strength of opposition in our midst. When you consider that half the members of our Assembly will lose by our Revolution and don't want it. When you further consider the number of ways, intrigues, money, calumnies at the disposal of those whom this great Revolution is depriving of part of the advantages they have usurped, you can well imagine all the obstacles they are putting in its way. Nevertheless, they will not have the victory though they will make us pay dearly for ours and those above all whom they consider their most determined adversaries will incur terrible enmities.[17]

These disputes were picked up by the intendant, present in an honorary capacity and relayed back to Versailles: 'The nobility is beginning to realise the extent of the grip that the Third Estate has gained over it and is trying to break free . . . the clergy which hitherto has had no influence has joined the nobility'.[18] At one point the first two orders seceded and threatened to bypass the Assembly and send their proposals directly to Versailles, 'because it would be more dignified and more advantageous to obey the royal authority than the Third Estate'.[19] The cracks were papered over but remained.

The first session of the Romans Assembly was prorogued on 28 September until 2 November to consider the king's reaction to the proposed constitution of the Dauphiné estates. Necker was grumpy: 'It is important for the general wellbeing that people stop thinking of the king and the nation as being perpetually at war.'[20] He presented the proposed Dauphiné constitution to the Conseil d'état on 22 October and minor changes were required. The Dauphiné negotiators at Versailles made the general point that Necker's 'personal situation', as one whose loyalty to the absolute monarchy was in doubt, 'required that he tread more carefully than anyone else'.[21] This perceptive remark is relevant to the whole of Necker's past and future ministerial career.

The Romans Assembly met again on 2–8 November to discuss the government's modifications and rejected them.[22] The government climbed down. But Necker's proposed changes, minor though they were, indicated a slight bias towards the position of the nobles and away from provincial independence. In rejecting them, Barnave opened up a crack in his relations with Necker which, over the coming months, would develop into a chasm.

The second Assembly of Notables met from 6 November to 12 December. By six of its committees to one – that presided over by the king's brother, Provence – they advised against granting the Third Estate *doublement* and as an obiter dictum (Necker had not asked their opinion on this) opined that voting should continue to be by order. With minor changes these were the same men who in the spring of 1787 had been feted as patriots for their resistance to Calonne's egalitarian plans. Now they were denounced as selfish aristocrats. The noble revolt had turned into a noble reaction. In fact, it had always been one as Brienne, Caze de la Bove and the archbishop of Vienne had convinced half of Dauphiné. The less vociferous half.

Necker was in a dilemma. He was later to say: 'All my contacts, all my habits had been contracted among the order of society which rejected *doublement*.'[23] But he was a realist. Thinking, as Barnave had written, merely in terms of 'credit', he knew that the Third Estate had and would exercise the power of the purse. He knew that the king's authority had been permanently weakened and that he must manage its decline by concealing the extent of it through timely concessions. So he could not simply follow the advice of the Notables, and he turned to the Conseil d'état, which debated the matter over several days. Finally, a double session of the Conseil des Dépêches was convened on 27 December. The queen was present: the first time a queen consort had attended the council. 'The queen maintained total silence; it was easy, however, to see that she did not disapprove double representation for the Third Estate.'[24] The words are those of Barentin, who had replaced Lamoignon as justice minister and who had voted to reject *doublement*. Marie-Antoinette had been stung by the nobility's opposition to the policies of 'her' minister Brienne. For the moment and for longer than people realised or realise today she supported the Third Estate. This may help to explain her alliance with Barnave in 1791.

The *Résultat du Conseil* consists of five short paragraphs providing: (1) that there should be 'at least a thousand deputies' in the Estates; (2) that the electoral unit should be the *bailliage*, the number of its deputies being determined by its population and taxation; and (3) that *doublement* should be granted. This is followed by Necker's lengthy report which had formed the basis of the council's discussions. It was redrafted for popular consumption when the *Résultat* was published as a twenty-six-page pamphlet. The report emphasises that by granting *doublement* there is no intention of prejudging the question of voting by head or by order (which the minister seemed to favour).

If voting was by order, the nobility and clergy would have a permanent two to one majority; but under voting by head, the commoners would have the majority since they were bound to win adherents from the 'liberal' nobility. Compromise was impossible – unless the nobility and upper clergy formed one chamber and the Third Estate another, as in England. This was Necker's favoured solution but he lacked the courage or the power to enforce it. In any case, would deadlock have been better than domination?

In the last section of his report, Necker has the king thinking aloud with his ministers and promising to become a constitutional monarch. His pledges include regular meetings of the estates, their consent to taxation and control over the budget (including the king's personal expenditure) and consultation with them on *lettres de cachet* and freedom of the press. These events overlapped with the meeting of the Estates of Dauphiné (1 December to 26 January). The estates tried to influence the outcome by declaring that if the Notables opined in favour of following the forms of 1614 and in particular voting by order, 'His Majesty should not hesitate between following their advice and that of public opinion'.[25]

THE ESTATES OF DAUPHINÉ

The leading roles in the estates were taken by Mounier, the secretary and the president, and Barnave's old sparring partner, Le France de Pompignan, the archbishop of Vienne. After the fall of Brienne, the archbishop dropped his advocacy of the divine right of kings. Maybe he was an archbishop of Bray, but Necker had always supported the episcopacy. He had made them presidents of his provincial administrations, and was to make the archbishop of Bordeaux justice minister and Pompignan himself minister for ecclesiastical appointments (*ministre de la feuille des bénéfices*). Pompignan maintained his moderate stance until his death in December 1790. He calmed passions in the Romans Assembly. Chosen to be president by acclamation, he insisted on a regular election. He headed the list of those chosen to represent the province in the Estates-General. Mounier drafted all the key documents with some input from his principal lieutenant, Barnave. Both favoured English-style institutions, suitably modified for France, though Barnave required greater modifications.

The primary purpose of the estates was to elect the deputies of the province to the Estates-General but, controversially, the Assembly decided also to give them a binding mandate. Barnave was appointed to a twelve-man commission to report on 'various matters' and in particular how many deputies the estates claimed in the Estates-General – they asked for thirty, which the government reduced to twenty-four.[26] They were elected by secret ballot and, as Barnave explained to his father, 'only those gaining more than half the votes went straight through and are deputies to the Estates-General. . . . I had 169 votes; the number necessary being 134 [*sic* for '144']'.[27] Mounier topped the list with 264 votes followed by the archbishop of Vienne with 160.

It would seem that Barnave, described as 'Barnave fils, avocat', came twelfth out of the thirty chosen. His relatively modest showing, given his renown, may in part be explained by the hybrid nature of the elections. Deputies were chosen for an order but by everyone. In most of

France nobles elected nobles, and so on. Malesherbes had hoped that everyone would elect – and therefore represent – everyone. Barnave's radical views may have alienated some of the noble and ecclesiastical electors. It may also be the case that just as the Barnave family were not universally popular in Grenoble, Barnave himself may have been considered too big for his elegant English boots at Romans – who did he think he was, bagging 'the most commodious apartment'? The electoral system made for a bias towards compromise candidates. The nobles and clergy would cast their votes for the less radical members of the Third Estate and Barnave, as he told his uncle, had incurred 'terrible enmities'. Similarly, 'the influence of the Third Estate meant that the choice of the deputies for the nobility and the clergy fell on men most favourable to the rights and interests of that order'.[28] This made for a more homogeneous deputation to the Estates-General.

Mounier drafted the 'imperative mandate' to be given to the deputies to the Estates-General but it closely followed the report (9 December) of the twelve-man committee on which Barnave sat, including verbatim the commission's directive 'forbidding . . . [the deputies] from considering any subsidies before the principles and outline of the constitution have been established' and to 'seek the appropriate means to restore order and economy to the finances'. We have seen Barnave insist that redress of grievance comes before supply. The mandate forbade the Dauphiné deputies from participating in the proceedings of the Estates-General until *doublement* and voting *par tête* had been accepted.

In public Barnave was decisive and his recommendations clear-cut. But private jottings which probably relate to this time reveal his doubts:

> Dangers of mixing the orders [at least] to begin with. Surviving prejudices will resume their course the moment the nobility is strong enough in the national body to dominate there. The union of the orders must be preceded by the admission of the Third Estate to all offices, the suppression of pecuniary privileges; the suppression of *dérogeance*; *annoblissements* made easier; the three ways by which each order will attain to dignities – birth, popular election or choice by the prince – must first be settled.

This was putting the chicken before the egg: the reason that the first two orders did not want voting in common was precisely to avoid Barnave's prerequisites for union. He cannot decide whether he wants to beat the nobility or join it –'facilitate *annoblissement*' – a dilemma with which we have already seen him struggle. But he wants the nobility to engage in 'useful' activities such as trade by abolishing *dérogeance*. This two-way 'passage' will blur the orders so that their political union would be less momentous. His fear of the aristocracy dominating the 'national body' would still haunt him in August and September 1789.

Then in a firmer, less tentative hand, Barnave seems to resolve his doubts: 'I think the orders deliberating together will be stormy at first but they will finish by getting on together whereas separated they will grow further and further apart.' And three pages later he scorns his own fears: 'Those who fear that the Third Estate will be intimidated if the orders deliberate in common completely misunderstand it.' 'Those', he continues, 'who doubt the Third Estate's fidelity to the king are making an even bigger mistake. It is a remarkable thing that in the multitude of licentious writings emanating from this order, there is not to be found any which attack the reigning prince or respect for the monarchy. Indeed, the Third Estate of several towns has even gone much too far.'[29]

The Romans assemblies had been stage-managed by Pompignan (a Briennist) and Mounier, a social conservative who favoured a strong constitutional monarchy. Brienne moved leftwards as he was leaving office and the Briennists formed an important part of the Monarchiens, the party Mounier was to lead in the National Assembly. These men ensured that the Romans assemblies would not be marred by the disputes between the orders which had led to the abeyance of the Estates of Dauphiné after 1626 and the Estates-General after 1614.

Cleverly, Pompignan and Mounier had the mandate drafted before the election of deputies. But after the elections the archbishop of Embrun, who had chaired the twelve-man commission on which Mounier's draft was based, now challenged it, 'thunder[ing] against every article in the mandate'. We learn this from a letter Embrun sent to Necker, so presumably he was confident that Necker disapproved of the mandate too. Embrun told the minister that he had led seventy-eight delegates to vote against the mandate, but 'when I saw that I was outvoted I protested and seceded together with forty clerics and gentlemen.'[30] During a tempestuous session he exclaimed: 'the first two orders are fucked – my prophesying soul proclaims it'. To which La Blache replied: 'you have spoken like a trooper; I will reply like a bishop'.[31]

The seceders were won back by an important concession. The mandate was amended to recognise that since the purchase price of 'noble lands' had reflected the fact that they were not subject to the *taille*, should the Estates-General decide that they must pay the tax, their owners – whether noble or *roturier* – must be compensated. One deputy noted that rather than being preoccupied with being 'less poor', they should 'begin by desiring liberty'.[32] The tension between liberty and equality, posed starkly in Calonne's programme and Barnave's writings, was, in the Dauphiné estates, not yet resolved. One hundred and twenty nobles and clergy signed a memorandum for the king protesting against the proceeding of the Dauphiné estates and it was lodged in the records of the Parlement of Grenoble, now in full reaction.

The achievements and tensions of the Estates of Dauphiné represented *in petto* those which the Estates-General would exhibit, but in the provincial estates, as a concession to the nobility, *annoblis* and parish priests were all but excluded. In the Estates-General the curés were to dominate the first order and swing the balance towards the Third Estate. Egret's study suggests that the nobility's very real fears of voting by head centred less on political power per se than on the use to which it would be put: the nobility and clergy, whatever the liberal nobles at Paris said, had not entirely given up on the idea of some fiscal privilege, while they were haunted by the fear that the seigneurial regime would be abolished. Pressure for this was coming up from the rural communities but both the bourgeoisie and nobles had minimised their influence at Romans by instituting two-tier elections for the countryside but direct election by towns.

'Such an assembly', Egret concludes, 'had only touched the financial privileges of the first two orders with extreme prudence, while it had alluded to seigneurial rights only in order to guarantee them.' The minutes papered over these cracks as minutes do but in reality 'hearts and minds were divided and the work of the Assembly was touched by an irremediable fragility'.[33]

Barnave had time to kill. There were four months before the Estates-General were due to open. It was inconceivable that he should pick up the threads of his legal practice – the gates to the wider world had opened. He would take his chances. He could not know how long he would be away; events would both shorten and lengthen its duration. There was riding and socialising and the composition of a curious pamphlet, his last, a riposte to Calonne's book-length *Lettre au roi* of 9 February, a vain attempt by the minister both to win back the king's affections and secure his election to the Estates-General: he actually turned up in his native Flanders but was met with such hostility that he was forced to scuttle back to his English exile.

Barnave, on the contrary, *had* been elected and a month before he left home to take up his seat in the Estates-General, he published his *Coup d'oeil sur la lettre de M. de Calonne*, not anonymously like his previous productions but proudly proclaimed as '*Par M. Barnave, Député de la Province de Dauphiné aux États-généraux*'. Calonne's *Lettre au roi* was an attack on his old sparring partner, Necker, and in particular on the *Résultat du conseil*.

Calonne saw voting by head as a regrettable but logical consequence of *doublement* and sought ways of mitigating what he regarded as a disaster for the king's independence of action. His solution was a bicameral legislature, such as obtained in England. A two-chamber system would preserve the king's independence particularly if the two chambers were at odds. But Calonne considered that a two-chamber system could only be instituted for future estates because some of the deputies for the present one had already been elected.

Calonne considered that there was no need for the clergy to have a separate house: the deputies from the nobility and upper clergy (bishops and 'gentlemen' clerics) would be fused in an upper house, as in England. A two-chamber system would also stop the proliferation of new nobles, which Barnave also favoured. The ministers could be elected to either house depending on their status and this could lead to a blurring of the distinction between *noblesse d'épée* and *noblesse de robe*, because ministers, like himself, were a 'sort of lawyer'. Ministers would have seats both to present royal legislation and to answer for their conduct. This would be a vexed issue in the Revolution.

Barnave did not think that a bicameral system would suit France as he had told the Dauphiné estates, because the peers, unlike the French noblesse, were 'not a distinct order but hereditary magistrates with family members in the House of Commons and had no other rights than those belonging to all the citizens'.[34] However, like Calonne, Barnave saw the dangers to the royal authority of a unicameral system. To counter these, he insists that the king should have an absolute veto over legislation. Otherwise, he would be little better than a 'Stadholder' perpetually seeking to safeguard his position through intrigues.[35]

Though Calonne re-affirms his 1766 credo that 'legislative power' belonged with the king 'unfettered and undivided', his views on the practical application of such power were not so very different from Barnave's. Calonne makes a sophistical distinction between different categories of legislation, each one requiring a different colour of wax seal. But for the main constitutional and financial legislation he advocates the same procedure as Barnave: measures should be passed by the Estates-General and accepted by the king (who could also propose legislation) before being automatically registered without remonstrances by the Parlement.

Calonne was taxed, as Barnave would be, with inconsistency. Maybe they were kindred souls. Calonne, the 'artful' architect of the crown's policies in 1787–8, held an involuntary fascination for Barnave, much as Satan has for Milton. Looking back in old age on the exciting events in which he had collaborated with Barnave, his best friend and political partner, Alexandre de Lameth concluded that Calonne 'had the greatest capacity of all the ministers of the old regime and maybe of the new'. Both Calonne and Barnave were brilliant intellectuals who could have had an academic career.[36] Both were socially insecure. Calonne, though the only noble of the robe to have mastered court manners, still resented the distinction between robe and sword. His nobility was of recent extraction.[37] Barnave's mother was *noblesse d'épée*, his father *bourgeois de robe*. Calonne's perceived inconsistency lay in his having attacked the privileges of the nobility and clergy in 1787 and defending them in 1789. He answered that an abuse was not a legitimate privilege.

And he was consistent in his defence of royal authority, which his egalitarian policies furthered, as Barnave was quick to realise. For, Barnave argued, egalitarianism is a basis for despotism – the example of

Napoleon would bear him out. The Revolution, by consummating Calonne's work, would create what Calonne's collaborator, Mirabeau, called a surface equality which facilitated the exercise of power, though the king was slow to grasp this. In his *Introduction à la Révolution française*, Barnave would write that Louis XV was 'moving towards that kind of equality which gives despotic governments security'.

We considered Barnave's comments on the 'excessive equality' of Calonne's provincial assemblies when considering the minister's proposals. That Barnave wrote this not in 1787 but as late as March 1789 is curious and may throw some light on a section of the Dauphiné mandate which can be attributed to Barnave and which demonstrates his nuanced approach to the nobility: 'And as everything which affects the dignity of man matters to this Assembly, it forbids its deputies (while respecting the legitimate prerogatives and rank of the Clergy and Nobility) from consenting to those humiliating distinctions which degraded the commons in the last Estates-General of Blois [1576] and Paris.'[38]

Barnave's 'glimpse' at Calonne affords us one of himself in the transition between two worlds. His pamphlet made Barnave define his position in some detail and together with his activity at Romans enables us to know more about his views on the eve of the Revolution than we do for most of the other 1,200 deputies.

Timothy Tackett argues that the deputies to the Estates-General did not arrive at Versailles in May 1789 as revolutionaries but rather 'became' ones through the force of unexpected events. Shapiro goes as far as to say that these events 'traumatised' the deputies.[39] Barnave was not immune to these processes but with this difference: despite his extreme youth, he had already developed a position. Events certainly made him temporarily a radical but they merely overlaid a corpus of political beliefs he had already achieved, his *acquis* so to speak, to which he would return after the Revolution had been 'finished', to use his word.

His letter to his uncle refers to a Revolution already achieved, at least in idea; if it was not exactly 'finished', it only required the finishing touches. So, looking at his position as he packed his best clothes for Versailles, we see a social conservative radicalised by barriers to his personal advancement. He wanted to pull the Third Estate up, not pull the nobility down; to create a situation in which there was no point in a rich bourgeois buying ennoblement.

In 1788 he had outlined what should be the objectives for the 'restored' Assembly. They would 'moderate financial depredations and public expenditure; eliminate with the audacity of a despot the following abuses: judicial and police abuses and *lettres de cachet*, inquisitions and restrictions; undeserved favours calculated to ruin the nation and snuff out merit'.

These are all conventional demands stemming from criticism of Calonne's administration and Brienne's repression. But his list gets more personal. He thought it necessary to 'diminish the *éclat* of military posts', by which he meant that the army would be more professional and effective with bourgeois officers like his late brother without the swagger of aristocratic ones. He also thought that the estates should 'change attitudes towards *dérogeance*', which forbade nobles from engaging in retail trade.

Warming to his theme, Barnave outlines plans for the moral and intellectual reform of the nation. The Estates-General

> would also be able to assign greater importance to the choice of [educational] curricula and development of the mind. They would create high reputations and turn opinion away from the frivolity and imbecility of its idols – not that they should cease taking pleasure in trifles but they should not perhaps take puerile pomposity so seriously. [Then] respect for genius and the true elevation of talent would take wing. [Thereby] they would raise up the new generation far more than the present one which dates from the explosion of philosophical opinions.[40]

One consequence of this was the attack by Raynal and his philosopher friends on the concept of a European balance of power, culminating in the partition of Poland by their hero (and Barnave's bugbear), Frederick II.[41]

Barnave, like Saint-Just, believed that the present generation was incorrigible and that the next must be moulded by better institutions. But his condemnation of the *philosophes* – which would continue for the rest of his career – was unusual, especially as he argued that they had sapped the moral foundations of the *ancien régime* and paved the way for the new one.

— FIVE —

FROM ESTATES-GENERAL TO NATIONAL ASSEMBLY

Barnave was not unacquainted with Paris, nor Paris with Barnave. He had spent three months there tending his brother and his fame had spread from Dauphiné; and though the Estates-General were to be held at Versailles, 12 miles away, the pull exerted by the capital was to be a constant factor in the Revolution. He went to Paris soon after his election, writing from there to a friend who had forwarded to him the proceedings of the local patriotic society. Barnave replies that the best way he can thank them is by providing inside information that cannot be got from the newspapers 'during my remaining time here' – he may have gone back to Grenoble and returned in time for the Estates.[1] In which case the letter to his mother dated 23 January 1789 should read 'April'. He told her that he had taken lodgings at Versailles for 200 livres (£8) a month at 5 Rue de Noailles, off the Avenue de Versailles, where the Estates were to meet. He lodged with Revol, another Dauphiné deputy, who had secured 139 votes in the election and told his mother 'we shall be fairly comfortable'.

That Barnave had access to information not in the public domain is borne out by an extraordinary claim he makes in a fragment in his papers dating from the early summer. His possession of 'very great personal advantages', he claims, stems from: 'Intimate relations with the first personages of the kingdom – and it is to be remarked that my standing with these persons is very superior to my standing in the Assembly, for I have an ascendancy over several of them which no one else has, and which depends a good deal on the reason that my indifference to putting myself forward . . . [excludes] all idea of rivalry.'[2] Clearly Barnave does not mean the king and queen by 'the first personages of the kingdom' – the king had only heard of a few of the Third Estate deputies, such as Target, who had defended Cardinal Rohan in the Diamond Necklace Affair, and Bailly the astronomer.

Rather, he should be taken to mean his relative, Necker, and Necker's daughter, Germaine de Staël. We will see him already closely involved with them in September over the question of the king's veto over legislation. Madame de Staël would have introduced him to others through her famous salon. It is not clear whether Barnave's 'ascendancy' refers to the 'first persons' or Assembly members – the sense would imply the former, but again that would be an even more extraordinary claim. This at least can be said: that Barnave's subsequent and clandestine dealings with the government and the king and queen would be at least as important as his role in the Assembly.

The Estates-General were scheduled to be opened by the king at Versailles on 27 April. Barnave wrote that he was not 'unduly elated' as he set out for the gathering. But apart from that stay at Paris and two overnight ones at Orange to collect his degree, he had lived at home. He must have felt like a student that day setting off for his first term at university. He must have been excited. And so must the rest of the 1,200 deputies who began to arrive in the course of April. True, the hundred or so court noble deputies were familiar with the surroundings: they had bedsitters in the palace but spent most of the week in their grand Paris *hôtels*. Many of the forty-six bishops would have haunted the gilded corridors of power in search of preferment and a few were favourites of the royal family.

The total eclipse of the Parlements was measured by the number of their representatives: a mere twenty-two. They had gambled – and that is the right word – on dominating the Estates and they had lost. They already regretted asking for them. The bulk of the noble deputies were not exactly backwoodsmen, more leaders of provincial society, a county set, but more insistent on their rights than the courtiers because more in need of them. The big surprise – in contrast to the Romans assemblies – was the large number of parish priests – three-quarters of the 303 clerical deputies. From their point of view, the nobles had been right to restrict their numbers at Romans.

Of the 600 Third Estate deputies, about 400 had some kind of legal qualification – lawyer was a broad term in *ancien régime* France – even the king had judicial functions and ministers were in Calonne's phrase a 'sort of lawyer'. Administration and justice were inseparable and many of the 400 were office holders of one kind or another. There may have been 150 lawyers in our sense of the word, plus of course the *parlementaires*, who had humiliated them in the exercise of their profession. There was one peasant and no artisans. Though election was by adult (over the age of twenty-five), male suffrage there was a two-stage electoral process and turnout had been low.

The Dauphiné contingent presumably travelled up to Versailles together, planning while dining at the *tables d'hôte* along the route. At Versailles they continued to meet every day to discuss tactics. They even drew up a *Journal des Etats-Généraux tenu par la Députation du Dauphiné*. Barnave did not have 'the most commodious apartment' this time and the deputies met either at Archbishop Pompignan's or those of the comte de La Bache. On Sunday 26 April they were at the archbishop's when they learned that the opening ceremony had been delayed until 5 May to allow stragglers to arrive.

On the 27th the deputies were informed that each order had been assigned a different costume for the ceremonies. The clergy could hardly appear without their soutanes, but why should the nobility and Third Estate dress differently when they did not in ordinary life? The nobles wore finery and plumes in their hats but the Third Estate wore black with short mantles and had 'their hair curled and powdered in front and hanging down loose behind as lawyers wore it in court'.[3] Barnave had thought he was done with all that. But the marquis de Deux-Brézé, the master of ceremonies, must have thought: since they were mostly lawyers, why not have them dressed like lawyers? Except that Barnave had packed a full wardrobe of English clothes, now cheaper after the new commercial treaty with England – something at least for which he could be grateful to Calonne!

Still, hitherto Barnave had not begrudged the nobility their distinctions, provided they were purely honorific and the deputation had more important matters to consider, chiefly their mandate not to participate in the Estates unless the deputies of all the three orders voted by head and sat in the same chamber. In April the mandate was challenged: Barnave writes to a friend, 'just as I was finishing this letter, I have been informed that we have been re-convoked to Romans, where it will be proposed that we water down the imperative clause in our mandate'. Nothing came of this and the Dauphiné deputies held firm.[4]

A foretaste of trouble ahead came on 30 April when the deputies were told that they would be presented to the king not by delegation but by order. The Dauphiné journal notes on 1 May: 'The deputation of Dauphiné, desirous of being presented as one body, with the three orders together, made representations to this effect to the ministers and particularly to the Grand Master of Ceremonies but to no avail.' When the members of the nobility and clergy were ushered into the king's cabinet to be presented, both wings (*battants*) of the doors were opened, but for the members of the Third Estate one remained firmly shut – in their face, it must have seemed. It was only a matter of protocol but protocol mattered to these touchy provincials, and it also seemed to indicate where government thinking lay on the big issue of voting procedure.

Barnave had always been suspicious of 'devil ministers' and around this time he wrote: 'With separate chambers, if the royal power sides with the aristocratic ones as there is every reason to fear since the Magistrates in the Conseil d'état and the ministers are always taken from the first two orders,[5] all that remains for the Third Estate . . . is war.'[6] This is perceptive: the *conseillers d'état* had been pushing for authoritarian measures since 1787.[7] Barnave may have had in mind Jean-Jacques Vidaud de la Tour, born in Grenoble, the *avocat-général* of the Parlement of Grenoble whom Maupeou had made its *premier président* as part of the 'revolution' of 1771. When Louis XVI reversed this policy, Vidaud was compensated by being made a *conseiller d'état*. He was therefore for Barnave the local incarnation of Louis XV's final corrupt years. Vidaud would play a key role in trying to thwart the Third Estate. But Barnave must also have known that the ministry was split on this issue.

On 2 May the Dauphiné deputation met to discuss 'the different courses of action available in the eventuality that the orders should be separated after the opening of the Estates'. On the 4th the agenda was 'continued discussion of same'.[8]

The Dauphiné deputies were not the only ones to discuss tactics. On 30 April the Breton deputation had their first meeting. It usually met in the basement of the Café Amaury, 36 Avenue de Saint-Cloud, owned by a lemonade seller of that name who was noted for his advanced views. Because the nobility had boycotted the elections, Breton deputies were either members of the Third Estate (forty-six) or from the lower clergy (twenty-seven), whose views tended to be more radical than those of most of the Dauphiné deputies. The diary of one deputy notes on 14 May their 'implacable hatred of the nobility'.

The government, however, had supported the claims of the Third Estate and the Breton deputies told the Intendant of Brittany, Bertrand de Molleville, of their desire 'to do everything for the king, so to re-establish his authority that the nobility and the Parlements could never damage it again'. He passed on their request to Necker, 'who declined all communication with these deputies as . . . [constituting] a species of corruption'.[9] Molleville's editor, or perhaps the ex-intendant himself, further commented: 'This Breton Club which could have been skilfully directed to saving the monarchy, turned diametrically against it and this gathering which had been disdained' became a 'formidable' enemy. It had spies within the palace 'and this form of espionage penetrated into the innermost workings of the king's mind'.

A contemporary notes: 'the members of this committee [the Breton Club] thought they should associate the deputation from Dauphiné in their endeavours, a province which had deserved so well of the country'.[10] The Bretons' seventy-three deputies always 'voted as one bloc';[11] so did the Dauphinois delegates, with twenty-four. When in mid-June they were joined by Siéyès, the theoretician of the dictatorship of Constituent power, they formed an irresistible combination of numbers and ideology. The junction between the Bretons and the Dauphinois became possible as the former's disillusionment with the king began to take root. Each had a shattered dream: the Bretons that the king still supported them against the nobility; the Dauphinois that the nobility and the commons could yet be reconciled. And for Barnave there was the collapse of his theoretical position of an alliance between the king and the Third Estate. But before that there were ceremonies and tactical manoeuvres.

On the 4th there was a mass at Saint-Louis's, the main church of Versailles. It was only the second time Barnave had set his foot in a Catholic church. The first had been in Grenoble Cathedral to obtain the certificate of Catholicity needed to practise as a barrister. And that had been a visit to an austere building under cover of dusk. At Saint-Louis's all the opulence and luxury of the court was laid out before him. Barnave thought you could dress well without luxury – a hate word for him. The Third Estate entered the church pell-mell with the others – to the impotent rage of the Grand Master.

But ceremonial order was restored for the grand opening of the Estates in the same hall as that used for the 1787 Assembly of Notables. The first two orders sat on seats separated by a barrier from the Third Estate, who sat on benches. There were loud murmurs and 'MM de Mirabeau, Le Chapelier, Barnave, Le Mounier [*sic*], du Bois de Crancé and others drew attention to themselves by their agitation.'[12] All five would play a major part in Barnave's story.

Proceedings were opened by three speeches: from the king, from Barentin and from Necker, extending respectively to three, ten and sixty pages of print. The king's speech was an anodyne amalgamation of nine drafts, including ones from Necker, Barentin, the king himself and Marie-Antoinette – symbolising her increased influence over the king.[13]

Necker's two-hour speech was mostly taken up with technical details about the financial crisis which he incongruously both claimed to have solved and thought should be the deputies' priority. It was difficult to disentangle from it any marked preference over voting procedures. He seemed to favour a mixed system depending on the matter to be discussed. But he let out – inadvertently – by referring to *two* or three orders that ultimately he favoured a two-chamber system, as in England.

We learn more from examining the genesis of this speech. In the *Résultat du conseil* the king had effectively promised to become a constitutional monarch. In a draft of his speech to the Estates, Necker proposed to reinforce the king's promises with 'legislative authority'. But Louis objected – and he had obviously raised this matter before, because he writes that he '*still* insists on changing the phrase' endowing his promises with legislative authority. 'At the beginning I have added "at the request" of the estates because . . . they cannot make law on their own.'[14] Necker believed that the Estates-General could make laws – elsewhere, he wrote 'with the opening of the estates, legislative power begins'. Not only that but 'the king, while speaking of the new constitution, should pronounce only on the suitability indeed the necessity of maintaining [*sic*] a bicameral legislature. For the rest, he should content himself with the arrangements presented to him' by the Estates. Barentin thought that the king was overly 'indulgent' in putting Necker's error down to a mere 'slip of the pen'. He thought it was a mistake for the king to concede (whether by promise or legislation) 'periodic' Estates because it 'stripped him of the right of convoking and dissolving them and above all of not assembling them at all'.[15]

For we have now reached the final phase in Barnave's schema of the triangular relationship between the king, the nobility and the Third Estate over the centuries. The noble revolt had brought the king low as in the Middle Ages, but in order to rescue him this time the commons would not be duped into paying taxes to equip a standing army and buy the nobles off. This time the nobility would have to pay its fair share, but to make sure there was no backsliding from the king, he must be bound by a constitution which would enshrine regular meetings of the Estates-General, whether the king convoked them or no. The Estates would also seize legislative power which the kings, and in particular the Bourbon branch of the dynasty, had always considered their sole prerogative – and still did (witness Louis's criticism of Necker's draft speech). The cardinal point is that once the differences between the orders had been resolved – from fancy dress and feathers to feudalism – the central issue in the French Revolution stood out: the location of legislative power. Everyone knew this: the king and queen, Barnave, Mirabeau and Robespierre, who thought that this was what the storming of the Bastille was all about.

The gradual realisation that the Third Estate would exact a heavy price for its support began to exert an influence on the king. But he was pulled in different directions, according to whether he listened to Artois and Barentin or Necker. An important factor was a shift in the positions of his other brother, Provence, and of Marie-Antoinette.[16] This implied a balancing act. The government did not know whether the aristocracy would be a threat or a victim. Necker, for example, as late as April 1789 said that the nobility was 'still a great weight in the balance', that is, still a force to be reckoned with; whereas the king realised their vulnerability, saying 'I will not desert my nobility'.

Barnave put it well: 'The military aristocracy . . . is somewhat analogous to the monarchy in that it considers itself as forming the branches of the monarchical tree of which the monarchy forms the trunk; and though it constantly strives to attract the sap towards itself, it can never allow the trunk to be cut down.' But he immediately qualifies this: 'However, is the military monarchy (as has been said so many times without proving it) necessary for a civilian and organised monarchy? If I can believe all that I have learned so far from many observations and reflections, then I reply in the negative.'[17]

Marie-Antoinette was influenced, though never uncritically, by the Austrian ambassador, the comte de Mercy-Argenteau. As anyone could have foreseen, the granting of double representation to the Third Estate only shifted the focus to 'the manner of voting in the Estates', by head or order. 'The clergy and nobility feared the preponderance of the Third Estate [if voting was by head] and it is very probable that the latter will win the day.'[18] This led to Mercy-Argenteau's dawning realisation that the victory of the Third Estate would 'threaten the royal authority which has already been reduced to the point that it does not know how to resist the disorder which worsens every day'. The idea that the Third Estate could represent a threat had never entered the royal head before 1789. The abbé de Véri gained the impression that the plan was to see how Necker fared in the Estates-General before deciding whether to move against him,[19] which is exactly what happened.

Most provincial deputies came to Versailles with an idealised or theoretical view of the king. Most had never seen him in the flesh and their image of him, derived from the coinage, was of a slim youth. Some Breton nobles had seen him and spent time at his pleasure. The three noble Dauphiné commissioners had spent much of 1788 at Versailles. Barnave may have seen the king in 1783 – anyone could enter all but the inner sancta of Versailles provided they were well dressed and Barnave was certainly that. His writings, though, and his speeches had dealt with a theoretical king or an archetype – good but deceived by evil advisers. Only once, in August 1787, as we have seen, does he attempt to describe a real person – a 'prince, feeble and badly advised . . . imprisoned in his frigid tone and wooden conduct'.

On 16 May Barnave told his mother that the commons should 'keep a journal which soon we will publish'. On 22 May 'a deputy from Dauphiné [Barnave] proposed that the record of all the sessions held to date should be read out. He was asked to do it and followed the operations of the Assembly day by day up to Wednesday 20 May. A member asked whether the recital which had just been made be published or not. The Assembly replied that it should not.'[20] The king had in any case banned publication of the Estates' proceedings. Adrien Duquesnoy thought that Laborde had first proposed the journal. On 24 May he notes, 'Barnave had the cheek to say yesterday: "I adopt the motion of Laborde which was rejected without its being understood." The next speaker said: "I reject the motion of Laborde because I understand it only too well." . . . Extreme disorder reins in the Assembly . . . schoolboys are better behaved.'[21] Duquesnoy thought the proposal was rejected partly because publication would reveal the chamber's ineffectual time-wasting.

Laborde de Méréville, son of one of the richest bankers in France, was to become a close associate of Barnave's in a grouping which has been dubbed the 'quadrumvirate',[22] and the friendship probably dates from this time. Laborde had been elected as a deputy for the Third Estate, though his father had been ennobled – indeed made a marquis in 1784. Méréville had been a member of the committee of thirty which met at Adrien Duport's. It was likely through Laborde that Barnave made the seminal friendship with Duport, a *parlementaire* who had proposed the impeachment of Calonne and now sat as a deputy for the nobility. Barnave writes, 'after two or three months my friendships were formed'.[23]

Within a week Barnave had made his mark – at least according to the vainglorious account he gave his friend Rigaud on 15 May:

> I am already as well known in the Assembly as Mounier and Mirabeau, that is to say much more than the others, but Mounier and I are objects of esteem whereas Mirabeau only one of curiosity. In my case all this stems from two reasoned opinions of mine, but I already know the Assembly well enough to be sure that I will be numbered among the three or four whose voice and ease of expression will give the greatest advantage. I shall certainly not seek a reputation but rather let it come to me. I have absolutely refused to let Mirabeau publish the resumé of my first speech in his journal.[24]

On 10 May Mirabeau published the first of his *Lettres à mes commetants* (precursor of his *Courrier de Provence*) to get round the government's ban. This is the first recorded instance of the admiring rivalry between Mirabeau and the man who would in a sense be his heir. Adrien Duquesnoy was not the only one to resent Barnave's bumptious attitude.

The deputies of the Third Estate decided to stall proceedings in the Estates until voting by head had either been accepted by the other orders or commanded by the king. But they proceeded by indirection, 'manoeuvring as before a battle to gain the most advantageous ground'.[25] *Doublement* had implied voting by head. Now they devised an intermediary stage. The deputies of the Third Estate insisted that the credentials of all the deputies should be 'verified' in the Third's chamber as a step towards meeting together and voting by head. The Third deputies had the tactical advantage of having been assigned the main hall of the estates. Barnave told his friend Rigaud that 'the Third Estate would, with imposing inertia await the other orders in the main hall'.[26] In pursuance of this tactic of masterly inactivity, they refused to constitute themselves as a separate order, as the nobility quickly did, the clergy 'tergiversating' as Barnave told his mother in a letter outlining the Third Estate's tactic of 'temporising in order by our patience . . . to demonstrate the nobility's bad faith . . . and bring the clergy on board'. In the days immediately following the opening ceremony, the Third Estate sent deputations to ask the other two orders to join them, but Barnave thought that this implied recognition that the other orders were properly constituted. Instead, a 'summons' (*avertissement*) should be sent to them to join what he termed 'the National Assembly'.[27] Le Chapelier for the Bretons proposed the same.

The manuscript diary of de Vismes, deputy for Laon, gives a version of Le Chapelier's proceedings. On 14 May he notes that 'several members of the third have declared that if the other orders refuse to join us, our chamber should be declared *l'Assemblée nationale*'. Vismes puts these words in block capitals and underlines them for good measure, 'The idea of a civil war holds no terrors for them.' Their spokesman was Le Chapelier, a 'Breton' who agreed this with all the Bretons with 'their implacable hatred of the nobility'. This somewhat neglected episode demonstrates the early, not to say immediate, radicalism of the group which would dominate proceedings over the coming months. These men did not become revolutionaries: they arrived as such.

However, Rabaud de Saint-Étienne, a Protestant pastor (Barnave spells him phonetically 'Rabot') proposed that the clergy's proposal of a conference of delegates from each order be accepted. The two motions – Rabaud's and Le Chapelier's – were debated over the next three days. It took so long, Barnave tells his mother, because 'of the appalling way of conducting' debates – every deputy being asked his opinion, whether he had one or not. Rabaud's motion won the day but the conferences between the orders were a solemn farce as Barnave, who voted with Rabaud, told his mother: 'You will appreciate that there is nothing to be hoped for from these conferences but it is very important that we cannot be reproached for refusing them and that we can in publishing all that has been said prove that it is only after having exhausted the resources of persuasion that we have been driven to extreme measures.'

Barnave not only voted for discussions but was chosen sixteenth and last of the 'commissioners' to meet their opposite numbers. Others included Rabaud himself, Mounier and Thouret. It was also thought wise to include the Bretons Le Chapelier and Volney. Another deputy, Creuzet-Latouche, commented on each of the choices, including 'Barnave, a young and very skilful orator from Dauphiné', but Adrien Duquesnoy's verdict on him was: a 'golden phrase-maker without big ideas. Fairly dangerous.'[28] Vismes refers on 16 May to 'M. Barnave, a very young advocate from Dauphiné who speaks very pleasantly. But ought not his youth debar him from a committee of grave conciliators?'[29] Duquesnoy listed eight men who had come to prominence in the early debates: 'Mirabeau, Malouet, Mounier, Barnave, Target, Legrand, Rabaud [de Saint-Étienne], Laborde. Unless I am very much mistaken . . . the role of most of them is already played out.'[30] Duquesnoy was mistaken – very much.

The delegates met on 23 and 25 May. On the 23rd one delegate – Barnave it has been suggested – said that the nobles' claim that their mandate forbade them voting in common on verification was bogus: it applied only to voting when the Estates were in full session.[31] Barnave himself made notes on the second meeting and, unlike the official record, attaches names to the speakers.[32] He was bored and heads his page with an elaborate doodle of nine circles hanging from an architectural pediment. He records some heated exchanges. Bouthillier said that all the nobles could propose was to communicate the *arrêté* of their chamber to vote by order: 'we cannot go back'; to which de Loup replied, 'therefore there is no point in conciliation'. Bouthillier agreed: 'conciliation is impossible because our decision has been taken'.

The duc de Mortemart said that the nobility and clergy had made several suggestions and that if the Third Estate rejected them, it must come up with proposals of its own. Rabaud said, 'let's reason it through', but an exasperated Target summed up the acrimonious atmosphere by saying: 'We have come here to convince you. MM. of the nobility have announced that they are in honour bound to abide by the *arrêté* [for separate chambers]. I believe that honour lies in not resisting the truth. Otherwise, the conference is useless.' Five more equally 'useless' conferences were held.

Soon they were abandoned, having – predictably – achieved nothing. One deputy opined that 'the nobility will only come amongst us when it is in their interest. Likewise, they only marry our daughters for our gold.'[33] Alexandre de Lameth, a disaffected courtier soon to be Barnave's closest ally, wrote: 'On 28 May the king expressed the desire that the conferences be resumed . . . under the chairmanship of the keeper of the seals [Barentin] . . . Barnave strongly opposed this because the nobility would be no more convinced at the second time of asking than at the first and . . . the clergy had wrapped itself in a mysterious veil playing the conciliator in order to attract partisans in both the other orders'.[34]

Nevertheless, the king's arbitration was accepted by 420 votes to 70 and the conferences were restarted, continuing from 28 May to 9 June. The seventy included the Bretons and 'the proselytes they were gaining'. From Lameth's account – and his *Histoire de l'Assemblée Constituente* is built round his friend Barnave's speeches – this is the point when Barnave 'crossed the floor' to join them, but this is not certain.

The decisive moment came on 10 June when Siéyès proposed that the commons issue one last appeal to the other orders to join them and then proceed to verify their powers in the name of the whole Estates-General. Any nobles and clerics who refused the invitation would not be considered valid deputies. Siéyès's 'motion was the result of a big conference held yesterday by the Bretons and their partisans . . . who formed a separate grouping'.

> [Vismes] more than ever feels the necessity of a coalition to oppose the Breton league and their adherents. Not that I think the motion bad but that it may open the door to more dangerous motions which are running in certain heads and may necessarily lead to the dissolution of the Estates-General. I even think that the terms of the motion [which passed by one vote, 247 to 246] suggests that we are constituting ourselves as a National Assembly and it is hard to believe that the king will ever accept this.[35]

Barnave later wrote: 'I made vain efforts to bring Mounier and the abbé Siéyès together . . . two imperious men who came [to Versailles] to make two opposing systems prevail'. It seems likely that Barnave had this occasion in mind, one which found him in the process of making the transition from moderate to radical. And so it was appropriate that when the commons, nervous about taking this step, also voted to send an address to the king explaining their actions, they chose both Malouet and Barnave to submit drafts. That of Malouet, an ex-naval intendant and friend of Necker's, was considered too servile and Barnave's was adopted. It consists of interminable pages devoted to the 'blame game'. One can only agree with Duquesnoy's verdict: 'In my opinion it would be hard to find anything more feeble, more cowardly, less elevated, more lacking in nobility. In short M. Barnave is a young man of twenty-seven or twenty-eight, full of pretension and pride, spoiled by the praise he has received in his province. The address was heavily criticised and had to be corrected . . . but the second version is no better than the first.'[36] Duquesnoy seems to have had Barnave in mind when he wrote: 'Unfortunately the Assembly is composed of a gaggle of lawyers who having enjoyed a petty reputation in the petty bar of their petty towns thought that they were going to play a big role and be noticed.'[37] Barnave would come to detest Duquesnoy in equal measure. De Visme writes: 'We said in the address that there was a natural alliance between throne and the commons against aristocracies of all kinds.'[38] The king's reception of the address was 'rather dry'.[39]

On 15 June the roll call of the *baillages* was completed and since *les absents ont toujours tort*, the commons now *were* the Estates-General and could at last proceed to action. But first they had to give themselves an up-to-date name which would reflect more accurately their composition and ambitions. Siéyès himself proposed the cumbersome title 'the undoubted representatives of the nation'. In his memoirs Barnave wrote: 'As long as there was some hope of reconciliation between the orders I supported, against the most ardent party in the commons [the Bretons], all the conciliatory steps. But having realised their futility through my participation in the conferences, I saw the need to press on and I supported the famous motion of the abbé Siéyès.' However, de Visme thought Barnave supported Mounier's even more cumbersome motion: 'the legitimate assembly of the representatives of the major part of the nation acting in the absence of the minor part'. Vismes records that 'MM Target, Thouret et Barnave supported . . . [Mounier's motion] in the most arresting manner'.[40]

Barentin reported the session to the king the same day; and he picked out Barnave for special mention: 'M. Barnave advanced the boldest propositions and ones most opposed to the king's authority. Among other things he said that the sovereign authority resided exclusively in the Assembly and that the king did not have the power to dissolve the Estates-General.'[41] It is interesting that the king's introduction to Barnave came through an accurate distillation of his thinking. Louis, who had a prodigious memory, was unlikely to forget that. And if he did, Barentin mentioned Barnave several times to make sure, though one of his informants called him 'Bordenave'.

Arthur Young calls him 'Bernave'. For Young, in the course of his celebrated *Travels in France*, also witnessed the scene. He noted: 'M. Bernave a very young man from Grenoble, spoke without notes with great warmth and animation. Some of his periods were so well rounded and so eloquently delivered that he met with much applause, several members crying – *bravo*.'[42]

Neither Siéyès's nor Mounier's cumbersome titles for the emergent new entity were chosen. Vismes thought, 'we need to find a term midway between Chambre des Communes and Assemblée nationale. The problem is more important than it appears even though it is only a question of a word. Let's hope we find an elegant solution.' He saw the full implications of 'National Assembly' as many did. But the king, reportedly at first said, 'it is only a phrase' when, on 17 June, 'National Assembly' was indeed adopted on the proposal of Legrand, an obscure playwright who had sat on the conciliation committee but seems to have played little part thereafter.

Reading the traditional account, one comes away with the impression that after flailing about for a title a certain Legrand popped up with the name 'National Assembly' and everyone just said, 'Why on earth didn't I think of that? It seems to fit the bill.' In fact, the radicals had tried to force it through on 16 June at a deserted evening session, as radicals do; but the decision was put off till the morning on the grounds that there was barely a quorum present. This is de Visme's account: '16 June (evening). A prodigious mental volte-face has just come about. Hitherto everyone seemed in agreement that the constitution of an *Assemblée Nationale* should be avoided as too dangerous. This formula proposed towards the end of the morning session found little favour. The Bretons who had dreamed it up before urged it again.' 'Siéyès who had gone over to them' had previously written that the people 'were not yet ready for a National Assembly'. But 'worn out with lengthy debates', people were about to vote for a National Assembly without proper scrutiny. Many, however, pressed for an adjournment. There was a 'scandalous' debate which risked demeaning the Assembly. The Bretons 'incited the people in the galleries against those seeking an adjournment'. 'I left early with several respectable deputies equally afraid of what they had seen as anxious about what was going to happen . . . and at midnight it was decided that the vote should not be taken with so many absentees.'

On 17 June 'the decisive blow was struck'. Target changed sides, as Siéyès had the day before, and presumably Barnave too. The voting in favour of 'National Assembly' was 491 to 90. The phrase '*Assemblée nationale*' had been kicking around for a year or two. Barnave, Calonne and Malesherbes had all used it. But it was now sited in a new context. It replaced that of 'Estates-General'. And the Estates did not possess legislative power – only the ability to present the king with grievances, which after their session had ended, he could choose whether or not to address. If the new Assembly, after giving itself a new name, had left it at that, many, including the king, may not have realised the implications which de Visme had feared and the Bretons had been planning for over a month.

However, they 'unanimously' followed the declaration with another decree which 'declared null and void all hitherto existing taxes and established the principle that even in the past, the tacit consent of the nation had not been sufficient to legitimise a tax, that its formal consent was necessary and that registration by the Parlements had not been a substitute'.[43] The *ancien régime*, 1614–1789, defined by the abeyance of the Estates-General, had never been a legitimate one. The abbé Siéyès said that 'on this day of the 17th we jumped forward two centuries' – or back to 1613.[44] Of this second resolution Vismes writes, 'its aim was to draft the constitution' and adds, 'it would be very interesting to know what the king thinks about the two decrees of the 17th. It must be said that the position of the king is embarrassing.'

On 19 June he writes, 'the court is in turmoil over our two decrees of the 17th. There was a very long meeting of the council at Marly today. Nothing has transpired as to its decision.' Barnave picked this up, possibly through Necker's daughter Madame de Staël, with whom he was on intimate terms. The 'council has been very stormy these past days', he told Rigaud on 21 June; 'it is said that vain attempts have been made to make the king take violent measures. The plan was to remove six or seven deputies from among our midst. Those are rumoured to be the abbé Siéyès deputy for Paris, Le Chapelier, deputy for Rennes, Bailly, president [of the Assembly], La Borde de Méréville, deputy for Etampes and you friend.'[45] Barnave, like many deputies, still believed that the king was on their side.

There were in fact several 'very stormy' meetings of the council to decide how to react to the Assembly's actions. Necker had been planning to intervene in the dispute between the orders but was overtaken by events. His draft proposal has not survived, but he later summarised it. Voting was to be in common on most matters, but: (1) the feudal and honorific privileges of the nobility should not be discussed in common; (2) the king would not accept a single chamber legislature; (3) the public should not be allowed to attend sessions; and (4) the king 'reserved to himself the full exercise of the executive power, especially the administration of the army'.[46] Necker wanted to 'overlook' the declaration of the National Assembly in the hope that, once voting procedures had been settled, it would go away. But there was no guarantee of success. Saint-Priest, a ministerial ally of Necker's, told the king: 'I fear that the Third Estate in its present state of exaltation will reject those absolutely just restrictions to be imposed on deliberating in common. I even fear that it will complain about the sovereign intervention of Your Majesty at this juncture.'[47]

This confession played into the hands of the reactionary party – Barentin, Artois, the Councillors of State and now Marie-Antoinette – who in order to corner the king had spirited him off to the château of Marly 4 miles away, on the grounds that he needed space to mourn the dauphin, who had died on 4 June. The council modified, perhaps denatured, Necker's draft. The final version retained voting in common on matters of general interest but the king suggested that motions should be carried only by a two-thirds majority and insisted that the organisation of future estates should be decided by the orders sitting separately. The king promised provincial Estates and approval by the Estates-General of taxation, loans and even the royal budget – all in all, a recipe for an aristocratic, decentralised, constitutional monarchy. This compromise of royal authority would not have been necessary if Necker had not allowed the case for the active alliance with the Third Estate which Barnave advocated to go by default. An important difference between Necker's and the final version which would have disgusted Barnave was that Necker's promise of a 'career open to talents', for example, no requirement of nobility for commissioned entry to the army or to the Parlements, was omitted.

Mirabeau's collaborator Étienne Dumont said 'democracy in royal wrappers' had been transmuted into 'aristocracy in despotic wrapping'.[48] Vidaud de la Tour, who made the final version, told Angiviller that the changes 'were not considerable but essential'.[49] Barentin told the king on 22 June, 'Your Majesty will find enclosed the new project which he instructed M. Vidaud de la Tour to draft. It has the advantage of clearly maintaining the constitution but in a conciliatory way, thereby achieving the same effect without using imperative language.'[50] Vidaud, it will be remembered, had been the *premier président* of Maupeou's 'puppet' Parlement of Grenoble. His role in the *séance royale* was known to the deputies. On 21 June Duquesnoy notes: 'Our anxiety is increased because it is thought that the plan that is about to be announced is the work of M. Vidaud de la Tour, a man servilely devoted to authority and the personal enemy of M. Necker.' The king's decision was to be announced to the Assembly in a *séance royale*.[51]

Orders were given to the troops to bar entry to the hall in which the Assembly met. A note from Barentin to the king makes clear that the purpose of closing the chamber was to prevent the clergy from defecting to the National Assembly before the *séance royale*.[52] The Assembly, wrongly concluding that the king intended a dissolution of the Estates, took a further, decisive step: repairing to an indoor real tennis court, they took the famous oath not to separate until they had given France a constitution (20 June). Mallet du Pan explained this radical step as the price paid by the moderates for preventing an even more decisive one:

> Siéyès, Barnave and the Club Breton had determined to profit from the occasion to transfer the Assembly to Paris without delay. They came to the tennis court with this plan. M. Mounier and other deputies were forewarned of this stratagem and to prevent so dangerous proposal as an immediate relocation, M. Mounier inserted the motion of not separating until the constitution had been accomplished. This motion suspended the coup planned by the Breton Club and if the votes in the most moderate section of the deputies had been divided, the Club would have won the day.[53]

For Louis, this was the critical move: he had already showed his concern over legislative arrangements during the drafting of Necker's opening speech; ultimately, he would be driven to contemplate flight in order to secure a say in the framing of the constitution.

The architects of the *séance royale* were far from confident. De Visme writes: 'The circumstances give us a great deal of force and the government has very little of that commodity to halt our proceedings. Anxiety can be read on the faces of our opponents.' Nevertheless, the duc d'Orléans, the king's cousin, who was suspected of wanting to seize the crown and who was urging the nobles to join the National Assembly, was nervous about the following day, according to Vismes, who dined with him on the 22nd.[54]

He need not have been. The *séance* itself, in which for the last time the king appeared in his full regalia, was a fiasco. Along the streets of Versailles, Louis was treated to complete silence – the 'lesson of kings', as the phrase went. The use of Lamoignon's unfortunate terminology –

séance royale – suggested that the king was treating the Estates-General with no more respect than a disobedient Parlement. In his *discours-programme*, similar in form to those he had recently pronounced in the Parlement, reference was made to the king's *volontés*, while the first clause began '*le roi veut*'; even the nobility, the beneficiaries of the *séance*, jibbed at forms which would have been regarded as highly irregular at the height of the *ancien régime*. As for the Third Estate, they simply refused to obey the king's order to 'disperse immediately and proceed tomorrow morning each to the chamber allocated to his order'. To the master of ceremonies, Mirabeau addressed his famous apostrophe about only moving at the point of the bayonet. The versions of Louis's reactions to this are at total variance, ranging from 'No, not bayonets' and 'So they want to stay? Damn it let them' to 'Clear them out!' The very criers refused to proclaim the new laws, claiming that they had colds.

Though the sittings of the National Assembly continued almost as normal, the building was surrounded by troops. Consequently, as Barentin told the king on 24 June, 'M. Barnave said . . . that in these circumstances they should write directly to the king and all the ministers and that if within twenty-four hours the Assembly's hall was not free and disposed according to the will of the nation, the Assembly would meet elsewhere. This motion received some support.'[55] Elsewhere meant Paris.

The next day, when 'the crowd tried to force an entry to the Assembly, the guards stopped them', but Duquesnoy reports that 'a young Barnave, of whom I have often spoken, got up with his usual torrent of words to denounce this attack insisting that a deputation should immediately traverse the town on foot to ask the king to withdraw the troops'. Seeing the 'risks' in such a procedure, it was proposed that the archbishop of Vienne should tell the crowd that 'all was going well'.[56] Barentin also reported the incident to the king, who must have been building up quite a profile of Barnave: 'Following the noise made at the doors by the people, M. Barnave proposed sending a deputation to the king, asking in the name of the Estates-General that they alone should be responsible for policing their chamber and the right to admit or exclude the public as required.'[57] Barentin had complained to the king that the Assembly members were playing to the gallery.

Necker had absented himself from the *séance*, which refurbished his fading popularity. After the *séance*, as rumours of his resignation swirled through the streets of Versailles, a vast populace poured into the palace, reaching the doors of the royal apartments, where, on this occasion, the bodyguards were able to halt them. Marie-Antoinette summoned Necker and for twenty minutes begged him not to resign. He agreed and weakly did not insist on remodelling a ministry of which he had lost control. Arthur Young notes: 'It is positively asserted, that abbé Siéyès, Messrs. Mounier, Chapelier, Bernave [*sic*], Target, Tourette, Rabaud, and other leaders, were almost on their knees to him, to insist peremptorily on his resignation being accepted, as they were well convinced that his retreat would throw the queen's party into infinitely greater difficulties and embarrassment than any other circumstance.'[58] This suggests that the Dauphiné–Breton blocs were now agreed on forcing some sort of a conclusion and may have been equally disappointed when, to buy time, the king, suspiciously supported by Artois, ordered the noble deputies to join the others, which they did on 27 June.

Necker had returned to office the previous autumn. He was de facto prime minister, that is, other ministers could not raise important matters with the king without his knowledge. But for some months, this had no longer been the case. This meant that two important measures related to the *séance royale* were taken without his knowledge or consent, through the agency of two ministers who had escaped his control: Puységur, the secretary of war, and Laurent de Villedeuil, the minister for the interior (*Maison du roi*). The first measure was the summoning of troops and its link with the *séance royale* is shown by the timing. On 22 June, the day Necker's version was finally jettisoned, Louis signed the first order, for the Swiss Reinach regiment to leave Soissons and arrive at Paris on the 26th. On that day, the day before he ordered the nobility to sit in the National Assembly, further orders were given, so that by 14 July there were some 30,000 troops assembled in the Paris region. This was far short of the 100,000 intended. Barnave saw through the deception: 'the government has treated us fairly graciously for several days now' as cover for 'surrounding us with a mass of troops.'[59]

There is considerable debate about the exact purpose of summoning the troops. But it is quite clear from the instructions from the generalissimo Broglie to Besenval, his field commander in Paris, that the measures were mainly defensive. On 1 July, for example, Broglie writes:

> The King consents that you assemble all the forces on which you can rely to safeguard the Royal Treasury and the Discount Bank and that you confine yourself to defending these two positions . . . at a time when we are unfortunately not in a position to look to everything. I shall authorise the marquis d'Autichamp to remain in his command at Sèvres and then, if it becomes necessary, to bring up the Salis Regiment as reinforcements to protect Versailles, falling back on the palace if necessary.[60]

But there was more to it than that: though the troops were not designed to subdue Paris, they *were* intended to prevent Paris from subduing the king – to force him to accept the National Assembly's demands. And with a cordon sanitaire placed around the capital, it was hoped to 'sell' the measures outlined in the *séance royale* to the rest of the country. A letter of Barentin's of 1 July to the king makes it clear that he still regarded the provisions of the *séance* as valid.[61] The method was exactly the same as that adopted to promote the coup d'état of 8 May 1788, as is shown in intercepted correspondence between the government and the intendants. On 25 June the deputy Biauzat got wind of a meeting of the royal council confirming what he had already learned from 'several letters opened in the post', namely that a 'decision was taken to circulate the sort of minutes [*procès-verbal*] of the so-called *séance royale* which soon will be called the *séance despotique*. I send a copy of a letter which will soon reach M. notre intendant.'

The letter runs:

> Monsieur, I hasten to send you some copies of the king's speech and the Declarations of His Majesty in the *séance* he held on the 23rd instant in the Estates-General of the kingdom. The king's intention is that you will immediately have the enclosed reprinted and distributed to the municipal and even the parish authorities. People may have been given a false impression of the objectives of this *séance*; and the knowledge of the truth can only confirm and reinforce confidence in the paternal intentions of His Majesty.[62]

On 13 July Barnave denounced the 'king's Declaration [on 23rd June] fraudulently sent into the provinces'.[63]

We have seen that in 1788 royal propaganda enjoyed a degree of success even in a rebellious province such as Dauphiné, and it would be interesting to know what success the government was enjoying in 1789 when the experiment was halted by a disastrous miscalculation by the reactionary faction, which played into the hands of those, such as Barnave, who had begged Necker to resign on 23 June: on 12 July the king's dismissal of Necker lit the fuse leading to the storming of the Bastille.

The dismissal of Necker was the centrepiece of a ministerial reshuffle – a reshuffle rather than a 'revolution' Barnave called it since Barentin and Villedeuil kept their key portfolios to continue their work of winning over the provinces. Breteuil headed the new ministry as *chef du conseil royal des finances*, La Vauguyon replaced Montmorin at foreign affairs and Foulon had a junior post. Puységur was pensioned off and Broglie added the war ministry to his position as generalissimo. A unified ministry, then, at last – but one whose chances of success were slight: the king was averse to violent measures, the troops were unreliable and money was in short supply to pay them, as Saint-Priest had reminded the king. Nevertheless, Barnave was worried: 'It is generally accepted', he told Rigaud on 11 July, 'that the plan to arrest a considerable number of the members of the three orders has been formed several times.'[64]

Barnave did not witness the storming of the Bastille, as his father happened to die on that day, relying on information from a new friend, the vicomte de Noailles, from an influential court family at odds with Marie-Antoinette.[65] So he can be forgiven for some of the errors he made in his report to a correspondent in Dauphiné, including the assertion that the besiegers had scaled the wall of the prison by climbing up the massed bodies of their fallen comrades! The interest in his letter of 15 July, probably to Aubert du Bayet, founder of the popular society of Grenoble, lies in its last paragraph. He urges the need for 'multiple addresses [of support] to the National Assembly and the formation of bourgeois militias ready to march', on Paris if need be. He adds that 'the rich have the biggest incentive to support the general good. The major portion of the Paris militia is comprised of the *bonne bourgeoisie* [underlined] and it is this which makes it so effective both in preserving order and as a bulwark against tyranny.' 'Bourgeois militia' – its original name – underlines the character of the National Guard formed to maintain order in Paris as royal authority collapsed. But Barnave goes further: it is formed of the upper middle class, the *bonne* bourgeoisie, people like himself and it is designed to keep the people in place as well as to resist the government. It is an updated equivalent of Montesquieu's *pouvoirs intermédiaires*, a two-way buffer.

He concludes his letter by saying: 'you must not lose a moment in circulating these ideas throughout the whole province. I rely totally on the energy of your town to whom it falls to be the mainspring of action. The same applies to all the provinces, *it is concerted from here*.'[66] This is the remains perhaps of the Necker network we noticed between Paris and Dauphiné before the Revolution. We do not know who, apart from Barnave, is doing the 'concerting'. The methodology is the same as the Jacobin network Barnave would play a leading part in creating later that year. The organiser may have been its precursor, the Breton Club, or some unknown steering group. A letter from Barnave to Bayet in February suggests that he may have had such an organisation in mind even then, as a provincial movement developed into a national one.

On 19 July he writes a more joyful letter to his friend Rigaud, also in Dauphiné, recounting the gains of the popular party:

> The Bastille stormed; the king having no option but to throw himself on the loyalty of his people, first in the Assembly then at the Hôtel de Ville in Paris. The former [Neckerite] ministers recalled in three days; the comte d'Artois, the Polignacs, the abbé de Vermont [Marie-Antoinette's reader] forced to flee in disguise. . . . More than 600,000 people of all ages and conditions . . . shouting *Vive la nation, vive la Liberté* and more spasmodically *Vive le Roi.*

The fall of the Bastille logically entailed the fall of the Breteuil administration and the return of Necker's. But it was a bitter pill for the king to swallow and involved some neat mental footwork from the deputies. Mirabeau wanted both to demand the dismissal of the Breteuil ministry and the recall of Necker, but Barnave 'wanted us to denounce the ministers without asking for the recall of M. Necker'.[67] His reasoning was subtle:

> Although in principle we have no right to demand either the dismissal of a minister or the re-appointment of another, it is none the less true that when a minister does not enjoy the confidence either of the nation or of its representatives, the National Assembly can and must state that it will not have any dealings with him over the concerns of the nation and that then the dismissal of such a minister becomes necessary.
>
> But the case is not the same with the recall of a minister who has been dismissed because by the same reasoning that one cannot force the National Assembly to have dealings with a councillor of the king who does not enjoy its confidence, one cannot force the king to recall a minister who has had occasion to displease him. I think we cannot demand the recall of M. Necker and that in this respect we must confine ourselves to expressing the opinion of the Assembly and that of the city of Paris which has been so emphatically proclaimed and in so terrible a fashion.

He is here feeling his way towards advocating a full-blown English parliamentary system, which worked by an apparent contradiction: if Parliament disliked the king's ministers, he was obliged to dismiss them if he wanted to get his business through. But once he had obliged Parliament, his business sailed through. The convention was that one should not put excessive pressure on the king – that was called 'storming the closet'; as with the 'infamous [Fox–North] coalition' of 1783. Parliament had forced George III to dismiss Lord North so that peace could be concluded with the Americans, but when it went on to force him to appoint Fox and North, it was felt it had gone too far, in making the king swallow 'a bitter pill' as he called it. For he regarded Fox as a rebel and North as a traitor. Parliament had outstripped feeling in the country and Pitt the Younger, whom George had installed as prime minister, won the general election of 1784. Barnave may have had this episode in mind – Louis XVI, who, perhaps in another's fate foresaw his own, had avidly followed the crisis and hoped that George would 'win through to the end'. Louis called the appointment of the coalition a 'personal pain' for George and it was known that Louis personally detested Necker.[68] 'Personal' was the key word. Paradoxically, the French monarchy, which had been growing more impersonal over the century – few knew what Louis XV actually thought but the machine functioned – became more personal during the Revolution. Kings come and go and Madame de Staël lamented that the Assembly did not look beyond the presumed personal hostility of the man Louis XVI towards the Revolution in order to frame a durable constitution in which the institution of monarchy had sufficient power to govern effectively.

The drafting of this constitution, Barnave told his friend, was in train; an eight-man committee had been set up and promised to report back in a fortnight. These preliminaries would quickly be examined in depth and then 'all they would have to do is deal with very subordinate matters, much less interesting especially for the spectator'. Rigaud was planning to visit in November but by then the fun would be over. All that would be left would be 'to tie up loose ends'. His friend would 'never be able to forgive himself . . . for having missed out on the finest spectacles which the annals of humanity afford'. November came and went and the Assembly was still in session; and on 15 December he told his mother that 'the moment when I can see you again is put off again and again'.[69]

⚜

It is instructive to note how various Third Estate deputies recorded the murders of the royal officials following the storming of the Bastille: de Launay, governor of the prison; de Flesselles, *prévot des marchands* (mayor) of Paris; Foulon, a junior minister aged eighty; and his son-in-law Berthier de Sauvigny, the Intendant of Paris, who, before his own execution, was made to kiss the bloodless head of Foulon. Barnave simply writes that they were 'put to death'. Biauzat says that Flesselles was 'convicted of having betrayed the city and summarily punished by death'. Foulon was 'condemned by the populace and hanged on the Place de Grève at 5 p.m. this evening'. After he had been cut down, 'a butcher's lad was forced to cut off his head, which was paraded for the delectation of the Palais Royal. His body was dragged through the mud for nearly an hour, after which not only his cordon rouge but all his clothes down to his shirt were cut to ribbons. Everyone wanted a bit.'[70]

Two hundred mounted men were sent from Paris to Compiègne to arrest Berthier. 'I trust I will be able to tell you in a few days', Barnave writes home, 'that he has been punished by death.' He adds, 'among the multiple crimes of which he stands accused I mention one, that of *lèse-nation*'. The apotheosis of this sort of pseudo-legalism comes in Robespierre's letter home: 'M. Foulon has been executed by a decree of the people' – he was lynched. Only Duquesnoy, a centre-right deputy who thought Noailles's account of the storming of the Bastille 'a trifle overblown', shows a concern that the people might '*acquire a taste for blood through shedding it however impure and with whatever justification*' (my emphasis). Duquesnoy wrote this on 16 July.

Barnave would paraphrase Duquesnoy on 23 July with words that would haunt him for the rest of his life. Barnave himself gives the context. On 22 July Foulon and Berthier were murdered, not in the heat of the moment, as de Launay had been, but after 200 men had trawled the Île-de-France looking for them. Berthier's son had asked Lally-Tollendal, whose own father had been unjustifiably executed under Louis XV, to intervene. He could not because the Assembly was closed for renovations. But he exploited the occasion to demand a proclamation threatening disturbers of the peace.

Barnave was angered by the theatrical way Lally deployed the *style larmoyante* for which he was famous, and which he himself eschewed – 'talking about himself, his feelings, his father' rather than Berthier and the 'state of Paris'. Barnave, whose 'nerves were on edge', lost control of himself (a rare thing) and said 'that all revolutions were accompanied by bad incidents and that it was fortunate that this one had so few victims and that the blood of these etc.' – his readers could fill in 'etc.' with 'was not that pure'.

Two things are clear about this speech. First, that Barnave did utter the infamous words and second, that he did not plan to. The *Moniteur* devotes only a short paragraph to Barnave's speech; but de Visme quoted both Lally's speech and Barnave's reply *in extenso*:

> M. Barnave said that the only precautions needed were the establishment of free and regular town councils and the bourgeois guards throughout the kingdom. He was moreover little affected with the incidents which so greatly exercised the Assembly. They were merely

> the inevitable consequences of a great revolution and then he added 'and in any case is the blood which has just flowed all that pure?' It caused us great pain to hear a young man raise himself so coldly against the general *sensibilité*. We must assume that his feelings were led astray by the desire to shine but what awful times we live in when ambition can serve itself with such deplorable means![71]

This witness clearly thought that rather than an uncharacteristic spontaneous outburst, as Barnave later claimed, his intervention was a cold calculation.

Most of Barnave's speeches were delivered impromptu and the draft for this part of his speech suggests that in the heat of battle he shifted his focus from the citizens slain in the rising to the royal officials: 'They talk of the blood that has been shed but this blood is rather that of the citizens who have defended the laws and the French nation. They suffered aggression and, reduced to defend themselves after having seen several of their comrades die, prudence and moderation accompanied their [faded word]. . . . They spared blood and, in this battle . . . in which eight of their comrades had fallen before their very eyes' – here he breaks off. The draft is actually just as insensitive, but one likes to think, with Madame de Stael, that Barnave was acting out of character. Three days after he made his speech, Barnave, in a letter to Rigaud, rows back a little: 'These past days the people of Paris have put to death M. Foulon and M. Berthier de Sauvigny, Intendant of Paris, without judicial process.'[72]

The royalist press made hay with the 'impure blood' and the phrase soon spread across the Channel when Edmund Burke quoted from a French source referring to Barnave's quip: 'M. Barnave laughing . . . when oceans of blood surrounded us.'[73]

⚜

Tackett's thesis that the Third Estate deputies did not arrive as revolutionaries but 'became' so should be modified. The Breton delegation led by Le Chapelier – and soon joined by Barnave and others such as Siéyès – wanted a sovereign National Constituent Assembly almost from the beginning: the first definite evidence dates from 14 May, that is, a week after the opening of the Estates. Many others, such as Vismes and even Duquesnoy, wanted the same thing but were afraid that if they took this step, the king would dissolve the Estates. They were not sure of the relative forces at play. It took them a month to come round to the idea but, as Barnave had told his uncle back in the previous autumn, the Revolution had already been accomplished in idea.

The question then becomes not so much *when* as *where*. Dauphiné and Brittany were already in Revolutionary mode in 1788. And the ball was kicked off at Versailles by the Assembly of Notables in 1787. Some places, perhaps Bourg-en-Bresse, never accepted the Revolution – at least not in their hearts. Moreover, the apparent paradox of Brittany, the most conservative of all the provinces, radicalising first can be resolved. The towns were revolutionary and the countryside – both nobles and peasants – conservative. As Barnave said, the nobles and peasants were natural conservative allies. Is there much evidence of châteaux-burning in Brittany in 1789? In 1793 the country districts of the former province rose up in defence of throne and altar.

— SIX —

THE DECISIVE PHASE, 14 JULY–6 OCTOBER 1789

The decisive phase of the French Revolution began and ended with transformative violence. It began with the fall of the Bastille and ended during the night of 5/6 October with the attempted assassination of the queen, who escaped from her pursuers dressed only in a shift. The popular mentality was the same on both occasions. For as Malouet says: 'If the court had been at Paris instead of Versailles [in July] it would have been the ministers, the princes, who would have been slaughtered instead of Foulon, Berthier and de Launay. It was as the agents of the Government that they were pursued . . . here was a ferocious populace in search of victims and it would have taken them indiscriminately in the street or on the throne.'[1]

The October Days brought home to the king the full, personal implications of the fall of the Bastille. Only then did he confide (to his cousin Charles IV of Spain) that the violence had robbed the whole revolutionary experience of legitimacy. Before 5/6 October there was a chance to build a new consensual system. The July revolution justified a major reordering of France which was accepted by the bulk of the population; the October Days justified resistance, and resistance justified a repression which, until comparatively recently, was justified by the French academic establishment.

In this period, when the foundations of a new constitution were laid, the political parties took shape: on the extreme left were a few men such as Pétion and Robespierre who thought that the new constitution should be derived entirely from the Declaration of the Rights of Man, which formed its preamble. At this time a rift also developed in the centre: Barnave, Alexandre de Lameth and Adrien Duport and the

Bretons on the left centre; and Mounier, Malouet and the group known as the *Monarchiens* on the right. On the extreme right were the ultras, diehard defenders of the old regime.

Everything hinged on devising a workable constitution. Duquesnoy despaired at the Assembly's failure to concentrate exclusively on this task: rather than being side-tracked by receiving endless sycophantic delegations and attending to disturbances in remote mountain villages, they should tackle the root cause of the trouble – the lack of a workable constitution. But if they could have tackled the problem of the constitution, its solution would have been less urgent. The first dilemma concerned the role of the king in the framing of the constitution. The bulk of the *cahiers* – and Mounier made a digest of them – insisted that the process should be a collaborative effort between the king and the Estates-General. But they no longer were the Estates-General – they were the *Assemblée nationale constituante*, the National *Constituent* Assembly, itself the result of the king's failure to resolve the dispute between the orders in favour of the Third Estate. The implications of this metamorphosis were realised immediately by Barentin and they were made palpable, as Robespierre was quick to realise, by the fall of the Bastille, by which 'the nation recaptured the legislative power'.[2]

But was 'legislative power' the same as 'Constituent' power? And was 'Constituent' power 'dictatorial power', as Siéyès asserted? This was the king's view when he was finally able to speak his mind:

> When the Estates-General, having styled themselves the National Assembly, began to occupy themselves with the Constitution of the Kingdom . . . the deputies reneged on one of the main clauses in all their *cahiers* providing that *legislation would be carried out in conjunction* with the king: in contempt of this stipulation, the Assembly has denied the king any say in the constitution by refusing him the right to grant or withhold his assent to the articles which it deems constitutional, by reserving to itself the right to place such articles in this category as it sees fit.[3]

And many from all sides of the Assembly agreed that this is what had happened, that a 'religious veil' had been drawn over this usurpation. This was recognised by Barnave's two closest allies: Alexandre de

Lameth, who coined the phrase 'religious veil', and Adrien Duport, who told the Assembly that had the king refused his sanction to any of the constitutional decrees, 'you would have declared . . . that you had no need for any sanction on the king's part to establish your constitution'. But the king's refusal would have been embarrassing because his sanction had smoothed the passage of legislation which the country would otherwise have regarded as too radical since it was not yet 'ready to trust its destinies to your zeal'.[4] Barnave argued that since the king's future powers would derive from the constitution, they could not be exercised over the actual framing of that document. A creature had no part in the act of creation.

In some jotted fragments Barnave claimed that 'Constituent power is sovereignty itself', delegated by the real sovereign, the people, to whom it must 'give an account of its exercise either explicitly or tacitly'. But he does not demonstrate that the nation *had* delegated Constituent power to the National Assembly – indeed, he admits that the Assembly had seized it. He draws a contrast between France in 1789 and England in 1688. Although James II had fled, though he had thrown the Great Seal into the Thames from his barge, the old institutions still existed. So, even though Parliament was a 'Convention Parliament', its ability 'to operate the good' was limited. In France, however, 'the abuses which originated with the government' had led to the collapse of that government, so the National Assembly had a free hand 'to operate the good'.[5] They were confronted with a *tabula rasa*; they were midwives to the birth of a new universe.

Not only was the king's constitutional and legislative power in doubt – even his executive action was restricted. Barnave had inaugurated his public career back in 1783 with his allocution, which stressed the need for the separation of the executive, legislative and judicial powers. In 1789 he starts a section on the three powers and in a revealing sentence argues 'that the first [legislative] power is so closely allied to sovereignty that if it . . .' – and there he breaks off. But whatever he was reluctant to say, he is clear that the executive was the junior of the three powers. In the high summer of 1789, the executive power had collapsed of itself with no help from the Assembly. It was a collapse both of its spirit and its mechanism. As early as spring 1787 the naval minister Castries had written, 'The mood [in the Assembly of Notables] tends to restrain authority in such a way that monarchical government will no longer be able to reconstitute itself.'[6] By July 1789 this process had progressed to the point where, Barnave was able to write, 'All the elements of the former structure had collapsed even before the National Assembly had laid the first blocks of the new one.'[7] The superb administrative system of the *ancien régime* was in ruins, from the intendants – 'the best part of my system', Louis had put it – downwards. The Intendant of Paris had been brutally murdered, the Intendant of the Île-de-France had taken refuge in England and the Intendant of Brittany had escaped the mob by jumping over a garden wall. The army, unpaid and mutinous, was no longer a reliable instrument, as had been shown on 14 July.

Barnave blamed the government. Its actions had caused the troubles, forcing the people of Paris and 'some' towns to exact a 'cruel vengeance', and now it 'groaned' and expected the Assembly to end them by a simple 'word' of command. They were aided and abetted by 'some' members of the Assembly, who, like Lally-Tollendal, imagined that a stern 'proclamation' would do the trick. The heart of the troubles was that the unelected authorities had no authority since they were discredited and 'hated'. What was needed was to 'urgently set up' elected municipalities, provincial assemblies and judges. This was what the 'circumstances demanded'. It 'would have linked in detail all the parts of the body politic before linking them with each other with an overarching relationship to the constitution; it would have created a nation before creating a government'. A precious fortnight had been wasted before even addressing this issue, but at least the armed forces had been required to take an oath to the nation as well as the king and a 'bourgeois [erased] national guard' set up.[8]

However, even these new entities were powerless in the face of rural unrest, which spread, Barnave wrote, with 'a rapid vibration' throughout the country. The peasants were simply refusing to pay feudal dues, burning the documents recording them and the châteaux which housed them. Mounier and Barnave felt a special responsibility for what was in effect a peasant revolt because in order to preserve the 'irredeemably precarious' unity at the Romans Assembly, they had agreed to the 'Addition' to the mandate which guaranteed feudal rights or fair compensation should they be abolished. On 23 January a member of the Estates of Dauphiné had written a letter to Mounier (which he probably communicated to Barnave) saying that the Addition had 'struck everyone to the quick' and that the village communities should have a right to revoke it. In September Barnave wrote of 'misfortunes – especially in our province'.[9]

There was panic and misinformation at Grenoble. Madame Barnave told her son that 'M. de Villedeuil's letter' did not help. It will be remembered that Villedeuil, the reactionary minister of the interior, had told the provinces that the programme of the *séance royale* was still in force. Madame Barnave did not know whether the royal troops had been withdrawn from Paris and Versailles. She feared they were 'halfway from Paris' – to where? Were they making for Metz, as the diehards wanted? Were they passing thorough Dauphiné? All the peasants working on Barnave's estate – it was his now after the death of his father – got it into their heads that the king was sending artillery from loyalist Valence to confront them. No belief in good king Louis here. Fully armed, they all set off at 9 a.m. The new National Guard tried to stop them. Some could not afford to miss a day's wages so Madame Barnave sold some silver to help them out. Her example was not followed.[10]

She had become an ultra-patriot, though she signed all her letters 'de Presle-Barnave', implicitly reminding her son every time that he was half-noble. The nobles and *parlementaires* of Grenoble had all fled to Chambéry, she related, but attempts were being made to coax them back with the promise of an escort from the National Guard. Madame Barnave's beloved brother had been besieged in the Citadel of Montélimar, where he was commandant. He, his sister affirmed, was now a patriot himself. He had supported the Parlement (as had Barnave), but turned against it after it had ruled that the Estates should follow the 1614 pattern. Now he was all for the 'Third Estate' and the 'commons'.[11] Since 'you have been in Paris', he was 'full of praise for the commons and blame for the first two orders'. And so was his proud mother: 'How many fine things have been enacted, my friend! How many fine things you have done! My heart overflows with joy.'

But Barnave and the Revolution were not universally popular in Grenoble. Barnave put it all down to the 'aristocrats', but his mother said that 'the solicitors complained that they were ruined and the barristers that there was nothing for them to do'. She was obsessed with the burning of châteaux. The peasants went in search of parchments recording feudal dues but she thought it was unlikely the *seigneurs* kept them there. There were 'attempts to discover who was inspiring the burning of châteaux. I am assured that M. Montauban de la Tour du Pin is one of them' – conspiracy theories abounded.

Barnave received a vitriolic letter dated 'Grenoble September 1789':

> If the châteaux in Dauphiné are attacked, Monsieur, you can expect to see your residence at Saint-Robert burned to the ground. It is the fruit of rapine. It will be no great loss if it is destroyed because you will be able to build a finer one with the money which M. de Mirabeau has received from the English and surely shared with you – they assure us that he has been well paid. His incense at first led you astray ['you perverted' crossed out]; his money corrupted you – there is no other explanation of your strange conduct. Every day I groan that I misplaced my confidence in you and contributed to your election. One could put it differently but [you secured your seat] by dishonest means . . . which you should never have employed if you had been in good faith. I am perfectly happy that you should know my way of thinking on your account.[12]

This rancorous letter is a harbinger, during the period of Barnave's popularity, of the accusations that would come to haunt him: his mysterious association with Mirabeau and the unexplained sources of his apparent wealth or wealthy lifestyle, and his perceived political volte-face or two faces.

⚜

The twin July crises, in Paris and in the countryside, had left the Assembly drained – even 'traumatised', it has been suggested; 'tired' according to Barnave – with the financial resources of most of its members 'exhausted'.[13] Apologising to a 'dear friend' in Grenoble for his long 'silence', Barnave explained that 'for some time we have lived in a mighty whirlwind which has left us – actors and spectators – neither the time nor the possibility of collecting our thoughts'.[14] The terrors and triumph in Paris had given way to apathy and the 'aristocratic party' was beginning to reassert itself, using the chaos in the countryside to win over 'the faint-hearted'. Nevertheless, Barnave 'confessed to being not all that upset' by the break applied by the faint-hearted because 'I am pretty certain that the Assembly would have gone too far if it had continued with its initial élan.' It needed to be 'moderated' by 'circumstances'.

However, there was good and bad moderation: moderation through 'foresight' was desirable, but moderation through 'lassitude' less so. The committee dominated by Mounier which was drafting the constitution fell into the latter camp. 'It is not working hard and its members are quarrelling among themselves.' And they had let slip a golden opportunity: 'when it was entirely the master to make the constitution all by itself, it let it slip right out of its hands and handed it over to us' – the rest of the Assembly.

Barnave is clearly ambivalent about whether this is a good thing. On the one hand, he regrets that the supine behaviour of the liberal 'minority of the nobles' had allowed the aristocrats and the conservative members of the Third Estate to gain control during the hiatic period between the fall of the Bastille and the completion of the constitution; but, on the other, he feared that but for their influence the untrammelled radicals would have carried the Revolution 'too far'. Half of him wanted the committee to found a strong constitutional monarchy – it would have saved him a lot of trouble two years later when he tried to do the same. Perhaps he wanted the committee to do the moderating so he would not have to do it himself. This draft letter provides a pivotal insight into Barnave's political career: there was no volte-face – just an abiding ambiguity which could be resolved by 'circumstances' either way. As it was, he was ready to let the force of 'circumstances' override 'the nature of things'.

Barnave takes up 'circumstances' again in a private memorandum, a pep talk, an interrogation with himself which he wrote at this time. There are two versions, each entitled '*où en sommes nous*' – 'where do we stand' – in early August. He talks again of the collapse of the old order, 'with the result that the bonds of positive laws are completely sundered. If public order is maintained; if the various parties in the body politic still deliberate together, it is due to lingering habits; it is due to the national character that it' – and here he breaks off.

Then in a firmer hand he writes, 'the moment where we stand is the most propitious of all to constitute a people'. But how, since he realises that it could go either way: 'I am trying to unravel the true situation. I am seeking what is the good or what is the evil that we must expect; and I am applying to circumstances the plan of conduct which they seem to me to necessitate. I am seeking to prove to the representatives of the nation that everything is fine and that the future is secure if only with a bold hand. . . .' He breaks off again.[15] What is at issue here for Barnave is the relationship between 'circumstances' and 'the force of things', or, as we would say, triggers and underlying causes. But 'circumstances' are more powerful than mere triggers – they are a halfway house to Barnave's fully developed theory of the force of things. He does not know what in fact was just round the corner.

Barnave's draft letter was written in the fortnight ending on 3 August – it can be dated from his reference to 'the two noble secretaries' of the Assembly. This suggests that he was mentally unprepared for the dramatic way that the crisis would be resolved by the renunciation of all privileges on the night of 4 August.

Even had the army been a reliable instrument, the National Assembly was reluctant to allow the king the use of it to restore order in the countryside, lest he turn it against the Assembly afterwards. So, a stage-managed surrender of feudal rights was arranged in the Breton Club. 'The motion had been devised by a few of the commons', but for maximum effect it was decided that the motion should be proposed by the richest feudatory, the portly duc d'Aiguillon, one of Barnave's inner circle. D'Aiguillon was pipped to the post in the Assembly by the vicomte de Noailles, who had no property and was nicknamed John Lackland, a grandstanding cousin of the grandstanding Lafayette, the commandant of the Paris National Guard. Noailles made the same point as Mounier's correspondent: that at the village level it was feudal rights that were the issue, not the constitution, which was dealt with in the *cahiers* of the next level, the *baillage*.

The surrenders, competitive virtue-signalling, took place in a sitting on the night of 4/5 August lasting until 2 a.m. 'People were pressing round the bureau' to make renunciations. Ecclesiastical tithes were abolished without compensation since they were not property and the clergy became state-salaried officials. The full implication of this was not at first appreciated, though ecclesiastical deputies led by Siéyès protested on 10 August at what they regarded as expropriation. The

August decrees also saw the entire implementation of Calonne's 1787 programme; indeed, in some respects, it went further, with the abolition of privilege in taxation, the sale of office and the different privileges of the towns and provinces of France. The Dauphiné deputy, the marquis de Blacons, was the first to surrender the privileges of his province.[16] Seigneurial justice, which Barnave had so stoutly defended in 1788, when attacked by Lamoignon was also swept aside. In short, the entire 'corporate' organisation of France disappeared overnight, though the customs union Calonne had proposed was not achieved until 1791.

However, as de Visme observed, 'It was not just enthusiasm which determined this great event but politics – fear and spite have served us well. But what matter the motives when the actions are fine and useful. It is clear for example that spite directed M. de Foucault when he proposed the reduction of court pensions. It was directed principally against the House of Noailles. The vicomte de Noailles and [his brother] the prince de Poix submitted with good grace.'[17]

On 6 August Barnave's ally Duport proposed the grandiloquent and inaccurate decree proclaiming that 'the entire feudal regime is abolished'. Inaccurate because it was only serfdom, or what was called *servitude personelle*, that is, anything which implied that the *seigneur* had some ownership over his peasants, that was abolished outright. It was rare and, where it existed, much attenuated by 1789. The king had abolished it on his crown lands in 1779 together with *mainmorte*, which prevented the serf from transmitting his land to any but his children. Dues on peasant properties, which were really the equivalent of rent, were to be redeemed. There was a grey area between servitude and rent which was never defined; nor was the rate of compensation for dues. Nevertheless, Vismes observed, 'What a blow struck against the nobility'; and added, 'they did not seem to realise the consequences'.

When the king finally gave his response in his message to the Assembly of 18 September, he found little to criticise in the August decrees, only making five observations of substance.[18] Louis said that where serfdom had in the past been replaced by a money payment, this should not be abolished without compensation; Barnave agreed. Louis also observed that seigneurial justice should remain until, as Lamoignon had provided in 1788, something had been put in its place; if tithes were abolished, they should be replaced by a tax payable to the state. Otherwise, the operation would merely result in the random redistribution of a windfall to landowners of 60 to 80 million livres that the treasury could well use.

Finally, Louis addressed the implications for foreign policy: the Treaty of Westphalia guaranteed the seigneurial rights of foreign princes with possessions in the former German province of Alsace, the '*princes possessionés*' and Louis informed the Assembly that they had already lodged strong protests. Also, the pope needed to be consulted over the suppression of annates – the revenue from vacant sees was paid to the pope.

Most of these were reasonable points and would have saved a lot of trouble, especially those relating to foreign policy, the king's area of expertise. The rights of the *princes possessionés* gave the Holy Roman Empire an excuse to interfere in the Revolution and the cancellation of annates gave the pope an additional reason to condemn it. By 1792 Barnave had come to think that this running sore was the fundamental stumbling block to maintaining peace with Austria. Louis commented bitterly on what happened when he volunteered an opinion and refrained from giving any in future. The Venetian ambassador wrote that the king's 'very pertinent' observations on the August decrees as a whole 'clearly demonstrate that the sphere of expertise of this Assembly is very limited'.[19]

Privately, Barnave thought the decrees had gone too far: in a draft letter dated 5 September he wrote: 'I will not dispute that some of the decrees of 4 August are excessive or precipitate.'[20] Precipitate indeed: Mirabeau said that they 'had spent an entire month discussing syllables [in the Declaration of Rights] and in one night they overturned the entire structure of the monarchy'.[21] Barnave also agreed with Mounier and the king that there should be compensation for money payments in lieu of *servitude personelle* because, though unjust in origin, they had become legitimised over time and some families relied on them. Barnave no doubt felt bound to honour the undertaking made by the Addition to the Dauphiné mandate.[22] The acts of the Assembly should be compensatory, not confiscatory. Feudal dues were property in a way that tithes had never been. Barnave's views and the king's were not so very far apart but the king wanted to assert his right to modify legislation whether constitutional or not; Barnave wanted to deny him that right.

THE DECLARATION OF THE RIGHTS OF MAN

The Assembly had been working on a Declaration of Rights since the fall of the Bastille. But they were continually distracted by more urgent matters. Barnave hoped that in time the Declaration would become a 'national catechism' like the American one drafted by Thomas Jefferson, now ambassador to France, on which it was modelled. But the French version never caught on in the way that the American one did, copies never having the vitality of the original: 'We hold these truths to be self-evident' is more euphonious than the didactic 'Men are born and remain free with equal rights. Social distinctions can be based solely on public utility.'

Barnave hoped that the Declaration would act as a bulwark against the Scylla of aristocratic revival and the Charybdis of popular incursions. We have seen that even before the Estates-General opened, he was worried that if the orders sat together, the aristocracy would become dominant. Now, in September, he believed that his fears had been justified: 'the union of the aristocracy with the commons', he told a friend, 'has totally changed the spirit of the Assembly'. 'You would be convinced of the truth of this', he went on, 'if you considered the present spirit of our Assembly. The clergy and the nobility have gained such an ascendancy there . . . that if the principles were not laid down, we could answer for nothing.' 'Principles' for Barnave (and Robespierre) was code for the application of the Declaration to general policy. 'If those who spurned ministerial favours or court etiquette' had not suffered the slings and arrows of 'calumny' to fight for the Revolution, it would have been lost. For most people – and this would become a refrain – 'preferred peace to liberty'.[23]

That was in a private letter. In his speech concluding the debate on the Declaration, however, Barnave stressed the Charybdis of demagoguery: 'I conclude with a powerful consideration. If a man of genius and audacity, abusing his hold on the legislature [Mirabeau?] were to propose the levelling of fortunes by the adoption of an agrarian law, the Declaration of Rights would be there to counteract the baleful effects of his eloquence.'[24] The history of the Roman Republic was the textbook of the Revolution and none of Barnave's auditors would have missed the reference to the agrarian law introduced by the Gracchi brothers which redistributed any estates above 125 acres.

Nevertheless, in one of the four articles he would have liked included in the Declaration he modifies this position: 'The social order requires that all property be respected, but it must also guarantee all its citizens a subsistence such that everyone should be able to procure the necessaries for life, whether by working – if he can – or in any case if he cannot.' For Barnave the ownership of property was both an inviolable right and the motor of history, but it carried with it a sort of bourgeois *noblesse oblige*. This would become a commonplace in the next century but was not in Barnave's.

Barnave listed privately – he spoke little in the debates – five more articles he thought should be in the Declaration of Rights. These included the following:

> 1 No one is bound by a law to which he has not given his consent either in person or by his representatives.
>
> 2 . . . the people cannot alienate the right to make or alter constitutional laws; thus its representatives can only exercise this right with an express authorisation from the major part of the nation. [When the constitution was finally – in the summer of 1791 – reaching its completion, Barnave wanted to make it very hard to change this.]
>
> 5 Public force must be directed by the magistrate in conformity with the law and if he uses the force he has received in order to protect the laws to infringe them instead, then those under his command must refuse to obey and the people are entitled to repel force with force.[25]

THE CONSTITUTIONAL BATTLE

The Declaration was finally presented to the Assembly on 27 August. It was to form Chapter 1 of the constitution. On 31 August Mounier, in the name of the constitutional committee, presented its draft of Chapter 2, 'Of the government', and Chapter 3, 'Of the legislative body', to the Assembly. Chapter 2 simply maintained the succession as traditionally defined. This was at once uncontroversial and problematic: no one considered replacing Louis XVI, so they were saddled with an incumbent king whose powers had to be restrained because he was distrusted.

Barnave put it like this: 'the Constituent Assembly undertook that most difficult of things: a great revolution without changing the king. It built a new ship but retained a main mast made of old timber.'[26] But since the old timber was rotten, the Assembly thought it could not be relied on. Madame de Staël, however, thought the Assembly should 'have established the royal power independently of what might be feared or hoped from its actual possessor'.

Baron Wimphen went out on a limb by saying that France should be defined as a 'royal democracy' instead of a monarchy. Like 'enlightened despotism', this was a paradox – as de Visme observed: 'it is very surprising indeed to see these two words in conjunction'. Duquesnoy claimed that 'our present ideas cannot be expressed by the old terms representing old ideas with no relationship to present principles . . . we must find a new definition'.[27]

The main proposals in Chapter 3, 'Of the legislature', were that there should be two chambers, a lower elective one and an upper chamber, called a senate. This would be chosen by the king from shortlists selected by the provincial estates from all classes of citizens. The king would have the power to dissolve the lower chamber, but would have to call elections for a replacement. He would have an absolute veto over the Assembly's measures. However, he would not have the right to initiate legislation and this would have prevented the development of parliamentary government on the English model: ministers with seats and commanding a majority in the Assembly, initiating legislation and thereby obviating the need for a veto. The very existence of a veto was a mark of failure.

The Assembly rejected its committee's proposal that the king should have the right of dissolution. Barnave fully realised, even exaggerated, the implications of this: 'To give or deny the king the power to dissolve the Assembly is to threaten either the existence of the monarchy or that of liberty . . . This problem was insoluble.' He later admitted,

> In England the king alone convokes, adjourns, prorogues, dissolves and orders new elections to Parliament. In the French constitution of 1789, the National Assembly had the sole right to adjourn itself and could never be dissolved. This totally autonomous and independent existence of the legislative body was the essentially republican

basis of the constitution and . . . it has to be confessed that over time it would have to be modified or it would destroy the monarchy.

Barnave argued that the king of England could safely be allowed to exercise the power of dissolution because the existence of an upper house meant that he would not be ruling alone during the hiatic period of elections.[28] However, in 1789 he argued vigorously against the proposed senate, revisiting arguments he had already deployed in the Romans assemblies and against Calonne. In England, unlike in France, the peers were 'too elevated and too few in number to humiliate the mass of subjects'. Again, that word 'humiliate'. Moreover, their relatives did not enjoy their privileges, 'being to the contrary mixed in with the other citizens' and often sitting in the commons.[29] Madame de Staël thought that this could be replicated in France by staffing an upper house with scions of 'the 100 or 150 historic families' and that this was an elegant way of 'quietly consigning to obscurity the minor nobility so numerous in France, a nobility in no way consecrated by history or recommended by public utility in any shape – and which discovered, much more than its higher brethren, a contempt for the Third Estate because its vanity always made it fear its not attaining sufficient distinction'.[30]

When he surveyed the course of the Revolution in 1792/3, Barnave had come to 'consider [a two-chamber legislature] to be the only solid and reasonable way of organising the national representation of a large country'. However, it was a way of 'terminating' a revolution, not inaugurating one. 'If the thirst for equality gags on [a second chamber] today . . . after a few years' experience one will be established out of a love of order when equality no longer feels threatened.' Back in August 1789 the aristocracy's intransigence was too raw for them to be accommodated in the new arrangements.

⚜

Private discussions were held on the linked question of bicameralism and the veto between leaders of the two wings of the centre party, Mounier on its right, and Barnave, Duport and Lameth on its left. Both wings were also in discussions with the government – meetings between

Mounier and individual ministers, including the foreign secretary Montmorin, and between Barnave and Necker through the intermediary of his daughter, Madame de Staël. The main sources for these gatherings are Mounier's published *Exposé*,[31] Barnave's interchange with Madame de Staël and Necker's published account of the advice of the *Conseil d'état* to the king.[32] This was the last chance to hold the centre together and, by his own admission, it foundered on the rock of Mounier's intransigence. The peace broker was Barnave, who tried to reconcile Lameth and Duport with Mounier and Lafayette, who wanted an elective senate as proposed by the constitutional committee but were against a veto.[33] It pained Barnave to quarrel with Mounier, his mentor, but thought he was stuck in 1788 and did not realise there had been a revolution.

Lafayette arranged three meetings at his Paris residence and when they proved inconclusive, he wrote to Thomas Jefferson, who was known for his hospitality, suggesting that a convivial dinner at his house might be conducive to an agreement.[34] Lafayette had squared this meeting with Montmorin. After dinner, 'the cloth being removed and wine set upon the table', the participants negotiated from 4 to 10 o'clock. They were, 'Lafayette himself, Duport, Barnave, Alexandre de Lameth [in favour of a single chamber and a suspensive veto] and Blacon, Mounier, Latour-Maubourg and d'Agout [who favoured two chambers and an absolute veto]'. Barnave, Mounier, Blacon and d'Agout had all worked together in Dauphiné.

The two sides differed on what had been agreed. On Saturday 29 August the gathering reconvened at Versailles and the grouping of Barnave, Duport and Lameth, who were beginning to be called 'the triumvirs', presented Mounier with 'a convention' and told him that if he refused, they would convene 'a numerous committee [the Breton Club?] to agitate in favour of a suspensive veto' and that the propaganda would be extended to Paris. This was the first acknowledged use of the Parisian lever. On 31 August there was a big demonstration against the veto at the Palais Royal residence of the duc d'Orléans, though there was little understanding of the issue. For as Madame de Staël put it, 'they spoke of the veto in the streets of Paris as of a monster that would devour little children'.[35] Mirabeau's collaborator Étienne Dumont wrote that the question of the veto 'was the first constitutional question on which the people took a lively interest'.[36] Would they have done so without prompting from Barnave and his allies?

Mounier was by now thoroughly alarmed, claiming that he was on a proscription list of those who supported the absolute veto, but that the name Mirabeau, who had also supported one, was mysteriously absent, the implication being that he was in league with Orléans. There was talk of 15,000 men marching on Versailles then and there to bring the royal family to the capital. Mounier turned to Lafayette, who managed to contain the Paris rising, which was confined to the precincts of the Palais Royal and petered out in the evening.

Nothing daunted, the same day Lally-Tollendal and Mounier presented the constitutional committee's recommendations to the Assembly unchanged: two chambers, absolute veto, right of dissolution. Simultaneously, their ally Clermont-Tonnerre proposed that if it was threatened, the Assembly should move to a provincial town, which was understood to be Soissons.[37]

Having contained the Paris rising,[38] Lafayette wrote again to Mounier on 1 September saying that it was essential that he 'made a coalition [with the triumvirs] and yielded on certain articles [. . .] he went as far as to say that otherwise he would be responsible for the bloodshed'.

Madame Barnave did not think that the king should have a veto at all, absolute or suspensive. She told her son:

> I have read M. Mounier's book on government. There are some excellent things in it but he has not convinced me that the king should be above the laws nor that his sanction should be necessary for their formation. I find it deeply offensive that one man should outweigh everyone else and block the wishes of all. He should be allowed to examine laws and make observations but nothing more. I could say more about [Mounier's] book but I don't want to miss the post.[39]

Barnave had already come to the same conclusion: 'The people delegates legislative power to its representatives. It would be against the nature of things that the monarch should share legislative power with them because the law is not a force or an action but rather a reason, a judgement. It would be absurd for the nation to repose the same confidence in the opinion of one man as in that of 1,200.'[40] On Sunday 6 September Lafayette repeated his warning to Mounier; on the 7th the Assembly closed the discussion on the legislature (Chapter 3 of the constitution); and on Thursday the 10th it voted for a single chamber by 849 votes to 89, with 122 abstentions. One reason why a second chamber was rejected by the National Assembly, and that decisively, was because the provincial noble deputies stood no chance of being selected for a putative upper chamber.

Attention now turned to the question of the royal veto, which, with no upper chamber as a buffer, had to take the strain of countering the Assembly. Through Madame de Staël, Barnave negotiated what he thought was a deal on the veto between his allies and her father, the *premier ministre des finances*, Jacques Necker. It will be remembered that Barnave's mother was very distantly related to Necker's wife and therefore to his daughter Germaine, then married to the Swedish ambassador, baron de Staël-Holstein. This is not just a genealogist's discovery: a letter of Barnave's father dated 19 June 1780 to one of his two sons shows that the family were already in contact with the Neckers.[41] The Barnaves had been part of a strong Neckerite faction in Dauphiné during Necker's first ministry. Only one letter apiece survives of Barnave's correspondence with Madame de Staël, but Barnave's letter suggests an established intimacy with its mock formal jocular tone redolent of his youthful letters to his sisters. It ends with 'Mme l'Ambassadrice . . . will I hope not leave this letter lying around on the mantelpiece'! Barnave must have been a regular visitor to the ambassadress's famous salon.

Madame de Staël also writes fondly of Barnave. She calls his 'apostrophe' 'is their blood then so pure?' unfortunate, totally at variance with his 'upright, delicate and even feeling character'. She considered that this 'young advocate from Dauphiné of the greatest merit was more fitted by his talents than almost any deputy to figure as a speaker in the English [Parliamentary] manner'. She adds tellingly, 'these elegant leaders of the popular party aimed at entering the government'.

Barnave's letter to Madame de Staël can be dated to the evening of Thursday 10 September. Beylié, who published this letter, omitted the superscription: 'The king and the assembly of representatives are both, the one and the other, delegates of the people.' This idea forms the structure of his notes for a speech on the veto. As delegates 'both are accountable to the nation and if one of them alters what had been confided to them, then the other appeals to the people as . . . sovereign judge and it is this appeal which gives the king the right to suspend' the law. His conclusion is elliptical but clear-cut: 'If the king refuses the law proposed [there must be a] new Assembly.'[42] In other words, the king is given not so much the power as the obligation to dissolve Parliament.

Barnave took a lot of pains over drafting his letter to Madame de Staël, with numerous crossings out, mixing the formal with the intimate. The letter runs:

> M. Barnave has the honour of warning Mme l'Ambassadrice de Suède that to ensure the success of tomorrow's initiative, it is very important that the letter which will be read [from Necker to the Assembly] states that the king will not exercise his suspensive veto in relation to the decrees [*arrêtés*] of the present Assembly but only to any laws which may be proposed by the successor ones. The importance placed on the decrees of 4 August by a portion of the Assembly could be a major obstacle to the success of the proposal if there were any lingering doubt on this matter.
>
> Mme l'Ambassadrice will I hope ['be so kind as to' is crossed out] pardon M. Barnave for troubling her so late in the day with matters of this kind and, in making the best use of this warning as she sees fit, she will be so good as not to leave it lying around on the mantelpiece.

The 'initiative' to which Barnave refers is a plan coordinated with the left-centre deputies that Necker should communicate to the Assembly the proceedings of the *Conseil d'état* in which he advised the king to opt for a suspensive veto, together with the covering letter to which Barnave alludes, which should make it clear that the king does not intend to use his new veto during the life of the present Constituent Assembly, especially over the decrees of 4 August.

Bradby considers that the letter from Madame de Staël which follows this in the archive is probably a reply.[43] It is dated simply 'Wednesday evening' but the president of the Assembly asked to read Necker's letter on Friday the 11th. Madame de Staël asks Barnave 'to call on her for a moment in the morning at 11 a.m. A matter which deeply concerns me obliges me to ask for this kindness. Also, I do not want M. Barnave to talk to *anyone* about this note. I need only to have mentioned the matter to be sure that it will remain a secret. I must sign it to avoid confusion with another person who I will have the pleasure of discussing with you.'[44] This does not sound like a reference to the veto, rather a question of patronage. The marquis de Ferrières notes Staël's method: 'secret meetings, notes sent in the morning, evening rendezvous'.[45] The association between Barnave and Madame de Staël was sufficiently well-known to figure in a satirical pamphlet play in 1791. Staël greets her 'Chevalier de la liberté'; they both joke that they are lax Protestants; but Barnave says that her favours are 'a foretaste of paradise'.[46]

In his report to the council,[47] Necker argues that the 'majority for an indefinite [absolute] veto is to say the least uncertain' and a small majority could lead to a 'dangerous commotion'. In this situation, 'will ministers who have been made responsible and whose prestige will inevitably decrease with their power, will such ministers, I say, dare to expose themselves to the representatives of the nation' by deploying an absolute veto?

Necker's covering letter makes no mention of not using the veto over the constitutional articles nor of the sanction of the August decrees which the king was still withholding. Rather he stresses that the veto must be for three, not two, legislatures; a mere two 'would render it null'. He urges the Assembly to respect traditions 'consecrated by the centuries and past generations' – they are not working *ex nihilo* as Barnave believed – and concludes: 'I see resistance on all sides to the executive power. You have created more liberty than in the English constitution which is admired throughout Europe. If you do not maintain the executive, I see disorders and unknown revolutions will destroy the edifice you have erected with such care.' 'Nothing would do more to undermine the dignity of the throne than the necessity of implementing laws of which the king would appear to have disapproved.' The English constitution works because the king, the magnates and the people are all contented.

There is a striking resemblance between Necker's report to the council and Barnave's interventions in the Assembly in favour of a suspensive veto. They both deploy the same arguments, the same examples and sometimes almost identical words. As one would expect, they both draw extended parallels with the English system to demonstrate that the absolute veto is appropriate for England but not for France, both citing the political maturity of the English and their entrenched habit of liberty.

Necker argues that if the king refused his sanction, the Assembly could put pressure on the king to break the impasse by 'deploying all the forces at its disposal such as a riot, popular petitions or the tardy renewal of taxes'. Barnave says 'the people would have no other recourse to overcome this resistance than the disastrous ones of insurrection and the refusal to pay taxes'.[48] Necker, having considered the case of a weak minister not daring to use the absolute veto, turns to ones 'of a different stripe'. Audacious and reckless ministers 'would have in their hands the means of bringing back disorder to the kingdom'; because they felt they had 'legitimate right' on their side, they would not want to climb down. Necker surely had the Breteuil ministry in mind. And Barnave spelled it out: 'All it would take would be a Richelieu [a favourite Barnave bugbear] or the men you saw recently in the ministry to throw the fate of the monarchy into the hazard.' Both Necker and Barnave equate the inauguration of an absolute veto with a return to the lurches between climb down and 'acts of authority' which characterised the last two years of the *ancien régime*.

⚜

Necker's letter was never read because on 11 September Mounier had it blocked on the spurious grounds that the advice that ministers had given the king in his council was inappropriate 'when a vote on the veto was about to be taken'.[49] In fact he wanted to conceal the fact that the government had accepted a suspensive veto. Mounier's ruse did not affect the outcome: the principle of a veto was accepted, by 733 votes to 143, but the absolute veto was rejected, by 673 votes to 329. Twice beaten, on the second chamber and the absolute veto, the constitutional committee resigned. The members were: Bergasse, Champion de Cicé, Clermont-Tonnerre, Lally-Tollendal, Mounier, Le Chapelier, Siéyès and Talleyrand. Le Chapelier, Siéyès and Talleyrand were re-elected on 12 October and were joined by Rabaud, Target, Thouret and Tronchet.[50]

That still left the length of the suspensive veto to be decided. Necker's letter had not been read but its contents were soon known; by 13 September it had been published, together with his report. There was no mention of what Barnave considered to be a quid pro quo, a gentleman's agreement, the king's not applying a veto to the constitution, including the August decrees, which still awaited his sanction. This betrayal, as Barnave saw it, was compounded when the minister of the interior summoned the Flanders regiment from Douai to protect Versailles as an alternative to flight, which had been debated in the *Conseil d'état*. These events wrought a change in Barnave's attitude to Necker and the monarchy. He now thought that it was legitimate to put the pressure of a riot on the king. In his 1788 *Esprit des Édits* Barnave had said that insurrection was 'the last and worst of all resorts'.[51] Now he was not so sure.

On 12 September the August decrees were sent to the king for his sanction. He said he would ponder the matter. 'Then', on 14 September, Duquesnoy relates, 'M. Barnave (a young man endowed with some talents but who praise has given more pride and who the mania for playing a role has made atrociously callous for a man of his age) proposed to suspend all discussion of the veto until the king has given his response to the decrees of the 4th [August]. . . . Thus, on a question such as this we have lost an entire session: the sad and annoying effect of stubbornness and pride.'[52] But Barnave claimed that the August decrees 'were constitutional in the sense that the constitution could not be made until the debris of the old regime have been swept away'; also, since the veto was accorded to the king after the August decrees, it could not be applied retroactively.[53]

THE DÉNOUEMENT

At this time Duquesnoy writes of a plan by some deputies to topple Necker, though this was made more difficult because on 5 August Necker had achieved a high degree of ministerial unity by placing a long-term ally, the archbishop of Bordeaux, Champion de Cicé, as justice minister. He had sat on the previous constitutional committee. The marshal de Beauveau, who became a minister without portfolio, was also a friend and ally.

The ring leaders of the plot were Talleyrand and Mirabeau. They were joined by Dupont de Nemours and Barnave, whom Duquesnoy calls Mirabeau's 'disciple', though the relationship was more complicated than that. The plot against Necker worked in tandem with pressure on the king to sanction the Declaration of Rights and the first articles of the constitution. On 20 September he had given his grudging assent to publish the August decrees, but in a letter of the 21st he made it clear that 'I don't think that I could with a clear conscience authenticate with my sanction all the [constitutional] laws which you have decreed on the various matters contained in your *arrêtés*'. De Visme, however, noted on 18 September: 'We are assured that the king and queen were of the opinion that the decrees should be sanctioned on the spot but that the council on the contrary thought it was as well to preface it with some observations.'[54] Not satisfied with the king's reply, the Assembly decided that it was not for him to quibble – he must just give his assent 'pure and simple'.

⚜

The Flanders regiment numbered only 1,000 men and could have no offensive objectives. Nor was it loyal, as was proved on 5 October. It was in order to cement its loyalty that on 1 October the ultra-loyal bodyguards gave a banquet for the officers of the Flanders regiment, during which the queen appeared with the dauphin and an air was sung by her favourite composer Grétry: 'Oh! Richard my king, the universe is abandoning you.' Visme was shown a woman handing out white cockades in the Oeuil-de-boeuf. There was 'a second similar very long banquet' on 3 October.[55] And on the 4th a Parisian deputation asked the minister of the interior, Saint-Priest, to send troops away. They were met with 'a formal refusal'. Saint-Priest relates that 'MM. Alexandre Lameth and Barnave asked me to get the king to cancel the arrival of this regiment of the line. I replied in such a way as to remove any hopes they may have entertained on that score.'[56]

Rebuffed by two ministers, Necker and Saint-Priest, on 4 October Barnave began a pessimistic letter. It consists of a single very long sentence built around a series of conditional 'ifs' but he breaks off before saying to what conclusion the 'ifs' must lead.

> If you had seen with your own eyes that the ministry not excepting M. Necker and the majority in our Assembly have never wanted the constitution; that whenever they got the upper hand even for a moment they tried with incredible bad faith to overturn everything which they appeared to have accepted; that their kingdom-wide network includes everyone who exercises any authority anywhere; that since the passing of the decrees of 4 August nearly the whole governing part of the nation had become our enemy and that of liberty; that in such circumstances to give the old order any great energy would be to resurrect it, to give it the means to crush us without a fight since it would have on its side the government and the majority of our Assembly which is ready to come out into the open the moment it is no longer restrained by fear or the wishes of the nation strongly expressed; if you were to reflect that we are not in a normal state where we are freely able to exploit all our advantages and where we are obliged to withstand an enormous countervailing force always ready to overwhelm us; that in order to force a constitution on the government and on a large part of the nation who don't want it, they must be made to feel that they needed this constitution to get them out of a worse predicament, you would have felt. . . .

Mathiez, who published this letter in 1898, thought that it showed that Barnave, Lameth, Le Chapelier and the Bretons were in league with the popular movement in Paris to organise the march on Versailles which occurred the following day. He notes that Le Chapelier was in Paris on the morning of the 5th. Members of the French Guard whose defection had led to the government's loss of Paris in July were paid 25 sous a day to attend the National Assembly and liaised between its radical deputies and the capital.[57] But, however suggestive, this evidence is only circumstantial. Barnave vehemently denied any knowledge, let alone any role, in the march on Versailles.[58] But then he was capable of straight lies when necessary.[59] Bradby disagrees with Mathiez's 'assumption that the letter refers to the disturbances in Paris and the coming insurrection' and concludes, rather lamely, 'that it is clearly an answer to a friend who had been criticising the acts of the Assembly'.[60]

Barnave would have continued his letter: 'felt that we were justified in' – but justified in what? Certainly, in severely constraining the king's use of the executive (by committees shadowing the ministries) and the army; and in welcoming the municipal revolutions and the creation of national guards throughout the kingdom and outside the king's control. But all this was avowable and avowed. What was more difficult to admit was the use of Paris by the Assembly to overawe the king. In July both wings of the centre – Mounier quite as much as Barnave – had recognised that the Paris rising had ended the stand-off between king and Assembly. Mounier had made a Faustian bargain with Paris and soon the devil would claim his due. The king had summoned troops not to subdue Paris but to prevent Paris from subduing him. In July when the troops proved unreliable, he had cleverly defused the situation by going to Paris to forestall Paris fetching him back. Marie-Antoinette would wryly remark that the people were far nicer when she came to them than when they came to her![61]

As long as the king was safe at Versailles, he could hold out indefinitely and, as Barnave admits, he now, by timely concessions, had something he had lacked in July: a majority in the Assembly. They may have had a majority for an absolute veto but, as Necker feared, not one big enough to prevent Paris causing a riot. On 31 August a riot had nearly developed into a march on Versailles. But Lafayette had it in his power to stop them. Though Mounier's party, the Monarchiens, had lost the votes on bicameralism and the absolute veto, the Assembly had chosen one of its members as president in all the fortnightly elections in September and Mounier was in the chair now. Furthermore, the events of August had driven the right and the centre-right closer together. Barnave believed that without the intervention of Paris the king and the conservatives and moderates in the Assembly would win out. The logic of the situation required that the royal family be brought back to Paris. And Lafayette, according to Necker, wanted 'a direct and habitual influence on the king's decisions' which was easier if the king was in Paris, where his duties as commander of the National Guard detained him for weeks on end.

Why did Barnave break off his letter? Was he interrupted by the events of the 5th? Or, more prosaically, is the next sheet merely missing? The letter, with only one correction looks more like a copy than a draft.

⚜

On the morning of 5 October a motley crowd mostly consisting of women marched on Versailles. They probably just wanted bread and their quarrel was as much with the Assembly as with the government. The king had written his response to the constitutional decrees the day before. It was delivered to the Assembly. Then he went shooting. Louis accepted the Declaration of Rights but contented himself with the observation (made by several deputies) that a declaration of principle should not precede its practical embodiment. Similarly with the constitution itself: he accepted the first nineteen articles provisionally but thought that the constitution could not be judged piecemeal but only when it had been finished.[62] But then he added that even his provisional acceptance was given 'only on the positive condition, from which I will never depart, that the general result of your deliberations is to leave the executive power entirely within the hands of the monarch'.[63] The Assembly had honoured this more in the breach than in the observance but the Assembly did not think it was up to the king to set any conditions.

And the Assembly was sensitive on this issue because it *had* usurped many of the king's executive powers. It is to this usurpation that Barnave probably refers in his letter. Lameth proposed that the Assembly remain in session till the king had clarified his position. His motion was not carried and Mirabeau argued that the king should not be pressed further because if his concession seemed forced, 'it would go down badly with the country'.[64]

The king's council discussed flight. Saint-Priest proposed withdrawing to Rambouillet and was supported by the maréchal de Beauveau, La Luzerne (Marine), and La Tour de Pin. All four, as Saint-Priest observed, had been soldiers. The civilians – Necker, Montmorin (though a camp-marshal, he had not seen active service) and the archbishops of Vienne and Bordeaux – opposed, Necker warning that if the king abandoned Paris there would be no money to pay the *rentes* or the troops.[65] With the council, as so often, evenly divided, the king cast his vote for staying. The officers on duty overheard the king pacing up and down the council chamber, exclaiming, 'A fugitive king! A fugitive king, never!'[66] A factor in Louis's decision was that midway through the council meeting he had met a deputation of five of the women, given them wine and promised to rush in grain supplies to Paris. Most of the women were preparing to traipse back to Paris.

But at 6 p.m. a message arrived from Lafayette that he was marching to Versailles at the head of his troops. This force posed more of a threat than the women. The debate in the council now veered towards flight. Orders were given for the carriages which had been waiting ready – harnessed in the Grande Écurie – to be brought round, but the crowd cut the traces.

At 8 p.m. confused firing was heard and Louis ordered the carriages to be readied again, but this time the grooms refused. The Assembly sent its president, Mounier, to ask the king for his acceptance 'pure and simple' of the constitutional articles. Mounier spent the entire evening waiting for the king's decision. At 10 p.m. the king finally told Mounier that he would accept the articles. The irony of the situation was not lost on Mounier, who had no more liking for the articles than had the king. Dutifully, Mounier asked the king to put his sanction in writing. Louis 'went to his desk, [and] wrote it out in full: "I accept, purely and simply, the constitutional articles and the Declaration of the Rights of Man which the National Assembly has presented to me."' Then 'he handed his sanction to him, weeping'.[67] As Necker was to observe: 'We had to yield, but posterity will never forget the moment that was chosen to consecrate the theory of the rights of man and to insert the cornerstone of the temple of liberty.'[68]

Fearing the sinister loyalty of Lafayette, Louis told Mounier to assemble as many of the deputies as he could in the château. Barnave argued that it was beneath the Assembly's dignity to wait on the king. Mounier ordered a drum roll and rustled up 200 deputies, but by the time they turned up, at about 1.30 a.m., Lafayette was already there. On his arrival the Hero of Two Worlds exclaimed, 'Sire, I thought it better to die at your feet than pointlessly perish' trying to stop the National Guard from marching on Versailles.[69] Louis must have winced at such fatuous grandiloquence. Having tried to persuade Louis to return with him to Paris, an exhausted Lafayette finally left the château at 5 a.m. and went to his grandfather Noailles's townhouse in Versailles. Then he threw himself on to a sofa and fell into an exhausted sleep.

About half an hour after Lafayette's departure, daybreak on a misty autumn morning, a portion of the crowd broke into the palace, made for the queen's apartments and hacked down two of her bodyguards outside the door, shouting, 'We want to cut her head off, and fry her heart and liver and it won't stop there.' One of the bodyguards just had time to reach the queen's apartments and shout to a lady-in-waiting: 'Madame, save the queen, her life is in danger.' Then he was cut down and left for dead. Behind the queen's bed, concealed in the panelling, was a door opening onto a secret passage leading to the king's apartments. 'The frightened queen, wearing only a chemise, clutching her petticoat, took refuge in the king's apartments.'[70] Some accounts have the furious populace, disappointed at missing their prey, slashing the mattress of the queen's bed to ribbons.

In the morning, under pressure from a mob demanding that he go to Paris, and with Lafayette ill-concealing his similar desire, the king asked the Assembly to send a deputation to advise him. Before they set off, Barnave, who was one of the thirty-six chosen, made a speech proposing 'that the person of the king and the Assembly are inseparable', that is, that the king and the Assembly should always reside in the same location. Mathiez considered this to be 'a roundabout way of transferring ... [them both] to Paris'.[71] He deduces as evidence Barnave's bitter and despairing letter of 4 October. However, a fuller extract from his speech paints a different picture: 'You are going to have to advise the king ... whether ... [he] and the Assembly should remain here, go to Paris or transfer themselves somewhere else.'[72] Duquesnoy put it more neatly: 'no one dared advise ... [the king] to go to Paris; but all concurred in determining him to stay at Versailles which amounted to going to Paris'.[73] A cynic would say that Barnave planned this outcome all along. If Barnave had indeed planned to relocate the king to Paris back in June, he had now achieved his objective.

The royal family were forced to set off to Paris at 2.30 p.m., their carriage preceded by the severed heads of their bodyguards on pikes. 'On the news of the king's departure for Paris', Vismes notes, 'M. Barnave proposed that the person of the king was inseparable from the National Assembly during the present session. This motion was carried, from which I conclude that if the king remains in Paris (which there is reason to believe), we will transfer ourselves thither.'[74] Barnave had told a friend that the Constituent Assembly would have finished its work by the end of the year. Perhaps Barnave was leaving open the possibility of the king's returning to Versailles thereafter.

Something more must be said about the word 'session' – the same in French as in English: as in the 'current session' of Parliament. In August and September, the Assembly debated whether the legislative body should be 'permanent'. By this they meant that towards the expiry of a legislature – which they fixed at two years – elections should automatically go out for the next one without being convoked by the king: an important but overlooked difference with the English polity. They did not mean that the Assembly should be in permanent session. Indeed, durations of between three and eight months were considered. In the event, however, the Assembly – unlike the English Parliament – sat every day of every month in every year from February 1790, even on Sundays. When the English Parliament was adjourned, the king governed; with the French Assembly in permanent session, it did.

AFTERMATH

Duquesnoy wrote of the scandal of 'a king snatched from his palace, dragged to Paris as a prisoner of his capital city'. Installed in the Tuileries, Louis did indeed consider himself a prisoner and, as Mirabeau had warned, not bound by any promises made under duress. On 12 October he sent the abbé de Fontbrune on a secret mission to Madrid to give Charles IV 'this solemn protest against my enforced sanction of all that has been done contrary to the royal authority since 15 July of this year'.[75] Significantly, the king did not send this missive on 15 July: until 5 October he was seeking to find a *modus vivendi* with the Assembly. For Louis the October Days projected a shadow onto the previous episodes of the Revolution.

This letter was not intercepted but Barnave was able to gauge the king's feelings in greater detail in the manifesto he left behind on his escape from Paris on 20 June 1791: 'His Majesty by giving his sanction to all the decrees indiscriminately – a sanction that he was well aware he could not refuse – was motivated by the desire to *avoid any discussion which he had learned from experience would be useless to say the least*' (my emphasis). The italicised clause refers to observations he had made on the August decrees and the constitutional articles. Consequently, 'all his proceedings after October 1789 were nullified by his complete lack of freedom'. The constitution in his eyes was not yet a valid document. Did this matter?

The October Days were the original sin of the Revolution. The 'magical union' of 1789 was shattered. This was immediately symbolised by the secession of Mounier and several of his colleagues. Madame Barnave informs her son of the state of play at Grenoble; of his enemies and friends – she says that he is accused of belonging, with Mirabeau, to 'the faction of the duc d'Orléans'. She relates Mounier's attempts, aided by Virieu and d'Agoult, to reconvene the Estates of Dauphiné on 2 November, including the supplementary deputies, whose sole role was to elect deputies to replace the current ones, such as Barnave. Virieu and d'Agoult had refused to sign the letter written by Barnave and signed by all the other Dauphiné deputies urging the standing commission of the Estates not to reconvene the estates and reassuring them that the king was perfectly happy in his new Paris home and that the queen 'was treated with the respect due to her rank', and so on. In his draft of this letter Barnave even wrote that 'the king and the royal family . . . have drawn a curtain over the deplorable details of the events which brought them thither';[76] but he did not have the brass neck to include this part in the printed version. This is because it was nonsense – Marie-Antoinette existed in a state of terror and the king hated his new quarters; it was nonsense also that the 'Assembly was about to complete the constitution' – but it did the trick: the Dauphiné estates did not proceed further. Barnave also complained (in a letter to a friend in Grenoble) that the supplementary deputies were not qualified to choose replacements as elections were now to be conducted without distinction of order – *doublement* was no longer enough. Barnave concluded this letter: 'If as I never give up hoping all this has a happy outcome, how happy I will be to enjoy peace back home.'[77]

But for all his bluster, Barnave was worried. He thought that Dauphiné was ready to secede and warned that the 'most courageous province of the kingdom would become a little state whose proximity to France would oblige it to seek protection from foreigners'. Dauphiné had seen some of the worst of the châteaux-burning; now it made the strongest protest against the October Days. The unity of 1788 was 'irredeemably precarious' indeed. His private doubts are found in some notes he wrote at this time: 'Disorders fomented, plots hatched, bread thrown into the river etc. have been rightly attributed to the enemies of the Revolution, who have never ceased to hope for disorders, for the dissolution of the Assembly and the return to the former system. The information found [from] the persons arrested have justified these suspicions.'

He continues with words which should dispel the suspicion that he was in the pay of the duc d'Orléans: 'The departure of M. le duc d'Orléans for England has made many people think that he was mixed up with those guilty [of the October Days]. Others think that the mission with which he was charged is genuine and important. Still others think that the object of his departure is the approaching revolution in Brabant' – the Austrian Netherlands. He told another correspondent that the departure of the prince was designed 'to remove even a pretext for . . . fear'.[78]

⚜

Having vainly attempted to incite Dauphiné to rebellion against the Assembly, Mounier emigrated to Switzerland and wrote increasingly bitter denunciations against the Assembly. Barnave chose not to reply.[79] Returning to France in 1801, Mounier was made prefect of the Département of Ille-et-Vilaine by Napoleon and then a *conseiller d'état*. He died in 1806. Writing thirty years later, Alexandre de Lameth wrote of 'the only too tragic events which soon would further accelerate the march of the Revolution. I refer to the *journées* of 5 and 6 October.'[80] Barnave may have realised it even then. He certainly did later when in his 1792 account of the Revolution, he called the October Days 'a catastrophe'.[81]

FRIENDS AND ALLIES

Barnave had said that the king and the Assembly must be 'inseparable' so, though many members were reluctant, the Assembly moved to the capital on 19 October. First, they sat in a hall in the archbishop's palace and on the 26th moved to permanent quarters in the Manège (riding school), which had been built in 1721 for the boy king Louis XV during his residence in the city. Barnave was one of the secretaries of the Assembly for the fortnight starting on the 26th at the changeover.

Charles de Lameth invited him to lodge in the family's grand town house in the 'cul-de-sac de Notre-Dame-des-Champs' near the Luxembourg Palace, the residence of the king's brother the comte de Provence. It had extensive gardens. The Hôtel de Lameth was a *hôtel* in both senses of the word: it was grand and it put up guests. Apart from three of the four Lameth brothers – comtes Charles and Théodore and Chevalier Alexandre (the youngest) – and their mother, the boys' tutor, now a deputy, and Barnave lodged there rent-free. Barnave had his own suite of rooms, two servants and a secretary. Madame Lameth was a sister of the duc de Broglie, generalissimo of the royal troops when the Bastille fell. She did not share her sons' advanced views but there was no quarrel.

Her husband had died young and the family were not well-off for a court family. However, Marie-Antoinette took them under her wing and the three brothers and their mother drew a pension of 60,000 livres (£2,500).[82] It was probably the queen who arranged Charles's marriage in 1784 to Mlle Picot, the daughter of a rich planter in Sainte-Domingue. But there was a falling-out with the queen, possibly because the boys' mother, as a Broglie, belonged to the anti-Austrian faction at court. This falling-out may explain Barnave's curious (in view of his democratic beliefs) observation: 'Louis XV's profoundly corrupt court was succeeded by a young court which displayed a lack of foresight. It [Marie-Antoinette] played with abolishing all etiquette and pulling down all prominent people.'[83]

We do not know exactly how Barnave got to know the Lameths – I have suggested it was through Laborde de Méréville, who, though a noble, sat with Barnave in the commons chamber. But it was a lasting bond. He wrote of it: 'After experimenting for two or three months my friendships were fixed and did not vary thereafter. They linked me to men full of faults to be sure but with great probity, character and courage.' Few such combinations survived 'three years at the centre of great affairs'. His did 'without a single instance of misunderstanding'.

Through the Lameths, Barnave got to know the duc d'Aiguillon, who was very young, very fat, very bald and above all very rich. Descended from Richelieu's sister, he was the son of Louis XV's hated minister, along with Terray and Maupeou one of a more notorious 'triumvirate'. Barnave flared up once when his friend was taxed with his father's misdeeds. D'Aiguillon's great friend was baron Menou. These men formed the nucleus of Barnave's party. The inner group – the proton, as it were (the 'triumvirate') – consisted of Barnave, his 'particular' friend Alexandre and Adrien Duport.[84] Duport and Barnave were the only two to have enjoyed a nationwide reputation before 1789 – Barnave for his pamphlets and Duport for having Calonne impeached in the Parlement where he sat as a judge. He would go on to introduce the jury system to France and propose the abolition of capital punishment. The wags had it that he was the 'thinker', Barnave the 'speaker' and Alexandre the 'doer', that is, the fixer – both he and Duport were considered by their enemies to be 'intriguers'. As said, Laborde formed with them a 'quadrumvirate' in the early part of the Revolution.

Charles and Laborde owned major sugar plantations and Barnave, as rapporteur of the colonial committee, was and is accused of being influenced by his friends. All these men came from the very top echelons of society – 'les grands' as they were called; a fusion of wealth (Laborde) or birth or, in d'Aiguillon's case, both. Duquesnoy has his own explanation of why these courtiers turned against the regime. When Charles de Lameth returned from the American war where the three Lameths had fought, he 'was piqued that his good looks had failed to turn the head of the queen'. As for d'Aiguillon, he 'only harried the court with such fury because the queen had persecuted his father, which he richly deserved'.[85]

Barnave was mocked for social climbing. Mirabeau's confidant, the comte de La Marck, wrote:

> This young man, scarcely out of college, was sought out by the most remarkable members of the revolutionary party such as the duc d'Aiguillon, the duc de la Rochefoucauld, Laborde de Méréville. . . . He had been feted, cajoled by these people so much above his station. He had especially become the particular friend of the duc d'Aiguillon, MM de Lameth and M. de Laborde. They had associated him in their pleasures and their political intrigues, in which his fine talent had been useful to them. It is remarkable that when they allowed him to follow his natural instincts, Barnave ceased to show

> himself as an extremist. . . . Before Mirabeau designated him to the court to be one of his auxiliaries, Barnave had already taken the step if not of breaking with his friends or at least of ceasing to depend on them.[86]

La Marck admired Barnave but Dubois de Crancé, soon to be democratised as Dubois-Crancé, detested him. Barnave regarded him as one of a handful of hard-line republicans and therefore an enemy of the strong constitutional monarchy he espoused. Edmond-Louis-Alexis Dubois de Crancé's early life represents almost a caricature of why people turned against the *ancien régime* – a heightened version of Madame Barnave's snub in the theatre. He entered the elite King's Musketeers at fourteen with an age-dispensation through the court connections of his family, but was then forced to leave because the nobility of his family was successfully challenged. No wonder he could describe himself as a man 'who despised the favours of a court he had frequented in his youth and which he knew to be both corrupt and corrupting'. Consequently, 'he had shown himself to be in the Estates-General an athlete ready to fight *unguibus et rostro* [tooth and claw]'. This comes from his self-portrait in his anonymous *Véritable portrait de nos Législateurs, Ou Galerie Des Tableaux Exposés À La Vue Du Public Depuis Le 5 Mai 1789, Jusqu'au Premier Octobre 1791*. This production had been preceded in October 1789 by his satirical *Supplément à la galerie de l'Assemblée nationale* (the first edition is hard to find).

The fourteen rogues in this gallery are given pseudonyms – Barnave is 'Bavenard', but this is only a tease since a key is provided at the end. Some of the nicknames are obscure, but Bavenard suggests '*bavardeur*' (prattler) and 'Iramba' is an anagram of 'Mirabeau'. 'Inordinate pride. A disagreeable [Midi] voice, an insignificant self-conscious countenance are the portion of Bavenard.' 'He never enters the chamber without arranging his features in a grotesque way; his lower lip jutting out, flashing eyes, his head inclined towards one or the other shoulder, as if he wanted to return contempt for contempt.'

'He . . . frequents *les grands*, caresses them. Barnave is insanely familiar with dukes, counts and marquises. . . . It is difficult for a young provincial to resist their advances.' Crancé thinks Barnave was merely the mouthpiece 'of the Lameths, Duport, Menou, and all that portion of the minority of the noblesse which has played so singular a role in the Revolution. He was merely their representative at the rostrum. We will excuse Bavenard who knows nothing of high society for falling into so alluring a trap; but let us also censure him for being so proud when he has no reason to be.'

Yet Crancé had the snobbish pride common to those who have stooped to conquer. Crancé then makes a more telling point: 'People are beginning to notice that all the motions are simply the result of his conversations with Iramba. Though he makes a point of sitting miles from him in the Assembly, it is a well-known fact that they frequently meet up after the sitting.'[87] Barnave's ambivalence towards Mirabeau would remain until he bade him farewell on his deathbed.

FINE DINING

High society and high politics were mediated through the dinner party (mid-afternoon) and the supper party. Several salons were specifically hosted by members of Barnave's group. 'The most sumptuous table, perhaps, in Paris was that of M. de Laborde, over which presided his wife, a sensible woman, who, wiser than many others of the financial set, took with pleasure and graciously the advances of the grandes dames, but withal maintained her dignity.'[88] We will see the protagonists, Barnave and Mirabeau, try to settle at Laborde's the question of who – the king or the Assembly – should decide the question of peace and war.

Laborde's elder sister, the baronne d'Escars, also entertained deputies from the 'patriotic party', as did Charles de Lameth's and d'Aiguillon's wives. Alexandre de Lameth was particularly associated with the salons of his pretty cousin Mme Victor de Broglie and Mme de La Châtre, an especial friend.[89]

Presumably Barnave also attended Madame de Staël's famous parties, though Gouverneur Morris (a snob) does not mention him. Morris resided in Paris off and on from 1789 to 1798, becoming the American minister plenipotentiary in 1792. Like his Europhile compatriot Henry James, Morris was an inveterate diner, attending the functions of de Staël and Laborde de Méréville and the larger dinners of Lafayette. He also was a regular at Madame de Staël's Tuesday evening supper, 'when not more than a dozen or fifteen covers were laid, and her chosen friends were admitted into the little salon . . . [it] was the great feature of the week'. Madame de Staël's salon now eclipsed that of her mother, which had done so much to further Necker's career. But Morris notes, 'On Sunday, the 25th, spending the evening in Madame Necker's salon I encountered for the first time since I arrived in Europe Count Fersen, whose merit consists in being the Queen's lover. He has the air of a man exhausted.'[90]

BARNAVE AND NECKER

Necker was weakened by the October Days which were directed as much against him as against the king. He had reneged on his promise to Barnave that in return for the suspensive veto the king would sanction the Assembly's decrees. Instead, the ministry had allied itself to the Monarchiens and these in turn (Barnave believed) had allied themselves to counter-revolutionaries. Necker was the great disappointment of the early phase of the Revolution. The Third Estate had seen him as their champion against the nobility – he was a half-hearted one at best – and as the financial wizard who had fought a war without raising taxes and could undo the damage done by Calonne. To be fair to him, from the outset he thought his task was almost impossible. After several attempts to oust him, Necker finally resigned on 4 September 1790. Sometime before that Barnave drew up a crushing list of his failures as principal minister of finance. The fragment begins:

> Do you recall his complaints about the National Assembly that he always sought to decry – the Assembly which always adopted his projects without the situation being any better for them?
>
> He asked for two loans [30 million on 9 August 1789 and 80 million on the 27th]; he got them and who is not left with the thought that the bad success of the first which signalled the collapse of our credit was due to the resentment of this minister about the minor changes the Assembly made to his proposal [reducing the rate of interest from 5 to 4.75 per cent] which could so easily have been withdrawn. . . . He asked for a tax of one-quarter of [one year's revenue]. It was voted.[91]

Necker could plausibly blame the Assembly for the failure of his loan. So when he came up with a proposal for a 'patriotic contribution' of 25 per cent of revenue to be paid over three years by everyone except workmen, the Assembly faced a dilemma. Reject it and the country faced bankruptcy; endorse it and take the blame for failure. So a group including 'MM de Mirabeau, Duport, Castellane, Barnave, Lameth, le duc d'Orléans, Latouche, Lauzun, Menou, d'Aiguillon, Le Chapelier' devised the wheeze of accepting Necker's proposals 'on trust' (*de confiance*) without debating their merit, so Necker would have no excuse to blame the Assembly if the 'contribution' flopped. If, on the other hand, the tax was a success, the Assembly could equally take credit for letting it proceed unhindered.[92]

'He asked', Barnave continued, 'that the *gabelle* should continue to be levied provisionally – we were feeble enough to let him have it'. 'He put forward a proposal to meet the expenses of the year. It was voted through.' 'The Church lands were put at the disposal of the nation; the monasteries were dissolved [February 1790], which put an immense mass [of property at] his disposal.'

Barnave had been one of the initiators of the confiscation of Church lands. When Necker proposed his loan for 30 million, 'Barnave while recognising the necessity for a loan, wanted steps to be taken to ensure it did not lead to increased taxes'.[93] In a coordinated move, 'the M[arqu]is de Lacoste said that to obviate the need for increased taxation the lands of the clergy should be put at the disposal of the nation to serve as collateral for the loan'.[94] Tithes should also be abolished without compensation. And religious orders suppressed. In preparation for the suppression, [Alexandre] Lameth and Lacoste proposed that religious houses should provisionally not accept novices.[95] Lameth had also supported Lacoste on the suppression of tithes without compensation. Lameth's intervention roused the most opposition from the clergy, who said the motion was irrelevant to the matter in hand: the loan. For good measure, Laborde 'gave a very extended sermon on religious toleration'.[96] There the matter rested until 2 November, when, the ground having been prepared by Barnave's group, the confiscation of the Church's property was formally proposed by Talleyrand and seconded by Mirabeau.

Under the heading 'Great and decisive moment', Barnave wrote that 'the secret' to all their problems 'lay in the property of the clergy'. He explained in note form: 'The constitution is nearing completion. The Revolution is advancing. But how to consummate it – how to give it momentum – how to reunite the parties – tax – work – prosperity – attaching the people to the Revolution – the clue lies in the property of the clergy.' The purchasers of Church lands would have a vested interest in the Revolution.

Barnave said that confiscating Church lands put 'an immense mass' at Necker's disposal – but a mass of what? 'All depends on the method of selling them.' The lands were virtually unsaleable because hard currency was being hoarded. Barnave outlined the consequences: 'when there is a lack of capital; when there is a lack of coins in circulation; when land is put on the market; idem [the redemption of] feudal rights . . .', the economy, to complete his thought, seizes up. And there was nothing 'for the needs of industry' – investment. So Mirabeau proposed that a paper currency – the *assignat* – be issued to the presumed value of the Church lands. But to prevent inflation, on the presentation of an *assignat* to buy a piece of land, it should be withdrawn from circulation. 'Therefore', Barnave argued, 'the *assignats* will not lose their value from distrust; therefore, they will not lose their value through over-issue.'[97]

After months of prevarication, Mirabeau's ideas were implemented after a major speech by Barnave on 28 September 1790. In this he demonstrated how the *assignats* could be used in a non-inflationary way to pay off the national debt, increase circulation and win adherents to the Revolution. The *assignats* should be convertible, not into gold but into portions of the confiscated ecclesiastical property. On presentation of an *assignat* to buy a piece of land, it should be burned so that at any one time no more than a billion should be in circulation, in addition to the 400,000 already issued. A billion was a guess – one of the notes for his speech has 1.2 billion; another 800 million. He admitted that they were guessing the value of the Church lands – as they had been guessing the size of the debt – but his proposal would have the incidental value of discovering it. Barnave put to good use his 1788 purchase of Smith's *Wealth of Nations*, quoting his theory of circulation. Prior to their being redeemed for land, the *assignats* would boost circulation to make up for the dearth of metallic currency.

The issue of *assignats* was a precursor of quantitative easing. But like quantitative easing, the authorities did not dare to unwind, and inflation followed. Barnave had always inveighed against the issuance of non-convertible paper money – what we call *fiat money* – and he cannot be blamed for the subsequent over-issue of *assignats* with no backing and the resultant galloping inflation. Similarly, President Nixon's ending the convertibility of the dollar to gold in 1972 led to higher inflation and the devaluation of the currency. In Barnave's time what he called the '*assignat louis*' had only depreciated 25 per cent against its gold equivalent, the guinea, but he tried to work out the implications for foreign trade, about which he was characteristically optimistic.[98] And as originally conceived the issuance of convertible *assignats* was better than the piecemeal expedients which Necker offered then (as in his first ministry). Barnave concluded his indictment of Necker: 'So what more can he want? What more can he ask for? Whence comes our distress if not from his incompetence?'[99]

The logic of 6 October was that, sooner or later, the Necker ministry should be ousted. This was put brutally by Adrien Duport in a footnote to the printed version of his report on provincial assemblies: 'The state can never recover any energy given the feeble and equivocal conduct of the present ministers imbued with the former ideas of authority, seeking to exaggerate the faults of the Assembly, executing its decrees negligently' to give the impression that it is acting under constraint; 'in short, whether by feebleness or calculation leaving the government without strength . . . in order to be ready to exploit any circumstances which many arise' to recover its former power. 'The kingdom is threatened with dissolution . . . unless the government changes its conduct or is itself changed.'[100]

Duport's refrain was taken up by Alexandre de Lameth: the ministers 'without being partisans of absolute monarchy could not entirely detach themselves from the *ancien régime* under which they had already grown old in their ways.' In short, old dogs could not learn new tricks. Lameth (and here Barnave's influence can be detected) extended the anathema beyond the ministry to 'the ambassadors, provincial governors and military commandants, intendants etc. [*sic*], in short all the functionaries were those of the *ancien régime* and it was evident that they would not use their authority to found a new one.' A new establishment was needed.

These comments by Alexandre de Lameth related to a discussion between Lafayette and his inseparable adjutant Latour-Maubourg, on the one part, and the 'quadrumvirate' of Lameth, Duport, Barnave and Laborde de Méréville, on the other, sometime between the October Days and the Assembly's (somewhat reluctant) move to Paris on 19 October 'during the preliminary discussions on the Church lands'. The company assembled at the house of Mirabeau's niece at Passy who, exceptionally for such ladies, 'did not hold a political salon'. They discussed the entire replacement of the ministry, as in England, and the top civil servants. However, 'the project did not go any further', Lameth concludes, either because Lafayette had some residual loyalty to Necker and Montmorin or because the king vetoed it.[101]

For Necker's son-in-law, the baron de Staël, the Swedish ambassador, the driving force had been the triumvirs who 'stirred up revolts in Paris and the provinces; they sought to frighten the ministers in order to replace them, retaining Necker alone because of his financial credit and his popularity; or at least keeping him in place until he had degraded himself by sacrificing an honest ministry only to be contaminated by association with a culpable one'. For Staël, Duport had gained a good reputation 'for never having been imbued with the prejudices of his corps', the Parlement, but was false, 'a bad speaker', a 'zealot', a 'Frondeur', 'ambitious without the means [to succeed], forever talking of liberty, forever coveting the ministry'. Barnave had been Mounier's disciple and owed to him his election to the Estates-General. But 'weary of a secondary position doing good preferred to take the lead in doing ill'. 'A man of talent, intelligence and character, but without independent means, he rendered himself odious by the harshness he displayed at the time of the Paris massacres.' Staël's harshest criticism is for Alexandre de Lameth, 'a young man ruined, ambitious, undaunted, who being blessed with neither talent nor a superior mind' resented all those who were.[102]

For the moment Lafayette and Mirabeau decided in their many conversations that the Necker ministry should be retained – though Necker himself was useless, his popularity was useful. Barnave's group, however, wanted them all out and 'to form one to their liking'. They would use the war minister, La Tour du Pin, a fellow Grenoblois of Barnave's, as a bridgehead.[103] Lafayette writes, 'Alexandre [de Lameth] the mouthpiece, I think, of M La Tour du Pin speaks of giving me the Army of Flanders' to get him out of the way.[104] Omer Talon, the Lieutenant Civil of the Châtelet court, was probably referring to two of the triumvirs when he told Mirabeau's confidant La Marck on 20 November that he had been approached by 'two men I have no need to name' – Duport and Lameth? – who told him 'the result of a conference at M. de La Tour du Pin's this morning was that he had been offered the post of keeper of the seals'. The triumvirs had told Talon: 'There has been a change of plan. We are no longer thinking of entering the ministry ourselves. None of us will be ministers, even Mirabeau. But the ministry is going to change and though people think that we have been side-lined we are the ones who will determine its composition. We are instructed to make you a proposal. The keeper of the seals will be ousted. Will you serve as his replacement? You have until 8.00 p.m. tomorrow to decide.'

Talon wondered whether to go along with the plot in order to learn its details and told La Marck to 'talk it over at the Assembly with Mirabeau, who is presently with Lafayette'. 'Lafayette will expect you at 5 p.m. precisely. It seems that one of the projects is directed even against him. So, he must . . . join with those who are in a position to support him.'[105]

⚜

These obscure discussions, which went nowhere, generated lists of potential ministers. The only full 'shadow cabinet' we have is Mirabeau's, who includes also in his handwriting a few names supplied by Lafayette and Marie-Antoinette. It was drafted before the decree of 7 November, barring deputies from becoming ministers and before the attempt to oust the justice minister Champion de Cicé and Necker – so mid-October.[106]

Mirabeau's list runs:

> M. Necker, *premier ministre* because he must be made as impotent as he is incapable but [we must] preserve his popularity for the king.
>
> The archbishop of Bordeaux, Chancellor,[107] choosing with great care the men who will draft legislation. [Mirabeau complained that Cicé either did not transmit the Assembly's measures or added the king's commentary.]

The duc de Liancourt for the war ministry because he is honourable, firm and has personal affection for the king, which will give him security.
The duc de la Rochefoucauld, Maison du roi and Paris, with Thouret under him.
The comte de La Marck for the Marine (Navy and colonies) because he cannot have the war ministry and he is faithful, a man of character and swift execution. (La Févalaye under him.)
The Bishop of Autun [Talleyrand], finance minister, his motion on the clergy['s lands]? Has won this place for him . . . [Laborde with him]
The comte de Mirabeau, minister without portfolio.
Target, Mayor of Paris where he will always be led by the lawyers [*basoche*].
Lafayette, minister without portfolio, Marshal of France and generalissimo for a fixed period to restore the army.
M. de Montmorin, Governor of the Children of France, *duc et pair*, debts paid off.
M. de Ségur, ambassador to Russia, appointed foreign secretary.[108] [Barnave would recommend him to the queen as prime minister as enjoying both their confidences.[109]]
M. Mounier, Royal Librarian.
M. Chapelier, Director of the King's buildings.

Surprisingly, perhaps, the queen was in on the discussions and had her own proposals, also in Mirabeau's handwriting, entitled '*Part de la Reine*' (the queen's share):

Minister of War – La Marck
Head of the Council of . . . Public Education – the abbé Siéyès
Keeper of the king's privy seal – [left blank][110]

The 'queen's share' section provokes two observations. First, Mirabeau is working closely with Marie-Antoinette six months before he was paid to send her written advice. Second, the presence of Siéyès lends credence to some spiteful comments from the well-informed spy master the comte d'Antraigues. He reproaches the vicomtesse de Laval (late of the

Polignac set, now a constitutional monarchist) with trying to broker a deal between the queen and Barnave's group: 'with the queen accepting all and even more than was asked, the duchesse de Luynes and that whore the vicomtesse de Laval, mistress of the Bishop of Autun are her intimate friends and thereby set up the correspondence with Barnave, Lameth, Siéyès and others of the same stripe'. We will see that at the same time that Mirabeau was making his lists, he suspected Barnave of sending memoranda to the court.[111]

This and the other dream cabinets reveal a very wide spectrum across all but the far-right and far-left, even including the queen. Duquesnoy thought that Mirabeau and Talleyrand would pave the way for Calonne, the man with whom they had collaborated on his reform projects: a wild if interesting guess. Le Chapelier, the doyen of the Breton Club, was about to found its Jacobin successor with Barnave, but he is included here, with Thouret, Siéyès and Target as leading members of the constitutional committee. He is slated to replace Angiviller as Director of the King's Buildings. The queen's 'share' of the spoils naturally also included La Marck, the link between her and Mirabeau and between the latter and her 'mentor', Mercy-Argenteau. She wanted Siéyès in charge of a new post in tune with the times – public education – something which should provoke further reflection. Interestingly, the mayor of Paris is included among the ministers, in addition to the duc de la Rochefoucauld, Maison du roi and Paris, with Thouret under him. Though Duport notoriously wanted to be justice minister, Malesherbes is considered unless Cicé survived but stripped of the role in drafting legislation. Of Barnave's group only Emmery and Laborde (under Talleyrand at finance) are mentioned. But at this stage they intended to rule through proxies rather than in person.

Mirabeau was given to rainbow coalitions – he would construct one including the two counter-revolutionary rivals Calonne and Breteuil in 1790. But this does seem like a viable way of satisfying all parties at a time when the completion of the constitution was thought to be imminent and life outside the Assembly had to be considered. It is in some ways an *ancien régime* construct – a division of spoils: the marshal's baton for Lafayette, a semi-sinecure for Le Chapelier, a peerage for Montmorin, with debts paid off. And the deputies too were acquiring debts, and they were about to acquire more with the Assembly moving to Paris. It is not perhaps unduly cynical to wonder if the satisfaction of all these ambitions might have ended the Revolution sooner. However, all these pipe dreams went up in smoke with the decree – 'the fatal decree' of 7 November barring deputies from becoming ministers.

THE FATAL DECREE

'Shortly after the translation of the National Assembly to Paris', Barnave writes, 'thirty people of whom eight or ten were deputies formed a political union whose object appeared to be to form a new ministry and install its members in it. With this object in mind M. de Mirabeau, one of the thirty, made a proposal which caused quite a stir at the time and was rejected by the National Assembly' – culminating in the 'fatal' decree. This society enjoyed no success and as soon as it was known was scathingly referred to in the National Assembly as the 'Comité des Trente'.

Barnave writes as if he had no involvement in the plot against Necker but on 20 October, he and Mirabeau made a joint assault on the ministry when Mirabeau and other deputies complained that the Assembly's decrees were not known or implemented in several provinces – in some places all that was known of the August decrees was the king's critique. On the 21st the keeper of the seals, summoned to the Assembly, defended his conduct on the grounds that the status of the decrees had been uncertain before the king's 'pure and simple' acceptance of them on 5 October.

The Assembly followed up its complaint with particular reference to the crisis in the grain supply by decreeing that 'having done all that it could on this matter, unless its decrees were executed the ministers and other agents of authority be held responsible'. On the 24th the ministers, collectively, struck back by sending the Assembly a memorandum defending their conduct – God should be blamed for the weather and many countries were banning wheat exports, which in any case would make little difference in a country of 26 million. They then collectively went on to the offensive in dramatic language, unleashing all the pent-up frustrations of the previous months: 'When the whole country from one end to the other is falling to pieces you expect the ministers to . . . be responsible for the execution of the laws! In that case the king's ministers, Messieurs, declare frankly that they will make no such undertaking . . . and would rather resign in favour of men rash enough to make such promises.'[112]

Mirabeau resolved to bring down the Necker ministry for failing to deal with the twin grain and financial crises and then present the dithering Lafayette with a *fait accompli*: a new ministry capable of surviving the ensuing uproar as Necker was still popular, especially in the provinces. He would begin with 'an evolutionary tactic' on 5 November, beginning with a further attack on the ministry for non-implementation of its decrees. Duquesnoy thought that Barnave's group was behind the attack and 'that the comte de Mirabeau appears to have joined them'. They exhibited 'the petty passion of men who want to dislodge the ministers in order to replace them was revealed in broad daylight: MM. Barnave and [Alexandre de] Lameth, young men who had barely started shaving, were savaging ministers whose talents, virtues and loyalty they cannot hope to emulate!'[113]

De Visme also picks up the support of Barnave for Mirabeau on the 5th. Some, Barnave said, blamed the Parlements for not implementing the Assembly's decrees, but he insinuated 'that perhaps the principal agents of the executive power were not entirely innocent'.[114]

Mirabeau then – completing his 'evolutionary tactic' – proposed that ministers should be available in the Assembly for questioning – rather than just reading statements and departing, as the archbishop of Bordeaux had. This was taken to be a step towards making members of the Assembly eligible for the ministry so that Mirabeau could retain his ascendancy over it after becoming a minister. The deputies were beginning to suspect that 'MM de Mirabeau and Duport had a marked desire to be ministers; the same intention was attributed to Le Chapelier; the Bishop of Autun had clearly shown his own; . . . MM de Lameth, Barnave etc., complicit in these intrigues, hoped to gather the fruits of them'.[115]

So, when Lanjuinais proposed that no member of the Assembly could be a minister during the present session and for four years thereafter, the motion was carried by a large majority: 'The extent of the applause showed how much the Assembly was enchanted by Mirabeau's discomfiture.' When Mirabeau said that the talent of France resided in the Assembly and that the government stood in need of some of it, he was booed. 'M. de Castellane who supported him was mauled by the Assembly in the same way.'[116] When Mirabeau highlighted the ad hominem nature of the proposal by ironically proposing an amendment to the effect that he alone should be excluded, he was hissed.

The pathological distrust of the 'Executive Power' which resulted in this 'fatal decree', as Mirabeau's friend La Marck called it, was both a symptom and a cause of the failure of parliamentary government to be established in Revolutionary France. It meant that ministerial ambitions could not be avowed. This is why Bradby never considered that her hero Barnave wanted to be a minister and rejected the evidence that he played a part in government in 1791. He was obliged to deny it, and she believed him. Mirabeau's point that it should be possible to take ministers from the biggest pool of talent (the Assembly), which Barnave would urge in 1791, was valid given that the Assembly was forever complaining about the poor calibre of ministers. La Marck summed it all up: 'In studying the revolution of 1789, one should never lose sight of the fact that the Assembly combined all the talent, all the energy, all the intelligence of the kingdom, whereas in the ministry virtually all one saw was lack of ability, lack of foresight and lack of prudence and certainly inadequacy for the circumstances. They maladroitly let slip the reins of government and the Assembly seized them.'[117] The decree was 'fatal' because, with no adequate channel of communication between them, it guaranteed entrenched war between executive and legislature. It also forced Mirabeau into clandestine relations with the king and queen, as it would shortly force Barnave.

Though the deputies could not be ministers *de jure* they became ones *de facto* through their committees, which shadowed the official ones. Of the 1,315 deputies, 315 sat in the 34 committees set up by the Assembly. Barnave's group were prominent in the committees: Alexandre de Lameth and Menou sat in seven; Duport in six; d'Aiguillon in four; and Charles de Lameth in three. Barnave himself sat in five, including Avignon, colonies, diplomatic and revision. He was the rapporteur of the colonial committee. Of others who figure prominently in this book Mirabeau sat in six; and of those prominent as Barnave's opponents, Dubois-Crancé sat in five, Pétion, Prior and Rewbell in four. Of those working with Mirabeau and later with Barnave, Talleyrand sat in seven, Le Chapelier sat in five, and Beaumetz and d'André sat in four.

In his 1791 manifesto the king complained that the Assembly 'by means of its committees, constantly oversteps its own self-appointed limits and concerns itself with matters relating exclusively to the internal administration of the kingdom and of justice and thus combines all the powers'.[118] Apart from the king, this usurpation was lamented by many on all sides of the political spectrum: Regnault de Saint-Jean d'Angely (who said the diplomatic committee was unconstitutional), Duquesnoy, Brissot and (apparently) Barnave, though his party had dominated the committees and, hence, to a degree, the Assembly and the government. Alexandre de Lameth put it succinctly: 'The executive power divested itself of its power in favour of the various committees which were created by the legislative power.'[119]

Barnave has a variation of this in his *Introduction à la Révolution française*: the Assembly had to step into the vacuum caused by the breakdown of government in the summer of 1789. But he also wrote, as a note for his *Introduction à la Révolution française*: 'Restore the Executive Power to the plenitude of its functions. Suppress the committees, etc. – the Assembly was against.'[120] It is not clear whether the section after the dash is connected with 'Suppress the committees'.

Brissot, like Duquesnoy, saw dangers in 'the anarchical and despotic committees of the National Assembly; in their ubiquitous invasion of the administration; I see them in the interminable delays in [completing] the constitution which are the despair of thinking patriots'. Though this was far from Brissot's point, the delay in completing the constitution, by prolonging the provisional situation, allowed the rapid deterioration of the political one.[121]

— SEVEN —

THE YEAR 1790

'The year 1790 presents few great events,' Barnave writes in the *Introduction à la Révolution française*; 'but it was fertile in important works and was the only one that was not marked by any great catastrophes. The [drafting of the] constitution made great strides and the Revolution was stationary. A multitude of political and administrative matters [were dealt with]: assignats, colonies and armaments for Spain.'[1] He omits to mention two disastrous measures – the abolition of nobility and the Civil Constitution of the Clergy – which alienated large and important sections of the population and which consumed time better spent in completing the constitution which *pace* Barnave did not make 'great strides.' You cannot be 'stationary' in a revolution. With skill you can end one but you cannot stand still.

⚜

The 'fatal decree' put paid to Lafayette's coalition-building and the attempts to topple the Necker ministry. As Staël says after the decree 'the plotting seems to have died down a little.'[2]

So Necker soldiered on and on, a lame-duck premier. Even within the ministry he was not unchallenged. Over dinner on 12 November Montmorin, Necker's chief ministerial ally, told Morris 'that their administration has no head, that M. Necker is too virtuous to be at the head and has too much vanity; that he himself has not sufficient talents, and even if he had he could not undergo the fatigue.' And that 'evening' Necker's plan to turn the Discount Bank into the Bank of France 'was disapproved of . . . in the council.'

Necker gained a respite by persuading the king to take several steps publicly to identify himself with the Revolution. On 4 February 1790, Louis went down to the Assembly and made a speech in which he 'placed himself at the head of the Revolution' and swore to uphold the constitution. Of this proceeding, however, which amounted to a speech unaccompanied by a policy, it has justly been observed: 'If one merely utters sentimental phrases, one obtains only fleeting applause. . . . Necker raised a peristyle which did not lead to any building.'[3] The king's request that the Assembly attend to the deficit was ignored. When Malouet, seeking to profit from the enthusiasm produced by the king's speech, asked the Assembly to confirm the king as head of the army and the administration, the Assembly did not even vote on his proposals.

Barnave thought that the king's speech was a trap: its

> effect . . . is to give those opposed to the Revolution a natural pretext to appear to have changed tack and consequently a powerful means to trick innocent patriots . . . to lull them into a dangerous sense of security. Never, however, has such security been more foolish and more dangerous because the number of discontents has been swelled by those who dislike the new geographical divisions of the country,

replacing the historic provinces with eighty-three Départements. How could anyone feel any emotional attachment to the Haute Garonne or Seine Inférieure – inferior indeed to Île-de-France?[4]

However, the speech bought Necker time, though little use was made of it. The king was allowed to spend the summer at Saint-Cloud, on parole, as it were. And on 14 July the anniversary of the fall of the Bastille was celebrated with delegates arriving from all over France. Barnave later said that if the king had exploited the euphoria and accepted the numerous requests to tour the provinces 'we would all have been lost'. But he did not.[5]

Nor did the Assembly use the time well. Though there were superficially no 'great catastrophes', the measures of the Assembly (which Barnave applauded) paved the way for them. The Revolution was in remission, rather than 'stationary', and in the summer of this quiet year

– the one in which Barnave's 'extravagant' popularity peaked – the Assembly introduced three entirely unnecessary and almost inexplicable measures which created the potential for civil war and, coupled with the October Days, sealed the fate of what he would call the 'first' Revolution: the abolition of nobility (19 June) and the Civil Constitution of the Clergy (12 July).

A REPUTATION WON AND LOST: FOREIGN AND COLONIAL POLICY

In May occurred the famous debate between Barnave and Mirabeau, hitherto uneasy allies, on the question of whether the king or the Assembly had the right to declare war and sign peace. In 1790 Britain established a trading settlement at Nootka Sound off Vancouver Island in their Canadian colony on land claimed by Spain. The Spanish seized two ships there; Britain demanded redress and armed an expeditionary fleet. Montmorin asked the Assembly for additional funds to support France's Spanish ally. The request led to a debate in the Assembly on the whole question of whether the king or the Assembly had the right to declare war and sign peace. The obvious answer, reached after seven days of acrimonious debate, in which the protagonists were Barnave and Mirabeau, was both: the Assembly decreed that 'the right to make peace and war belongs to the nation. War can only be declared by a decree of the legislative body, passed on the formal and necessary proposal of the king and subsequently sanctioned by His Majesty' – a role which Barnave had never denied the king, though Mirabeau rhetorically claimed that he had.

Generally, the outcome of the debate was considered a success for Barnave and Alexandre Lameth, who were escorted home in triumph, but for Desmoulins it was a defeat. He noted 'on Saturday 22 May the little dauphin clapped Mirabeau's decree with wisdom well beyond his years' – he was five; Desmoulins further noted that Robespierre was more farsighted than those applauding Barnave: 'Gentlemen, what are you cheering for, the decree is detestable in the extreme? Let the brat clap his hands at the window, he knows better than us what he is doing. Ever since [the voting of the article] the king has started taking the fresh air and hunting.'[6]

The issues were trivial, not just *sub specie aeternitatis* but in the context of the Revolution, especially since the constitution would go on to forbid wars of aggression and all the king wanted was to conduct peace negotiations away from the public glare. Moreover, Barnave believed the Spanish alliance was vital for France. In his analysis there were two European power blocs: the Triple Alliance of England, Prussia and Holland; and the alliance of France, Spain and Austria. 'France by her geographical position' – but actually by her superior wealth – gave a 'helping hand, as it were' to our 'maritime ally' (Spain) and our continental ally (Austria). Spain was totally reliant on a stable France to stop England seizing her colonies.[7]

Like Louis XVI, Barnave had a love-hate relationship with England. While admiring her institutions, he believed (wrongly) that 'it was in her interests never to allow a free and regular constitution to be established in France'. He believed that without French support she would turn Spain into a client state like Portugal. 'Although the Austrian alliance was far from having the absolute and obvious utility of the Spanish, it was no less to England's advantage to break it up . . . for Austria, being our continental rival', England could divert French resources from the overseas struggle by weaning it from France. More will be said of the Austrian alliance because Barnave sensed that it could either be the rock on which the constitutional monarchy would founder or the one on which it could be founded. Barnave was well aware that neither the Spanish nor the Austrian alliance was popular, but he stuck his neck out in support of both.

Barnave made some notes for the debate which though skeletal reveal more of his thinking than the speeches he delivered:

> On the right of [declaring] war and [making] peace.
>
> Difference from England – it does not fear either the introduction of a large army nor a foreign invasion.
>
> The commitments made in treaties are really legislative acts.
>
> Absurdity of secrecy [the king argued that no foreign power would negotiate in public with an assembly].
>
> The place of the executive in diplomacy.
>
> The king can never be a general [command in person]. Nature of royalty, inviolability [the king can do no wrong], [he is] a fallback [and can] never direct action.[8]

Now, as ever, it came down to a question of trust. Barnave said in open Assembly, 'you are being asked willy-nilly to take the word of men [the ministers] whose designs are dubious to say the least'.[9] Barnave and Alexandre believed that perhaps for the first time since the October Days a ministerial party was being assembled in defence of the king's prerogative to conduct foreign policy, which he regarded as the jewel in his crown. The ringleader was Mirabeau, who, since 10 May, had been sending the king and queen written advice in return for the settlement of his debts and a bonus for success at the end of the session.[10] Some twenty deputies were involved, including Barnave's ally the vicomte de Noailles, whom he challenged to a duel. On the eve of the debate, La Marck told Mirabeau that 'Dupont, Chapelier, Lauzun, le vicomte de Noailles, and Lafayette all want to speak in support of the ministry. Perhaps Dupont will speak in favour of a descent on England.'[11]

On 27 July, as part of a coordinated effort by Barnave's group to bring down the ministry, Dubois-Crancé alerted the Assembly to rumours of the passage of imperial troops through the frontier province of the Ardennes on their way to suppress the rising in the Austrian Netherlands. Montmorin told the Assembly that this was a treaty obligation and on the 29th, as a popular demonstration brayed 'down with the ministers', a six-man committee was set up to review all treaties concluded in the previous thirty years. The committee comprised Fréteau, Dubois-Crancé, Menou, Mirabeau, Châtelet and Barnave.

Its powers were entrenched when it was instrumental in settling a flare-up in the Anglo-Spanish dispute. William Pitt, the prime minister, was happy to avail himself of the offer of unofficial mediation by Hugh Elliot, an admirer of the Revolution and a friend of Mirabeau's. 'I am extremely glad', he told Elliot, 'to find by your letter that you have succeeded so well in establishing a confidential intercourse with the leaders of what appears to be the ruling party of France.' Elliot told Pitt that he had had 'a private Conference with a Select Deputation of the Diplomatic Committee. The persons appointed to meet me were M. Menou, M. Fréteau and M. Barnave – since elected president of the National Assembly.' It was agreed that this sub-committee would make a report to 'the Diplomatic Committee *in pleno*' and that Menou would tell Elliot of their conclusions. The committee informed Montmorin 'who agreed to the propriety of this representation'.

Then to strengthen his negotiating position Montmorin asked for further assistance: he asked for thirty ships and Barnave got him forty-five. But in a revolution, there is always a price to be paid and, as Masson observes, 'when that disastrous affair was finally concluded on 25 November, it is easy to see what ground the Assembly had gained: it had set up a permanent diplomatic committee, a committee of government if ever there was one'. Masson called the diplomatic committee a 'committee of government' because the core attribute of monarchical government had been the conduct of foreign policy. And Masson adds, 'the monarchy without protest allowed itself to be divested of its essential attributes.' And the fall of the keep completed the Assembly's control of the castle.

THE COLONIAL IMBROGLIO

The popularity Barnave won in the peace and war debate he lost as the rapporteur of the colonial committee on the troubles in France's lucrative sugar islands, Martinique and (the most important) the French half of Saint-Domingue (modern Haiti), which by slave labour on its plantations accounted for three-quarters of French sugar production and was accordingly called 'the pearl of the Antilles'. The historiography of this subject is vast and I have chosen to confine myself mainly to the material I have found in Barnave's papers.

There were four related issues in French colonial policy during the Revolution: (1) slavery; (2) the slave trade which fed it; (3) the political rights of the mixed-race 'free men of colour'; and (4) the obligation of French colonies to trade exclusively with France – '*l'exclusif*'. In 1788 the *Société des amis des noirs*, led by the journalist J.-P. Brissot, had been established in order to promote the immediate abolition of the slave trade and the gradual abolition of slavery itself. It found some resonance in the country at large: of the 482 consolidated *cahiers de doléance*, 23 demanded the end of the slave trade and 10 the abolition of slavery itself; 19 raised the matter.[12]

However, though these matters were referenced in its debates, the Constituent Assembly sought to legislate on (3) and (4) only. On Barnave's recommendation, the Assembly by its decree of 8 March, embodied in instructions to the colony of the 28th, accepted without debate his proposal that the status quo in the colony would remain until the planters voted to change it – which they were unlikely to do.

This was not his original intention: a draft in his papers begins: 'Immediately after the reception of the decree . . . all the freemen paying taxes and domiciled for over a year in the parish *without distinction of colour* ['*sans acception de couleur*'] will assemble to elect their representatives to the colonial assembly' (my emphasis).[13] Why did he change his mind? This is a historian's question: few if any of his contemporaries knew that he had. His opponents just assumed that he was becoming reactionary and was influenced by the fact that Charles de Lameth, with whom he lodged, had acquired large plantations through his wife. But the historian can use Barnave's archive to show how his policy evolved – in this case in a less liberal way; and if one could do this for other political leaders, one might get a more contingent view of the development of the French Revolution itself.

There were two counter-currents generated by the Revolution. The new spirit of liberty emboldened the planters to demand what Britain's American colonists had demanded and achieved: freedom from the old colonial system restricting their trade to that with the mother country. The other, epitomised by the Declaration of the Rights of Man, implied emancipation of the enslaved population and, as a preliminary, the abolition of the slave trade and full political rights for the freemen of colour. When it came to the pinch, Barnave opted to buy off the planters' desire for free trade by acceding to their demand that the 'free men of colour' be denied full political rights. In later private reflections Barnave made a connection between (1) and (4): 'The two revolutions in the colonies: freedom [of the enslaved population] and independence [that is, free trade] necessarily go hand in hand. Policy and humanity both require that the process be gradual.'[14] But it was far from that: a major slave revolt broke out in 1792 and in 1794, the National Convention abolished slavery in French colonies.

BARNAVE AND BRISSOT

The foreign policy debates (Barnave accused Brissot of being in league with England to destroy the Franco-Spanish alliance) and especially the colonial issue brought Barnave into conflict with the influential journalist J.-P. Brissot. His *Patriote français* was perhaps the most popular journal, but he also devoted a book-length pamphlet to an attack on Barnave – not just his policy but his personality.[15]

Human rights, he thundered, were anterior to the constitution; they could be declared but not decreed: 'one declares a right but one decrees a law'. Barnave 'seemed to think that the Declaration only applies to a locality, is merely a matter of maps', whereas it was universal. Better, he concluded, 'to lose our islands . . . than turn them into an impious laboratory . . . [for a virus] calculated to infect the soil of liberty'.

Brissot chided Barnave for prizing practicality over philosophy.[16] 'You think my arguments are philosophically correct but bad politics.' But a little more philosophy, he claimed, would have improved Barnave's oratory because the philosopher 'would have been careful not to improvise or deliver long perorations on matters of which he was ignorant; nor to luxuriate in sterile offerings on commerce, *assignats*, taxation, speculation, diplomacy which are no more pardonable than bad manners'.[17] But it was not just the substance of Barnave's speeches which Brissot criticised – it was his 'oratorical style'. He granted that Barnave had 'adroitly grasped the ideas of others; arranged them logically; developed them lucidly; that in short you speak with facility; but it must also be agreed that your ideas are neither new nor elevated; that your body-language is cold, your ideas lacking in energy and your style lacking in precision'. He warned him that unless he worked on these points, he would justify the epigraph that placed at the beginning of his pamphlet read: 'You who are so jealous of your gloire / Tremble lest it cease *before* your hour.' Brissot changes 'after' to 'before', adapting the line which Cicero addresses to Catiline in Voltaire's verse play *Catalina*.

Brissot had a strong personal animus against Barnave, hating him for lording it over the Jacobins and neglecting his own *Société des amis des noirs*. 'A patriot shuns luxury like a poison, like a crime. He does not affect to have a numerous court of clients in his anti-chamber, giving audiences with a cold and studied dignity. He leaves these insolent charades to despots.'[18] It was true – people had to make appointments to see Barnave if they could not catch him leaving the Assembly. An antechamber – like a king. Access was everything – in the old dispensation and the new. A filter. The panoply of power. Though the colonial issue was the origin of the dispute between the two men, soon we will see Brissot, a republican, attacking the Austrian alliance which Barnave considered essential for the preservation of the constitutional monarchy.

ABOLITION OF NOBILITY

Though Barnave played little part in it, Alexandre Lameth, who led the debate over hereditary nobility, was obviously influenced in his conclusions with contact not only with Barnave's thinking but also from observing him at close quarters at meals, seeing how he held his knife and fork, how he relaxed in their shared house. What he says could have been written by Barnave himself. 'The leading class of the Third Estate had already obtained all the material satisfaction that it could desire' – the blocks to advancement Barnave so bitterly criticised – 'by the immense changes operated by the Revolution; but when you are living comfortably, when you have received a good education, when you have acquired learning, you experience needs of another kind and you find social superiority without inadequate foundations intolerable.'[19]

Lameth specifically says that it was the elite of the Third Estate – Barnave's class – who felt their exclusion – the way Madame de Barnave treated her husband's clerks showed that the social gap between them and her family was as great as that between the Barnaves and the nobility; and Alexandre makes it clear that 'for some time the notion of suppressing nobility had fermented in the minds not of the people but of the elite of the Third Estate'. The differences within the Third Estate were mirrored by the chasm between the provincial nobility, who had hissed at his mother in the theatre and the court nobility who befriended him – the Lameths, d'Aiguillon and Laborde. In the provinces, where Barnave had spent most of his life, the upper bourgeoisie were often better educated and richer than the local nobility. Lameth thinks this was particularly true of Brittany (and Le Chapelier was a prominent speaker in the debate), a poor province where the nobles were poor. Barnave had defended the legal rights of two such Dauphiné families against the fisc, but it cannot have escaped his notice that their rights were attacked because 'narks' thought these families were in no way superior. Lameth thought that the Breton nobility, 'deprived for the most part of the advantages of wealth, were not in a position to receive a superior education which confers tact'. Of course, he was talking about himself and, of course, that is what Barnave encountered – 'the softened edges of asperity'.

The debate on the abolition of nobility was a set-up job, like the night of 4 August. Alexandre Lameth admits that 'a large number of court nobles were in on the secret' – their social standing, unlike that of their provincial brethren, was secure. Alexandre began by proposing that the chained captives under Louis XIV's horse in the Place Vendôme, representing the four provinces he had conquered, should be removed before the representatives of these 'generous' provinces arrived for the 14 July celebrations. This proposal was greeted rapturously and followed inconsequently by the demand that noble titles should be abolished. Alexandre's elder brother Charles demanded that armorials should be banned and Lepeltier de Saint-Fargeau, a president in the Parlement of Paris and, as he said, the proud possessor of several marquisates and comtés, should use only their surnames.

Feeling that this virtue-signalling had proceeded too far and too fast, a deputy demanded an adjournment until Monday as constitutional matters should only be discussed in the morning and certainly not on a Saturday night. Barnave claimed that these were not constitutional matters and that they should proceed straight to a vote, which they did when titles, armorials, even livery were outlawed. Funerary monuments were spared.

This appears to have been Barnave's only intervention in the debate. But he was closely involved. In his papers there is a draft of Charles's speech entirely in his hand with numerous corrections. I thought at first that Barnave might have written the speech for him. But it begins 'M. Ch de Lameth', who refers to 'the previous speaker' – Alexandre. It would seem that Barnave is preparing Charles's speech for publication or, not liking the *Moniteur*'s version, improving on it. It is similar to that version but there are interesting differences which reflect Barnave's concerns. At first, he wants to stipulate that nobles should not employ 'these puerile distinctions ... in their letters and calling cards' but changes this to 'the language of polite society'. Either way, he thinks 'that the law should decidedly not carry out an inquisition' against offenders; but then thinks the fact 'that public opinion marks them out as among those who still do not understand our happy revolution' suffices.[20] These additions – visiting cards, the language of polite society – suggest that the abolition of nobility was a personal rather than a doctrinaire matter.

Later he realised the disastrous consequences of a measure which gratuitously alienated 250,000 nobles. The decree turned the Revolution from being 'an individual matter to one of caste and corporate consciousness'.[21] It alienated 'especially the army officers who, wounded in their pride as gentlemen were more so as commanders by the indiscipline of their troops'.

The decree created a new wave of émigrés, who, dishonoured in their own country, settled in new lands as 'colonists' or 'pilgrims', in Barnave's colourful words, and dreamed of returning as conquerors. 'Thirty-two of the 168 nobles on the right present in the Assembly in June 1790' left to join the émigré armies. Ferrières puts it well: 'honour was placed in opposition to the national interest'. 'From this moment a chimerical pride made the nobility irreconcilable enemies of the constitution. A league was formed between the nobility, the clergy and the Parlements, these three bodies, who had detested each other before the Revolution, came together and worked to undermine . . . an order of things in which they were no longer allowed to have a place.'[22]

Lafayette, who had not wanted to be outdone by the Lameths and had supported the decree, now joined Necker in asking the king to veto it. He refused, whether in pursuance of a *politique du pire* – allowing the Revolution to caricature itself, though it needed no help from him – or because he was scared to veto a popular measure or thought his observations would be ignored, we do not know. A clue may be found in Ferrières's observation that the decree was motivated by 'puerile bourgeois vanity'. A year later, explaining to his émigré brothers why he was going to accept the constitution, Louis said 'the lower portion of the people see only that they are reckoned with; the bourgeoisie sees nothing above them. Vanity is satisfied. This new possession has made them forget everything else.' Louis XVI had a deeper understanding of the Revolution than is generally realised.

THE CIVIL CONSTITUTION OF THE CLERGY

If the abolition of nobility was motivated by vanity, it was also motivated by spite, with past grievances compounded by ever-present opposition.

The motives for that other spiteful measure, the Civil Constitution of the Clergy, are less obvious, for they had accepted, if some with bad grace, the loss of their lands and their tithes and being paid by the state. It is generally accepted that the driving force behind the measure was Jansenism and Gallicanism. As Tackett puts it, 'the reform package which the ecclesiastical committee presented [was] a complex mixture of Jansenist, Gallican and Physiocratic proposals'.[23]

Jansenists, strong in the Parlements, had been persecuted by Beaumont, the archbishop of Paris, after the pope had been induced to condemn Jansenism as a Catholic heresy in 1711. The Gallicans, who did not support the new heresy, did not like the pope's interference either. The backers of the measure, including the Jansenist Martineau, the rapporteur of the ecclesiastical committee and the Jansenist theologian Camus, claimed to represent a return to the ideals of the early Church by instituting popular election of bishops and curés by all active citizens of whatever faith or none. This was also in conformity with the election of military and naval officers and judges introduced at the time.

Just as Barnave, a *roturier*, may have thought it was not his place to attack noble titles, so as a nominal Protestant and actual atheist he may have felt a qualm about attacking an institution already on its knees. He never formed part of a Protestant bloc in the Assembly. He 'confined himself to the brief reflection' that there was no need to restrict the electorate to the faithful since, wading briskly into deep theological waters, he ventured that it was not the election itself which conferred spiritual authority since that quality 'could only be transmitted by those who already possessed it'.[24]

It was not this doctrinaire measure, though, which led to difficulties but the new boundaries for the bishoprics, which were to be co-extensive with the new *départements* that had replaced the old provinces: as there were 135 old bishoprics and only 83 *départements*, some bishops would have to resign, and others be assigned new sees. This rational change required papal institution and though the king tried desperately to secure this, it was not forthcoming.

The matter lay quiet for six months, but then on 27 November the Assembly compounded its error by decreeing that all priests must swear an oath of allegiance to the constitution, including the civil constitution, or resign their livings. Louis postponed giving his sanction while he desperately, and in vain, urged the pope to baptise the civil constitution and thus save France from schism.[25] Then, on 26 December, with 'death in the soul', he finally sanctioned the decree. About half the curés took the oath but only seven bishops. Schism was thus a reality, with France divided into jurors and non-jurors.

It was at this point that Barnave entered the fray, insisting (1) that the ecclesiastical deputies should take the oath, and (2) that otherwise the king should be asked to fill their livings. He then complained to the *Moniteur* for 'attacking the decree of 26 December for the second time'. 'This criticism', he added, 'was the occasion of a violent diatribe against me. Doubtless the decree has no need of defenders but they would still be useful.'

THE JACOBIN AND CORDELIER CLUBS

The year 1790 also saw the development of Barnave's power bases outside the Assembly and his concomitant ability to put pressure on it. In the previous chapter we found hints that Barnave used popular pressure in Paris to influence the royal government and the Assembly itself. These were indications only but in 1790 the pressure took a concrete, almost institutional, form in the shape of the Jacobin Club, which Barnave co-founded, and in the popular movement centred on the Cordelier Club, through which the whole of the Left Bank was controlled by Danton, with whom Barnave had demonstrable links for the rest of his life. In 1787 Georges Danton, a powerfully built man with a scowling face like Beethoven's, had purchased an office involving the presentation of cases to the *Conseil d'état* and, though it did not confer nobility, he styled himself 'd'Anton'.[26] We will see that Danton was secretly in the pay of Montmorin, the foreign secretary. Barnave also had secret relations with Montmorin, though the minister could not find an opportunity to offer him a bribe. A complicated secret network underlay the surface equality of Revolutionary politics.

It is generally accepted that the Breton Club provided the nucleus of what became the Jacobins after the Assembly's move to Paris.[27] Accommodation near the Assembly was rented from the Dominican friars on the Rue Saint-Jacques, which gave the club the name by which it is generally known, first as a right-wing jibe, soon as a badge of honour. Its official name was 'Société de la Révolution', but in February 1790 this was changed to 'Société des amis de la Constitution'. The change was less significant than at first appears since on all sides 'Revolution' and 'Constitution' were interchangeable.

At first the new club rented the Dominicans' chapter house, then, as the membership swelled, the chapel and finally the library, which became its home till the dissolution of the club after the fall of Robespierre in 1794. The room had an exaggerated barrel roof which must have given strange acoustics and made it hard for Robespierre's thin voice to penetrate. His dominance, however, dated only from the middle of 1791. Before that Barnave's faction controlled the club.

The inaugural session in early November contained about 100 members, the second 200. They were all deputies but soon others were allowed to join if proposed by six members. The first president was a close ally of Barnave's, the baron de Menou. The secretaries were, according to Alexandre, 'Target, Barnave, Alexandre de Lameth, Le Chapelier, Adrien Duport and three others whose names I forget'.[28] No minutes of the meeting were kept until June 1791 and knowledge of the early officers is sketchy, but we know that d'Aiguillon was elected president on 8 February; Charles de Lameth was president on 15 March and Barnave on 3 June 1790.[29] Elections were monthly.

Barnave drew up the rules for the society, which were adopted on 8 February. At least that is the accepted view.[30] But though there are drafts similar to the final result in his papers not corrected by him, they are not in his hand; whereas a draft entirely in his hand bears little if any relationship to the final version.[31] Though the printed rules are comforting and self-congratulatory, the earlier draft borders on the hysterical and is concerned entirely with the underhand rear-guard action of the aristocracy, whom the Revolution had robbed of their spoils: the time when the constitution is about to be completed is also that 'when wicked citizens are redoubling their efforts to destroy it . . . with all the resources of perfidy . . . arming the people against their own interests'. Barnave's mentality is binary: France faced either 'the most brilliant destiny or the most frightful anarchy'.

However, the heart of the matter lies not in the preamble but in the rules themselves. There were two salient features outlined in the first article: 'to discuss in advance the matters that are to be decided in the National Assembly' and 'to correspond with such like-minded societies as may be formed throughout the kingdom'. The first article was only a codification and systematisation of what, as Alexandre said, had been done since the start of the Revolution. The second was new, though we have seen from his letter of 15 July that Barnave had been thinking of provincial pressure groups 'concerted' from Paris for some time. The combination of preparing debates and the Jacobin network, attempting to give the whole country the same constitutional heartbeat, was transformative. It was Barnave's most original contribution to the Revolution, perhaps his only truly original one.

It was not just the mechanism but also the spirit in which it operated from the start which made it distinctive. Robespierre, who was not original, took over a going concern. Even the famous purges which characterised the society in 1794 are envisaged in Article IV:

> If a member is convicted of having manifested whether verbally, in writing and a fortiori by his actions, of having displayed principles which are clearly against the spirit of the constitution and the Rights of Man, in a word against the ethos of the Society, then (depending on the gravity of the offence) he shall be reprimanded by the president or excluded from the Society by majority vote.[32]

Camille Desmoulins, an early member of the Jacobins whose journal *Révolutions de France et Brabant* supported Barnave, fleshes out the bald objective of Article 1:

> We know that the Breton deputies meet at the Rue Saint-Honoré. . . . The Jacobins meet three times a week. Their session is truly, literally a rehearsal for the next day's sitting of the National Assembly. There the motions are proposed and discussed, decrees drafted, presidents and secretaries of the Assembly and the members of the different committees nominated and as they have the majority all they have discussed in the evening is done and dusted.[33]

Barnave himself is equally explicit: in a letter to the Jacobins of Grenoble in June 1790 he refers to 'the Comité des Jacobins who have it in their power to fix the elections in the National Assembly' and the jealousy of those deputies in the Jacobins 'who had not yet been elevated to the honour of the secretariat or committee membership [in the Assembly]'.[34]

One of the best contemporary analyses of how Jacobinism worked was made by Louis XVI:

> In nearly all the cities and even in several country towns and villages associations have been formed with the name *Société des amis de la Constitution* [Jacobin clubs]. In defiance of the laws, they do not permit the existence of any other clubs that are not affiliated to themselves, thus forming an immense corporation even more dangerous than any of those which previously existed. Without authorisation, nay in contempt of the laws, they deliberate on all aspects of government, correspond with each other on all subjects, make and receive denunciations, and post up their resolutions. They have assumed such a predominance that all the administrative and judicial bodies, not excepting the National Assembly itself, nearly always obey their orders.

Nevertheless, the reach of 'the elegant and respectable Jacobins' only went so far. They could not call up a riot. For this the popular movement, whose members were soon to be called the *sans-culottes*, was necessary. The link between Barnave's party and the popular movement was provided by Danton.

The origins of the popular movement lay in the sixty districts which had elected the Parisian deputies to the Estates-General. After the elections, the districts remained in being and claimed the right to call the deputies, or 'mandatories', to account in virtue of the direct democracy they espoused. The most vocal of the districts was that of the Cordeliers and Danton was its semi-permanent president. The Cordeliers' district was the home to most of the radical journals: Loustalot's *Révolutions de Paris*, Brune's *Journal de la Cour et de la Ville*, the *Mercure National* and two which especially supported Barnave, Fréron's *Orateur du peuple* and Camille Desmoulins's *Révolutions de France et de Brabant*. The district provided a safe haven for radical journalists.[35]

Arguing from the legitimacy conferred by direct democracy, Danton claimed that the real authority in Paris lay not with the mayor Bailly but with the districts which 'by communicating their resolutions to each other and electing ad hoc executive committees as necessary' could put pressure on the mayor, the Assembly and, ultimately, the king.

The town hall struck back in May 1790 when they persuaded the Assembly to replace the districts with forty-eight 'sections'. The Cordeliers' district was now incorporated into the Théâtre Français section but to preserve its geographical identity a Cordelier Club was formed. For two years,[36] Danton continued to control both it and the popular movement. But he now also joined the Jacobins, making his first recorded speech there in May 1790. Thus, two pillars of Barnave's pressure group were united.

There was also a third, which overlapped with and complemented the Jacobin network: the municipalities. The idea for the development of municipalities had been trailed by Barnave in his 'impure blood' speech: instead of a proclamation castigating the murders of Foulon and Berthier, he had said 'the only precautions needed were the establishment of free and regular municipalities and the bourgeois guards throughout the kingdom'. Ferrières offers the best analysis of the objectives of what he calls 'les Lameth' in establishing these entities, which created a country-wide network which he plausibly estimates at 'about 1,300,000 officials to propagate their ideas' – a sort of nomenklatura.[37]

What distinguished the municipalities, Ferrières observed, was that their officers – 1,175 of them, including 'notables' – were directly elected, whereas the district officers were chosen in primary assemblies and the departmental ones were chosen by the districts. 'It was above all in the attributions given to the municipalities', Ferrières continues, 'that the revolutionaries showed their predilection for these bodies': tax collection, public works, cleaning streets, and so on, 'but the most important right, which made them a veritable power, was that to requisition armed force', whether national guards or troops of the line.

⚜

From 1790 splits in the Jacobin Club arose reflecting the fact that, as Barnave lamented, 'the unity among the members of the popular party in the National Assembly is less than could be desired' – for which he blamed Lafayette.[38] On 15 March 1790 Duquesnoy notes that a steering committee or 'directorate' of the Jacobins had emerged consisting of 'MM. Barnave, d'Aiguillon, the two Lameths, Laborde and the baron de Menou'. Duquesnoy complained that they had not gone to the trouble of overthrowing one aristocracy 'only to replace it with another'. The dominance of Barnave's 'directorate' was 'one of the causes of the comte de Crillon's club' – a short-lived rival to the Jacobins.

However, from its ashes 'The Society of 1789' emerged. And to emphasise that it was mainly for deputies, they paid no membership fee, whereas others paid 120 francs (£5) a year, £1,000 in today's money. The society – the 89 Club – held an inaugural dinner with 124 covers on May 13, with Siéyès presiding. Barnave is scathing about the members of the rival club, whose mainstay was Lafayette. There were some forty or fifty deputies – 'the rest mainly comprised very rich bankers and financiers . . . and above all a large number of young courtiers who having left the aristocratic party, now thoroughly discredited, attached themselves to this society to integrate themselves in the new system without risking losing the advantages of the court or fashionable salons by their association with the Jacobins'.

The main stumbling block to a reconciliation between the two rival clubs, the Jacobins and the 89, was Lafayette, the dominant force in the latter. Lafayette cynically thought that Barnave's group, though not corrupt, 'wanted power over political matters and influence at court' – exactly what he had achieved. Lafayette was aware that the struggle between himself and the Jacobins pitted the two dominant 'patriotic' forces in France against each other. Lafayette had the National Guard and the guardianship of the king and queen in the Tuileries, and with it the disposal of the civil list that the Assembly gave the king as compensation for putting his crown lands 'at the disposal of the nation'. But above all it was the National Guard. Barnave's group had the Jacobins, with its nationwide network, strong but never total control over the National Assembly, and influence in the popular movement through their ally Danton. Neither group had much of a presence in the other's strongholds.

Lafayette believed, with some justification, that Barnave's group – and Alexandre in particular – were trying to loosen his hold over the

1. The château of Saint-Robert purchased by Barnave's father in 1755. Barnave grew up here and returned in 1792. He was arrested here at the break of dawn on 19 August. The château has extensive grounds going down to the Isère. Barnave inherited the property after his father's death in 1789.

2. Barnave wrote of Louis XV: 'In the end [of his reign] such was the success of the systematic degradation of the nation that it no longer cared for anything but the love of gold, the delights of pleasure and the most frivolous vanity; and when it was finally put to the test by the violent acts which marked the end of the reign it combined such obedience with such contempt for its master that it seemed ready to suffer everything'.

3. Miniature of Barnave as a young man, by Louis-Marie Sicardi. The Louvre has an earlier miniature on ivory also by Sicardi, signed and dated 1782, housed in an enamel and two-coloured gold snuff box. Barnave may have been referring to these in his undated letter to a presumed fiancé. It was unusual for a provincial bourgeois to employ the king's miniaturist, particularly at such a young age.

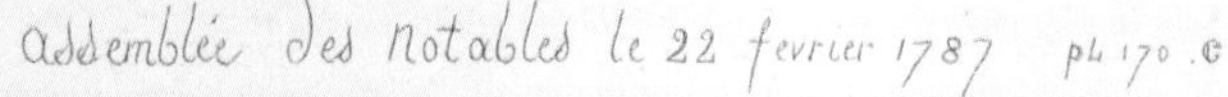

4. Calonne (monkey) asks, 'With what sauce would you like to be eaten?' The Notables (fowl) reply, 'We don't want to be eaten at all.' Barnave wrote: 'From the convocation of the Notables my whole attention was directed to political matters. The thought of seeing my country freed from its chains and the caste to which I belonged raised from the state of humiliation to which an insane government seemed to be increasingly condemning it stirred all my mental and spiritual faculties.'

5. Barnave called Calonne the 'artful' architect of all the crown's policies between 1787 and 1788. Barnave's longest pamphlet was his *Coup d'oeil sur la lettre de M. de Calonne* of March 1789 in which, curiously, he attacks Calonne for attacking the status of the nobility.

BARNAVE.
L'homme De la Cour 1791
L'homme Du peuple 1789
Tantot Froid, tantot Chaud, Tantot Blanc, tantot noir,
A Droite maintenant, mais autrefois à Gauche,
Je vous disois bon jour, et je vous dis bon soir.
6.26362

6. No wonder Barnave called this cartoon an 'infamous caricature'. In 1791 an English visitor saw a realisation of it 'at the waxworks in the Palais Royal', adding that already 'the caricature was entertaining all the taverns in London'. In a sense the Janus accusation was true. Barnave was 'the man of the people' and 'the man of the court', but concurrently, not consecutively. He served the one by serving the other.

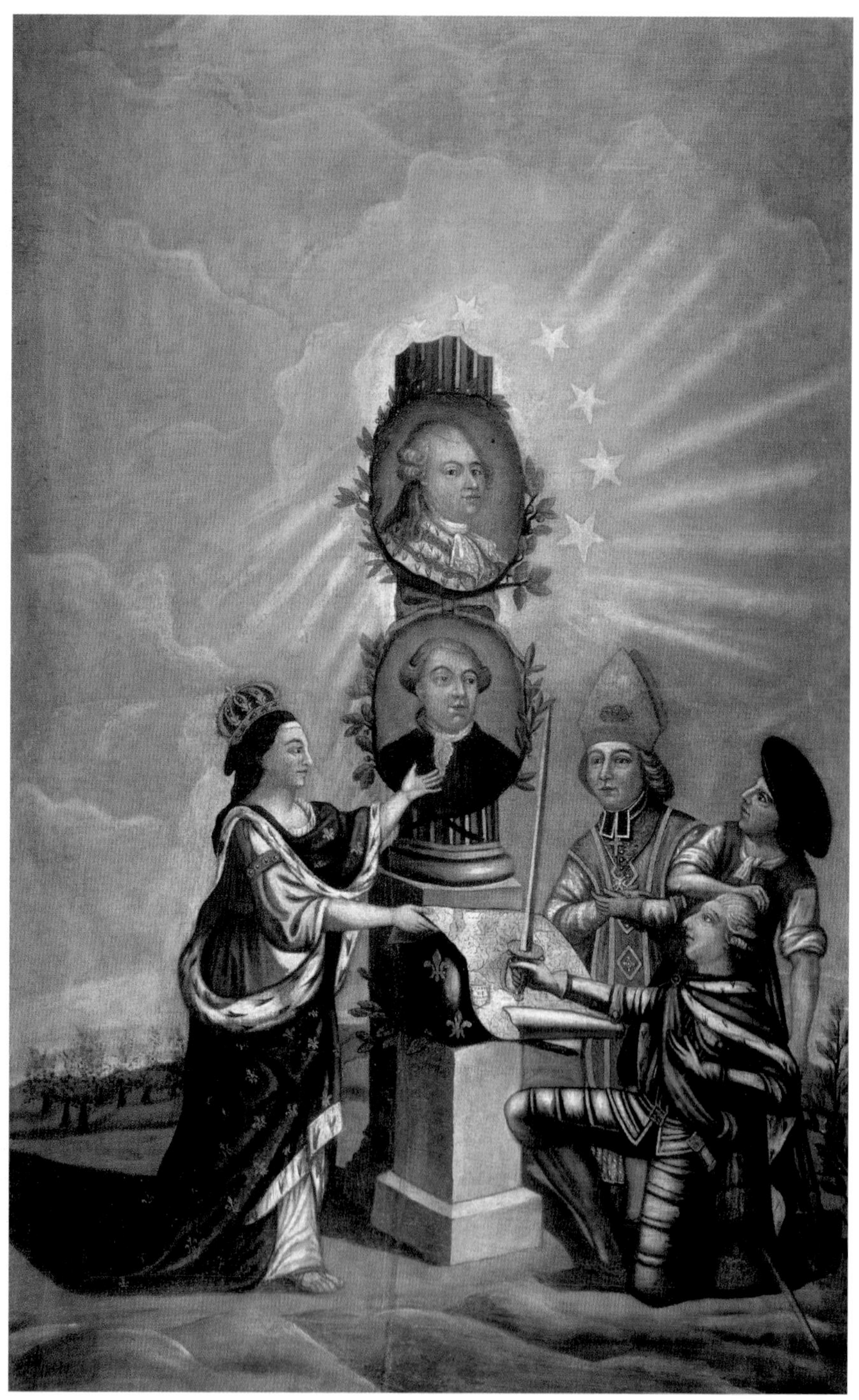

7. Barnave's distant relative Jacques Necker is the focus of this allegory of the three estates – the peasant on the right (actually there was only one in the Estates-General) gazes up at him in admiration. Barnave thought he had the minister's word that the king would accept the August decrees and the Declaration of Rights in return for a suspensive veto. He called Necker a 'charlatan' and asked: 'Whence comes our distress if not from his incompetence?'

8. Barnave (far right holding a tricorn hat), Mirabeau (massive frame), with support from Dubois-Crancé (top, hand on sword pommel) and Père Gérard (praying) were behind the commissioning of David to commemorate the oath not to separate until they had given France a constitution. So their faces alone are painted in this preliminary sketch. The first draft has them clothed, this naked, and the next was to have them re-clothed, but the picture was only completed after David's death (exiled as a regicide) in 1825. The man with puffed out chest is Robespierre. Mounier actually proposed the oath to forestall a plan (probably supported by Barnave) to have the Assembly move to Paris.

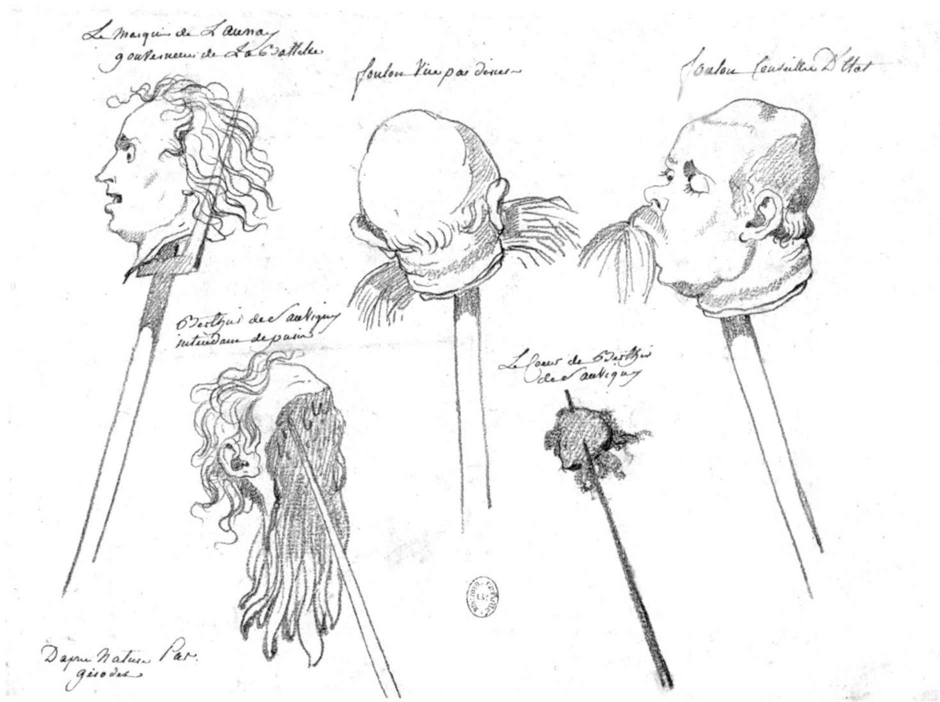

9. Barnave notoriously said of the murder of these royal officials in July 1789: 'So, is the blood that has been shed all that pure?' A draft for his speech transfers the blame to the victims: 'They talk of the blood that has been shed but this blood is rather that of the citizens who … [were] reduced to defend themselves'.

10. Through his distant cousin Madame de Staël Barnave negotiated a deal on the king's veto between his allies and Necker her father. Later he backed the appointment as war minister of her lover Narbonne. 'Thousand-tongued fame', he told Marie-Antoinette, 'was not her equal'.

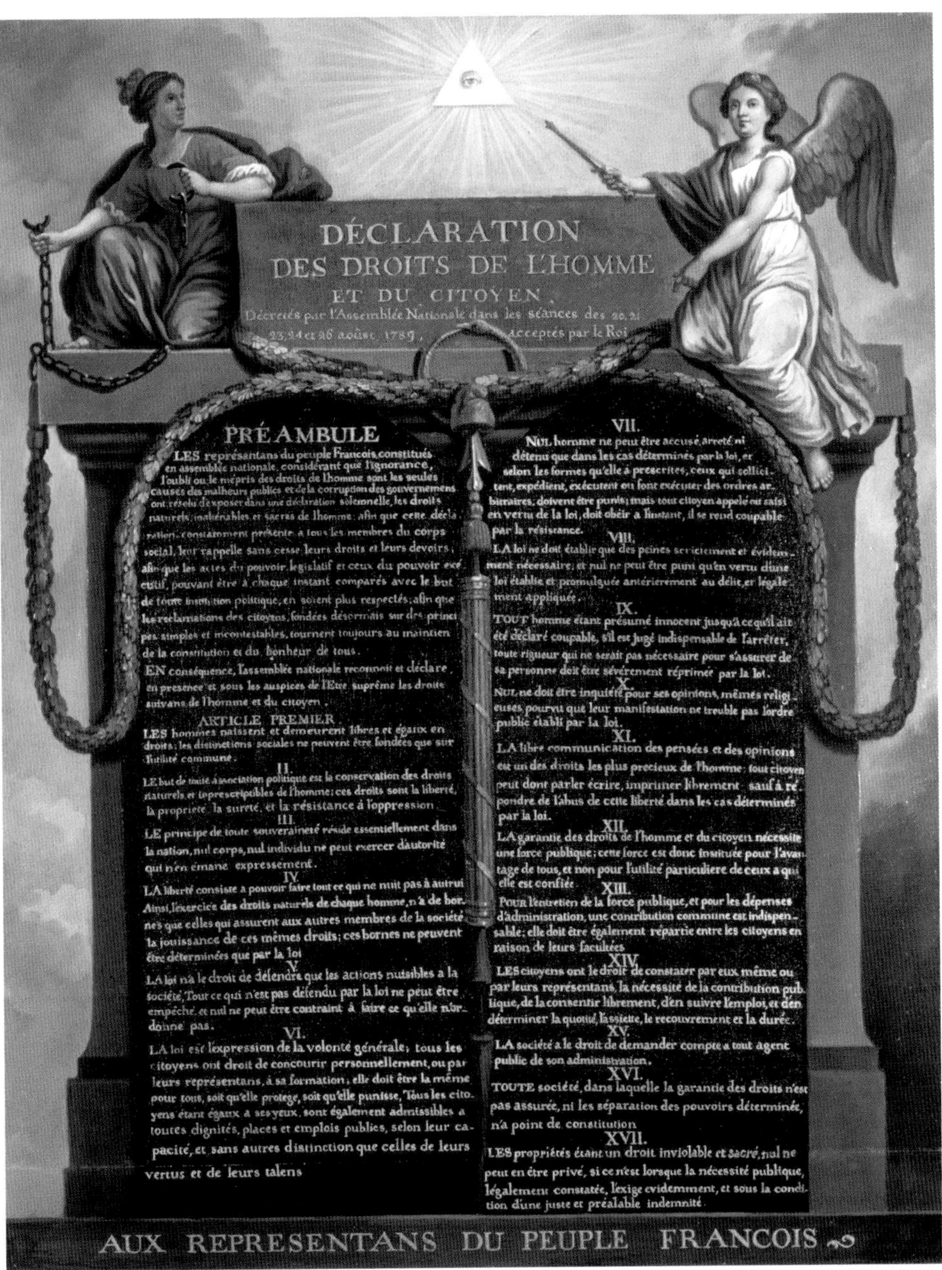

11. Barnave hoped that the Declaration of the Rights of Man would become the 'national catechism' of the new France, acting as a bulwark against the Scylla of aristocratic revival and the Charybdis of popular incursions. Robespierre thought it should be applied literally and mocked Barnave for advocating a limited franchise. The Declaration was indeed more honoured in the breach than in the observance.

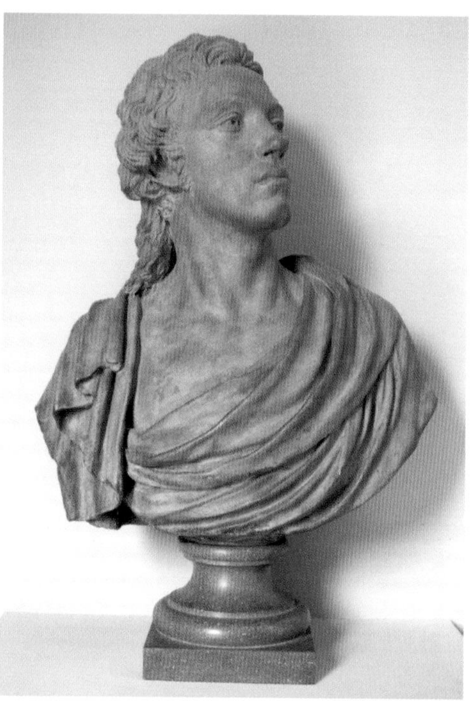

12. Houdon was the only artist to capture the vein of arrogance which ran through Barnave and so infuriated many of his colleagues who could not see the sweetness which captivated his intimate friends.

la nation la loi et le roi.
département de l'isere district de grenoble
municipalité de St Egreve laissé passer
M. Barnave françois domicilié en cette municipa-
-lité de St Egreve district de grenoble
département de l'isere commandant en
chef de la garde nationale de ce canton
agé de trente ans taille de cinq pieds
quatre pouces cheveux et sourcils châtains
yeux bleus, bouche moyenne, front grand
visage maigre et prêté lui assistance en cas
de besoin.
délivré à la commune de St Egreve
le dix sept juin 1792 l'an quatrième de la
liberté.

Barnave

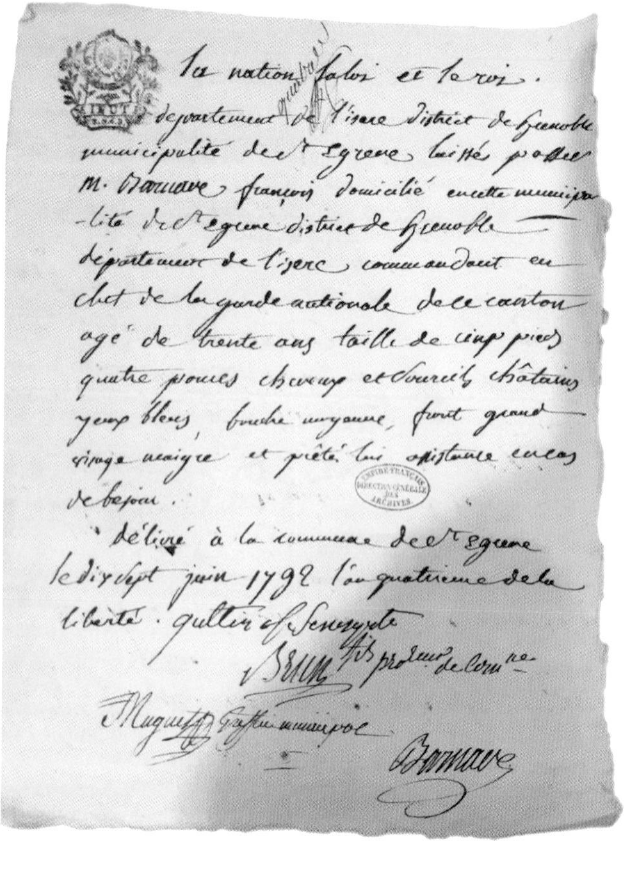

13. Barnave's passport aged thirty, two months before his arrest, with signature. He is described as having 'dark blond hair and eyebrows, blue eyes, medium mouth, large forehead, thin features'. Lévis is more poetic: 'blond hair in buckles harmoniously framed a large and high forehead', a proud chin and a slightly retroussé nose. He had a large voluptuous mouth and a smile of disdain played on his lips, revealing dazzling white teeth.

14. Of the 'triumvirate' it was said that Duport 'originates it, Barnave speaks it and Lameth performs it' – that is, Duport was the intellectual, Barnave the orator and Lameth the wire-puller. Barnave's originality is to be found in his writings rather than his speeches. Duport advocated a jury system and the abolition of capital punishment.

15. Barnave supported Mirabeau's idea of issuing a paper currency backed by the confiscated Church lands. The interest-bearing notes could be used to buy the land, upon which each one would be destroyed to prevent inflation. Barnave argued against over-issue but the temptation was too great and the *assignats* depreciated by 25 per cent against gold in his time, much more later. By the fall of the monarchy in August 1792, 3.2 billion *assignats* were in circulation. By the fall of Robespierre on 27 July 1794 the total was 11 billion. Galloping inflation was the inevitable consequence. It is easier for its elected representatives to cheat the nation than it is for its king.

16. Barnave and Mirabeau had a stormy relationship though both believed in a strong constitutional monarchy. Barnave was to have been the linchpin in Mirabeau's grand project and was in a sense his heir. After sparring in the foreign policy debate Barnave invited him to dinner with a view of outflanking Lafayette.

17. The royal party was stopped at Varennes and they were sent back to Paris under guard. The Assembly sent commissioners who met up with the coach at Epernay. On the return journey Barnave 'who was fairly slim' sat wedged between the king and queen in the front seat of this berline carriage, 'the hearse of the monarchy'. In snatched conversation he and Marie-Antoinette agreed that he would try to implement the programme of the king's manifesto and she would persuade her brother, Emperor Leopold II, to get international recognition for the Revolution.

18. Danton was Barnave's link to the popular movement. Barnave warned Danton and Desmoulins to get out of Paris just before the Massacre of the Champ de Mars. Danton reciprocated by allowing Adrien Duport to flee to England after the fall of the monarchy and he made two attempts to have Barnave released.

19. Louis is depicted as a pig with the horns of a cuckold, Marie-Antoinette as a panther with the head of a gorgon and her infamous feathers. The caption 'The two are but one' seems to contradict the image of a left-leaning king dragged rightwards by his wife, and may be true at least until 1792. Compare with the Janus cartoon of Louis (plate 22) and of Barnave (plate 6).

20. Du Tertre, minister of justice 1790–2, was responsible for transmitting the policy hammered out between Barnave and Marie-Antoinette to a cabinet committee with its own room in the Tuileries, which the king rubber-stamped in the Conseil d'état. Du Tertre's arrest was ordered at the same time as Barnave's and he stood trial and was guillotined with him. After his conviction he told the tribunal: 'You kill me today, that is the result of the Revolution; posterity will judge between us.'

21. The Swedish nobleman Axel Fersen probably became Marie-Antoinette's lover in 1785. He believed (wrongly) that she was sleeping with Barnave. To this sexual jealousy was added political: he was a counter-revolutionary giving the queen different advice from Barnave's. Bizarrely, Marie-Antoinette entrusted her correspondence with Barnave to Fersen for safe keeping in 1792. He wrote, 'Barnave died like a coward'. Untrue.

Je soutiendrai la Constitution
Je détruirai la Constitution

22. This Janus head and that of Barnave both appeared in the summer of 1790. Louis told a minister that the best way to highlight the failings of the constitution was to apply it faithfully. For lack of right-wing support Barnave was not able to increase the king's constitutional powers as much as he had hoped and had promised Marie-Antoinette, who knew he was 'beaten'. Nevertheless they had to make the best of a bad job.

23. The fall of the Tuileries was not a foregone conclusion, and Barnave believed that if he had returned to Paris he could have stiffened the resolve of the Assembly 'whose despicable feebleness had given a fistful of men the audacity to subjugate it and make a great revolution in the state by means of a popular riot'.

24. Barnave refused the pleas of Théodore Lameth to ask the Convention for his release from prison because 'to ask them for justice would be to recognise the justice of their previous acts and they have killed the king'! He concluded, 'No, my friend, I would rather suffer and die than lose one scintilla of my moral and political character.'

25. Brissot was Barnave's nemesis, bitterly attacking his colonial policy in his lengthy *Lettre à M. Barnave* and destroying the constitutional monarchy by driving France to war with Marie-Antoinette's bother Leopold in the hope of smoking out her treason. 'We need great treasons' he proclaimed; he was guillotined a month before Barnave.

26. As he surveyed dukes and beggars thrown together pell-mell in the over-crowded prison, Barnave told a fellow inmate, '[W]hen you consider these high mightinesses, these philosophers, these legislators, these miserable wretches all thrown together, does not that infernal stream of legend come to mind, from whose bourne no man returns?'

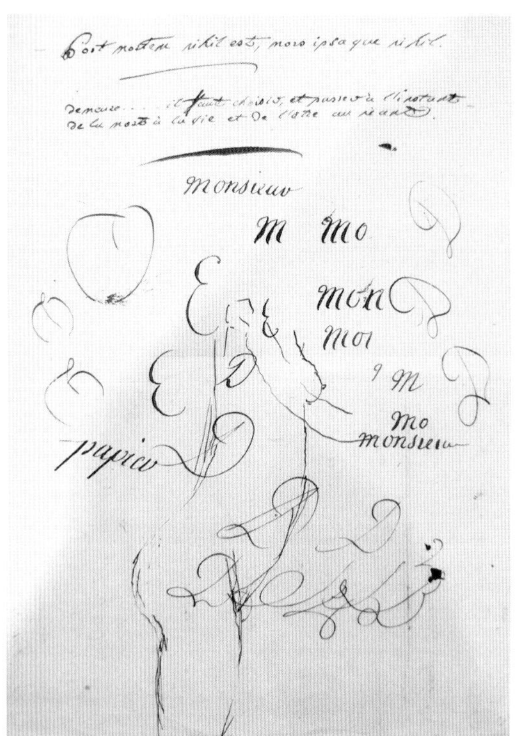

27. Barnave was a great doodler. Here, above the profile of a naked woman and the words 'monsieur' and 'papier', he writes: 'Post mortem nihil est, mors ipsa que nihil' (There is nothing after death and death itself is nothing). Beneath it he writes Voltaire's execrable translation of Hamlet's soliloquy 'To be or not to be'.

28. The execution of Robespierre and his supporters on 28 July 1794. Note: the beheaded man is not Robespierre, but Couthon; Maximilien Robespierre is shown sitting on the cart, dressed in brown, wearing a hat, and holding a handkerchief to his mouth. His younger brother Augustin is being led up the steps to the scaffold. Robespierre was the presiding genius of the Revolutionary Tribunal which condemned Barnave.

National Guard, the ultimate basis of his power and a means of challenging his rivals' control of the municipalities. Barnave wanted to enforce the decree stipulating that 'no one could command the national guards of more than one département' and noted that several areas had petitioned Charles de Lameth to be their commander.[39]

In June there was an attempt to end the schism with the 89 Club. On the 8th deputies from both clubs meet in the Jacobins 'to advise as to ways to finish the drafting of [the main parts of] the constitutional decrees between now and 14 July so that a solemn oath can be taken to abide by the constitution' by delegates (*fédérés*) from the départements celebrating the first anniversary of the fall of the Bastille.[40] Barnave had told Lafayette that although his views were 'fixed' on certain 'fundamental bases' on 'a large number of subordinate ones, he was flexible'. But on 13 June Barnave drafted a bitter letter to a friend about the collapse of the negotiations: 'M. de Mi[abeau] has never given up the absolute veto. M de L F has never given up the American idea of two chambers and the choice of judges by the king.' They and their associates have subjected Barnave's group 'to their base intrigues these six months'.[41]

Barnave was still smarting from Mirabeau's conduct in the debate on war and peace, and in particular from his giving a distorted version of his speech to the press. He also blamed Lafayette for an opportunistic alliance with Mirabeau on this issue. He claimed that since the beginning of the Revolution, but particularly in the last six months, these two had been defaming true patriots such as Lameth, Duport, Menou, his good self and Pétion. They had been tarring them with the slur of republicanism, whereas they stood for a 'free monarchy'. In a hysterical section of his letter, Barnave accuses his enemies of paying even the 'reputable journals' to slander him and of sending out emissaries throughout the land, even 'besieging' 'taverns and cafés' with their propaganda.

Barnave relied on public opinion to shame waverers into rejecting this revival of the Monarchiens' aims; otherwise, 'the nation would be forced to new insurrections'. 'If public opinion does not manifest itself', Barnave claims, 'the ministry will soon have an assured majority in the Assembly' – as in September 1789 when an insurrection had also proved necessary. 'This combination' – a ministerial majority – he continues, 'is acceptable in an [ordinary] legislature but it is absolutely disastrous in a constituent assembly' – altered from 'convention'. Barnave's anger and bitterness is the grit in the oyster which has produced a pearl – his most concise summation of his political principles during the Constituent Assembly.[42]

However, the pearl, like Barnave's anger with Mirabeau, was synthetic and he was disingenuous in his peace negotiations with the 89 Club: his real aim was to break up the coalition between Mirabeau (whom he admired but distrusted) and Lafayette (whom he despised). This emerges from an undated and unaddressed draft of a letter from this time which can only be to Mirabeau: 'I could certainly justify my character and condemn yours, but in writing I think I would be at too great a disadvantage. Come to dine at my place tomorrow. I do not have 30,00 men under my banners as M. de Lafayette does but if I were to range you under them as well, I think I would have more power. Adieu – see how inconsequent I am: I love your letter despite the insults it contains.'[43]

The familiar badinage is similar in tone to that which he employs with Madame de Staël and other women. His claim that his 'power' – based on the Assembly, Jacobins and popular movement – is greater than Lafayette's, which derives from the National Guard, looks like an offer of alliance. Lafayette's star is waning. By the turn of the year, we will see Mirabeau writing as if Barnave was his heir – and in a very real sense he was. Both men essentially believed in a strong constitutional monarchy. Lafayette did not. This letter also shows, uniquely, that despite a noisy rivalry stretching before and after this incident, Barnave *liked* Mirabeau. Here is displayed the charm with which he captivated his friends and which he withheld from the world. Two more faces. Nothing immediate seems to have come from this invitation to form the dominant coalition of the broad left, but it sowed a seed in Mirabeau's mind.

Attempts to reconcile the two clubs, the Jacobins and the 89, were renewed in late August and September. Lafayette took the initiative in asking Danton to invite Barnave, Duport and Alexandre, Danton himself and Durand, president of the Gravilliers section, round to his house. There they met for 'three consecutive evenings'.[44] The aim, according to Danton's friend Desmoulins, was to end the schism between the Jacobins and 'the 89 Club that baleful tree, that boon upas [a poisonous Javan tree] which spreads its liberticide branches over the

National Assembly [which] will be killed at the root.'[45] The hope was to detach Lafayette from the 89 Club and if Lafayette is to be believed, it succeeded in its object: on 3 October he told Bouillé, 'I recognised in my conversations with the leaders of the [two] clubs that their ideas are closer than their personal animosities; at the moment I do not go to either club, staying with my friends and receiving everyone.'

Mirabeau gave Marie-Antoinette an analysis of these events under the heading 'What must we do to topple him [Lafayette]': 'His enemies in the Assembly include all the enemies of the 89 Club, or rather, since he is accused of having thrown in his lot with this society in order to give himself a party with which to fight the Lameths, he is the one who is blamed for the division of the patriotic party in the National Assembly.' He concludes that the 89 Club is doomed to extinction because it can only win by allying itself to the right.[46]

If agreement could have been reached, it would have embraced the commandant of the National Guard, the Jacobin leaders and two dominant figures in the popular movement, Danton for the Cordeliers, with his links to the ministry through Montmorin, and Durand, an influential figure in the sectional movement. Moreover, as Lafayette's letters make clear, the king and queen were informed: 'I then told them [the king and queen] how I stood with the Jacobins. I saw them in the evening.'[47] Lafayette informed his cousin Bouillé, commander not only of the main armies of the line but of the only one in which, for the present, discipline was still intact after the recent suppression of the mutiny at Nancy. Thouret, the rapporteur of the constitutional committee, visited Duport, the Jacobin leader Lafayette liked best, with Lafayette's proposed constitutional 'articles.'[48]

Bradby considers that these meetings ended in failure because Lafayette wanted to slip a second chamber into the constitution at the last minute. But on the larger constitutional discussions, there was agreement, which culminated on 23 September in the National Assembly's addition of seven of its members to its constitutional committee to 'examine all the decrees passed by the National Assembly, separate those which are properly constitutional from those which are merely regulatory and in consequence make a corpus of constitutional laws, and revise the drafting of the articles so as to rectify any errors which may have slipped in.'

On 3 October Lafayette gave Bouillé his take on the two most important features of the decree: the codification and the addition of seven new members: 'A revisory committee has been formed whose work will have an almost total impact on the drafting of the constitution. . . . If the members of the committee come to an understanding, they could do a useful job particularly as it is made up from members of both wings of the popular party and for that reason its proposals will be passed more quickly by the Assembly.'[49] The seven additional members were: Duport, Barnave, Alexandre de Lameth (the 'triumvirs'); Pétion and Buzot, slightly to the left of them; and Beaumetz and Clermont-Tonnerre, from the remains of the Monarchiens.

Barnave shared Lafayette's optimism that the constitution would soon be completed. In a draft of his speech accepting the presidency of the Assembly, which he occupied in the fortnight 25 October to 8 November, he thanked his colleagues for the confidence they had placed in him 'at the moment when your labours are advancing towards their conclusion and those remaining to be run through have already been prepared by long meditation.'[50] It would, however, be another year before the constitution was completed and it would be at the centre of Barnave's concerns. Uncertainty as to when the constitution would be finished and what he would do afterwards was responsible for Barnave's havering over acceptance of the mayoralty of his native town.

MAYOR OF GRENOBLE

Barnave was mayor of Grenoble from 1 August to 14 November 1790. He was elected on the first ballot with 215 votes out of 397. He had been in continuous correspondence with the popular society of Grenoble, many of whose members were also town councillors who wanted favours from a powerful deputy. It was a stitched-up job. We know this from a letter Barnave wrote to a friend on 25 July, that is, a week before his election: 'I have not changed my mind on my election to the mayoralty of Grenoble, so, I beg you to do all in your power to spare me the very painful step of refusing the choice which would have been made of me.'[51]

Barnave's friend was unable to prevent his election but on 13 August he declined the honour on the grounds that his duties in the Assembly would not allow him to take on the mayoralty.[52] Undeterred, on 22 August Grenoble renewed their offer and agreed to wait until the Assembly had finished its work. Barnave then gave his friend a conditional letter of acceptance to give to the town council only 'if you think . . . [my acceptance] is absolutely indispensable'. The friend obviously did, for Barnave's letter of acceptance was delivered. It was provisional – to be reviewed in November – when Barnave resigned.

Barnave was chosen as mayor not only because of the influence of the local Jacobin Club but also in the expectation that he would obtain benefits for the town. In 1790 Grenoble had a current account deficit of 12,000 livres and a debt of 130,000. The town council required authorisation from the National Assembly to borrow such a sum. They asked for his help and on 1 June – two months before his election as mayor – he replied that he had given the request to 'the finance committee. Although the sum you want to borrow seems fairly considerable . . . I managed to get the committee to present to the Assembly on Friday a decree authorising you to borrow 130,000 over six years starting from now for pressing needs' and to raise the money with local taxes.

Grenoble made a second request which Barnave thought 'very difficult to grant'. We do not have their letter, but they were making another three demands of the Assembly: (1) a temporary local salt tax before the *gabelle* (salt tax) was abolished; (2) a request to the '*Comité de l'alénation des biens nationaux*' to buy nationalised Church lands valued at 8 million livres (no wonder they were indebted!); and (3) that the Assembly overturn its order removing the battalion of Royal Corsican Chasseurs from Grenoble where it had mutinied. Barnave promised to 'omit nothing however to see it through either by the Assembly or by external means which perhaps will have more chance of success' – presumably pressure on ministers.

He continues, 'I would have already given you a clearer picture if M. de la Borde, whose credit in the finance committee and in the administration, I need for this matter, had not been on his country estate for a week on the occasion of the marriage of one of his sisters.' Laborde de Méréville, of course, was one of the quadrumvirs and through him Barnave controlled the finance committee.

Charles de Lameth, who was influential in the military committee, was enlisted for the third request and also for keeping two artillery companies from Valence in Grenoble. The town was fearful of an invasion from Piedmont. Barnave wrote to Grenoble: 'I have not been able to deliver the letter you sent me to give to M. de Lameth because the very day I got it the health of his father-in-law obliged him to go to attend on him some miles from Paris.' But Barnave was able to assure them in advance that Charles would respond very favourably to the trust they had put in him.[53] On 5 August Barnave intervened to endorse Grenoble's claim to be the seat both of the Assembly and the directorate of the new département of Isère.

A NEW MINISTRY

The Necker administration was not finally winkled out until the autumn. The proximate reason for its collapse was two mutinies: one military (at Nancy), the other naval (at Brest). In August the Châteauvieux, a Swiss regiment in the service of France, mutinied over pay. Mirabeau told Marie-Antoinette that Duport and Menou were responsible: 'Swiss nationals living in the capital have formed a club directed and animated by MM Duport and Menou and always guided by their incendiary political machine they have proselytised disorder among the Swiss regiments.'[54] Though Bouillé, the army commandant at Metz, shared Mirabeau's view,[55] there is no hard evidence that they were right and when Bouillé suppressed the mutiny, breaking one of the soldiers on the wheel and hanging twenty-eight for good measure, Barnave did not dissent from Lafayette's letter of congratulation and when in 1792 the mutineers were pardoned and feted by Robespierre, Barnave was scandalised.

In assembling the forces needed to suppress the insurrection, Bouillé had relied on the départements in the area of his command rather than the municipalities. For Barnave the former were 'aristocratic', the latter 'democratic'. Barnave's party had ensured that only the municipalities could call out troops, whether national guards or troops of the line. Bouillé was aware of all this,

> observing that the members of the départements, composed of nobles, and in general of landowners were royalist but did not dare to profess it. They were in Alsace, Lorraine and Franche-Comté. . . .

> Thus of the nine départements six were entirely . . . at my disposal. But their functions did not extend beyond administration and having nothing to do with policing they had very little influence on the people who were directed by the clubs and the municipalities, the rivals of the former, whom they regarded as aristocrats.[56]

At the heart of the Nancy affair was a struggle between the départements and the municipalities, represented at the national level as one between the ministers, Bouillé, Mirabeau and the queen against Barnave and the Jacobins, with Lafayette floating between. La Tour du Pin, the war minister, once an ally of Barnave's, at Bouillé's request gave him a circular letter to all the départements under Bouillé's command to authorise the passage of troops. There were several départements involved since 'at the same time the king' had extended Bouillé's command to constitute an Army of the East.

On 2 September Bouillé's suppression of the mutiny provoked a rising in Paris; the mob threatened to march on Saint-Cloud, where the royal family were still in residence. Lafayette advised a terrified Necker to 'seek refuge with a friend'. Instead, Necker fled to his estate at St-Ouen, sent in his resignation both to the Assembly and the king, and retired to Switzerland, having lost all control over the direction of the Revolution. The king's sister, Madame Elizabeth, commented: 'Have you heard the great news that does not cause a stir in Paris? M. Necker is gone. He took such a fright at the threat of being hanged that he was unable to resist the tender solicitations of his virtuous wife to take the waters. The Assembly, on reading this phrase, laughed and passed to the order of the day.'[57] Necker's dismissal had caused the storming of the Bastille, his resignation merely laughter.

Necker was not just scared – this time he was glad to go. Barnave and his mother paid their taxes, but many did not: the fisc only received some 40 per cent of what it was due so, once again, Necker resorted to loans, but with little success: by 1792 the loan issued on 24 September 1789 had only yielded 32 million of the 75 million livre target.

In 1792 Necker published his *Du pouvoir executif dans les grands états* and Barnave penned a withering critique of it. 'It is a beefed-up pamphlet. . . . A rehash saying nothing that he hasn't written a thousand times before.' It is full of 'colourless stock images'. 'His amour propre is ridiculous and totally lacking in dignity.' 'Spite and resentment . . . are the dominant tone throughout.'[58]

The pretext for the assault on the remaining ministers was the naval mutiny at Brest in October 1790. La Luzerne, the naval minister, had given orders for eight ships to sail to Saint-Domingue to suppress the rebellion of planters seeking free trade. But the crew saw this as an assault on liberty and on 11 September refused to sail. The Brest Jacobins and municipality (whose personnel overlapped) backed them up and forced the captain of the expedition's flagship to hand over his instructions from the minister. Royal commissioners were sent to investigate but La Luzerne was scared to take decisive action and told the port commandant to liaise with the municipality. Barnave decided to make this the pretext to bring down the government.

On Friday 15 October Mirabeau warned the queen that on the following Monday 'three of its committees have resolved jointly to get the Assembly to ask the king to nominate a new ministry'. Mirabeau told her that a new one was certainly necessary but that the king should forestall the Assembly by dismissing the ministers first. Otherwise, it would set a dangerous precedent. On the Saturday he repeated his advice to pre-empt the Assembly's demand and added that the important thing was that Lafayette should have no role in ministry-forming.[59]

The king made no move over the weekend and on the Monday Mirabeau joined forces with Barnave's group in the committees. This may have been his intention all along. The committees decided to 'make the disturbances at Brest the pretext' for asking the king to dismiss his ministers. They put up Fréteau to be their spokesman, but he declined. 'Barnave decidedly did not want to accept' what he regarded as a poisoned chalice.[60] In the end his ally Menou was roped in and spoke (badly, La Marck thought) for the three combined committees. His tactic was denounced by Clermont-Tonnerre: 'By what perverse logic have your committees under the guise of a report' on the naval disturbances 'turned your attention to a ministerial . . . holocaust?'

Undaunted Barnave rehearsed his constant refrain that the ministers were 'slow and timid in executing your decrees'. Camille Desmoulins detected a lack of sparkle in Barnave's speech and thought 'his peroration feeble', though 'it was no crime for an orator to have an off day'.[61]

Another reason why Barnave had not wanted to introduce the measure was that the committees were actually divided and that, presumably tipped off by the queen, the ministers had spent the weekend recruiting forces. Barnave's assertion that the condemnation of the ministers by the four committees was unanimous was challenged. He answered that 'the only division was over the form the Assembly should adopt to force their dismissal'. Clermont-Tonnerre said that the vote of the committees had been stitched up when there was barely a quorum: 'four of your committees, the number of whose voters happened to be reduced to 25 [out of 48] decided by a bare majority of 15 to 10 that the only way to restore [naval] discipline was to dismiss the ministers. If that were the case, gentlemen, . . . you would not find a single honourable man ready to accept the post of minister.'

The debate was clearly not going all Barnave's way, and Beaumetz sought to soften Menou's motion by excepting Montmorin from the 'holocaust' on the grounds that it was illogical to blame a foreign secretary for home policy. Menou (who was secretly working with Montmorin) accepted the amendment but the government supporters were still able to insist that individual votes were taken, which Desmoulins thought made a hundred of the left wing reverse their vote because they relied on ministerial patronage. Some absented themselves (such as Bailly, Lafayette and even Camus), some covered their faces as they voted on the ministerial side.[62]

Defeated in the Assembly, Barnave turned to Danton and the popular movement to put pressure on the king. Danton appeared before the Assembly at the head of a deputation of the Commune to demand the dismissal of the ministry. La Marck told Mercy-Argenteau that if the Paris deputation did not winkle out the ministers, the Jacobins would organise petitions in every municipality; he thought that the real target of the protests was the queen, who had been constructing a ministerial party.

A terrified La Tour du Pin had been refusing to sign any papers for days to make the king accept his resignation, and on the night before Danton appeared before the Assembly he simply cleared his desk, which did the trick. The king accepted his resignation on 28 October, but his successor, Duportail, was not appointed until 16 November. The other ministers were of sterner stuff: Cicé wanted all the rest to go but himself, Montmorin was clinging on like a limpet and Saint-Priest wanted to hang on until he could become ambassador to Sweden, where his brother-in-law was the Austrian ambassador.[63] All to no avail: Cicé resigned on 22 November and though Saint-Priest manged to cling on until January, when he left for Sweden, it was not as ambassador.

Not content with the dismissal of the ministry, Barnave put direct pressure on Montmorin to get Cicé replaced as keeper of the seals by Duport du Tertre, the man who would be with Barnave at the very end. He was appointed on 22 November. Desmoulins, his antennae sensitised by his school friend Robespierre, asked: to whom do we owe this nomination of the keeper of the seals? 'I swear it is M. de La Fayette', replied someone who ought to know – in that case 'here we are reconciled with La Fayette', said the patriots. By their deeds shall you know them. No, said the *Journal des Jacobins*,[64] 'this appointment is due to Jacques Menou and André [*sic* for 'Antoine'] Barnave, who have pestered M. de Montmorin for eight days to propose this citizen friend of the revolution to the king'. Barnave, who regularly met Montmorin in the diplomatic committee, could have done this openly.

Condemning the power of the committees, Desmoulins adds:

> But all are evidently agreed on one point, that it is not the king who is doing the choosing. Now, if he cannot even choose the keeper of the seals, who can he choose? Does anything better demonstrate that the constitutional committee by swelling the number of offices technically in the hands of the prince has deprived the nation of the right to nominate without giving it to the king?[65]

The triumvirs dominated the constitutional committee but theirs was not the dominant influence in the forming the new administration. It was Lafayette's and their suspicion that the whole thing was stitched up in a committee of Lafayette, Montmorin and the king and queen seemed to be confirmed. La Marck wrote that 'despite [his declining influence] Lafayette managed to populate the new ministry with his creatures. M. Duportail one of his most devoted friends became war minister. Even the Lameths managed to get one of their own in the cabinet in the shape of M. Duport du Tertre, appointed keeper of the seals.'

Mirabeau must also have had a role in du Tertre's appointment. He told La Marck on 22 November, 'So there we have Duport du Tertre with the seals. That is to say Cassandra instead of Crispin.' Crispin was a stock character in French comedy; Cassandra the Trojan princess doomed to make accurate prophesies which were not believed, to whom both Malesherbes and Louis XVI have also been compared. The same day he reiterated: 'I will see Cassandra after I have given him a few days to settle into his job. I will press Pellenc's case strongly.'[66] Pellenc was Mirabeau's secretary for the letters he wrote to the queen. Part of Mirabeau's deal with the court must have included payment of Pellenc's expenses.

La Marck characterised du Tertre as 'a mediocre advocate of an extremely weak character, incapable of acting on his own initiative. He could not have been and in fact was not otherwise than the spokesman of the Lameths, who were responsible for his entry into government.' He concluded that such men 'over the next eighteen months dismantled the monarchy bit by bit'.[67] Whether this would be the case the next chapters will show, for he was to be the linchpin in Barnave and Marie-Antoinette's system of government.

— EIGHT —

BARNAVE'S PRIVATE LIFE

BARNAVE AND WOMEN

To judge by his private comments and one or two of his public ones, Barnave was a misogynist. In 1788 he sketched some apothegms in the La Rochefoucauld mould:

> Women are capable of any amount of good or evil where the passions are concerned. But they are incapable of impartiality and all that flows from it. With them: no passion at stake = no action, no volition, no thought.
>
> I do not know if women, by turns heroic but never fair, are more egotistical than the majority of men but they are certainly much more blind in their egotism.
>
> Women's feelings are very deep but almost always egotistical.
>
> With our modern . . . education women's character is corrupted more slowly but I think it is corrupted more generally than in the case of men – no girls are pure after eighteen nor men honest after forty.
>
> The main blot on the character of women is instability – besides their natural feebleness, their virtue never survives trials and experience; rarely too do their principles and ability to reflect; but much of their natural inclination to inconstancy and their even more wavering imagination does survive.
>
> Just as business/politics corrupts men, so flirtation and amour propre corrupt women. The pretty ones become egotistical and vain. The ugly ones become wicked and mean.
>
> How with women amour propre does not affect their dignity – when all that is said to flatter one of them tends to wound another, Result: they are in perpetual conflict.[1]

Women have more weakness than flexibility. They more often grant to force what they deny to prayer.

Women pride themselves more than men on social status. . . . They have entirely forgotten primitive equality.

Women, like the great of the earth, set such store by the respect that they are used to receiving that when they cease to receive their due all their confidence evaporates. Thus, they prize form over substance and in their eyes errors of etiquette constitute the greatest offence.

Women are often like the gambler who starts by thinking it is permissible to cheat at cards to level the odds and ends up getting into the habit and winning the lot. Women are not the only ones whom in the belief that they are at a disadvantage strive to win by the most blameworthy means.

Women display another characteristic in the belief of their inferiority – it is the glory they take in a multitude of things. They prize equally everything that comes their way – knowledge, credit, honours, power, reputation – and they never enjoy any of them.

There are very few women who are not weak but there are many who give themselves an impression of strength by a powerful . . . [unreadable word].[2]

Barnave wrote these reflections when he was twenty-seven. Two years later he had not revised his opinion. He was heard to say in the Jacobin Club: 'When the devil grows old he becomes a hermit; when a woman loses her looks, she becomes a religious bigot.'[3] In the section of 'Des femmes' entitled 'coquetry', Barnave extends his musing on the ages of woman. Only after the age of twenty are women tired of teenage 'coquetry' and ready to love. By thirty 'their vanity is rekindled' and they seek reassurance from younger lovers that their beauty has not faded. 'Then they slave over their toilette and parade their lovers.' 'Then comes the moment when the lovers flee away and they must give up everything. Then at the same time they become embittered.'[4]

How did such misogyny affect his known relations with women? Was it affected by them? We know that Barnave broke off an engagement and strung his fiancée along for some time while he was conducting more than one passionate correspondence with other women. These are full of reproach and misery and the accusation of 'coquetry'. At the outset of their correspondence, Marie-Antoinette noted: 'The two friends [Barnave and Lameth] did not attempt to conceal that they thought me very frivolous, incapable of undertaking anything serious, incapable even of thinking logically.' However, Barnave soon came to revise that opinion and they dealt with each other as intellectual equals.

The evidence that Barnave was engaged to be married comes from an unfinished draft letter referenced by a private letter Barnave wrote to a friend dated 25 June 1790, which tells us that his inamorata's name began with an S: 'Tell S . . . that I never stop thinking about her. I will write to her soon and send her what she has asked me for' – a portrait. He explains that he is 'overloaded with business and exhaustion and does not have a free moment'.[5]

He begins his letter with: 'rumours of my so-called marriage have been broadcast so widely here and in such an affirmative manner that I thought, dear love, that all your trust in me would not be enough to reassure you – especially after so long a silence on my part'. Some of these 'rumours' were far-fetched. The *Correspondance secrète*, having opined that Barnave had 'received money from all sides – the court, the colonies and probably from M. d'Orléans', thought he intended 'to enjoy his fortune in America' and 'will marry a rich creole who will give him four millions'. Another source noted that after the Constituent Assembly had closed, 'he married the only daughter of a former judge in the Cour des Aides with a dowry of 700,00 francs'.[6] On 26 August 1790 Madame Barnave told her son: 'the public have for a long time been talking of your marriage to a young widow, the daughter of M. Massère. She is said to be amiable, rich and pretty. Several people have sought to offer me their congratulations. I brushed them off persuaded as I was that there was nothing in it and that in any case it would not be through the public that I would be informed.'[7]

So Barnave felt obliged to reassure his fiancée that his 'heart had not changed' and he had not even considered marriage to anyone else. Her 'distress pained him' and her consoling 'image' looked up from the bottom of the 'whirlwind of troubles' which assailed him. 'Nothing equalled his wrong in not writing' – his friends and his mother made the same complaint – but he did not have the time to meet 'even basic obligations'.

However, and paradoxically, the 'extraordinary kind of life' he had been living 'enters the soul and imprints true feelings there indelibly'. Nothing would part him from her and he had 'learned by experience what I had always known intellectually that affections of the heart are the only source of happiness, that ambition is repugnant to my . . .' – nature, he would presumably have said; and if said, it would have been a lie – and one moreover he was not obliged to tell.[8]

Why feel the need to deny ambition in a love letter? Did he mean social ambition? Would Barnave have been 'marrying beneath' either his former or his present station? Michon thought that Barnave refrained from intense relations with other women out of loyalty to his fiancée; in short, he thought that 'he was not the Don Juan of certain counter-revolutionary' writers.

However, in the section he called 'Le Coeur de Barnave', Michon publishes a passionate letter and neglects three further letters of despairing love. All four are drafts, all unaddressed and undated. The published letter runs:

> I scarcely dare to say a word to you and that word compromises you. I suffer from not being able to talk to you because I make people stare. However, I must receive an explanation; you promised me one. The fear of acknowledging what I would fain not believe and what I tremble to know made me hesitate to ask you yesterday but today my mind is made up. A cruel anxiety torments me and if I must be unhappy, I would prefer to know my fate. Is your heart engaged? Tell me . . . you have shown me enough confidence, enough good will for me to expect a frank and sincere reply. If it is not true that your heart is engaged, if the most devastating notion was only a mistake! Let me see you just once in your life [alone] then at least I can talk freely to you. Sometimes you have shown interest in me. My happiness depends on talking to you for one hour.
>
> Adieu, Madame, tomorrow at nine I will send for your reply. I have complete trust in what you will say to me . . . and if your reply is not what I fear, deign to tell me when I can see you.

At nine o'clock Barnave's fears are confirmed in a short note – a '*billet*' – but not a billet-doux. Its arrival prompts the first of the unpublished letters:

Madame, I renounce not a project but the final pleasure to which I had raised my hopes. I did not expect a refusal and without expecting any great interest on your part I never thought that you could refuse a moment's attention and kindness to a man experiencing the most natural and sincere grief. All the feelings of my soul lay at your feet. I would have died a thousand times rather than cause you a moment of pain. How could I have imagined that I would not obtain what confidence, friendship and esteem never refuse. But no more of this. I would not obtain by pestering that which your feelings alone would make invaluable; that which for me had become the link of an inviolable and disinterested attachment.

Be happy! May the feeling which fills your soul compensate you for all that you are sacrificing for it. No! You are not unhappy since my own misery has not moved you. I do not wish to reproach you for anything but I have the right not to expect so much coldness and hardness. My conduct has been frank . . . and you . . . you who today refuse me the consolation of a brief encounter, have you not managed thereby to reinforce the trait which desolates me? Have you never seemed to reciprocate my emotion? Ah! Since you wanted me to think you were sincere, I had the right at least to expect that my misery would not have left you cold. But let us speak no more of it. I am not trying to find fault with you. I would suffer if I had to change an iota of the most seductive of images. I will seek consolation within myself.

There is your billet. I should perhaps have returned it to you sooner but I wanted to write to you and in my state of grief I needed time to make an irreversible resolution.[9]

The second unpublished letter runs:

An evening I had counted on spending with you would have been insupportable if I had not employed it in writing to you. I wanted to see you; you had gone out; however, you said yesterday that you would spend the evening at home. Can you imagine how cruel it is to abandon the hope which buoyed me up all day? I have never yet gone to yours without [palpitating all the way along the route] without trembling; getting past the porter; climbing the stairs; traversing the antechamber; passing into the obscurity of your apart-

> ment everything is the object of a new emotion, the strongest of them is the hope of finding you alone deep in your enchanted cabinet.

Another draft:

> On the day on which I counted most [to see you], to hear 'she has gone out'! You cannot imagine all the sadness of these words! Where should I have gone? What should I have done if I had not had the consolation of writing to you? What shall I do in short when I no longer have the hope of meeting you the next day? Although I restrain my feelings for you; although I force myself to think of something else; although I even struggle to hide my feelings from you; although I am fully resolved not to ask you to reciprocate them; nevertheless, it remains an unspeakable pleasure to tell you sometimes how much interest I take in you. It is a pleasure also to sacrifice the pleasure to which I like to think I had a claim and to talk of what concerns and touches you and to hear [you talk of] your melancholy. These are so many true pleasures. Someone will say some day that you fear me because of my taste for observation; but as I never speak ill of you, what would have been the point of discovering your faults?[10]

Who was this mystery woman who wreaked such havoc with Barnave's emotions and clearly displaced his fiancée? Or were there two? The third letter is clearly to a woman of high status, with a porter, a long stairway, an antechamber and a cabinet. I did for a moment think it could be Marie-Antoinette, who records in detail the difficulty of seeing Barnave in person. He fears if he is seen talking to her, people will stare and she will be compromised. But it is probably not the queen. For a start, Barnave knew she had a lover in Fersen. Another possibility is Madame de Staël and though she too had a lover in Narbonne, he was with the army. Staël records that despite Barnave's fierce reputation, he has a sensitive side. Whoever she was, it seems we are dealing with a 'political woman' whose dealings with Barnave, if known, would have embarrassed them both.

A third letter is even more fragmentary, and has no beginning or end. This time it is Barnave who is ending the relationship.

> Adieu. I took some pleasure in having told you the truth. I know enough about you to believe that at the moment when you – me it was not your coquetry that was involved. Could I not in granting it everything at least get in return that it would leave us free for one moment and that it would allow me to see you at least once as you really are? It would be the height of blindness to flatter myself that I could change you; it would be a ridiculous presumption and these thoughts carry an indefinable sadness into my heart.
>
> Such is my situation with you. I do not know how to express myself with greater truth. It does not even leave me the charm, the indescribable pleasure of saying I love you. To exhaust myself with dreams and regrets! To desire and fear that I will forget you! To see you would cause me more pain than pleasure, yet I suffer for not seeing you. That will be all that remains of the impression of a happiness which could have been profound.[11]

Here is another accusatory fragment: 'To move from seriousness to irony is no answer to my reproach of writing coldly; but when after so long a period of silence I see that writing which you accuse me of having forgotten I am far from seeing a more serious reproach in it; it is when you . . . me. . . .'[12]

There is a letter to another woman in a lighter vein: a draft with many crossed-out lines. It is a sustained jeu d'esprit built on the 'coquetry' of women – a piece which has something of coquetry itself. 'This miserable travesty which corrupts and destroys the majority of women is in you only a weakness which has no purchase on your heart.' But he warns her not to let her coquetry stray from 'the circle of her amusements' and penetrate 'relationships where it ceases to be excusable and destroys happiness. Can the indulgence of amour propre replace the charm of expressing your feelings and total trust [which constitutes] the only true happiness?'[13] Barnave had always liked to lecture women he considered 'flighty', whether it was his young sisters, Madame de Staël or Marie-Antoinette.

In another unaddressed letter reference is made to an intimate social friend, Marie-Charlotte, comtesse de La Châtre. The recipient was about to leave Paris and Barnave had been expecting 'for all these past days to have supper with you either at Madame de La Châtre's or chez moi'. La Châtre would be very sorry to miss Barnave's correspondent. She could name her day but must give him sufficient notice so he could lay in food 'because he did not want to make her die of starvation'. And she should try to bring along 'Théodore [Lameth] and M. Duport'. The inclusion of Duport – M., not Adrien – suggests a political supper. The comtesse was the daughter of the king's late *premier valet-de-chambre* and the heiress of a financier – so not quite 'top drawer', like several of the women in the Lameth circle. The comte Espinchal wrote that 'the comtesse de La Châtre is tall, pretty and very agreeable. She is destined by nature to grow fat but has succeeded, to the detriment of her health, in giving herself a slight and elegant figure.' He adds, 'she is good natured but given to flirtation and even gallantry . . . her boudoir became the rendezvous of all the dandies of the democratic party, prominent among whom were the Lameths, Barnave, the prince de Broglie, and so on. She is cited as one of the most zealous patriots.'[14]

MOTHER AND SON

Barnave and his mother were very close. She had lost both her husband and, in Dugua, a talented son, and 'trembled for the other in whom I place all my consolation, all my hopes, obliged to hide all my fears at the bottom of my heart without showing anyone' – except him. She calls him her '*cher ami*' and '*bon ami*' as well as her '*cher fils*'. But her surviving letters are mostly nagging ones. She chides her son for the paucity of his letters – 'excusable when you were secretary [of the Assembly]'. He replies that she can read about his doings in the press but he cannot know what is going on in Grenoble. Indeed, sometimes she can only learn of his doings from reading reports of the parliamentary debates; 'when you have not spoken for some time in the National Assembly, I am always worried that you are ill'.[15] She is fiercely patriotic and has no more time for 'aristocrats' than her son has.

Her letters to her son start with the death of her husband on the day the Bastille fell. Barnave told her to give herself a few 'pleasures'; for with 'careful management', they would have enough to live on without Barnave needing to pursue a career outside 'national assemblies'.[16] Madame Barnave also discusses business matters – the hard winter of 1788/9 had affected her silkworms so she got only 60 livres for their produce – and family ones: the marquis de Monteynard, minister of war 1771–4, had given her 'a pretty, fine diamond' (her husband had acted as judge in the seigneurial courts of Monteynard, the local magnate – a popular man in Dauphiné despite serving under Louis XV's last government). She had been keeping the jewel to give to her son's wife on his marriage. But if a patriotic subscription was opened in Grenoble, as it had been in Crest and Romans, she would donate it, providing Barnave had no objections.[17]

When it becomes clear that Barnave is a power in the land, she badgers him constantly for favours for her family and connections. He often ignored her efforts, to judge from their repetition.

But he got a relative a job in the tax department at Caen by sending a testimonial to the ill-fated de Lessart, then finance minister. When de Lessart was minister of the interior, he furthered Barnave's request to have a M. Clapper appointed registrar of Grenoble.[18] Barnave had influence through the committees on which he and his friends sat, and his particular interest was the army. So Madame Barnave was hopeful that he could do something for her two brothers, who were middle-ranking army officers. One was commandant of the Citadel of Montélimar, but was unpopular despite (his sister claimed) his patriotism and delight in his nephew's career. He wanted a transfer. Another brother's pension was late: 'I strongly suspect that you have forgotten to write to M. d'Hemeri to get my elder brother's arrears of pension totalling 400 livres and appointments of 600 paid – Jean-Claude Emmery spoke on military pensions.'[19]

The chief clerk of the Parlement of Grenoble had lost his job when that body was abolished. Madame Barnave thought, not unreasonably, that people should be compensated for losses caused by the Revolution and she wanted the man to have an equivalent position in the successor body. She presumed the post would be filled by the judges. They had not yet been appointed but she knew of three likely candidates and wanted her son to enclose 'individual letters' for her to give to each one to add force to the general petition she was organising. She did not think her son would 'be breaking any rules' and that 'it was his duty to do everything he could in a matter . . . to which she attached great importance.'[20] On one occasion, Madame Barnave sent two sons of a dear friend with a letter of introduction to Barnave in the vague hope that he 'would do something for them if the occasion arose.'[21]

His mother was just one – if the most persistent – of the many suitors, mostly from his native province, to lay siege to Barnave. The fall of the *ancien régime* entailed the ending of thousands of jobs. One lawyer complained to Barnave that he 'had been deprived of a permanent position and obtained a temporary and less lucrative one'.[22] But the Revolution created even more thousands of jobs as France became decentralised and then, in 1793/4, re-centralised.

Barnave thought that this explosion of jobs was a good thing 'momentarily' – it 'satisfied a lot of towns' by doling out 'salaries'. Moreover, the beneficiaries of 'the first elections' were keen. But if this continued for long, it would 'destroy the new regime' by diverting talent away from commerce and industry. What was needed was fewer but well-paid 'functionaries' – a perennial complaint.[23] For the moment, though, the floodgates were open – Barnave had his own list of protégés and his assistance was sought both by the dispossessed and would-be successors. He put pressure on the ministers, and the Assembly's committees, as seen in the correspondence between Barnave and the town of Grenoble at the time of Barnave's election as its mayor.[24]

Lest one be tempted to mock Madame Barnave's trivial and inept interventions, her eccentric orthography and phonetic spellings (errors from which her son was not entirely exempt), consider this letter Madame Barnave wrote on 15 March 1791. M. Bayez was coming to Paris. He was president of the newly created département of Isère and she had had occasion 'to write to him on the subject of our reparations' – for what? – and she 'could not have been better pleased' with his response. He was also 'one of our most zealous patriots'. He was travelling to Paris with 'our bishop M. [Joseph] Pouchot, who is going there to be consecrated' as a new 'constitutional' bishop on 3 April. Bayez had married the bishop's niece and Madame Barnave was 'enormously fond' of both men.

Madame Barnave had asked Bayez to write to his uncle on behalf of Barnave's old tutor abbé Laurent, currently 'curé of Vervin', who wanted to be one of the new bishop's *vicaires* (deputies). This was Bayez's reply, which Madame Barnave transcribes: 'It will always be a pleasurable duty to oblige you in all things whether essential or trifling. Consequently, you may assure M. Laurent that he will be one of my uncle's *vicaires* – I have his promise. My uncle accounts himself fortunate to have the good fortune to be of service to you. The tutor of M. Barnave has too well deserved of the *patrie* not to be welcomed by all those who cherish it.'[25]

Madame Barnave says that the appointment is 'uniquely because of you' 'because M. Bayez is one of your most zealous partisans'. When Bayez gets to Paris, Barnave would be his first port of call and the point of Madame Barnave's letter is that her son should be suitably grateful. Here we have the new establishment at work: the Barnaves, though Protestant, had always had good relations with the Catholic hierarchy, but now uncle and nephew were the heads spiritual and temporal of the new département. Suddenly Madame Barnave had found the social eminence she had so long desired – no one would dream of turning her out of a box in the Grenoble theatre now. Hitherto we have seen Madame Barnave as a suppliant to her son; this flash suggests that she was a power in her own right. How many more did she manage to place in the short window of opportunity available to her?

A letter of hers to Barnave that June suggests, though the details are obscure, that she and Bayez are working together to keep the Isère on the patriotic track. She has gone to Grenoble in order to invite a M. Ferrier to dine at St Robert and adds: 'I learn with great pleasure that [Ferrier] is establishing himself here; so, we agreed, M. de Bayez and myself, to give M. Ferrier free rein but to restrain him if it became necessary – since the aristocracy is so exalted here, we need someone who can abase it straight away.'[26]

FINANCING A LIFESTYLE

Barnave's deputy's salary of 18 livres a day could not sustain his fairly lavish lifestyle, though living rent-free in the Hôtel de Lameth certainly helped. His expenditure (apart from over 500 livres on books and 25–9 on postage for March 1791) was of the kind to get noticed. He was a dandy and dressed expensively; there are outstanding tailors' bills totalling 500 livres while he was in Paris. People exaggerated the number of great coats he owned but he bought three for 111 livres, one hazelnut in colour. Other purchases were for cravats, gilets and breeches. He favoured English material – casimere (woven merino wool) – and had one gilet made of English suede.[27] These needed buttons, of which he bought 192, 24 of silk, the rest gilt metal, probably shipped in from

Birmingham; 72 of these were 'little gilded patriotic buttons' with Revolutionary slogans or symbols. These cost extra – 50 sous, where the standard model was only 30. Like any aristocrat, he paid late: one bill for 179 livres of 27 October 1790 was settled on 8 April 1791. He admitted spending 1,200 livres on cabs when all the institutions of Revolutionary Paris were within easy walking distance.

Inevitably, people suspected him of having been corrupted – variously by England, Mirabeau, Orléans or (most persistently) by the court – as in the 'infamous cartoon'. Rumours abounded, which he was forced to deny, that he was buying up estates: 'I defy anyone to cite any investment I have made; any property purchased ... may my head fall if anyone can disprove it.' 'It is said that I have sustained huge gambling losses but the extent of my gambling is a few games of billiards for the price of a dinner.'[28] Dubois-Crancé, however, who detested him, wrote that he did 'not think that Barnave *sold* himself to the court – his pride was enough to corrupt him'.[29] And Lamartine put it more gracefully: whereas 'Mirabeau sold himself, Barnave gave himself'.[30] This must be the final verdict, so we must look for other explanations.

Barnave supported himself by borrowing: 10,500 livres from the banker Périer, who had provided his château of Vizille to the patriots in 1788. The money was raised in instalments as and when needed: 1,200 on 24 August 1789 and 1,200 on 30 December; 600 on 29 March 1790; and more tranches of 600 on 22 May, 2 July, 9 August, 22 October, 5 November and 29 December; and on 22 March, 7 and 27 April, and 16 May 1791. The sum was repaid in December 1791 when Barnave was sent a package of *assignats*: one of 1,000 livres and ten of 500 livres; he repaid 'the rest partly out of income and the rest from a loan from his relative Dejean'.[31]

His mother sent him 5,000 livres drawn from the estate of his late father and he received another 6,000 from this source. And this provides the clue to Barnave's financial situation. On 14 July the Bastille was stormed and Barnave became a double heir. His uncle Antoine died on 28 September 1788, leaving his property to Barnave's father with reversion to Barnave himself. Barnave's father left the bulk of it to Barnave, his only surviving son. Barnave borrowed against these assets while the estates were being settled.

From land tax returns it would appear that Barnave's father's wealth was mostly in investments. Barnave's land tax assessment for 1791 for St Robert was 221 livres.[32] This would have been for the two *vingtièmes* which were still being levied – valuing the estate at 2,200 livres, though the *ancien régime* assessments were notoriously undervalued. St Robert was a small estate with only one farm leased out. However, a semi-literate receipt dated 17 August 1792 from a tax collector for money paid by Barnave on Antoine's property at Vercheny is for 709 livres, suggesting a property valued at 7,009 livres.[33]

Just as it was a point of honour for a patriot to evade or avoid *ancien régime* taxes such as the *vingtième* – the whole point of the Assembly of Notables had been to secure a better assessment – so it was a point of honour to pay Necker's 1789 patriotic tax of a quarter of income. Accordingly, Barnave told his mother in December 1789 that they should rather err on the side of over- than under-payment. He told her to pay 3,000 livres, suggesting an income of maybe 10,000. That was for the whole family. Barnave told the Revolutionary Tribunal that his share was 6,000 livres.

By the new year, however, he was concerned about money. A draft letter to his mother dated 2 January 1789 [*sic* for '1790'], imagining 'that misery must be extreme in Grenoble just now', tells her to give more to charity than she usually did and people in similar situations were doing. He wanted her to 'stand out in this regard', but then confessed: 'I don't know if you have any money for this or for anything else.' 'I am writing to M de Lathune [his banker] and to [my agent at] Vercheny to send you what they can lay their hands on at the moment. I ask you, however, to employ it with the greatest economy, since besides the 1,000 livres I owe the province [the Estates of Dauphiné for printing],[34] I have drawn 2,400 livres from M. Périer's agent of which, truth to tell, I owe 2,000 to the royal treasury.'[35]

BARNAVE THE HYPOCHONDRIAC

Barnave was a hypochondriac and dabbled in quack cures which were bizarre even by the standards of the day. This may have resulted from the six months during which he watched his beloved brother die. In 1787 he had bought a book entitled *L'art de prologer la vie* – probably

J. B. Pressavin's *L'art de prologer la vie et préserver la santé ou Traité d'hygiène* (1786) – 'hygiene' being the ancient Greeks' word for natural health.

Barnave also wrote some observations entitled 'Hygiene'. They were solely concerned with drinking water and drinking water. The first observation is banal: 'Fresh water is very useful as . . . a relaxant, refreshment and an aperitif but taken in too great quantities its leads to flatulence. One must as far as possible put water in the blood. It needs humidity provided by water preferably taken with food.' 'Acidulated water' is less relaxing but has the same effect. 'The amount of water drunk should be proportionate to the temperature.' But in any case, 'it is better to drink too little than too much'. 'If the tendency to flatulence persists or has only recently abated, even a very little is enough to . . . start it up again.'[36]

Water, whether plain or 'acidulated', was tame stuff and soon Barnave was in correspondence with 'Doctor XX' – Pessavin? – over dangerous remedies. The doctor was having difficulties in passing water and was worried by both the colour and consistency of his urine. So he embarked on a series of experiments. At first, he combined nitrate powder mixed with his ordinary drink – wine at meals or in company – with mercury tablets. When his 'urine flowed better, was white in colour and less fibrous', he left off his mercury pills and turned to 'ferruginous spa water, two beakers full in the morning for twelve to fifteen days'; then he moved on to 'two spoonfuls of an astringent on retiring to bed' for three days, the same in the morning as well, 'until the flow was perfect'. The doctor was still persevering with his cure 'up to today and seems determined to stick with it to the end . . . [however] M. XX will do well to write to me if the slightest accident befalls him or has any anxieties above all.' The next sheet is lost.[37]

Barnave had every reason to be anxious: it was notorious that ormolu workers died young from mercury poisoning. Nevertheless, and whether he suffered from the same complaint or not, Barnave decided to take up one of the doctor's remedies: 'ferruginous water'. He even tells us 'how to make ferruginous water': 'Take half a dozen large nails which you soak in water. Take them out and let them dry for twenty-four or forty-eight hours during which these nails will soften. Put these softened nails to soak in a beaker of water for twenty-four hours and there you have ferruginated water.'[38] Even bread did not escape Barnave's concerns. 'Whatever M. Tissot says, bread produces a lot of blood. Fresh brown bread contributed powerfully to flatulence.'[39]

Barnave also fell under the spell of the influential charlatan J.C. Lavater, urging his friend Rigaud in September 1787 to purchase his *Essai sur la physiognomie destiné à faire connaitre L'homme et le faire aimer*, the third and final volume of which had appeared the year before. Get it unbound, he advised, 'because most bindings damage the margins irreparably and destroy nearly all the value of works of this kind'. The book featured copious engravings of the human head to illustrate Lavater's theory that physiognomy was about the specific character traits of individuals rather than types. These first state engravings would degenerate 'over the years' in later editions as the printer's plate got worn. So Rigaud should 'buy it direct from the publisher'. Lavater believed that the profile offered the best chance of assessing character and many of the Revolutionary leaders are depicted in this way. In 1783 he developed a machine for casting the shadow needed for a silhouette and these had a short-lived vogue.[40]

Lavater was, of course, a charlatan, but Barnave, who prided himself on his rationality, was, like many irreligious men at the time, an easy prey to quacks such as Mesmer with his theory of animal magnetism. But Rigaud, who also shared Barnave's interest in hygiene, was a serious scientist and went on to publish books on clean air and fertilisers. Whether he bought Lavater's work is not known.

— NINE —

BARNAVE AND THE COURT BEFORE THE FLIGHT TO VARENNES

We have seen that Barnave had made early contact with the government through Madame de Staël to negotiate a suspensive veto for the king. His most important contact would be that with the queen, who was increasingly taking over the reins from a demoralised king. This contact may have begun as early as October 1790 and relate to the ministerial changes discussed above. On the 25th of that month, Mirabeau wondered 'why I send these notes [for the court]' when the queen was receiving rival advice from 'Bergasse [a *monarchien*] and perhaps of Barnave and others with locks [of magic purple] hair' like those of the legendary Nisus.[1] At precisely this time Barnave, as president of the Assembly, travelled to Saint-Cloud to present his compliments to the king and queen and to have a working session (*travail*) with the king.

Mirabeau, however, could not make up his mind whether Barnave was his rival or his heir; and though 'the friends of Barnave are not . . . [his] friends',[2] he recommended that the king should make 'the lot' of them ministers. He thought that the Jacobin leaders were planning to do a deal with Lafayette over the composition of the next ministry and then double-cross him. Their aim was to have a weak ministry keep their seats warm for them 'until the end of the legislature', when deputies could become ministers. But the king should anticipate this process and, assuming he could revoke the 'fatal' decree 'appoint the Jacobin leaders as ministers, *all of them, the lot*!' 'All' would comprise Barnave, Alexandre de Lameth, Duport, Laborde, Menou and d'Aiguillon.

It is generally assumed that this was all part of a Machiavellian plot to discredit the Jacobin leaders with the rank and file. Mirabeau actually saw it as a two-way bet: what he actually said was, 'if they bed in well and good, they will be obliged to compromise [*composer*]; if they fail, they are lost and their party with them'.[3] He believed, as did Barnave that 'no ministry could govern without the support of the majority' in the Assembly.[4]

A month later secret negotiations were held between Montmorin and the triumvirs through two intermediaries – an unknown diplomat and Charles, marquis de Croix, a Jacobin deputy who later turned right. Both Croix and Charles Lameth represented the nobility of Arras in the Assembly. The correspondence was important enough for the king to keep and hide: the four documents were found in the king's safe (the famous *armoire de fer*) after the fall of the monarchy.[5] Their 'style' is deliberately elusive – 'forgive my style. I hope you will be able to interpret it' – with its initials: 'D' for Adrien Duport, 'AL' for Alexandre de Lameth and an indirect reference, probably to Barnave, who the marquis asked to find good seats in the press gallery.[6] This diplomat met Duport and Lameth together on three occasions in a salon and had breakfast with Barnave once and alone.

Two letters are dated 14 and 15 November. Cicé, the keeper of the seals, 'the agent in the soutane', was still in place and Duport, Lameth and their intermediary, the marquis de Croix, thought that getting rid of him would be a first step. But the Jacobin leaders feared a 'trap' and that unless certain conditions were met, Lafayette would exploit this proposal to depopularise them. The triumvirs insisted that they could do nothing 'unless the high personages [the king and queen] took their colour from the new order, and destroyed any doubts about their intentions, which [they conceded] have been only too greatly calumniated'. They acknowledged that if the king could not freely appoint his ministers, 'the executive power would be without resources'; but if they got up and said that the power to appoint and dismiss was 'not a matter for the [Assembly's] committees but for another power . . . it would be rejected without discussion unless lack of confidence in its agents and especially their inactivity had been previously dispelled'.

In any case, there could be no question of 'AL departing suddenly from a plan he had followed for twenty months . . . their chariot was bent on a route from which they could not deviate without falling down a precipice either to the right or to the left. . . . They could only return to the desired point by making a long detour.' Nor would they ever betray Revolutionary 'principles' – 'it was their great warhorse'. Croix 'concluded from his meeting with D.A.L. and myself that agreement could be reached provided neither side was too demanding'. The diplomat concluded: 'You [Montmorin] were thinking that the process could be speeded up. I do not think so.'

The unknown diplomat's 'breakfast' with Barnave was no more fruitful; nor his account of it more explicit: 'I made the exploratory operation on the flank [of the triumvirs] you wanted by inviting [Barnave] for breakfast on the pretext of recovering a diplomatic document to which I pretended I attached some importance. This did not succeed. Something else cropped up. I think that even if we could detach him, we must have [the triumvirs] all together.'

Despite this 'reluctance', when Barnave began to have regular secret meetings with Montmorin at the turn of the year, Lameth and Duport did not accompany him. Instead, he went with Menou, the sixth of the sextet. It is no accident that Menou had accepted Beaumetz's amendment that Montmorin be excluded from the ministerial 'holocaust'. There are hints that this reflected tensions within the tightly knit group. La Marck noted that

> before Mirabeau designated Barnave to the court as one of his auxiliaries, Barnave had already taken the decision if not to break with his friends at least not to depend on them. He had seen M. de Montmorin privately and been well received. M. de Montmorin communicated the details of this meeting to Mirabeau which confirmed his view that Barnave could be of great service. And that is why he is going to be kept apart in Mirabeau's plan.[7]

This 'plan' for a vast 'propaganda machine' arose from a long heart-to-heart discussion between Mirabeau and Montmorin between 10 p.m. and 1.30 a.m. on 5/6 December. Mirabeau gave Marie-Antoinette all the details in his forty-sixth note because he 'wanted her to be the hub of the correspondence'. Montmorin should be encouraged as the 'least bad minister given the quality of the new appointments so maladroitly chosen'. Montmorin believed that he was in a strong position because his 'colleagues arrived only yesterday'. Besides, Montmorin's 'links with the Jacobins [Barnave and Menou] offered good chances of success'.

Those links were on display when Montmorin's *valet-de-chambre* told Mirabeau at 9 a.m. to come somewhat later because 'MM Barnave and Menou were still with him'.[8] Montmorin would have preferred to see Barnave alone, but 'he only ever comes with Menou and confidences of a certain kind are impossible in the presence of a third party'. In Mirabeau's plan, Montmorin 'would always see Barnave alone and no one would know of their meeting'.

Montmorin told Mirabeau that

> the Lameths have never liked you and never will. I know that they have harmed you in a thousand ways and can prove it. . . . These men are irreconcilable because they are convinced that it is impossible for them ever to be forgiven [by the queen]. Only one of their sect merits exemption – it is Barnave. We must win him over to deprive them of him or [that failing] destroy him with them. I would prefer the former course to the latter.

Six months later Marie-Antoinette would say that Barnave's pardon was guaranteed.

The queen was the linchpin, the 'hub of the correspondence', in Mirabeau's words, 'the strongest part of the government', in Montmorin's; 'it is through her alone that I want to act on the king, because her influence is by far the surest and by far the most complete'. 'If I manage to organise a propaganda machine, its main objective would be to re-popularise the queen', who 'as far as I can judge . . . has renounced any idea of a Counter-Revolution [*Contre-Mouvement*] and, if the constitution can be improved, I don't despair of reconciling her to that which cannot be changed'.

Finally, Montmorin mentioned a few names of people he could count on in the Assembly: 'Thouret, Chapelier, and the Bishop of Autun [Talleyrand]. As for Barnave, I am not as sure' because he can never be got on one side. 'I have a man in his service [his secretary David?] but I have not yet managed to offer him money.' For his grand scheme – extending to ninety printed pages – Mirabeau put a great deal of flesh on Montmorin's skeletal ideas.[9] There were to be 'three foci on which this influence was to be brought to bear, the National Assembly, Paris and the provinces' – the last with a view to influencing elections to the successor Assembly, something which the government had neglected to do for the present one. Control of the Assembly was to be based on twelve deputies from the different parties: 'MM. de Bonnay, the abbé de Montesquiou and Cazalès for the right wing, Clermont-Tonnerre, d'André, Duquesnoy, Talleyrand, Emmery, Chapelier, Thouret, Barnave and me.'

The link between them was to be Montmorin; and the coordinating link between Montmorin and the deputies was to be Adrien Duquesnoy, but the deputies had to be consulted on this choice. Duquesnoy was the only one to know the names of the others and see Mirabeau every day; but even he was not to know the full plan. Barnave suspected Duquesnoy's role, later calling him 'the vile servitor and perhaps the pimp of all the ministers'. The whole picture should be disclosed to none of them:

> So, for example Montesquiou, Bonnay, Cazalès, Clermont-Tonnerre and d'André must not know that the others are involved. Chapelier and Thouret must not know that Barnave and I will be their auxiliaries. Barnave must always be seen [by Montmorin] alone nor do I want my links with any of them to be ostensible. . . . This tactic will inspire greater trust in deputies who think they alone are in the minister's confidence.

This was necessary because the deputies 'belong to three opposing wings of the National Assembly and this circumstance which makes them ideally suited to accomplish the various measures contained in this memorandum precludes their cooperating on a plan whose outcome will perhaps not be pleasing to any of them, still less to their party'.[10] In particular, Duquesnoy, the circus master, and Barnave, the star turn, detested each other.

The first number of Duquesnoy's influential journal *l'Ami des patriotes* appeared on 27 November 1790 and featured a vitriolic attack on the triumvirs. Barnave responded in kind: 'the same men who they denounce to the partisans of the monarchy as men of faction they accuse of royalism to the defenders of liberty'.[11] Duquesnoy had written:

> MM Duport, Barnave and Alexandre de Lameth, baffled on all sides in their projects, in despair at seeing that public opinion judges them, that the Revolution which they had thought was made for them was turning against them, their remaining hope is to do a deal with the court, by terrifying it with their power. They are trying to make the ministry a prop to support them. . . . All their schemes are known; only children are taken in.

As evidence of their weakness, Duquesnoy adduces their failure on two occasions to get d'Aiguillon elected president of the Assembly and their failure to stop Mirabeau being elected president of the Jacobins. He concludes: 'This is the fate which awaits them. They were seen to fight the court in order to frighten them; they wanted to oust the ministers in order to succeed them; the ministry eluded them and their weakness, starker with every passing day, does not even leave them with the shameful resource of giving themselves to the court.'[12]

Mirabeau, however, thought that Barnave's group controlled all the ministers except Montmorin. On 5 February he told the queen: 'The Lameths have to recognise that this minister [Montmorin] is not their valet like the others.' To evade their control Montmorin was showing sensitive material to the king alone and not the council.[13] Barnave's friendship with du Tertre further clouded Montmorin's relationship with Barnave. After saying he had never managed even to offer Barnave money, Montmorin continues, 'Moreover I know that I am being double crossed. I was promised [that is, by Barnave] to be allowed time to write to Rome over the decree . . . [forcing the clergy to swear acceptance of the civil constitution] but Alexandre de Lameth is agitating for [the king to give his] sanction.'

After the flurry of references to Barnave in Mirabeau's correspondence at the end of 1790 there are no more specific references to a leading role for him. Instead on 17 January Mirabeau told the queen that he had had 'a very interesting conversation with Alexandre de Lameth' in which he detected that he and his colleagues – '*ces messieurs*', an expression she would continue to apply to them – were 'embarrassed' by the radical stance which they still had to keep up to perpetuate their popularity. They now wanted 'to fight on another terrain. They are already talking of the ingratitude of the people and of the reverses suffered by the men who were most useful to their country.'[14]

⚜

Despite Mirabeau's guarded optimism, Alexandre was the rock on which Mirabeau's relations with the triumvirs would founder. In February he violently attacked Mirabeau in the Assembly and in the Jacobins over emigration controls. The root cause of these obscure movements was the desperate attempts by two wings of Mirabeau's plan to refurbish their fading popularity by attacks on each other and on Mirabeau himself. The emigration in question concerned less the 'aristocrats' than the royals. It centred on two departures: that of the king's aunts, 'Mesdames Tantes', for Rome and that of the royal family for Saint-Cloud. The latter had wide-ranging repercussions.

Barnave felt keenly his loss of popularity, mainly the result of his colonial policy. He attributed it in part to the preoccupation of himself and his friends with committee work – Barnave (colonies), Alexandre (military promotions), Duport (juries) – at the expense of debates in the Assembly: poetic justice, Duquesnoy must have thought, for playing collective ministers instead of getting on with drafting the constitution. Duquesnoy mocks the way that Barnave and his friends had been wont to saunter into the Assembly as a group at noon like the rulers of the universe. Now trying to recapture their popularity, they schmoozed up to the backbenchers they had previously neglected. 'I am not the only one to notice that *ces messieurs* are never so amiable as when their credit is in decline.'[15]

On 19 February the king's maiden aunts, Adélaide and Victoire, left their palace at Belle-Vue and headed for Rome. Mirabeau had warned the queen to stop them going as it would make people suspicious that the king would soon follow them, though not to Rome. It was good advice. On the 21st Barnave arrived early at the Assembly and proposed a law on emigration: 'considering that public opinion is worried about much more significant departures which are rumoured to follow, it is time to reassure the nation'.[16] The more important departures at which Barnave hinted were taken to be the king's brother Provence and his wife. A mob forced them from the Luxembourg Palace to the Tuileries.

Provence was not privy to the king's escape plans and the storm blew over until the 24th, when the Assembly was informed that the ladies had been detained at Arnay-le-Duc. The king sent a letter to the Assembly asking it to require the local municipality to allow his aunts to proceed on their journey. The Assembly agreed, but there was question of whether the municipality should also be censured. Most (including Barnave) thought it should be mentioned in mitigation that 'their patriotism was alarmed by circumstances calculated to worry all attentive people and all vigilant patriots'. This 'convoluted and vulgar amendment', as Duquesnoy considered it, was rejected 'on all sides'.

Mirabeau cut through all the verbiage and said simply that the ladies' 'departure was perhaps monumentally imprudent but certainly not monumentally illegal'. He proposed that 'since no existing law prevented Mesdames from freely travelling, there was no reason . . . [to discuss the proceedings of the local municipality] and that the matter be referred to the executive power'. This was ultimately adopted, but not before Alexandre de Lameth had made a grandstanding intervention, which led to an irreconcilable breach with Mirabeau. He thought that the ladies' journey 'was not so insignificant as some people thought. . . . Since several members of the royal family were fleeing from a Revolution which had conferred on them such great advantages [*sic*]'.

He then added some words which Duquesnoy transcribed 'word for word' and italicised: '*I am astounded that the speakers have not distinguished between a revolutionary moment and those which must follow. . . . If we act now in the same way as we will when the Revolution is finished, it will never be finished.*'[17] Beaumetz drew out the meaning: 'The previous speaker has declared that we should employ the same methods now [that is, insurrection] as those with which we began the Revolution.' However, there was all the difference between using force against despotism, in 1789, and against 'laws which we ourselves have made'. Alexandre was arguing in February for the continuous revolution which in July Barnave would seek to 'finish'.

During Lameth's speech, Mirabeau rushed up to the tribune and 'shouted at the top of his voice that he would not stand idly by while principles were being abandoned for popularity. Everyone could distinctly hear M. Barnave's emollient words beside M. de Mirabeau and several people heard him assure Mirabeau 'that Alexandre was not referring to you, that he only meant to attack d'André and Fréteau. I [Duquesnoy] transcribe his expressions.' Menou also tried to defuse the situation: 'I think that Europe will be truly amazed to learn that the National Assembly of France has spent four hours discussing the departure of Mesdames who prefer to hear mass in Rome rather than in Paris. Peals of laughter and applause echoed through the chamber.'

The debates soon widened into the question of emigration in general. On 28 February Le Chapelier, on behalf of the constitutional committee, proposed that in times of crisis a three-man commission should be given dictatorial powers to prevent all emigration and confiscate the properties of those émigrés who refused a summons to return. Desmoulins assumed that this was a trap to force the Jacobins to adopt terrorist measures; but it may equally have been an attempt by Le Chapelier's group themselves to regain their popularity.

Duquesnoy, the linchpin of Mirabeau's operation as its parliamentary manager, was now concentrating his attentions on this group – five deputies of the twelve mentioned in Mirabeau's plan: d'André, who had 'talent and application', Emmery, Le Chapelier, Thouret 'especially' and Beaumetz.[18] But no less than Barnave in this period, the five were themselves desperate to be popular. And because Mirabeau was aiming to discredit the Assembly by inducing it to pass ultra-radical decrees, the policies of all three groups are hard to disentangle; Mirabeau despaired of Montmorin's failure to control them even with money. 'For example', he complained, 'Beaumetz, Chapelier and d'André had secret dinners', and on 9 March, in Mirabeau's absence from the Assembly, 'proposed to demolish the dungeon of Vincennes to *popularise* themselves, refused to speak against the law controlling emigration so as not to *depopularise* themselves' and, 'to *popularise* themselves, asked M. de Montmorin' to get the king to circularise all the foreign powers with a statement that the king was content with the Revolution – the genesis of an important idea to which we will return.

This trio knew that the rival one, Barnave, Lameth and Duport, were planning to propose the demolition of the dungeon and for the same reason: both sides were more or less connected with the court. All needed to refurbish their fading popularity by radical gestures, partly because that connection was beginning to transpire, partly to increase their price, though only in some cases was this a monetary one.

A satirical pamphlet mocked the discomfiture of the triumvirs when Le Chapelier proposed the demolition and was supported by 'MM Beaumetz, d'André, Dupont, Regnault, Duquesnoy, and others' – their centre-right rivals. The triumvirs 'and their thirty friends had witnessed their credit falling and wanted to raise it a little' by a dramatic announcement. Now that their rivals had stolen their thunder, what did they say? 'Not a sausage. *Ne unum quidem verbum*.'[19]

During these 'secret dinners', Beaumetz, Le Chapelier and d'André received confidential information from Danton, who received 30,000 livres from Montmorin with which to generate support for the monarchy in the sections. Mirabeau did not think that Danton 'distributed' this money 'innocently' – whatever that meant. These months were punctuated by popular demonstrations for and against the monarchy and many were indeed orchestrated – an accusation regularly levelled against Barnave.

To return to the emigration question – one that would preoccupy Barnave for the rest of his career. Whether or not Le Chapelier's demand for a three-man commission was 'fed' to Mirabeau, he used this 'barbarous' law as a peg on which to demand that in a free society emigration should be allowed. This was challenged by an obscure Jacobin and, though none of the triumvirs had spoken, Mirabeau famously apostrophised them: '*Silence aux trente voix*' – the generally accepted total of Barnave's parliamentary following. That evening Alexandre made a withering attack in the Jacobins, not just on Mirabeau – hinting at his links with the court – but also on Le Chapelier, Beaumetz, d'André and Duquesnoy.[20]

Bridges would be rebuilt to them – too late for Mirabeau, who died on 2 April. As he lay on his deathbed, the Jacobin Club of which he had been president in December voted to send a deputation to enquire after his health. It included Barnave. Mirabeau was forty-two – what he called 'the sins of his youth' had taken their physical as well as political toll. But some said that the laceration he had received from Alexandre, who refused to be part of the deputation, had been a contributory factor.

Dubois-Crancé, writing in 1792, has an interesting take on the impact Mirabeau's death had on Barnave's political reputation. At his death, 'Mirabeau was about to declare himself openly for the court party; Barnave [who had lived under his shadow in the same party] would have fought him in order to differentiate himself and so remain faithful to [Revolutionary] principles; and if, after the end of the Revolution he had died, he would have been carried in triumph to the Panthéon of great men and Mirabeau would have had a ditch for a sepulchre.' Instead Mirabeau was placed in the Panthéon – and then thrown in a ditch when his 'apostasy' was discovered with the publication of the king's papers later that year.

After Mirabeau's sudden death, his devastated team regrouped to form what one might call Marie-Antoinette's kitchen cabinet. Duquesnoy took a prominent role through his journal *l'Ami des patriotes* and parliamentary management; he occasionally corresponded with and saw the queen, as did La Marck and Fontanges, archbishop of Toulouse, more frequently; there was occasional input from Mirabeau's doctor Cabanis and his secretary, Pellenc.

Mirabeau's death also led to a reassessment of the utility of his project. Both the two main elements, parliamentary management and influencing the popular movement, were expensive. Montmorin thought it was money wasted and Laporte, the Intendant of the Civil List, wrote to the king on the afternoon of 16 April: 'Your Majesty knows about the abbé de Périgord's [Talleyrand's] relations with MM. Dandré, Chapelier, Beaumetz, and others who have very badly honoured the undertakings which we thought they had contracted.'[21] Nevertheless, in time most of the twelve deputies on Mirabeau's list fused and worked more or less together – Barnave and Le Chapelier, for example, as they had in the summer of 1789. There was a regrouping of the old patriot party in a conservative sense.

The following day Montmorin pronounced the infiltration of the popular movement also to have been a failure. On 17 April he told La Marck: 'You must speak firmly to Talon and Sémonville [agents]. (I have just spoken to Jullien [another agent] that way) and you must tell them that there is no point distributing three or four million in Paris if we are still at the mercy of a fabricated insurrection and that if things continue like this, we will have to wind up the whole circus.'

The 'fabricated insurrection' Montmorin had in mind was one organised by the Cordelier Club against the presence of refractory priests in the royal chapel and the rumour that the king had received his Easter communion from one of them. On the 17th the Club drew up an *arrêté* 'denouncing the first functionary [the king] to the deputies and all the French people . . . as refractory to the constitutional laws of the kingdom'. The Cordelier's *arrêté* was to be printed and sent to all the patriotic societies and the départements. Danton was the president of the Cordelier Club and had been paid at least 30,000 livres to prevent just such measures. However, the attempt to influence Paris opinion was not called off for on 20 April La Porte wrote to the king: 'This evening I am going to try to dispel [this] notion [that the king had taken communion] in the Cordelier Club.'[22]

The king had in fact received his Easter communion on Easter Sunday in his private chapel from the hands of his grand almoner who had not taken the oath to the civil constitution. A grenadier on duty at the Tuileries held up the service for half an hour and though it then went ahead, he was applauded by his colleagues and it was these grenadiers who were behind the attempt to stop the king going to Saint-Cloud on Easter Monday.

We do not know why the king wanted to go to Saint-Cloud but we do know from the queen's lover Fersen that they were only planning to be away for Easter week – 'leaving on [Monday] 18 April and returning on Wednesday or Thursday week'.[23] So no intention to emigrate. But the crowd that stopped them on the 18th, while they sat in the coach ready to depart, thought that the journey was merely the first leg of one to the frontier or beyond: it has convincingly been argued that 'the religious issue' was merely a 'pretext'.[24]

After one and three-quarters of an hour sitting in the carriage, and seeing that Lafayette was powerless, Louis took his family back into the palace and they abandoned their plans. The crowd, led by the grenadiers of the National Guard, entered the vestibule of the palace and tried to follow Marie-Antoinette to her private apartments. But a furious king shouted: 'Grenadiers! Stop right there!' And, as Fersen relates, 'they all stopped dead in their tracks as if they had had their legs cut right off'.

An all-night crisis meeting was held in the Tuileries to work out what the king's response to this egregious infringement of his basic liberty should be. Duport du Tertre, the keeper of the seals, wrote to the king: 'It is three a.m. I have just left M. de Montmorin's where several members of the National Assembly were gathered, with whom we [that is, the ministers] conferred. We hit on the idea of a dramatic intervention by Your Majesty and we thought that it would be appropriate for you to go unannounced to the Assembly this morning. I enclose an agreed draft speech on the assumption that this measure meets with your approval.' The queen also received a copy.[25]

Du Tertre does not say which deputies were gathered at Montmorin's, but we may get an idea of the personnel from a letter which Cabanis sent to Marie-Antoinette: 'the king should, without delay . . . invite the opinion formers of all the parties to attend him including: MM Lameth, Barnave, Duport, Crillon, Pétion, Thouret, abbé Siéyès, Lafayette, La Rochefoucauld, d'André, Beaumetz, Le Chapelier and Emmery and all the ministers'. And he should tell them that 'the Jacobins and the 89 Club should reunite in a single body in order to save a monarchy on the verge of destruction'.[26] Five of these names are on Mirabeau's list of twelve.

Everyone was scared: even the centre-right deputies and the queen's kitchen cabinet thought the situation was so explosive that the king should change his household and publicly take communion from a 'constitutional' priest. Later that day Duquesnoy told La Marck: 'after a long discussion [among the deputies] it was decided that Beaumetz should see the king tonight . . . M. de Montmorin was to request this before the start of the council and he insisted that d'André be there too; he expected it to be about 11 p.m.'. They were to urge the king to say that illness prevented him from going to Saint-Cloud 'but that he hoped to be better in time to go to mass on Sunday' – that is, at the local church, Saint Germain l'Auxerrois. 'They set great store by this démarche and undertook *to make the king reign at this price*. But they did not want to speak to him unless the queen was there. If he refuses to take this step, they will say that it is impossible to save both him and the country . . . and so they would be forced to choose the latter' (my emphasis). Duquesnoy begged La Marck 'on bended knees' to 'use all his influence' with the queen to support the initiative.[27]

And he did. On the 21st he told her: 'I swear on my honour that the safety of the royal family depends on their attending the local parish without delay.' Fontanges was roped in; he saw the danger but how 'as a man of the [nonjuring] cloth can I advocate the course of action you desire? I will have to think about it.'[28] Subsequently, the king attended mass in Saint Germain l'Auxerrois and from a 'constitutional' priest, the abbé Poupart. It was a bitter pill – Poupart had been the king's confessor for fifteen years and Louis regarded his acceptance of the civil constitution as a betrayal. The king also dismissed his grand almoner and several members of his household.

The three deputies who crop up in the La Marck correspondence over the Saint-Cloud incident are Thouret, Beaumetz and d'André. The deputy Montlosier states that Alexandre de Lameth and Montmorin came to an understanding that the constitutional articles were to be revised so as to strengthen the monarchy and 'that the work should be mainly confided to MM. Thouret, Beaumetz, Duport and d'André, with MM. Barnave and Lameth naturally having a great input'.[29] These were the same men who had assembled at Montmorin's. Montlosier says only 'if my information is correct', but it is striking that the 'triumvirs' are also linked with the three deputies mentioned in the La Marck correspondence. The latter group had been taking a radical position since the Saint-Cloud incident, which suggests either a pre-arranged or a natural convergence. In the ultimatum they deliver to the king, the threat of abandoning him is coupled with the promise 'to make him reign' (*faire règner le roi*) – in other words, to give him real authority by revising the constitution. This is exactly the deal that Montlosier outlines.

Barnave had been in desultory communication with Montmorin since the turn of the year and George Michon claimed that Barnave 'imposed and drafted' the circular letter which Montmorin sent to all France's diplomatic representatives on 23 April stating that the king had voluntarily accepted the constitution.[30] Michon's sole evidence is provided by Bertrand de Molleville, who claimed that the 'parti Lameth' 'offered the king their advice and services' at a time of 'difficulties, worry and despair' in return for the circular letter.[31]

This is directly rebutted by Barnave himself when he told the queen on 19 October that 'M. de Montmorin, just when disturbances were at their peak had that letter written to the foreign courts which was so ridiculous by nature of its exaggeration'.[32] In his detailed correspondence with La Marck, Montmorin does not mention pressure coming from Barnave but rather from La Marck himself, from Pellenc, Duquesnoy and even from the queen who, according to her close adviser Fontanges, 'saw the necessity for the proclamation'.[33]

There is a dramatic irony here because the Saint-Cloud departure had removed any doubts on her part about the need to escape from Paris. As Marie-Antoinette told Mercy on 20 April:

> the event which has just taken place has confirmed us more than ever in our plans [for flight]. . . . Our very life is not safe. We must give the impression of yielding to everything until we can act and [*pace* the circular letter] our captivity proves that none of our actions is done of our own accord. . . . Our position is appalling. It must absolutely finish in the next month. The king desires it even more than I do.

Hitherto it was the queen who had urged caution because the king might weaken.[34]

The proclamation would and did act as a smokescreen. The king, however, was ashamed of the duplicity involved and wept at having to endorse a lie from which he stood to benefit. Montmorin wept with him – 'like a child'. He was not privy to the plans for flight but wept because what he was made to say in the name of the king was evidently not true – he had been forcibly prevented from going to Saint-Cloud. Poor Montmorin, slight of build, short of stature, short of money, weak of constitution and temperament. He had been an excellent ambassador to Spain and, as Molleville said, would have made a good minister in less troubled times or under a stronger prime minister.

Though Barnave disapproved of the circular letter, because of its transparent and humiliating dishonesty, he did want the king to demonstrate by actions his acceptance of the Revolution. On the evening of 24 April, there was a 'conference' between La Marck, Fontanges and the leaders of Barnave's party. It represented a concordance or capitulation spelling out in detail Barnave's price for saving the monarchy and '*faire règner le roi*'. As said, the actual phrase, though it summarised his position, was not his, but that of d'André, Le Chapelier and Thouret, his once and future allies, who were probably present as well. They were as exigent as the Jacobins, which narrowed the king's choice since the right deputies (according to La Marck) represented only 1 per cent of the population and were 'riddled with woodworm'.

La Marck gave Fontanges a resumé of the conference to pass on to Marie-Antoinette.[35] Fontanges found La Marck's conclusion 'desolating but inevitable'. La Marck wrote: 'CONCLUSION: [royal policy] must not just have a blood transfusion but grow a new skin'. Hitherto the king had made concessions only when forced to. That had given him a temporary popularity but that approach was 'played out and would not have the same effect'. The king must 'flatter the nation's vanity' as expressed in its desire for 'equality and liberty'. He must 'restore his throne by means of the strongest party [Barnave's]. There is no middle way. He must either reign through them or run all the risks.' But it was too soon for the queen to 'flatter the people. It would be put about that she wanted to betray them.' 'She must begin by persuading the public that she accepts that the Revolution is irreversible and keep the king in this persuasion.'

'These are the main demands of the leaders of the popular party', La Marck continued. If the king resists, they will 'popularise themselves at his expense . . . and it is always to the queen that the danger will redound'. The 'bullet points' were: (1) reduce the expense of the household; (2) leave no trace of distinctions conferred by titles in the household officers; (3) base future nominations to the Orders of Chivalry on civic merit; (4) the royal couple must show themselves in public; (5) once a week keep open court to anyone decently dressed – call it a 'social circle'; and (6) once a week the king alone, flanked only by two ministers, should grant audiences. These are almost identical to the measures which Barnave would urge on the queen in the months following the flight to Varennes.

There was a follow-through, though Gouverneur Morris exaggerates its strength. On 25 April he notes that Terrier de Monciel, with Brémond,[36] 'comes to see me and gives me an account of what he has done with the chiefs of the Jacobins. He is to have a further conference.' 'They [the Jacobin leaders] think it will be best to act in concert with the court, without appearing to do so, lest thereby they should lose their popularity. . . . He is to obtain, if he can . . . a list of the [constitutional] articles they desire; also, if possible, the [ministerial] places they aspire to.'[37] On 9 May Brémond tells Morris that 'he is employed by the Jacobin chieftains to form a selection of constitutional articles and also to consult on the means of restoring order'.[38] Like those with the unknown diplomat the previous November, these negotiations dribbled into the sand. For the king and queen were making detailed plans for flight.

This change of plan explains the petering out of letters between the members of Marie-Antoinette's 'kitchen cabinet', who, for their own safety, were kept in the dark. There are no letters between 28 April and 21 June, the day the royal family fled. Marie-Antoinette simply told Fontanges to lie low in the country for a while. She said no more, but they all must have guessed something was afoot. The flight to Varennes, Fontanges told La Marck, cleared up the mystery which had covered the previous two months.[39]

So, with hindsight, these two months have an air of unreality. And, when the mystery was revealed, they would entrench the view of royal duplicity engendered by the circular letter of 23 April. The manifesto the king left behind is a specific repudiation of that letter. Yet there is a paradox at work also: if one lays aside the petulant remarks about the way he has been treated, the bulk of the king's manifesto can be seen as a development of the ideas put forward by the Concordat group after 23 April – as a basis for action. A way 'to make the king reign'. One does not need to assume prior knowledge of the escape by the triumvirs (as Michon following Robespierre does) to see this continuity. How 'to make the king reign' (faire règner le roi) is the thread through the maze of this confused period. But, realistically, did the politicians mean the queen? And did it put Marie-Antoinette in mind of 'her' minister Breteuil's desire that ministers should be appointed 'who thought that they could only carry out their functions by making the queen reign?'[40]

— TEN —

BARNAVE ON THE DEFENSIVE

Was Barnave in the months before the flight to Varennes moving towards the court or was the Revolution moving away from him? In these months he sustained several defeats: as well as that of his colonial policy, he was also defeated on the question of the eligibility of ex-Constituents either to become ministers or sit in the next legislature. Finally, he lost control of and seceded from the Jacobin Club he had founded.

THE ELIGIBILITY DEBATES

Politicians in the French Revolution were wont to contrast themselves with their *ancien régime* predecessors, whom they regarded as ambitious, amoral and corrupt office-seekers – 'intriguers'. They regarded the current ministers as leftovers from that time. The Constituents saw themselves as Cincinnati (or Washingtons) who having given France a constitution would return to the plough or (since most were lawyers) to their office, if it still existed. The triumvirs were regarded by many as delinquent in this respect: Alexandre had the reputation of being an 'intriguer' – a strong term of abuse for Robespierre, among many. Duport was generally held to covet the place of keeper of the seals. Barnave was their mouthpiece. And though Barnave privately in his *Introduction à la Révolution française* praises 'emulation', only once did any of them publicly make the obvious retort: what is wrong with noble ambition? Duport asked in his dark but brilliant speech in the 'eligibility' debate: 'is there a surer way to weaken, to degrade the legislative body than to exclude capacity, talents, public virtues, even ambition and the love of glory?' Barnave privately wrote in this context: 'If one were not allowed to admit or indeed pride oneself on the desire to serve one's country in the most important posts and to win *gloire* thereby, honest men would confine themselves to their own affairs and a political career would no longer be pursued by any but ambitious hypocrites and men avid for gold.'[1] The most natural reading of 'most important posts' would be ministerial ones.

The Constituent Assembly was getting long in the tooth and weary. Many backbenchers were itching to go home, repair their finances and see their families again. But those who had tasted power and thought they had made good use of it did not want to 'return to nothing', as their enemies had it.[2] Duport, Robespierre and d'André were all appointed to the senior positions in the new central criminal court – Duport as its president – but they all resigned rather than serve with each other.

Apart from natural ambition, all the triumvirs believed, like fathers fearful for their children, that the constitution needed weaning, that the gains of the Revolution were not secure. They had witnessed a dynasty crumble which had just celebrated its 800th anniversary, one seemingly secure at home and abroad. In his speech Duport warned the deputies that they could not continue to rely on 'an unlimited supply of the lucky events which hitherto have served us so well'.

Part of Duport's gloom stemmed from the consciousness that his party was losing control of events, losing in short control of the Jacobins, which it had founded, to Robespierre. Robespierre, as Michelet brilliantly observed, calculated that if the successor Assembly were deprived of men of talent and experience, the Jacobins would easily overawe it.[3] The same could surely be said of the ministers and it was with them that Robespierre made his first move. The 'fatal decree' had barred Constituents from becoming ministers during the session of the Assembly, but what about when it ended? On 7 April Robespierre proposed – to applause – that 'no member of the present Assembly could be appointed to the ministry nor receive any place, gifts, pension, salary or commission from the executive power or its agents for four years after the end of his [constituent] functions'.

His authority was 'a philosopher [Rousseau] whose memory you honour and whose writings paved the way for the Revolution and your work'. Rousseau had thought that 'in order to inspire confidence and respect for the laws the legislator must detach himself from his creation'.[4] Most people would rather think that prior experience was a desirable quality in a job applicant. This was Barnave's considered opinion and he felt that this and Robespierre's associated law banning members of the present Assembly from being deputies in the next one (16 May) was the fundamental flaw in the constitution. But just as the 'fatal decree' had been aimed specifically at Mirabeau, Robespierre's proposal was aimed at Barnave and Duport.

However, whereas Mirabeau had poured sarcasm on the fatal decree, none from Barnave's party attacked Robespierre's motion at all. Robespierre had a knack (until 9 Thermidor) of both terrorising and shaming his opponents into silence, leaving it to others to make the direct accusation. On this occasion Barnave, with gritted teeth, went one better than Robespierre, proposing that the law be extended to jurors in the High Court and even those on the list who had not actually served. The whole day was a repeat of the emulation of the night of 4 August.

Everyone knew that Robespierre was planning a law banning Constituents from being elected to the Legislative Assembly. Bang on cue, when on 16 May Thouret for the constitutional committee turned to the question of the next legislature, Robespierre interrupted him to propose that members of the Constituent be barred from standing as deputies for the Legislative Assembly. This again was directed at the triumvirs, who were generally believed to want to prolong the session of the Constituent Assembly and/or be elected to its successor. On 17 January Mirabeau had told the queen: 'M. de Lameth draws the conclusion that they must prolong the session of the Assembly, place themselves in the département [of Paris] so as to avoid any interregnum prior to getting themselves elected to the next legislature.'[5] This seems a fair assessment of their aims.

As ever, Robespierre's timing was impeccable: the day before Barnave had suffered a humiliating defeat on the voting rights of people of colour. Silence from Barnave meant it was left to Beaumetz and Le Chapelier to defend eligibility. Beaumetz uttered a few words, 'but the rest of his speech was lost in murmurs'. Le Chapelier wanted to speak but cries of proceeding to a vote sprung up again. The discussion was closed and the motion adopted as follows: 'The National Assembly decrees that its members cannot be elected to the next legislature.'[6] The vote was almost unanimous.

This self-denying ordinance, with support from left and right, at first seems puzzling. But the right who had no chance of re-election wanted to diminish the prestige of the next Assembly, as did Robespierre – there was a general and justified belief that its members would be of lesser quality. As Michelet put it: 'For the two extremes, the Jacobins and the aristocrats, the common enemy to be destroyed was the constitution and the constitutional party, the fathers and natural defenders of this sickly child [*enfant peu vialable*].'[7]

We do not need to imagine how cast down the triumvirs must have felt. And their chagrin – bitterness at failure. For Desmoulins witnessed it and 'stopped seeing them'. After the vote he had encountered Alexandre and Théodore de Lameth. 'They were not the same men. I could not get a single word out of Alexandre, who seemed more guarded. But I shall never forget what Théodore told me: "This can't go on; Duport said last night that they must leave France." Camille reproached them for not staying to defend their work. "I mean it", Théodore replied, "one more decree like that and we will abandon France." '[8]

Bradby thought that Barnave was made of sterner stuff,[9] but it was Duport who returned to the fray the next day. Thouret tried to mount a counterattack but all he secured (and this he found unsatisfactory) was Barère's compromise that though the ex-Constituents could not be elected to the Legislative Assembly, they and anyone could be elected to the next two consecutively, though they could not be elected a third time until two years had elapsed. This would enable Robespierre to be a deputy in the National Convention which followed the Legislative Assembly. Desmoulins found Duport's speech 'so calumnious, so bilious' that it caused him to 'regard the patriotism of this [ex-]*parlementaire* as infinitely suspect'.

The first half of the speech is not devoted to the question in hand but is a gloomy account of the collapse of government and the impending collapse of society. Barnave's celebrated speech of 13 July is clearly modelled on Duport's. Barnave asked: 'Are we going to finish the Revolution or are we going to start it up again?'[10]

Duport said, 'the Revolution is finished. . . . I repeat, the Revolution is finished'. 'Do you think that the normal state of a country is one of permanent Revolution?' But on the question of liberty, Duport went deeper than Barnave. 'How should we envisage the twin fundamentals of liberty and equality?' he asked. 'Liberty should be limited', he replied, foreshadowing J.S. Mill, 'by the liberty of other people'. 'It is not a personal and absolute right with no relationship to our neighbours and fellow citizens.' For that way lies 'the vile passions of egotism'. 'Do not think', he concluded, 'that notions of liberty and equality ever retreat; much to the contrary they spread more and more. . . . [U]nless they are anchored to a strong government, they continue to flow, levelling all the way, always dissolving until the land is divided' – the agrarian law of the Gracchi. And, he added, foreshadowing de Tocqueville: 'Having levelled the mountains, the most insignificant ant hills are felt to be a restraint'.

'As for equality . . . some want equality of fortunes and property', others think 'capacity and talent are irrelevant'. Robespierre believed that patriotism was more important than talent in choosing officials and when he came to power was able to put these notions into practice, with disastrous effects – for example, putting a patriotic goldsmith, Rossignol, in charge of suppressing the rebellion in the Vendée. A veiled and not so veiled attack on Robespierre ran through Duport's speech. For example: 'Certain men . . . have not assumed any personal responsibility [Robespierre sat on no committees and was never elected president] – because attacking every reasonable proposal does not count – but have occupied a personal chair of human rights without interruption.'

Barnave thought that the success of Robespierre, this 'singular man', whose talents were 'well below the mediocre', lay in his 'integrated and constant character' and 'his concentrated interior passions, which made him a man set apart'. 'With him, there was a unity of conception and execution . . . bringing all his talents to bear on the means he chose.'[11] Elsewhere he wrote:

> He is the genius of anarchy. He would like the nation to exist without laws and recognises nothing but the Declaration of Rights. Essentially a tribune of the people, he loves only the power which comes from the extra-legal effervescence of the people. His *amour propre* is excessive and intolerant. His talent lies only in declamation and is mediocre even in this, but if history is just, it will recognise in him a primitive,

homogenous and inflexible character. I believe him to be above all sordid considerations.[12]

It was Duport's fear that the professor's theories would soon be put into practice. 'Have you not noticed this flock of stupid sheep mouthing that the first legislature should also be constituent and that it should draft a constitution more conformable with the Declaration of Rights. When these ideas have taken further hold, it will be too late to avert the danger.' In the declaration the king left behind when he escaped from Paris, he predicted that the elections to the next Assembly pointed to 'a metaphysical and doctrinaire form of government [a republic] which would not work'. Duquesnoy noted the similarity: 'I don't know if anyone has noticed that the [king's] depiction of the present state of France is exactly the same as that presented by M. Duport in his speech on re-election and M. Fréteau on behalf of the diplomatic committee. The National Assembly ordered that both should be printed.'[13]

Duport several times accuses his opponents of republicanism, whatever euphemisms they chose to employ – 'with such principles they set themselves up as republican heroes', he sneers. But he warns that to achieve the republic, 'it will be necessary to drown in the blood of the last defenders of the throne'. And finally an exhausted people will be only too glad to relapse into the arms of a despot. Indeed, this new despotism will be all the stronger than the Bourbon one because it will have popular backing. Duport, a sickly man, did not live to see his prophesy come true in the shape of Bonaparte. Duport advances a circular view of history, one which Barnave developed in his *Introduction à la Révolution française* and *Rèflections*. Liberty, the best form, is also the most unstable, sandwiched between 'independence', that is, the licence he fears, and 'slavery'.

Duquesnoy wrote, just before the debate on eligibility:

MM. Lameth, Duport and Barnave want re-election with incredible passion because they believe that, outside the Assembly, they will return to the nothingness from which they never should have emerged. So they took the most amazing steps to secure it. . . . There is not a Paris lady that they did not get to negotiate in their name with those members of the left they thought influential. . . . They

> negotiated both with the right of the Assembly and with another part of the left.

This, Duquesnoy concluded, 'was one of the main explanations for the silence *ces messieurs* have maintained for several months. They were afraid to speak lest they inadvertently offended one of the five or six parties with whom they were trying to do a deal.'[14]

SECESSION FROM THE JACOBINS

The rise (and fall) of the Jacobin Club was mainly due to three men: Le Chapelier (in its Versailles precursor, the Breton Club); Barnave (in its Parisian refounding as the *Société des amis de la Constitution* or Jacobin Club); and Robespierre (in its survival phase – during the summer of 1791 – and its later dominance when it gave its name to a regime). Two of these three (Le Chapelier and Barnave) sought to destroy the Jacobin Club, while Robespierre, by pitting it against the National Convention on 9 Thermidor, ensured that its destruction would follow his own. Le Chapelier, in the law which bears his name, sought to muzzle the club. Barnave seceded from it.

On 29 April Le Chapelier introduced legislation designed to muzzle the clubs (Jacobin and Cordelier) and the electoral sections. He would have liked simply to suppress these troublesome entities outright; instead, he sought to achieve a similar result without creating an insurrection by banning their main weapon (apart from the insurrection) – the collective petition which put pressure on the constituted bodies, including the Assembly. He argued, 'If these societies had the right of petition, they would become dangerous corporations.'[15]

The *ancien régime* was constructed of such 'corporations', from the Gallican Church, the network of Parlements, to the craft guilds and village structures. The state had relations with these rather than individuals unless they were very high-born, such as princes with *appanages*. The new regime smashed the corporations and had relations only with individuals. So, Le Chapelier argued, townsmen could petition, but their act must be individually signed, otherwise minority voices would be suppressed and the group would be 'elevated into rivals of the municipality'.

Barnave and his friends took no part in the debate. Their action and inaction must have seemed like a betrayal of the club they had founded.[16] And symbolised a change of face.

The colonial issue destroyed Barnave's hold on the club. On 11 May Brissot spoke for the first time at the Jacobins, specifically to attack Barnave's colonial policy: 'the colour of your skin should make no difference between one man and another', a comment received with applause. Someone interrupted Barnave's reply with 'get to the point', and he did in words which would come back to haunt him: 'You are claiming the Rights of Man for a tiny number of men [30,000 free people of colour], while in France millions of men are so deprived' – the 'passive citizens' who could not vote in the coming elections to the Legislative Assembly'.[17] This was too good an opportunity for Robespierre to miss, though he waited until the 13th to make the obvious retort: 'You tell us that we have not respected the rights of man in Europe – but for you we would not have violated them.' Fresh in Robespierre's mind was the exclusion of 'passive citizens' from the National Guard on 27 April following Alexandre de Lameth's report. Another speaker lamented 'that a man [Barnave] whom he had thought to deserve not one but a thousand laurel crowns' had 'broken his heart' by his betrayal of his principles in the Assembly.[18]

Circling nearer to Barnave, Brissot then sought to refute his accusation that those who defended the rights of people of colour and those who opposed the Spanish alliance were in the pay of England, countering, 'I too could accuse others of corruption, and I too know lots of anecdotes.' The relations of deputies with the court were transpiring. 'I beg you sir', replied Barnave, 'to be so good as to reveal them publicly.' Brissot continued, 'My publications have only attacked those men who have an agenda ulterior to patriotism.'

The link between the Paris Jacobin club and the affiliated societies in the country was the circular letter, drafted by the correspondence committee, usually Barnave himself. And here both Brissot and Robespierre (soon to be deadly enemies) managed to weaken Barnave's hold. In the first fortnight of March Barnave sent out one of his productions; the theme of this was his continual refrain that 'when a people is constituted, respect for the laws which it has given itself is the first of duties'. With this respect they would be able 'to surmount all the obstacles in the way of terminating the Revolution'. Barnave took immense trouble writing this bromide – there are at least four drafts.[19] But in the *Patriote français* of 17 March Brissot challenged all Barnave's assumptions. The constitution was not a final act; it could not be 'fixed invariably'.

Above all, Brissot attacked Barnave's devotion to the constitutional monarchy. It was ridiculous to say that the deputies' unceasing efforts were 'seconded by a king whose virtues impregnated' the constitution. The king's virtues were irrelevant since France had outgrown personal monarchy. A monarchy 'instituted for the good of the people and stable government. Bah! Puerile public law . . . It would be easy to prove that a free regime could be stable without a hereditary monarchy.' The affiliated societies 'will not be surprised' by the errors and bad grammar of the circular, 'when they learn that it was not discussed after its reading. . . . In vain did M. Robespierre raise his voice to demand questions. M. Barnave carried the publication of the letter by assault, as he has the decrees on the colonies. If M. Robespierre had managed to get a hearing doubtless, he would have combatted an error which overturned the Declaration of Rights.'

Maybe this experience prompted Robespierre on 27 May to challenge Barnave's hold on the correspondence committee and demand that its personnel be completely renewed (he did not at this stage in his career say 'purged'). Barnave replied: 'If this society is no longer a gathering of friends; if it is no longer a meeting of men united for the common good; if it is now just a theatre of calumny and pride, we can do nothing further for the country, there is nothing further for us to do here and it only remains for us to depart and take up arms for the defence of the whole country.'[20] With these heartbroken words, Barnave departed. As Michon said, 'The first phase of the Revolution was closing; the second was about to open.'

— ELEVEN —

VARENNES AND ITS REPERCUSSIONS

> In this correspondence they [Barnave and Alexandre] have fulfilled more than a duty: a lively and deep feeling has attached them to the interests of the queen. The more, during the course of the Revolution they had been obliged to fight against her, the more her courage and misfortunes have acquired rights over them and the more they saw themselves as favoured by a circumstance [the flight to Varennes] which engaged them to serve her in the interests of the Revolution itself.
>
> Barnave to Marie-Antoinette, 28 August 1791[1]

The king was an early riser and those who ministered to him had to follow suit. Nevertheless, on 21 June Montmorin must have been surprised to receive a visit 'at about 6 a.m.' from d'André. Fontanges, who gives us this information, explains: 'M. d'André who was currently very prominent in the Assembly and who had ended up enlisting secretly for the king from whom he was receiving 1,000 écus a month via M. de Montmorin was the first to be informed of the king's flight – I don't know by whom.' It was this anonymous man perhaps who 'while M. d'André was still with him or was on the point of leaving' brought Montmorin a letter from the king telling him to await further orders. This same man presumably 'sent or delivered personally a sealed packet' to La Porte containing the king's 'declaration' with orders to read it out to the Assembly – not to have it proclaimed but read to the deputies so that they could act on it.[2]

Robespierre would accuse the triumvirs and Lafayette of colluding in the king's escape – accusations we will examine not because they are true but because they accurately reflect the parameters of the king's dealings with Barnave. But an accusation against d'André would have been more convincing. Not only was he the first to know of the king's escape but he took his statement on his return to Paris. He also would be one of the inner committee of five which outlined the future relations between the queen and Barnave. Fontanges is our best witness because he was a member of the queen's kitchen cabinet and received her account of the flight to Varennes; he was also a member of Malouet's group, the Monarchiens. It is possible that if their escape had succeeded, the king and queen envisaged negotiating primarily with this group centring on d'André, Beaumetz and Le Chapelier, rather than with the triumvirs.

These groupings had begun to coalesce for some months before the king's flight, a process which was carried further in the interval between news of the king's flight and news of his recapture, that is, a period of thirty-six hours. Fontanges again:

> Despite the brave face the Assembly adopted, members of the left wing were already thinking of taking advantage of this event in order to terminate the Revolution through a solid accommodation with the king. They had even gone as far as to approach some of the principal members of the right and to propose to MM. Cazalès and Malouet that they [the left-wing deputies] be among the four deputies that they envisaged sending to negotiate with the king.[3]

According to the duc de Choiseul, the constitutional committee (containing Le Chapelier and Barnave) had chosen commissioners 'from all parties, including M. Cazalès, to go and treat with the king at Montmédy', the king's destination, where his lodgings had been prepared. M. Gouvernet was to go on ahead to announce their arrival.[4]

Another account has the research committee telling a clerical deputy that 'the orators of the left were going to propose a deputation of sixty to the king as soon as they knew his whereabouts'.[5] Alexandre de Lameth, hearing of the king's recapture at Varennes, lamented: 'What a disaster! In my terror at the speed with which public order is disintegrating, I hoped that a negotiation with the king, from a position of demonstrable and complete independence, could, through reciprocal concessions, give France the rest for which I seek in vain except through such a conjuncture.'[6]

These were private discussions. The most succinct account of the reaction in the Assembly is given by Madame Roland, one of Brissot's circle:

> A single member of the Assembly felt the need to shed light on the conduct of the commander-in-chief [Lafayette, suspected of facilitating the king's escape] and of those responsible. His motion was set aside primarily by Barnave and the Lameths (the latter have been reconciled with the queen for a week) who never have displayed their close union with d'André more openly than today. It is said that, tipped off about what has happened, they had their plans ready laid; they are the ones who have done everything and steps seem to have been coordinated to prevent Robespierre, Pétion and Buzot from speaking.[7]

The 'single member' was Rewbell. He had barely launched into his demand for an enquiry into Lafayette's complicity when he was interrupted by Barnave. Barnave did not like Lafayette but he saw the need for union with the man who was the commander of the armed force of the capital and the figurehead of the 89 Club. Barnave listed Lafayette's contributions to the Revolution and the Assembly heard no more of Rewbell's motion. Barnave later wrote that 'he had retained enough of his scandalous [*sic*] popularity to be able save Lafayette'.[8] Lafayette and Montmorin had been detained by an irate people – deputies went to rescue them. Barnave then proposed an anodyne proclamation telling the people to stay calm. Insurrection was appropriate in 1789 against despotism, he said, but now they should take their orders from the Assembly. His motion was seconded by d'André and passed *nem con*.

Barnave's defence of Lafayette is all the more generous because he did not know himself whether the general had foreknowledge of the escape. A few days later he asked the queen: 'Madame I know that I am about to take a great liberty but I cannot resist asking whether M. de Lafayette was in on the secret of the escape of Your Majesties.' Marie-Antoinette replied, 'On the contrary; though one is a queen, one cannot stop being a woman to some extent' – meaning probably that Lafayette's accusation of adultery had insulted her.[9]

Meanwhile it was learned that an extraordinary session had opened in the Jacobins – at noon, instead of the usual 6 p.m., Robespierre denounced 'the decree keeping the present ministers in place and placing the executive power in their hands jointly with the different committees of the National Assembly'. Barnave later wrote: 'My links with [Duport du Tertre] became much closer after the king's flight . . . when the diplomatic committee of which I was a member assembled at his place with the executive council.'[10] It was the links between this committee and Montmorin that Robespierre particularly denounced: 'It is to this traitor that you are entrusting your foreign policy under the surveillance of . . . whom? Of the diplomatic committee, of this committee over which a d'André reigns supreme.'

Robespierre then pointed out the similarities between the king's manifesto and the triumvirs' recent policies. Four times he employs the rhetorical refrain 'why did the king choose this precise moment' to go? And answers: 'he chose the moment' when the primary assemblies were in progress and with the prospect of a Legislative Assembly more radical than its predecessor and prepared to revoke a portion of its measures.

Robespierre did not think that the king's flight was meant to bring about the restoration of the *ancien régime*. Nor, he adds, 'could it have been upon Leopold and the King of Sweden and on the army [of émigrés] beyond the Rhine, that he placed his hopes'. No, Robespierre argued, something more dangerous, because more insidious, was afoot: the king intended to do a deal with the National Assembly which would enable the émigrés to return voluntarily to France. (Louis mentions this objective in his manifesto and Barnave wanted it too.) They would 'at first ask for very small sacrifices to bring about a general reconciliation'; and they would have little 'trouble in inducing a weary people to accept a deal, a halfway compromise'. 'You will have observed', he added, 'how [the king] distinguishes [in his manifesto] between those things in the constitution which he finds offensive and those he deigns to find acceptable.'

Robespierre, flushed with the success of his self-denying ordinance, unerringly found a spot where the triumvirs were vulnerable: the king 'chose the moment when the first legislature at the end of its labours looked on the successor in the way one regards one's heir' – an heir, moreover, 'which was going to oust it and exercise a national veto by annulling a portion of its acts'.[11]

At the climax of Robespierre's speech – when he was saying that his revelations would lead to his death and the *assistance* pledged that 'we will all die before you' – 'at the very moment' when hats and hands were raised in salute, 'Démeuniers, Chapelier, Lafayette, Beaumetz, d'André and all the leprosy of the 89 swept' into the club. They had rushed over during an adjournment of the Assembly and were just in time to 'catch the end of Robespierre's speech and he repeated the salient truths for their benefit'. Barnave wrote of Robespierre's intervention: 'meanwhile this – [blank in manuscript; Bérenger supplies 'odious'] man whose element is anarchy worked on the Jacobins to incite the hotheads against the National Assembly'.[12]

The Jacobin Club published an account of the session but omitted most of Robespierre's speech. Danton's attack on Lafayette, which followed it, is given in full. Alexandre de Lameth stopped him in his tracks. The balance of forces was equal and Barnave was able to secure his last '*triomphe d'assault*' in the Jacobins by getting the club to circulate the affiliated societies with a bromide similar to the Assembly's proclamation. It began with the official version of the king's flight, that 'misled by criminal advisers the king has distanced himself from the National Assembly', and concluded with the platitude: 'All divisions are forgotten; all the patriots are united; the National Assembly – that is our guide; the constitution our rallying point'.[13] Barnave put his all into this assault – one witness said that 'Barnave's voice sounded as if it were choked with emotion'.[14]

However, as Kuhlmann observes, 'The address, the official guide of the club only in form, must not be allowed to mislead us. The debates in the club show us that this attempted reunion was a complete failure'.[15] This became evident the very next day, 22 June. In the absence of the president, Prieur, who was attending the National Assembly, the chair was taken by the man who, more than Brissot or Robespierre, would be Barnave's nemesis – Pierre Chépy, one of the secretaries of the Jacobin Club. Robert had announced that he was bringing to the club 'an address' of the Cordeliers 'demanding the destruction of the monarchy'. When Gorguereau denounced the address as 'villainous', Chépy 'felt obliged to remind the previous speaker to mind his language'. 'Worn out' with the altercations, Chépy was replaced in the presidential chair by another man who would play a part in Barnave's downfall – Dubois de Crancé.[16]

It took time for these events to register in the provinces. On 23 June Barnave received a letter from a member of the Jacobin Club of Grenoble reminding him that he had overlooked his request to recommend him for membership of the Paris Club (the membership request had been turned down). By the time the letter reached him, Barnave had effectively seceded from the club, though on 27 June he received formal notification that the correspondence committee would be resuming its sessions on the 28th at 7 p.m. – they had been interrupted during the continuous session of the Assembly following the king's flight.[17]

⚜

Towards the end of the second day, the Assembly was taking a short break from its continuous session and Gouvernet, who 'was due to set out at 10 p.m. [to find the king] was getting ready to enter his carriage when news of the king's recapture arrived at 9 p.m.'.[18] He had been stopped by the local inhabitants at Varennes, some 25 miles from his destination, Montmédy – a small, fortified hill town in Lorraine near the border with Luxembourg. Marie-Antoinette asked the local authorities to escort the royal family to Montmédy, but they insisted on sending them back to Paris. Bouillé's troops, who had been waiting for him at Stenay, attempted a rescue but arrived two hours too late. Romeuf, Lafayette's aide-de-camp, arrived first and escorted the royal family on their long return journey.

The recapture meant a change in emphasis. If the king had reached Montmédy, he could, as Lameth said, have negotiated 'from a position of demonstrable and complete independence'. The commissioners would have been further to the right, though it is likely that Barnave would have been of their number. And they would have negotiated openly. Now the commissioners were taken from the whole spectrum of the original left of May–July 1789. Their choice was settled by a rare agreement between the triumvirs and the right, including Malouet and Cazalès.[19] The commissioners selected by the joint constitutional and military committees were Pétion, a republican, Latour-Maubourg, aligned with the 89 Club, and Barnave. Dumas, Lafayette's adjutant, was included to handle the military arrangements. Pétion called him 'the creature of the Lameths' and he was a close friend of Barnave's. His choice – at a time when the lives of the king and queen were in danger – was no accident.

Pétion thought that he had been selected 'as a man of known virtue' 'to give cover' for those less patriotic than himself. Maubourg was well known to Madame de Tourzel, the governess of the royal children who had accompanied her charges on the journey. 'Barnave had already laid his plans', wrote Brissot. 'Though the commissioners were not there to negotiate, their role was to protect the royal family rather than to further imprison them in their carriage.'[20] Barnave agreed: 'I drafted the powers of the commissioners sent to Varennes in these same [combined] committees; they were instructed specifically to ensure that proper respect for the royal family was maintained.'[21]

They were appointed round midnight and they agreed to meet at 2 a.m. at Maubourg's to finalise plans. 'Barnave was a very long time in coming', Pétion recorded, 'and we did not set off until 4 a.m.'. We do not know what detained him. Duport and Lafayette turned up together at Maubourg's, 'chatting together amiably'. This surprised Pétion: 'I knew they detested each other and their coalition had not yet been made public.' Lafayette 'sneered' at the king; they debated whether he should be imprisoned, dethroned or given a council. Duport kept his own counsel.

THE RETURN JOURNEY

Just before the commissioners met up with the king, Barnave drafted a letter to the president of the National Assembly. They had heard that the king had spent the night at Châlons and continued towards Paris in the morning. He expected to join the king in the evening. 'Along their route the commissioners had given the strictest orders to preserve the safety and tranquillity of the king.' 'Everywhere the response to the king's departure had been the same as in Paris: the countenance of the people had been tranquil and proud. They were inundated with expressions of respect and confidence in the National Assembly.'[22] The commissioners met the king's coach at Epernay, in Champagne country, just south of Rheims and 90 miles from Paris.

Dumas was beside Barnave when he delivered the Assembly's decree to the king, who said: "Gentlemen, I am very glad to see you. I had no intention of leaving the kingdom. I was going to Montmédy and intended to stay there until I had examined and freely accepted the constitution." Barnave then whispered to me: "If the king remembers to repeat the same thing, we will save him."[23]

Seating arrangements were then discussed. There were two carriages – the king's berline (not as big as in Varennes mythology) and the chaise containing the waiting-women. The king, Pétion and Elizabeth were all of ample proportions and Maubourg was of 'very great stature so there was some doubt as to whether they could all fit into the coach, but the king said that if everyone budged up, they could all squeeze in'. Maubourg volunteered for the ladies' carriage. Marie-Antoinette appeared to want him to join her in the carriage as the only one she knew personally. But he told her that she already had his loyalty and that the important thing was to win over Barnave, 'whose influence in the Assembly was considerable'. She knew this, of course, and if she had needed reminding, the previous month Laborde *père* 'had been sent by his son [Méréville] and his associates Duport and Barnave to get her to identify herself with the Revolution which they regarded as completed'. 'They were not so ill-disposed as she imagined and he sang the praises of . . . [Barnave] in particular, with whom he seemed enchanted.'[24]

Fontanges gnomically wrote that Barnave at this time was 'rather the friend of those who wanted to reverse the Revolution than holding this opinion himself'. Dumas notes that 'Barnave and Pétion took their place in the berline at the reiterated request of Their Majesties'. Pétion and Elizabeth occupied the back seat, either side of the king's thirteen-year-old daughter. The handsome Barnave, 'who was fairly slim', sat between the king and queen in the front seat. The women took it in turns to have the dauphin on their knees. Maubourg and Mme de Tourzel travelled with the waiting-women in the other carriage.

Marie-Antoinette told Fersen that Maubourg and Barnave had behaved 'very well' but that 'Pétion was disrespectful'. That was putting it mildly: he taunted her with her liaison with Fersen. 'Pétion said that he knew everything; that they had taken a hire-cab near to the château driven by a Swede called . . . (he pretended not to know my name) and asked the queen to supply it; she replied: "I am not in the habit of knowing the names of cabbies." '[25] Pétion, a blonde, big-nosed lawyer from Chartres, was 'quite good looking', Molleville said, 'from a distance'. He was consistently rude, talked of republics and regretted that France was 'not yet ripe for one'. On his return, he asked the National Assembly to put the king on trial.[26]

Having proposed himself for a commissioner and drawn up his own instructions, it was unlikely that Barnave would waste such an opportunity. Bradby makes much of Pétion's assertion that he never let Barnave out of his sight – even to the extent of sharing a bed with him at their first stop at Dormans. And in his *Introduction à la Révolution française* (and naturally at his trial), Barnave denies that anything happened on the return journey: 'On the road there were never less than eight in the same carriage. In the houses where we broke our journey, the commissioners stayed together. . . . The precautions we took to guard our consignment [the king] were very strict and did not permit anyone to get to him secretly.'[27]

This is nonsense. At the start of their correspondence, Marie-Antoinette refers on three occasions to their discussions – one of which took place at Meaux while the light failed in the bishop's summer gardens. Barnave in one of the series of forty-four secret letters he later sent her related that he had 'never known' her before the journey and it was only 'pure and noble sentiments' which had led him to take an interest in her. Their contact would have ended with the journey 'if the queen had not asked him to keep it up'.[28] But their relationship got off to a bad start when Barnave, thinking that one of the three bodyguards sitting on top was Fersen, gave a sardonic smile. Marie-Antoinette disabused him by smoothly giving their names.[29]

Michelet considered that Barnave was jealous of Fersen for organising the (successful) escape from Paris and was annoyed that the queen, whom he had been advising since December 1790, should have listened to Fersen rather than him. So far from conniving at the flight, it threw Barnave off course. Coming after the 23 April circular, this would have seemed like a kick in the face. According to this version, instead of a glacial queen slowly melting it was Barnave's susceptibility which had to be smoothed by the charm which the queen could put on.[30]

In 1793 Barnave told the parliamentary reporter C.F. Beaulieu that the queen treated him with 'delicate sensibility'.

> The two children ... played with him and seemed to implore his protection. The dauphin sat on his knees for nearly the whole journey and charmed him with his sweet friendliness. Barnave assured me that had the royal family belonged to the most ordinary class it would still have evoked his compassion. What sentiments must it have inspired considering the heights from which it had fallen! The young man could not hold out despite his extreme coolness: he promised himself to do all in his power to be of service to these unfortunate people.[31]

There was obviously some sexual attraction between Barnave and the queen, though no one except the jealous Fersen ever suggested that they were lovers. There was a dangerous rivalry between the two men who aimed to save the queen – two men with a passing resemblance, though Fersen's features were more pinched; and, despite a shaky start, an intellectual relationship also developed between Marie-Antoinette and Barnave.

Burke's *Reflections on the Revolution in France* had been published on 1 November 1790 and the French translation appeared on the 29th. Two passages must have seized Barnave's attention. One was Burke's quotation from a French source referring to Barnave's infamous 'is their blood so pure' quip, and the second was the famous passage about Marie-Antoinette: 'I thought ten thousand swords must have leaped from their scabbards to avenge even a look that threatened her with insult – But the age of chivalry is gone.'[32]

Barnave was offered an opportunity to show it had not when Marie-Antoinette noticed a priest being manhandled by the National Guard. She alerted Barnave who, in order to address the assailants, leaned out of the door of the coach so far that Madame Elizabeth, won over by his gallantry, grabbed his coat tails to stop him falling out! This astonished Marie-Antoinette, given that Elizabeth was a diehard counter-revolutionary. From this indecorous position, Barnave harangued the mob: 'Tigers! Have you ceased to be French? Nation of heroes, have you become one of assassins?' The priest escaped with his life.[33]

Barnave also got on well with the king. He told Beaulieu that 'the king chatted with him in a familiar way, discussing several important matters and revealed to him a prince whose intelligence was far removed from the public conception'. They must have discussed the king's manifesto. There was never more than 'a small dispute' – whether because Barnave pursued the discussion 'with the good manners of a man used to polite society' or, as one suspects, because there was very little actual disagreement. If it had not dawned on them before, the king and queen had before their eyes for three days a member of the Third Estate with manners as good as those of their courtiers, and an education that was better.

Throughout Barnave treated the king with innate tact, an important quality with Barnave, asking the king each day when he would like to set off, as if he was still in charge of the voyage. At their first meal stop after the commissioners had joined them (Fersen had provided food only for the voyage out), 'the king and queen noticed that the table had only been set for the royal family'. They asked the commissioners to join them; Barnave and Maubourg, out of delicacy, at first refused; Pétion was made of coarser stuff. During these long hours of conversation, Marie-Antoinette and Barnave worked out a concordat based on common needs.

As Marie-Antoinette's confidant, La Marck saw the situation, Barnave and his associates had twin fears: an invasion by the émigrés backed up by Austria and an attack on property at home. Marie-Antoinette could remove the first fear and a restored king the second. So the deal was briefly this: Barnave and his allies in the Assembly would try to revise the constitution along the lines suggested in the king's memorandum. In return, (1) the king would wholeheartedly accept it – why should he not if he could secure all he had aimed for by flight without civil war? And (2) Marie-Antoinette would ask her brother Leopold to mark his own acceptance of the Revolution by renewing the treaty of alliance with France. Deprived of the support of the emperor, the king's brothers and the émigrés, having no hope of overthrowing the constitution, would return to France, particularly if the king ordered them to do so.

The coach arrived back in Paris at 8 p.m. on Saturday 25 June. The Champs-Elysées was densely packed, but there was total silence.

Everywhere placards sententiously proclaimed: 'Whoever applauds the king will be thrashed; whoever insults him will be hanged.' Everyone left their hats on. Doubtless those who did not usually wear a hat acquired one. The arms of the National Guard were reversed, as for a funeral, drums gratuitously rolled – ritual humiliation. On their arrival at the Tuileries, d'Aiguillon and the vicomte de Noailles rushed to give the queen an arm. She knew that these members of Barnave's party hated her – d'Aiguillon because she had hated his father; Noailles because she had aimed to take his family, previously dominant at court, 'down a peg or two'. They took her a back route – to prison she thought; actually, to save her from the mob. She implored Barnave to save the lives of the three bodyguards who had accompanied the royal family, which he did.[34]

A few minutes later, Pétion entered the king's bedroom:

> All the valets were ready waiting for him dressed in their usual costume. It seemed as though the king were returning from a hunting-party; they did his toilet. Seeing the king, contemplating him, you never could have guessed all that had just happened: he was just as phlegmatic, just as tranquil, as if nothing had happened. He immediately put himself on show.

'He put himself on show', externally and internally; that is the clue. It was partly a matter of conditioning, the life on display he had known since a small child, partly a way of holding himself together. The flight to Varennes appears in his diary as an ordinary voyage. The detail is meticulous: there was no *coucher* at Dormans because there was no bed. He had slept in a *fauteuil*. Soon, too, Barnave was referring to the flight to Varennes as a 'voyage' rather than the ridiculous official version of a 'kidnapping' (*enlèvement*) or the embarrassing truth of a flight.

The Assembly decided to send three commissioners to take statements from the king and queen. Out of a possible 598 votes (the right wing abstaining in protest at the king's suspension from office), Tronchet received 400 votes, d'André 354 and Duport 351. The king made it clear to them that he had no intention of being interrogated and was told that was never the plan. Instead, he dictated a prepared statement, read it through and signed it. Clermont-Gallerande thought that the bulk of the statement was the king's own but that the final sentences were 'rent from the king's pen by the persistent hectoring of MM. Duport and d'André, perhaps also by the advice previously given by Barnave' on the return journey. These sentences were to the effect that the king had realised from his encounters that the people sincerely wanted the constitution. Gallerande (and Michon following him) thought that this was ridiculous: how could anyone gauge the mood of the people from sitting in a coach?[35] However, Marie-Antoinette confessed to Fersen on 31 October that her journey had convinced her that 'there is not a single town, not a regiment on which we can rely'.[36]

Ferrières thought the whole thing was 'the work of Barnave'. But given that Barnave intended to make the king's declaration the basis of the Assembly's revision of the constitution, the precise authorship is less important. The king made four points. (1) He had decided to leave Paris because the Saint-Cloud episode had convinced him that his family was in danger. (2) The proof that he had not planned to emigrate was that lodgings had been prepared for him at Montmédy – the house, a modest château with its plaque, was recently on the market. (3) The constitution did not leave him with sufficient resources to run the country. (4) Instead of being asked to sanction the constitutional articles piecemeal, he should be asked to sanction the whole.[37] The triumvirs intended to answer the first point by providing the king with his own bodyguard; the last three points echo their own sentiments.

That was the first hurdle cleared but there was also a move to declare a republic, or at least change the monarch. This came less from the extreme left than from the Fayettists and the 89 Club. Lafayette detested Marie-Antoinette, who more than reciprocated. Fersen's diary entry for 12 June, when he was seeing the king and queen every day to finalise the details of the flight runs: 'Planned trial of Lafayette changed to a court martial.'[38]

Unlike the right and Barnave's group, the initial response of Lafayette and his circle on learning of the king's flight had been not to treat with him, but rather to depose him and declare a republic. Lafayette wrote: 'One should not be surprised to learn that ... [the king's flight] gave birth in some and revived in some others the idea of a pure republic [as opposed to a republic with a figurehead monarch]. Lafayette naturally found himself among the latter.' 'A few days' after the king's flight a group of deputies assembled at the duc de la Rochefoucauld's to consider the situation. The host proposed a republic and was backed by his friend Dupont de Nemours, but the majority was against.[39]

Even some in the constitutional committee, by definition central to Barnave's plans, considered not a republic but a change of monarch – bizarrely, the reactionary Artois was considered. This move was championed by Le Chapelier and Beaumetz. According to Théodore, his brother Alexandre quashed all these notions by declaring: 'You are free to dishonour yourselves but if the strange idea which has just been rehearsed were to be adopted by the [constitutional] committee; if the Assembly itself were to adopt it and take the king's crown away, then I warn you, gentlemen, that my friends and I still have enough remaining popularity to be able to have the crown placed on the head of the royal child.'[40]

⚜

Marie-Antoinette did not know what to do – or what was coming next. How to continue those snatches of conversation with Barnave? 'Having thoroughly reflected since my return on the strength, resources and intelligence of the man with whom I chatted, I realised that it could only be beneficial to establish a sort of correspondence with him while stipulating as the first condition that I should always state my views frankly.'[41]

But how to communicate when you are effectively under house arrest, though that problem had never stopped her and never would. Lafayette was still in charge of palace security, despite the lapses for which he was blamed. She asked him to tell Barnave that she wanted to talk to him. But Barnave sent back that it would be too risky for all concerned. That would have been her 'preferred' route. Instead, she had to devise something more circuitous. She dropped a sealed letter into the pocket of a loyal servitor Oscar François de Jarjayes, who took it to Barnave. She employed a simple code based on A = 1. So Jarjayes, 'JA', was 10; Barnave, 'BA', was 2:1; Alexandre de Lameth was A:12 and Duport 4:15. The queen sometimes dropped this precaution, using initials and even full names. Barnave would dictate his reply to Jarjayes, so it would not be in his handwriting (this fooled scholars into thinking the correspondence was forged) and Jarjayes would return it to the queen, together with her letter re-sealed. Jarjaye's wife who, like Madame Campan, was one of Marie-Antoinette's *femmes de chambre*, was a link in the transmission.

The queen told Barnave: 'We cannot go on like this. We must certainly do something but what? I don't know and that is why I am addressing . . . [Barnave]. He must have seen from our discussions that I was in good faith.' Barnave 'read her note over several times with transports of delight' but said that he could not give an answer until he had consulted Lameth – they had 'a strict agreement' on this. The two friends decided that they must first get the idea 'past a secret committee of five which they would convene that very evening'. They listed its members as follows: MM Duport, Barnave, Alexandre de Lameth, d'André and Dumas. They added that 'there was another much larger committee but the same intimacy and trust did not reign there. In the latter committee, apart from the five, there were Messrs. de Lafayette, Maubourg, Lacoste, Emmery and some others whose names I do not recall. Having given this explanation [verbally to Jarjayes] they dictated letter no. 1.' Marie-Antoinette numbered all forty-four of the series, which would continue until January 1792. Back in the autumn of 1789 Barnave had entertained the notion of having Lacoste and Emmery as minister for foreign affairs and finance, respectively.

In her preliminary note the queen had said that there was not much she and the king could do; they were under virtual house arrest and the king was suspended from his remaining functions (these were exercised by the ministers forming an executive council). Barnave disagreed with her: the king would recover his authority only if he could 'procure great advantages to the nation' and the two he had in mind could be obtained from within a palace:[42] have the revolution endorsed by the emperor and the branches of the Spanish Bourbons; and persuade the king's brothers and the other émigrés to return to France. Barnave's whole enterprise was predicated on peace with Austria. He wanted to transform Marie-Antoinette's nationality from being a liability into an asset and revivify the moribund alliance which had brought her to France. Paradoxical as it may seem, Barnave thought he could do business with Leopold because of not despite his suspected involvement in the king's flight. Barnave thought that all those involved in the flight, such as Bouillé, were advocates of a strong monarchy rather than a return to the *ancien régime*: 'All the indications relative to the king's escape in 1791 and the camp at Montmédy . . . prove that it was coordinated with Leopold and that its object was the establishment of a strong constitutional monarchy (*un système mixte*).'[43] If the émigrés returned, the country would become less revolutionary because it was less threatened and the émigrés, as 'upstanding men of property', would further Barnave's plans for a property-owning democracy.

Barnave wanted Leopold to renew the 1756 alliance and Marie-Antoinette to get the credit for it. But would there be any credit? Most people in France detested the Austrian alliance; it had been the root cause of Marie-Antoinette's unpopularity. Would not its renewal further inflame an irritated nerve? The bulk of the evidence suggests that Leopold, his chancellor Kaunitz and Mercy supported Barnave, at least until the end of 1791.[44] But Leopold was too fine a player to declare his support openly.

Whether because of Marie-Antoinette, his dealings with Montmorin, his experience in the diplomatic committee or his youthful reading of Mably, Austria held a particular fascination for Barnave. In his *Introduction à la Révolution française*, he brilliantly analysed Austria's relationship to France and its Revolution. Austria was 'our natural rival on the Continent but our actual ally' (a similar point had been made by Vergennes). She did not need military assistance from France (which in the Seven Years War had been a bonus) but rather 'a guarantee of our inertia, which would enable her to deploy all her own forces' for her expansionist projects. France's '*demi-Révolution*' suited her perfectly. She did not want the restoration of 'despotism' because France's absolute monarchs had been a thorn in her side. But nor did she want the overthrow of the Bourbon dynasty on which depended 'the maintenance of our alliance'. She wanted, in short, a bourgeois revolution in which the 'martial' spirit of the aristocracy would be replaced by a 'mercantile' one – hence, Leopold's support for 'the camp at Montmédy'.[45] Both Barnave and Marie-Antoinette knew foreign affairs were crucial. They would settle the fate of the monarchy: its death in 1792 and its resurrection in 1814. Barnave's request to Marie-Antoinette was the mirror image of the circular letter of 23 April: it had told the European powers that the king was satisfied with the Revolution; now Barnave wanted the powers to say that they were.

But Barnave's request embarrassed the queen. She notes: 'After receiving this reply, I let several days elapse before taking up my pen. 2:1 asked if I had no news to give them. The two friends [Barnave and Lameth] did not attempt to conceal that they thought me very frivolous, incapable of undertaking anything serious, incapable even of thinking logically. 2:1 himself sent a short note which I have burned containing the assurance that affairs are looking better.'[46] She finally replied on 9 July, observing that she had not seen Leopold for twenty-six years and had never been close to him in any case, though the death of their brother Joseph in February 1790 had brought them somewhat nearer.[47] This prompted Barnave to try putting pressure on her through her mentor, Mercy-Argenteau. He was now in Brussels, with Blumendorff the *secrétaire d'ambassade* holding the fort at Paris. So next day Méréville's father Laborde gave Blumendorff a letter from Barnave to pass on to his chief.[48]

The letter expanded on the points he had made to the queen: the king would have to give the nation 'some services' to win back trust and these concerned the return of the émigrés and international recognition. If the king was able to survive 'a revolution such as this', he would be unassailable, but if he remained 'reviled on his throne then all the cords of government would be loosened, the nation would remain in a state of revolution and a republic declared for lack of suitable alternative candidates among the present dynasty and by the natural progression of notions of liberty and equality'. More immediately, if the elections to the successor legislature were held while the king was still under suspicion, that body would 'probably' be more radical.

Barnave threatened the emperor (none too delicately) with the prospect of social and political disintegration in France and 'the contagious example of a king cast from his throne, shaking those who were not too firmly seated on their own' – perhaps a reference to the ongoing rebellion in the Austrian Netherlands. An abbreviated entry in Fersen's diary would suggest that Mercy's reaction was cool: 'The 19th [July], Arrived at Spa 9 a.m. Alex. Lameth, Barnave, Lafayette, Duport, [Laborde] de Méréville in coalition, have broken with the Jacobins; have made overtures to Mercy through Laborde *père* to get the king to come to an understanding with them. Mercy replied that he had not had any communication with the king; told them some home truths.'[49]

It is doubtful, however, whether Mercy did, for he held back Marie-Antoinette's letters to Fersen until September, hoping to further her negotiations with Barnave.

After the initial exchanges between Marie-Antoinette and Barnave, the queen, as she told him on 20 July, had decided to wait 'until the great events which have occupied the last week were over' before taking up her pen again. These events were the debate on what Marie-Antoinette called 'the great report' on the consequences of the king's flight (13–16 July) and the popular demonstration known as the Massacre of the Champ de Mars (17 July) against the Assembly's verdict on them.

⚜

The king's fate, together with that of his accomplices – except that, to paraphrase Robespierre, this was a murder without a body – was decided by the combined committees (military, diplomatic, constitutional, revision, criminal justice, report and research). For the episode was multifaceted: the diplomatic committee was interested in the involvement of Leopold II, the military in that of Bouillé and his officers (some of whom stood accused); the role of the criminal justice and the sinister research committee was self-evident. The constitutional committee had to decide whether a king could violate a constitution which was not yet operational. In prior discussions of that committee, Thouret, Le Chapelier and Démeunier argued for inviolability and their conversation was reported back to the king.[50] In theory, some seventy deputies sat on these committees, though Barnave recalls 'fifty or sixty'.

Now that they had lost control of the Jacobin network, the triumvirs' dominance of the committees was the bedrock of their power. But they did not have it all their way. Barnave remembered that 'M. Pétion, Siéyès, Buzot etc.' proposed that the king be replaced by an elective executive council as a transitional stage to a full republic. When Beaumetz declared for inviolability, Sillery proposed the young duc de Chartres for king, his father Orléans having ruled himself out. Sillery's wife, Madame de Genlis, was Orléans's mistress and had directed the education of his children. That is all we know of the internal debates within the committees. Barnave sums up their conclusion: 'Those who held the principle of inviolability, whose opinion prevailed, wanted to preserve the constitution and saw no basis for dethroning Louis XVI either in any existing law or the national interest.'[51]

For the debate in the Assembly the triumvirs put forward a straw man, Muguet de Nanthou, as the spokesman of the combined committees, but his very long statement was a compilation – the input of Barnave and of Duport can be detected in certain sections. He began with a long factual reconstruction of the days immediately preceding the kings '*évasion*', his voyage and his recapture. Muguet said that the royal family had been taken to Bondy (where the berline was waiting) by 'an unknown man'. Everyone knew that this was Fersen – Marie-Antoinette warned him, 'above all don't return here under any pretext. They know that it was you who got us out of here; you would be lost if you turned up.' 'We are guarded day and night. Rest assured nothing will happen to us, the Assembly wants to treat us gently. *Calm yourself if you can. Look after yourself for me.* I won't be able to write to you anymore. *But nothing in this world can stop me adoring you until I die*.'[52] The omission of Fersen from the list of co-accused was presumably a service Barnave performed for the queen. This factual account of the king's escape (the earliest reconstruction we have) was almost value-free – it is not entirely clear why it was included.

Muguet then proceeded to the question of the king's guilt, proclaiming his inviolability on the grounds that if the legislature sat in judgement on the executive, it would violate the separation of powers. The king's declaration, Muguet argued, was an irrelevance – it was not countersigned, could have been forged, and so on. It had no *locus standi*. How could the sentiment expressed therein contradict his acceptance of a constitution of which he had had no role in the drafting? Muguet further rent the 'religious veil' which had shrouded the Assembly's seizure of power by baldly stating that the king's sanction was 'a simple formula which is in no way indispensable and from which you freed yourselves as soon as you were forced to by the king's flight'.

But this was a dangerous argument: to concede that during the king's suspension the country had been effectively governed as a republic threw in doubt the necessity for a king. Duport provided the best argument for the defence of the king – retrospective justice was against the rule of law: 'it would be contrary to all the rules of justice to apply a law which is not yet in existence to a current case'.

In general, the tone of the debate was clinical. There was some anger on the extreme left, though much of it was synthetic; and Robespierre's speech was one long snarl. The only man who expressed any sympathy for the king's predicament was Salle and his speech had the biggest impact.[53] Cleverly, he sought to exculpate but also blame the king. Most of his long speech was devoted to the king's declaration. Hitherto the memorandum, though of crucial importance, had been largely ignored by the Assembly, which had heard it read out by Laporte in stony silence. Salle was 'far from wanting to dissimulate the *incivisme* of this production', but he half-excused the king's complaint that the committees had usurped his executive role: 'I will go as far as to say that the Assembly confirmed his fears by exercising – though it had no choice – various administrative acts.' This admission was deliberate and paved the way for the Assembly to answer the king's points as Barnave had promised the queen. He concluded: 'How miserable is the condition of a king' – a view the king himself would have endorsed.

Barnave responded warmly to the 'magnanimity and generosity of soul' displayed in this speech.[54] The emotion of Salle's speech answered the newfound emotion of Barnave's own. Though his encounter with the queen had not changed his political views, it had endowed his enterprise with an emotional character, removed him from the lock of Artemis, the goddess of chastity, or rather fused the public and the private. He later said that witnessing the fortitude with which the royal family bore their sufferings equipped him the better to endure his own. Therefore, he spoke with passion in what is generally considered to have been his best speech.

Barnave said that Salle, by dwelling extensively on the king's memorandum, 'dispensed' him from the need to do the same. However, in preparatory notes for the speech, he wrote, 'it is necessary to re-read the king's memorandum. This [my] speech must be the resp[onse]', but before he had completed the word, he replaced it with the 'refutation of the various reproaches to our constitution' which it contained. First thoughts are illuminating. Barnave saw his policy as both answering the king's justified complaints – by strengthening the executive – and refuting his unjustified ones.[55] Barnave's notes move beyond the narrow question of the king's inviolability to a summation of the work of the Assembly: they are titled '*compte rendu*'; and the first word is 'missions – . . .: happiness is the aim [and] the constitution is the means'. The king told his émigré brothers that the constitution made the people of all classes happy. They were wrong but must be allowed to learn by experience.

Barnave's most original insight was that the Revolution had brought an end to personal monarchy: 'the personal wishes of the monarch are absolutely irrelevant to the establishment of the constitution'. Praise or blame of an actual sovereign was irrelevant, as was the accident of birth in a hereditary monarchy. Those who were ready to condemn the person of one king were just as likely to fawn on another they liked. Barnave attributes this idea to Duport, who 'has shown [yesterday] that the king can only act through his responsible ministers – his personal qualities cannot and should not decide the fate of a nation'. In fact, Duport had put it slightly differently: the constitution would be accomplished through the logic of the situation, whatever the king's personal attitude, though if the king and the Assembly had been known to be in 'schism', the task would have been more difficult.

Barnave asserted but did not demonstrate that a hereditary constitutional monarchy was essential for the safeguarding of property rights. He thought that a weak elective executive council or a federal republic (the only one he thought on offer for a large country) would not be able to resist 'this feeding frenzy for equality'. This led to his great affirmation, which drew applause even from the galleries: 'What you have accomplished so far is good for liberty and equality. But if the Revolution takes a further step, it cannot do so without danger. The next step towards further liberty could entail the destruction of the monarchy and the subsequent lurch towards equality would involve an attack on property' – 'Because that was all there was left to do.' He explains: 'You know that the night of 4 August gave more supporters to the Revolution than all the constitutional laws put together. But for those who would like to go further, what night of 4 August is there left to do but laws against properties?'[56] Barnave's notes for this famous passage include: 'On the conservative spirit which must succeed us – a step towards equality attacks property; a step towards liberty attacks the monarchy.' '*Esprit conservateur*' could be translated as a 'conservative reaction' as in the Thermidorian one, but he meant 'preservative spirit' – or even 'spirits' because, as we shall see, there was also an embalming mentality at work.[57]

The crux of his central argument for the inviolability of the king was taken from his reading of English history. 'England, because of its [unwritten] constitution, which is determined by events, has never made provision for eventualities which have not yet occurred; because not having a government based on law but on facts it is always obliged to derive its laws from circumstances.'[58] It was an ad hoc constitution depending on a power struggle – some kings had been unjustly deposed. But in France it would be against the rule of law to depose a king for a crime which had not yet been defined. In France the king should not be above the law, but neither should he be beneath it.

'After Mr. Barnave's speech', Earl Gower, the English ambassador, reported, 'the Assembly determined to finish the discussion. Those of a different opinion scarcely showed themselves as it is not the custom to proceed to any division or to number the votes except in very nice cases.'[59] Madame Roland thought 'there were no more than forty for the good cause'.[60] But though the 'case' was not 'nice' enough to require a vote, there was strong opposition to the committees. An unnamed deputy speculated that if the king were retained with his 30 million civil list, 'this terrible instrument of corruption', they could expect to see 'a Calonne at the head of our finances and a Bouillé at the head of the army'.[61] Robespierre was scathing about the so-called abduction of the king: 'I will not examine whether the king fled of his own accord or if from the extremity of the frontiers a citizen spirited him off by the force of his counsel.'[62] From Grenoble a well-wisher congratulating Barnave on his speech observed that those members of the constitution and the revision committees who wanted to resign were 'feeble'.[63]

THE 'MASSACRE' OF THE CHAMP DE MARS

The Assembly's semi-rehabilitation of the king on 15 July provoked a demonstration on the 17th and this in turn provoked a seminal event, known as the Massacre of the Champ de Mars. Barnave would tell the queen that if their arrangement did not work out, he reserved the right to take the necessary steps to preserve himself, that is, by veering to the left. But he was deluding himself because after the 'Massacre', that was no longer an option. The facts are well known. The Cordelier Club got up a republican petition and in the early evening of Sunday 17 July took it to the Champ de Mars to collect signatures. In the explosive atmosphere the gathering was likely to straddle the line between a demonstration and an insurrection, and the municipality replied to the petition by declaring martial law, in token of which Bailly, the mayor, Lafayette and the National Guard arrived on the scene with a red flag. The National Guard advanced. The crowd replied with 'a hail of stones' and one stray shot was fired. Lafayette ordered his men to open fire, killing some fifty of the petitioners. Nine of the National Guard were killed.

The contrast with the guards' stance during the abortive Saint-Cloud departure was stark and irreversible. The National Guard had fired on the people for the first time and in defence of, not against, the king. Like Barnave they had no way back. The dividing line now was between Parisian popular politics and the Assembly backed up by a National Guard which had reverted in spirit to its original name, the Bourgeois Guard. La Marck believed that the National Guard had fired on the people 'less to repel them than in self-defence' – in other words, if the gathering had not been dispersed, it would have marched on the Assembly and forced it to declare the republic.[64] Lafayette, having flirted with the republicanism which remained his ideal, was now committed to saving the monarchy, though always on his own terms. He, Bailly and Barnave had dipped their hands in the blood. They were committed in both senses of the word.

The evidence that the triumvirs were 'spoiling for a fight on the 17th and that the Cordeliers gave them the pretext they wanted' is stronger than that for their collusion or connivance in the king's flight.[65] On the 16th d'André had told the Assembly that to disobey the decree of the 15th exonerating the king amounted to an attack on the constitution; Charles de Lameth, who was president for that fortnight, ordered the département and municipality of Paris 'to employ all their means to repress disorders'. In response, Bailly wrote to Lafayette on the morning of the 17th telling him that 'last night . . . at the Jacobins it was proposed that . . . a large gathering meet on the Champ de Mars to sign a petition . . . to present en masse to the Assembly. I am asking you to be ready to receive them with sufficient force.'

In fact, Robespierre, playing a long game, cried off and withdrew the Jacobin petition. But the Cordelier one went ahead and with each draft their petitions became more radical, so that the one actually signed demanded that the Assembly 'overturn its decree of 15 July, null both in form and content, given that the crime of Louis XVI is proven; that this king has abdicated; to accept his abdication and convoke a new constituent body to proceed in a truly national way to the judgement of the criminal and above all to the replacement and organisation of a new executive power' – code for a republic or, as Barnave had said, a halfway house to one.[66]

At 9 a.m. on the Sunday the engraver Sergent, the president of the Théâtre Française section, called on his friend Danton and found there 'the general staff of the Cordeliers' Club,[67] including Camille Desmoulins and Fréron, editor of the radical *Oracle du peuple*, and Momoro the printer – all people with whom Barnave had cooperated in his more radical days. They were discussing the murder of two peeping-toms in the Champs de Mars earlier in the day and how it might be exploited by the authorities over the signing of the petition. As they were sipping their café-au-lait, 'the butcher Legendre rushed in and told the gathering that two people (whom he named but I only remember one, Lefèvre, a man devoted to the Lameths, Duport, Barnave and other deputies) had called on him and said: "We are charged to warn you to get out of Paris today; dine in the countryside. Take Danton, Camille and Fréron with you; they must not be seen in the city today; It is Alexandre Lameth who is urging it." '[68]

Danton, Desmoulins and Fréron duly left together and dined at the house of Danton's father-in-law in the country. (Danton would repay the favour in 1792 when he was justice minister and a warrant was out for Alexandre's arrest.) Momoro stayed in Paris and was arrested with six or eight others. 'What was the aim of the [Barnave] faction?' Sergent asked. 'To reject the dethronement [*déchéance*, of the king] and [promote] the revision of the constitutional act whose principles they perverted.'[69] In his no. 86 and last (he thought he was in danger), Desmoulins gives his own account of the escape to Danton's father-in-law's and gives its location – Fontenai-sous-Bois, two leagues (6 miles) from Paris – adding that he was pursued by cutthroats accusing him of being an aristocrat in the pay of Prussia. The rival journalist Prudhomme accused the three fugitives of cowardice, but Desmoulins protested that 'wherever they were they were more useful to the Revolution than they would have been in Paris'.[70]

Desmoulins showed no gratitude to Lameth. He thought Alexandre was the new organising intelligence behind Lafayette, who was somewhat deficient in that quality. He adds, 'Alexandre de Lameth and Barnave were seen strolling on the Pont Louis XVI while patriots were being shot on the altar of the *patrie*, joyfully listening to the fusillade and no doubt saying to themselves like Charles XII [the martial king of Sweden] "henceforth that will be my music".'[71]

There is in Desmoulins a mixture of shame at being helped to escape by a renegade and fear of discovery – Sergent told several people about the incident. Also, a sense of betrayal – after all, Desmoulins had lauded Barnave in several of his numbers. It was only in this, what he expected to be his last number, that Desmoulins saw that the 'key to all the liberticide events between 21 June and 17 July inclusive was that power had slipped from the Lameths and Lafayette and Duport could not be re-elected'. And, he added, he had not been the first to sport the tricolour cockade only to substitute decemvirs for monarchy, nor committees for ministers, nor a M. d'André or a M. Barnave as prime ministers, nor the co-dictators Lafayette and [Alexandre] Lameth for *lettres de cachet*.[72]

Of course, Barnave did not saunter on the bridge enjoying the sound of gunfire. Nor did he, as Dubois-Crancé wrote, 'rub his hands with glee in the Tuileries gardens at the sound of his fellow citizens being mown down'.[73] But the morning after, in the Assembly, Barnave was harsh and determined. Unapologetic would imply that he felt that an apology was due. The praise of Charles de Lameth, the president, for the conduct of the mayor and National Guard should, he said, receive 'maximum publicity'. The 'distinctive characteristic of a free man is the religious observance of the law. The time has come when those who for some time have been the torment of the country should finally be consigned to eternal contempt.' The nation should adopt the families of the nine national guards who had perished in the affray: 'their children are our children, their wives our wives and everything they have left on earth belongs to us'. When Pétion rose to object to further restrictions on placarding he was greeted with 'ironic laughter' from 'the left', which was now the new centre, and cries of 'curses on Marat, Brissot, Laclos, Danton'.[74] Danton was safely in hiding, while, as Barnave put it, 'a newly invigorated law' punished those who had not been tipped off.

THE FEUILLANT CLUB

It is ironic that Barnave was opposed to the creation of the new club which gave his party its name. In the *Introduction à la Révolution française* he gives a detailed account of the creation of the Feuillant Club. When the Jacobin Club refused to recognise the decree of 15 July declaring the king inviolable, those deputies present, with the exception of Robespierre, Pétion and Buzot, walked out and held a meeting in the Feuillant church adjoining the Assembly. There they decided to secede from the Jacobin Club and found another in the new locale. They would, however, appropriate the official name of the Jacobins, '*Société des amis de la Constitution*', and attempt to take over the provincial network. Barnave recalls: 'neither myself nor any of my friends had any part in the convocation nor the choice of where to meet. In the discussion I spoke tenth or twelfth in favour of seceding from the Jacobins. . . . But I was against the formation of a new club.' That was proposed by Rewbell, 'to prevent the Jacobins remaining the hub' of the affiliated societies and 'corrupting their ethos'. If Barnave did not oppose Rewbell, it was because he thought the harm of forming a new society was less than 'seeing a large number of our colleagues returning out of habit to the Jacobins' and making them even stronger.[75]

That, however, was precisely what happened over the coming weeks and for the same reasons that Barnave and Alexandre gave for not forming a new club. The people who joined the Feuillants lacked the fire and determination of the radicals, who were 'for the most part journalists and scribblers . . . with nothing to lose'. The Feuillants were 'peaceful men and proprietors' with much to lose and so, paradoxically, the very qualities which Barnave extolled doomed them to failure. They were, in modern parlance, 'wishy-washy liberals'. Moreover (another paradox), 'once the Revolution was finished' – again Barnave's aim – they thought that political clubs would no longer be needed. In any case, their political careers were coming to an end and there was no point facing the hostility of the Parisians. Alexandre thought that it would have been hypocritical 'to found a new political club when they themselves had contributed to the [Chapelier] law which had proscribed them' and that it would 'condone the culpable resistance of the Jacobins to the law'.[76]

C.F. Beaulieu, the parliamentary journalist–historian, throws more light on these events. After the 'Massacre', members of the National

Guard, especially the cannoneers, were all for forcibly closing the Jacobin Club, even training their mobile canons on their building where Beaulieu happened to have his lodgings. But 'Lafayette, Barnave and others thought that this would have been an attack on liberty . . . and that the secession of the deputies would be sufficient to neuter the Jacobins.' It nearly worked and Kersaint proposed 'closing their hall and handing over the keys to the Feuillants. But MM Pétion, Robespierre and Buzot opposed him; several deputies who had stayed away through fear gradually returned and the Jacobins reformed' – purged in fact – and were stronger than ever 'thanks to the state of unpopularity and abasement into which the Assembly had fallen'.[77]

Pétion, Robespierre and Buzot, together with Corroller, Royer and Roederer, stayed loyal to the Jacobins. One hundred and seventy-two deputies joined the Feuillants on 16 July but a canny or terrified seventeen waited until the issue of the Champ de Mars was decided before joining on the 18th. These included members of the group which had been associated with Mirabeau: d'André, Duquesnoy and La Marck. The late arrivals also included Emmery and Liancourt.[78]

— TWELVE —

THE REVISION OF THE CONSTITUTION

It would have been much easier for the triumvirs and their new allies d'André, Beaumetz and Le Chapelier to revise the constitution in order to 'make the king reign' had the king been able to negotiate with them from Montmédy in a position of demonstrable independence. But he had been stopped at Varennes and the allies had depleted their patriotic capital merely to save the monarchy. Many deputies who did not want to dethrone the king did not think he should be rewarded either. Moreover, many felt that the constitution on which they had worked (off and on) for two years should not be tampered with.

They found a voice in Buzot, who, on 11 August, declared:

> We demand that the constitution remain exactly as it is because we have sworn to maintain it. If you seek to change one article decreed after the most solemn discussion, there would be nothing to stop you also changing the decrees on non-re-eligibility or attacking the law which states that members of the National Assembly will not be able to become ministers [Barnave's precise aim]. (Applause from the extreme left of the left part of the Assembly – murmurs from other parts of the chamber.) If you reopen the discussion on all the parts of your constitutional act, it could take you two or three months.[1]

Moreover, Buzot sat in the revision committee, as did Pétion, and these men, whom Barnave called closet republicans, led an opposition within the two committees. In setting up the revision committee, the whole idea had been to give the revision authority by including a wide spectrum of opinion, but rainbow coalitions tend to fade like their exemplar.

Therefore, Barnave and his friends had to set about constructing a majority. Theoretically, there were 1,315 deputies all told in the Assembly; but 605 never spoke, 561 spoke only occasionally and only 53 spoke 'very often' and 96 'often'.[2] Duquesnoy makes much of the body of uncommitted but patriotic backbenchers who were swayed by the best arguments and their 'instinct' for the right conduct. He calls them the *bas-côtés*; in the Legislative Assembly, they were the 'stomach'; in the National Convention, they would be called 'the Plain', as opposed to the Mountain, where the radical Jacobins sat. Parties were equated with 'faction' since there was only one right course of action guided by patriotism. But they existed.

Everyone seems to agree that Barnave's party numbered about thirty, or, more precisely, thirty-three.[3] The group, led by Le Chapelier, Beaumetz and d'André, included most of the members of the 89 Club, say seventy. Their group included Duquesnoy, Siéyès, Talleyrand and Fréteau. In the last months of the Constituent Assembly the eight members of the constitutional committee (Talleyrand, Siéyès, Le Chapelier, Target, Thouret, Démeunier, Tronchet, Rabaud de Saint-Étienne), plus the seven of the revision committee – Duport, Barnave and Alexandre de Lameth (the 'triumvirs'), Pétion and Buzot (radicals), and Beaumetz and Clermont-Tonnerre (ex-Monarchiens) – were the nearest thing France had in the period 1789–91 to a government presenting a programme, though like many governments they contained an internal opposition in the persons of Buzot and Pétion.

These two were part of an emergent third party. Hitherto, Cazalès had called his own group (the right) 'the opposition' and, unlike the left, they usually voted as a bloc. They numbered about 300, but then on 29 June, in protest at the suspension of the king, 293 signed a protest against all the acts of the Assembly, saying they would sit but not vote.[4] Their place was taken by an opposition to the left of Barnave's group: the editor of the *Archives Parlementaires* 'noticed the emergence during this discussion [on the king's responsibility debate of 13–15 July] the formation in the Assembly of a third party, as it were, which had existed for some time [that is, since the Jacobin split] but now came out into the open. Robespierre and Pétion were its leaders.'[5] Barnave talked of 'a dozen deputies such as Pétion, Rewbell, Buzot, Robespierre, Dubois de Crancé etc.'[6] Madame Roland put it at forty, which seems reasonable.

Of a similar size was the last group, the Monarchiens, led by Malouet and Clermont-Tonnerre. In February Barnave had deeply wounded Malouet by ridiculing the charitable efforts of his club as offering the people 'poisoned bread'. Malouet was an honourable man who at the start of the Estates-General had shared his and Mirabeau's hope of a strong constitutional monarchy based on alliance with the Third Estate and who, like the other two, had been distressed by the king's apparent betrayal but, instead of attacking him, had remained silent. The two men now came together. Barnave told Malouet, 'I may seem very young to you but I assure you I have aged a lot in a few months.' Malouet replied: 'you have reached the age of maturity with no loss of powers and it is time to put them to good use, for which you have the means'.[7]

Barnave saw Malouet as a bridge to the hard right wing, the 'noirs' whose votes would be essential for major changes in the constitution in line with his agreement with the king and queen, since even if all those who joined the Feuillant Club could be kept in line, the backbenchers would need persuading. But the 'noirs', pursuing their *politique du pire*, preferred to sacrifice the king rather than renounce their hope of restoring the *ancien régime*. Their abstention was pure hypocrisy. All Malouet could offer Barnave was his group of forty. This meant that changes to the constitution would have to be smuggled in by sleight of hand.

⚜

On 8 August Thouret, the rapporteur of the constitutional and revision committees, presented their proposals to the Assembly for discussion clause by clause. On 16 August Marie-Antoinette wrote to Mercy-Argenteau that Barnave's party 'have realised for a week that they are beaten'.[8] Barnave gave the queen a somewhat different picture. The committees had only been defeated on three major matters and two of these defeats, he claimed, strengthened rather than weakened the royal position. The committees, having failed to secure right wing support, did not attempt to revoke the self-denying ordinance. All they aimed for was to repeal the clause preventing a deputy from serving in successive parliaments without a two-year interval between their second and third stints. But they were defeated even on that. Their second defeat 'limited a deputy to standing for election in the département in which he was domiciled'. These two constituted 'a severe wound to liberty but far from enervating government they had the opposite vice of giving it a decided superiority'. What he meant was that they made it more difficult to establish a political career.[9] The clause which Barnave considered to have weakened the monarchy was that which 'forbade the king from selecting the agents of the executive power [especially ministers] from among the members of an expiring legislature'.

But these were not the measures that the king and queen had at heart. Michon argues rightly (as Duquesnoy did at the time) that the king's declaration was the basis of the concordat between the triumvirs and the court.[10] In his declaration the king complained about threats to his safety and slights to his dignity. These matters were addressed by giving him a constitutional guard and by changing his title from 'first functionary' to 'hereditary representative' of the nation.

Louis complained at length about the Jacobin Club; these complaints had been answered by Le Chapelier's legislation and the secession. He complained about the licence of the press and this was addressed. He complained about the Assembly's committees shadowing the ministers and the contempt with which they were treated. But this was a convention, not a constitutional provision, and with skilful management could be addressed during the next Assembly. However, in a note for his *Introduction à la Révolution française*, Barnave wrote, 'Restore the executive power to the plenitude of its functions. Suppress the committees, etc. – the Assembly was against.'[11] It is not clear whether the section after the dash is connected with 'suppress the committees' – if so, it marks an unrecorded defeat at this time.

From within the committees, Buzot and Pétion tried to revise the constitution in a more radical direction. On the first day's debate, Buzot wanted to insert a clause into the Declaration of Rights to the effect that 'the king will not have the prerogative of mercy' – the king cared passionately about this and said so in his Declaration. Pétion thought that the guarantees of press freedom were insufficient. Duport tartly observed that if those two had honoured the committees with their presence, they could have spared the Assembly a fruitless discussion. On the 9th Thouret told the Assembly that 'the difficulties raised yesterday were ironed out in the committee which MM Buzot and Pétion attended' – the prerogative of mercy would be discussed when they came to the administration of justice.[12] But this was only a truce.

On 27 August Beaumetz, on behalf of the 'almost unanimous' finance and constitutional committees, proposed 'an amendment to article V.IV.II charging the ministers to give their opinion on the way to raise the funds necessary to provide for state expenditure' – in other words, a budget. Most of the seventy-seven members of the finance committee tended to be moderates. Those from Barnave's party included Alexandre Lameth, Laborde, d'Aiguillon and Noailles. Beaumetz's amendment was designed to be more acceptable to the Assembly, which the day before had adjourned his proposal that the king should simply be given the initiative in financial legislation. And in the evening Barère had denounced the measure in the Feuillant Club itself on the grounds that it 'would amount to giving the ministers the initiative in fiscal legislation'. 'Precisely', Beaumetz replied, 'this is an accusation to which we offer no defence. Since the king did not have a veto over financial legislation, he needed the initiative or the Assembly would be a one-chamber dictatorship.'[13] The amendment was defeated. It had been a serious attempt to answer the king's criticism in his manifesto that he had been 'rendered a stranger' to financial matters of which he had 'some understanding'.

The episode demonstrates the triumvirs' vulnerability towards the end of the revision process: with two strong dissentients in the committee, they were even attacked in the Feuillant Club, which should have been their power base. On 21–23 August there had been strong opposition in the Feuillants to a measure designed to answer the king's complaint that he had been left at the mercy of insurrections: the creation of a constitutional guard of 1,200 infantry and 600 cavalry. Malès, Tracy and Goupil said the guard should not be military! Rewbell, Salles and Viallard did not want a guard in any form. Duport defended the measure in the Feuillants and he and Alexandre de Lameth pushed it through the Assembly in the teeth of fierce opposition from Pétion, Robespierre, Roederer and Vadier.[14]

Throughout the month of August Feuillant members were drifting back to the Jacobins. The first to slip back was Antoine, who regaled the *société mère* with his tale of apostasy and recantation, generously accepted. Another was the honey-tongued Barère, who promised Robespierre future good behaviour and as the spokesman of the Committee of Public Safety would become 'the Anacreon of the guillotine'. Successive batches of apostates returned to the bosom of the *société mère*, including some who had absented themselves from the Jacobins but who had scrupled to join the Feuillants. On 21 August Robespierre proclaimed in the Jacobins that 'there was no longer a single patriotic member of the Feuillants who was not resolved to rejoin us'.[15]

On the 10th the Assembly voted on whether the king should be styled a 'hereditary representative' or merely the 'first functionary' of the nation, as in the first draft. Barnave was behind this change and he turned the debate with a subtle distinction: 'what distinguishes the representative from the public functionary is that the representative can will for the nation [for example, in exercising his suspensive veto or signing treaties], whereas the public functionary can merely carry out its instructions'. It was Thouret who on 28 March had proposed that the king be called 'a public functionary' and the dauphin 'first reserve'.[16] But he gamely proposed the change and was backed by d'André and Rewbel, as well as Barnave. Though Rewbel was a radical who had often opposed Barnave, for example on the rights of people of colour, it was he who proposed seceding to the Feuillants and he did not rejoin the Jacobins. They were opposed by Pétion, Buzot, Prieur, Roederer and Robespierre.[17]

On 11 August the Assembly discussed voting qualifications: the constitutional draft envisaged two-tier elections, with primary assemblies choosing electoral colleges, which chose the deputies. The committee proposed lowering the monetary qualification to be a deputy but increasing it to paying taxation equivalent to forty days' labour for the electoral college, a fourfold increase.

We have seen that Barnave believed that political power derived not just from wealth but from the education it enabled. Now he repeated that 'poverty prevents the acquisition of enlightenment for those who are perpetually struggling with want'. Such people would also be more open to corruption: 'poor electors could be bribed by as little as a pint of beer as in England. Corruption would multiply as flies on dung.' He was not, he explained, aiming to exclude 'farmers and artisans' from the electoral college, but rather 'scribblers and journalists' and this jibe was taken by all, including the man himself, to refer to Brissot, who was desperate to represent Paris in the next Assembly. This caused outrage and Barnave struggled to reply: 'I am going to say; I am going to say; I am going to develop' – each time interrupted by boos. Finally, he was allowed to make a long speech, distinguishing between direct democracy as in ancient Greece and representative democracy in a large country such as France. The decision was adjourned on Vernier's proposal to the end of the revision, when on 27 August the qualification for the electoral college was retained but changed from a taxation to an income one.

Those supporting the committee were: Thouret, Beaumetz, Barnave, Pison, Tronchet, Gérard, Lavie, Anson, d'André; and those against: Pétion, Buzot, Robespierre, Prugnon, Roederer, Salle, Maupassant, Gombert, Fréteau, Goupilleau, Camus, Grégoire, Guillaume, Goupil and the charmingly named Laville-aux-Bois. Salle had swung the debate on the king's inviolability.[18]

⚜

The key vote took place on 13 August. When Thouret read article VIII preventing deputies from sitting in three consecutive legislatures (an article from which the committee had minuted and published its dissent), Saint-Martin observed that no mention had yet been made of the article forbidding a deputy to accept an appointment in the gift of the crown for four years after leaving the Assembly. Forced onto the defensive, Thouret argued that in a time of revolution distrust of the executive was appropriate, but not in the settled state; therefore, he had not regarded the prohibition as part of the constitution. Duport weakly argued that the clause inserting the prohibition had been rushed through, maybe in an empty House. Lanjuinais, Guillaume, Saint-Martin, Goupil and Roederer argued that the four-year ban should be reinstated. Buzot proposed that the intervals between an ex-deputy returning to Parliament or taking a crown appointment should be standardised at two years and this was accepted.[19]

In the course of the session Guillaume, a little-known Parisian lawyer who had recently been asserting himself, caused a tumult by attributing the bad feeling in the House to 'several serious omissions in the committee's submissions which the *true* friends of liberty thought they could detect'. Stung by the insult, Barnave sprung to the main rostrum, but Guillaume from another one on the far-left continued his tirade. After twenty minutes this stereophonic row was finally ended by the president, who told each of the protagonists to say his piece separately. Barnave did not think Guillaume merited an individual reply but rather saw his intervention as an example of the general mistrust of the Assembly for the committee: 'I have to tell you that yesterday we met as a committee and only one question was raised: given what seems to be a general disposition of the Assembly towards us ought we not to resign.' Stunned 'silence was followed by murmurs and applause'. The committee had, Thouret explained, sat up till midnight, and concluded 'unanimously' that the obstacles put in the way of re-election, combined with the ban on the king appointing departing deputies, 'have removed the only means which remained for making the constitution work and establishing a real government'. Echoing Barnave, he said that the committee had already pared the resources of government down to the very bone.[20] All Barnave could obtain (on 15 August) was the right of the ministers to speak in the Legislative Assembly when they wished.

There was an interesting duel between Barnave and Roederer, an Alsatian ex-*parlementaire*. Borrowing from d'Holbach's *L'homme machine* (1747), Barnave was wont to describe governments as machines; now he wanted the constitution to work as a perpetual motion machine, one that was not tinkered with by later legislatures. If lesser constitutional articles were reclassified as ordinary statutes, later legislatures could change them without usurping constitutional powers. That would minimise the need for national (constitutional) conventions, which would have kept France in a state of perpetual revolution rather than regulated motion. But – to continue the analogy – he thought that (given the prohibitions the Assembly had inserted) the machine needed to be run in by those operatives who had set it up. He thought it was necessary for the Constituent Assembly to continue in session for another 'five or six months' to run in the engine. However, he could only find 'some fifteen or twenty' deputies to support him and the issue was not raised.

In his notes for the *Introduction à la Révolution française*,[21] he writes, elliptically, 'A mechanic . . . A doctor . . . It is by the same mechanism that a change in government is operated in the body politic. Both are needed.' Two constant themes in his writings are machines and prolonging life. Now it is the life of the constitutional machine which needs to be prolonged. In particular, it is the machinery of government, which, having been 'partially dismantled', needs to be reconstructed.

Roederer, however, 'wanted to examine the machine of government not through the eyes of a mechanic but as an artist, a social engineer'. So it was the spirit rather than the mechanism of the constitution that mattered. Liberty should be like a religion: if departing deputies were denied access to the ministry, there would be no excuse for the people to doubt their patriotism. And if (to answer Barnave) noble ambition needed an outlet,[22] such 'men would find enough places in the gift of the people without seeking those from the executive power'.[23]

Barnave believed that this indeed was the plan of Robespierre and Pétion: block the royal road to power to their opponents and gain an equal power through election. This is exactly what they did by being elected to the central criminal court and then, in Pétion's case, by becoming mayor of Paris. Barnave alludes none too subtly to this in his speech. The real enemies, he claimed, were not the aristocrats, but rather 'those who have wanted to remain in a state of perpetual revolution. Men who affecting the guise of patriotism . . . in order to reach the most august positions have presumed to take people in with this new mask and new name and have joined up with miserable scribblers', such as Brissot.[24]

⚜

On 29 August Pétion warned the Jacobins that the military committee (reporter Alexandre de Lameth) was going to propose sending deputies to the provinces as commissioners to enforce decrees. Michelet took this motive at its face value and as desirable,[25] but Pétion saw it as a pretext to get 'patriotic' deputies out of the way for the final stages of revising the constitution. Buzot added that this was no time 'to strip the Assembly of thirty or forty patriots' when they were 'needed at their posts'. Their decision, for example, on 'whether the decrees on nobility should be kept as constitutional or reclassified as ordinary statutes would decide whether the Assembly still merited the confidence it had hitherto enjoyed'.

Martineau called for Buzot to be called to order for insulting the Assembly. But all that happened was that d'André, hitherto the constitutional committees' staunchest supporter, got up to say that everyone acknowledged that the commissars should not be dispatched until the constitution had been finished and that it was a slander to suggest that any deputy wanted to reclassify the constitutional decrees. He for one would oppose this with all his strength – this was greeted with 'Applause'. Buzot's motion to defer sending the commissioners was adopted.

The whole episode cannot have lasted more than five minutes, yet it seemed to confirm the suspicion that Barnave and his friends were seeking to achieve by the back door what they had not this strength to demand by the front. Re-classifying was seen as a trick, as was denuding the Assembly of their opponents. They were shamed into silence. Michelet wrote of this episode, 'on the 30th [August] . . . they weakened, they scattered, their majority eluded them, and with it their power – forever, because power was the issue'.[26]

On 3 September, the revision was completed and Lord Gower concluded: 'the committees shewed a desire to give more energy to the executive power but all attempts at that kind have been strenuously resisted by the Assembly'.[27] Robespierre, however, considered that the king had obtained a good deal and in a withering speech on 1 September warned the triumvirs not to get the king to make his acceptance of the constitution conditional on changes which would remove the last 'debris of our original decrees' and give no alternative but '[for us] to resume either our chains or our arms'. 'Immediately', Montlosier relates – the official accounts are flat – 'the Lameth party, seeing where this attack was leading, roused themselves. Duport, the most ardent of them all, advanced towards the tribune and threatened Robespierre, hurling abuse at him. Robespierre, in no wise disconcerted, just said: "M. le prèsident, kindly order M. Duport to refrain from insulting me if he wants to remain standing in my presence." The extremity of the left wing and the galleries cheered fit to burst their lungs.'

Robespierre resumed: 'I presume there is no one in this Assembly so cowardly as to negotiate with the court on any article of our constitution, so perfidious as to get it to propose changes which he is too ashamed to propose himself . . . [because some clauses] block his ambition and cupidity . . . [thereby proclaiming] that he saw in the Revolution merely a path to self-aggrandisement'. Raising his voice, he said: 'I demand that each one of you swear that he will never conspire with the executive power to change any article of the constitution on pain of being declared a traitor to the *patrie*.' While the tribunes cheered, and Barnave's group 'fumed', 'all the right wing roared with laughter'.[28]

⚜

It is no surprise that Barnave could only find fifteen or twenty deputies prepared to prolong the session of the Constituent Assembly. Indeed, it was d'André who demanded that the deferred elections be finally held and the Assembly dissolved – he was greeted by rapturous applause.[29] All hope of obtaining emolument from a position in the gift of the crown having evaporated, he was anxious to set up a chain of grocery stores, thereby gaining the soubriquet *l'épicier*. The same feeling that Barnave wanted to change the constitution by sleight of hand went with the suspicion that he wanted a Long Parliament. But two years of revolution had left the country and the Assembly exhausted. And the same lassitude which Barnave detected in the Assembly and throughout the country meant that, as he acknowledged, the deputies 'were impatient to see their families again' or, as Dubois-Crancé said, rebuild their careers and their fortunes. Crancé thought it wrong to perpetuate the Assembly, 'an organisation of notables designed for the thirteenth century', in which 600 members represented constituencies which no longer existed and '400 at least would have stood no chance in elections opened up to all Frenchmen by the new constitution'.[30]

It was not just that election by orders, already obsolete in 1789, was now redundant but that the Assembly by its very achievements had rendered itself unrepresentative: the provinces had gone as well as the orders, but also the kind of office which had conferred the prestige that led to the election of many deputies from the Third Estate. When the king (and others) said the primary elections boded no good, he did not just mean that they were throwing up radicals but (which is not quite the same thing) that a different category of deputies was likely to result. The same motives which produced the eligibility decrees militated against Barnave's attempt to mitigate them.

This lassitude was reflected in attendance in the Assembly. 'It did not regularly number more than 150; on the most critical day, the morrow of . . . [the Champ de Mars Massacre] only 253 deputies sat.'[31] Michelet speculates that most members had gone home, or were in committees or brothels.

A striking feature of the revision debates was the absence of Barnave's core party. Michelet wrote:

> When I say the constitutionalists, I speak above all of Barnave. He alone seemed to preserve life, drive and hope. Nothing can express the weariness of the others, their ennui, their nausea, their discouragement. Patiently they awaited the blessed hour which would give them rest. . . . In the midst of a general malaise, the life of the Assembly, the hope of the monarchy, the desire to save it were concentrated in the head of a twenty-eight-year-old Barnave. The disparate coalition which had rallied four-fifths of the left of the Assembly, united two enemies, Lafayette and Lameth, [and] almost destroyed the Jacobins [had evaporated].

But why, Michelet asks, did Barnave 'throw himself into this enterprise . . . with hope, shall I say, or ardent despair'? And he answers, following the letter of Gouvernet to Bouillé that we have quoted, that his encounter with Marie-Antoinette had melted his heart. How else to explain the change in this man whose 'habitual self-sufficiency, whose noble, crisp and cold speeches' such as those on colonial policy 'were in no way those of a dreamer'? He did not pride himself on a sentimental discourse, 'unlike all the other men of the period from Louis XVI down to Robespierre.'[32] The reader will judge whether Michelet's verdict was itself 'sentimental.'

Michelet thought that the Champ de Mars incident had knocked the stuffing out of all the constitutionalists except Barnave; and that they felt a kind of shame in reversing much of their constitutional work. Though he did his best to hide it – from himself and from the queen – Barnave himself shared something of their pessimism. Encountering Barnave strolling in the Tuileries gardens 'sometime after the return from Varennes', Montlosier 'quizzed him on his hopes for the future; he made no bones about telling me in no uncertain terms that he regarded it as impossible to establish any kind of liberty in France. Perhaps it was just a passing mood . . . [brought on] by his exasperation at the bad disposition of the Assembly.'[33] However, the baron de Staël's dispatch of 4 September noted that the triumvirs 'now seem to think that the constitution is unworkable. I know for a certainty [from his wife Madame de Staël?] that *le sieur* Barnave said that future Assemblies should have no more influence than a council [*sic* for 'assembly'] of Notables and that all power should reside in the government.'[34]

The journal of the right, the *Actes des Apôtres*, was quick to pick up this change of attitude in a short satirical play: '*Conversation de ces Messieurs*' – the original triumvirate enlarged to a 'decemvirate' by the inclusion of committee members. The cast, in order of appearance, is: Thouret, Alexandre Lameth, Talleyrand, d'André, Beaumetz, Barnave, Le Chapelier, Desmeuniers, Duport. The trio of Le Chapelier, Beaumetz and d'André is lumped together with the triumvirate as it had been since Mirabeau's death. They all agree that patronage is the key to power. Desmeuniers argued that they must make not just the ministry open to deputies but 'all possible places in the Administration . . . municipalities, treasuries, tribunals' – the lot. 'Honours and profits', gloated Duport, always regarded as the most ambitious, 'we'll have it all! Desmeuniers, you will be mayor of Paris or royal librarian with 72,000 livres a year to sort out the king's [extensive collection of] books.' They would win over the deputies in the next Assembly 'by holding out the prospect of being ministers after two years because', d'André said, 'each of us will have made enough to retire with no regrets'.[35] Other sources give a full list of cabinet posts: Barnave, marine and colonies; Alexandre de Lameth, war; Duport, justice; Thouret or Beaumetz, interior; Le Chapelier, finance; d'André, keeper of the seals; Broglie, foreign affairs.[36] For the extreme right, as well as the extreme left, had come to the same conclusions about the motives of '*ces Messieurs*'.

DRAFTING THE KING'S LETTER ACCEPTING THE CONSTITUTION

On 3 September a torchlight delegation of sixty deputies took the constitution to the king for his consideration. They sported powdered wigs instead of the usual knee-length boots and canes. The king was given diverse advice on whether he should accept the constitution 'pure and simple' or make it conditional – rejection was tantamount to abdication and was not seriously considered. A memorandum of Pellenc's which 'was given to the king in the first days of September' states that the triumvirs 'desired the king to propose the changes [to the constitution] they could not obtain themselves, hoping thereby to revenge themselves on the Assembly . . . or to find a new way to force it to revoke its decrees which block their path to public employment – as if the king should be counselled by their ambition'.[37] The queen was aware of the accusation for on 1 September Barnave had told her that attacks in the Assembly were directed not at the ministers but at 'certain individuals who were suspected of wanting to leave a door open for their return to public life'.[38]

If the triumvirs entertained any such notions, they soon abandoned them. Bertrand de Molleville noted that

> in a [ministerial] committee in the apartments of the keeper of the seals [*du Tertre*], Duport and Barnave were alarmed at the attacks that the Jacobins were unleashing against them in all their journals and even in the Assembly itself, where Robespierre had denounced them by name as traitors to the *patrie*; they forecast such misfortunes if the king gave a conditional acceptance of the constitution that they and the ministers present determined the king to accept the constitutional act purely and simply.[39]

The elaboration of the king's letter of acceptance involved many hands. Barnave told the queen that it would have been far simpler if he had written one out for her to add her comments. But she told him that the king would make a compilation from several sources, his usual practice. There were drafts from: d'André, the Chevalier de Monsin, the abbé Maury (who counselled rejection), the finance minister de Lessart and two from Montmorin (bullet points and his draft). Louis also consulted Malesherbes as he had done through his reign and Malouet.[40]

There is a brief draft for the king's letter of acceptance in Barnave's papers – other sheets may be lost. Barnave provides the king with the sort of patriotic curriculum vitae which became increasingly necessary as the Revolution progressed, accumulating baggage on its way. The opening of the letter the king sent was taken almost verbatim from Barnave's draft but very little else – those passages that were are indicated.

> BARNAVE: I have carefully examined the constitution you have presented for my acceptance. I accept it and will see that it is enforced. This word satisfies the legal requirements but my character and the interests of the nation require that I explain myself with greater frankness [crossed through and replaced with 'development'].
>
> KING'S LETTER: I have carefully examined the constitution you have presented for my acceptance. I accept it and will see that it is enforced. This declaration would have sufficed in other times but my character and the interests of the nation require that I make known my motives.

> BARNAVE: Attentive to the voice of public opinion, I consulted it on the recall of the former bodies of magistrates [the Parlements]; on the choice of my ministers and on the major operations of government.[41]
>
> KING'S LETTER: The nation can have no doubt that from the beginning of my reign I have desired its happiness. This has been my constant rule.

Barnave's next page is in very condensed note form – just the phrases in quotation marks, which I have expanded where necessary:

> I instituted 'provincial assemblies' – under the administrations of Necker and Brienne.
>
> 'When the deficit' came to light, I convoked the Assembly of 'Notables'.
>
> I convoked the 'Estates-General' and 'doubled' the representation of 'the Third Estate'.

I ordered 'the reunion of orders' on 26 June 1789.

'Sadness at the disorders'.

I gave my 'acceptance to individual [constitutional] decrees in order to facilitate their execution'.

KING'S LETTER: I accepted its [the constitution's] parts even before I could judge the ensemble and if the disorders which accompanied almost every phase of the Revolution desolated me, I hoped that . . .

BARNAVE: 'I hoped that the completion of the constit[ution]'

KING'S LETTER: 'the constitution was about to be completed and yet the authority of the laws seemed to weaken each day'.

BARNAVE: 'All opposed' – obscure.

Of course, there may have been other drafts and Montmorin's includes a passage on the 'self-denying ordinance' which is almost identical to words and sentiments Barnave writes elsewhere:

> Finally, you have deprived me of the freedom to take any agents of execution from the members of the legislatures – neither when they are serving nor for two years thereafter. However, confidence is only enjoyed by those marked out by public opinion and this confidence is as necessary for all my agents as it is for myself. A generous sentiment inspired the National Assembly [to rule themselves out]; but the public interest was also a duty and the functions of the executive power are as essential to the common good as those given by the votes of the people. I can therefore only regret that public opinion can no longer guide me in my most important choices.[42]

If Barnave had hoped that the king would include this passage, he was disappointed. The king did, however, stress, though in less detail and with less emphasis, the changes which had been made to the constitution during the revision, without which he could not have accepted it and to achieve which he had 'distanced himself from Paris' – the same reference to the flight to Varennes occurs in Montmorin's draft and the king's message.[43]

To give the illusion that the king's acceptance was free, he was allowed to travel the 7 miles down the Seine to Saint-Cloud to ponder his decision, though d'André had advised him that this was a farce, especially as the dauphin was being kept in Paris as a hostage. He should give his assent in Paris – nowhere in France was any safer and if he gave it from abroad, he was doomed. Leopold, he said, did not care whether the king was free or not – the eighteenth century was not noted for morality in international relations.[44]

Marie-Antoinette knew perfectly well that the Declaration of Pillnitz of 27 August from the emperor and the king of Prussia was hot air. It stipulated that, provided the other powers assisted, 'then and in that case (*alors et dans ce cas*) the co-signatories would intervene to restore the king of France to his rightful position'. The emperor knew full well that English determination to remain neutral removed any obligation on his part to intervene in France. He wrote to Kaunitz: '"then and in that case" is with me the law and the prophets. If England fails us, the case is non-existent.'[45]

In fact, the emperor, Kaunitz, his chancellor, the quadrumvirs (for Méréville and his father were involved here), Montmorin and Pellenc were all working closely together. Kaunitz informed Montmorin that though he detested the constitution, Austria had no intention of intervening.[46]

What really concerned both Leopold and Marie-Antoinette was whether the constitution could be made to stick.[47] This, Barnave argued, all depended on the way the machine of government operated: 'an inept government would be able to derive little from these great prerogatives; but a clever one with public confidence' and given the king's permanence and the legislature's transience 'could become a virtual legislator', especially with his possession of a suspensive veto.

But would he be allowed to use it? Marie-Antoinette asked, prophetically:

> With what can we repress the anarchy which is erupting everywhere with renewed vigour? With the law? But it is nothing without force and does that exist. The same argument can be applied to the next legislature. Despite the decrees, the constitution and the oaths, who can guarantee that it will not want to change everything and that the republican party will not regain the upper hand? If that happens, where is the force to prevent it? I would not have these anxieties were it not that the next legislature is about to open.

It would be fine if '*ces Messieurs*' could supervise their work, but 'neither force nor the king's powers nor the stability [existence] of the ministry are sufficiently established to navigate all these rocks successfully'. To calm her fears, Barnave told her that 'there was every indication that the majority in the next legislature will be sensible'; but in his manifesto Louis had gloomily noted, 'if one can detect any disposition on the part . . . [of the primary assemblies] to go back on anything it is in order to destroy the remains of the monarchy and set up a metaphysical and doctrinaire form of government [a republic] which would not work'.[48]

⚜

On 13 September the king's letter was read out in the Assembly. It symbolised the link between the revision and the king's declaration. He said that if he had been presented with the constitution 'before I distanced myself from Paris' he would have rejected it! But subsequently, 'You have shown a desire to restore order, you have considered the lack of discipline in the army; you have recognised the necessity for curbing the licence of the press.' They had also downgraded to ordinary 'regulations', subject to repeal, 'several articles which had been presented to me as constitutional'. Foremost among those was the civil constitution of the clergy. He ended with a flash of candour: 'I should, however, be telling less than the truth if I said I perceived in the executive and administrative resources sufficient vigour to activate and preserve unity in all the parts of so vast an empire; but since opinions are at present divided on these matters, I consent that experience alone shall decide.'[49] 'The left part [of the Assembly] and all the galleries rang with applause.'

On 14 September, as king of the French rather than king of France and Navarre, wearing the red cordon of the Saint-Louis, the only order left, Louis XVI took the oath to the constitution before the Assembly, he standing, they, with the solitary exception of Malouet, seated with their hats on.[50] Both Louis and (watching in a box) Marie-Antoinette were mortified, especially as the king had not been provided with a throne – just an ordinary chair covered with blue velvet strewn with the lilies of the old France. Back home a tearful Louis apologised to the queen for the degradation he had brought to a Habsburg archduchess. She complained to Barnave, who tried to brush it off; it did not really matter – chairs, thrones, sitting, standing, hats on, hats off – were only symbolic. Yet he well knew the value of symbols.

The crowds had cheered them back to the Tuileries but a now cynical Marie-Antoinette was not fooled: 'I know how to reckon that; most of the time it is paid for.' Happiness was gone forever; she lived only for her son. Her hair had gone white at the temples on 6 October. But when she took her bonnet off after the return from Varennes, she revealed to Madame de Campan 'hair as white as a woman of seventy'.[51] Acceptance of the constitution meant qualified liberty, but with it came different problems: 'I am reduced to fearing the moment when they will seem to be giving us a kind of liberty. At least in our present state of total nullity, we have nothing with which to reproach ourselves.' Nevertheless, in the following months she would, with Barnave, be more actively engaged in government than at any time in her life.

— THIRTEEN —

GOVERNING IN SECRET

Barnave did not return to Grenoble until January 1792, setting off home on the 5th. The reasons he gives either for his staying on or for his departing tell us little. In the preliminary examination before his trial, he was quizzed about all this:

> Q. When did you leave Paris? A. At the start of January 1792, having before that lived alternately in Paris and on some of the surrounding country estates and in particular at Osney near Pontoise in a house belonging to Charles Lameth [18 miles from Paris]. Q. Why did you stay on in Paris after the closure of the Constituent Assembly? A. Initially to relax and enjoy the company of my friends and from the end of October I was detained by illness.[1]

We do not know the nature of the illness – perhaps sheer exhaustion, perhaps hypochondria. He could not give the most probable explanation: that Marie-Antoinette persuaded him to stay on.

The only contemporaneous references to his planned departure in October come in two letters to him from the queen. Crucially, the first, dated 13 October, implies that Barnave had intended to return to Paris and had promised to give her some memoranda to guide her during his absence: 'I await with impatience the papers which M. Barnave promised to give me before his departure and I hope that during his absence he will not forget the end of our conversation [on 5 October]. There can be no mistrust.'[2] A week later Barnave was still in Paris and still intending to leave the city. Marie-Antoinette made a cryptic reference to it: 'In our last conversation I predicted some of the things which are happening now. I was wrong only on the timing. I thought I would let M. Barnave arrive back in Dauphiné before arousing his suspicions. For my own part I have nothing with which to reproach myself, having employed every possible means to bring about a favourable outcome.'[3] The natural reading is that Marie-Antoinette predicted that the new Assembly would not be as docile as Barnave assumed – she actually warned him of this back in August – but did not want her concerns to put him off his planned departure for a well-earned period of recuperation. He would learn soon enough that he was needed back in Paris.

Then, he tells us, he stayed on another fortnight or so to keep an eye on the Feuillant Club, which had had an influx of new members. Naturally there is no hint here of what he was really doing – except this: 'It was during this sojourn that the crime was supposed to have been committed which has given rise to my accusation.' The 'crime', as we shall see, was that of advising the king on the use of his veto. But this was just the tip of the iceberg, one that remained submerged for more than a hundred years: for during this period, he and the queen were directing the government by letter.

BARNAVE AND MARIE-ANTOINETTE MEET AGAIN

The king was back on his tottering throne and the new Assembly opened on 1 October. For reasons both political and personal Barnave and Marie-Antoinette were desperate to see each other. Meeting was dangerous but it happened. The queen had not seen Barnave since their return from Epernay. One of the main things which needed to be discussed was the renewal of the ministry due to Montmorin's pending retirement – long delayed, it occurred on 31 October. 'These matters should be decided in a conversation', Marie-Antoinette told Barnave. Madame Campan's account of the difficulties and dangers of organising a meeting with Barnave would seem fabricated 'cloak and dagger' stuff did Marie-Antoinette's own account not match them.[4]

Campan relates that she had waited for hours 'hand on the latch of the little entresol door' where Barnave was to enter but that the queen had taken over the watch herself. Marie-Antoinette's corroborating account is:

> I finally decided to see *ces Messieurs*. The time fixed was Saturday 1 October at 7.30 p.m. It was Alexandre Lameth and Barnave who were to have come. I had waited at the door for three-quarters of an hour when Jarjayes came to tell me that one of his acquaintances had stopped him on his way just as he was about to enter; that *ces Messieurs*, already alarmed by the crowd and the visibility on their route, had run off even as he spoke. It was this account that made me write the following note:
>
> 'The person [Jarjayes] has just informed me of the contretemps. I can't make tomorrow as there is a game of cards scheduled. I will be in my private apartments at 7 p.m. I am trying to find a safer way you can enter undetected.'
>
> Barnave and Alexandre Lameth want to come. Duport is decidedly against.

Marie-Antoinette reciprocated this coldness of Duport's, telling Barnave that overcoming her reluctance to include him in the correspondence was proof of her sincerity.[5]

Barnave replied that they

> couldn't repeat the experiment until they found a less dangerous way. It is not only our lives which would be compromised the moment we were recognised but we would instantly cease to be of any utility. And the large number of enemies we have been obliged to make who are presently constrained by the force of public opinion would fall on us with renewed vigour since our mysterious proceedings would authorise their suspicions. The queen should see these fears as a new proof of our sincerity and zeal.[6]

The queen finally saw Barnave and Lameth on 5 October and again on the 12th – this time possibly Barnave came alone. He refers to this encounter several times in the rest of the correspondence.[7] For the queen the main point of the meeting was surely to persuade Barnave to stay on and help her to govern. But since meeting the queen was perilous, Barnave devised a system of government based on the letter, continuing the correspondence of the summer.

HOW GOVERNMENT OPERATED

To minimise what he called the 'shortcomings of government', Barnave devised a method of control. A minister who has the confidence of himself and the queen should 'transmit' his advice, '*after laying it before the queen by letter* . . . openly to the king and council' (Barnave's emphasis).[8] The comte de Ségur had been his first choice, a diplomat acceptable to himself and the queen, but they settled on Duport du Tertre, the minister of justice. He had been an enemy of the queen, but he had mellowed and was, according to Molleville, who now became the naval minister, 'attached to the constitution more by gratitude for raising him from being a lowly clerk to the most prestigious post in the kingdom after the king'. 'Lowly clerk' was a slight exaggeration: prior to being made justice minister, with Barnave's backing, on 20 September 1790, after the collapse of the Necker Administration, du Tertre had been deputy mayor and public prosecutor of the Commune.

We have seen his extensive dealings with Barnave during the session of the Constituent Assembly. And after the dissolution of that Assembly, du Tertre 'continued in intimacy with some of those who had composed it; namely the Lameths, Barnave and Adrien Duport, who were every day at his home: he did nothing without consulting them'.[9] Du Tertre was characterised by the finance minister de Lessart as 'the senior minister and in some respects the chief of the council' – 'chef du Conseil', an echo of its *ancien régime* namesake.[10] He became Barnave and Marie-Antoinette's conduit to the ministers, the mechanism being: letters between Barnave and the queen to thrash out a policy, transmission to du Tertre to be finalised in the committee, thence to the king in his council for a rubber stamp. Gouverneur Morris picked up something of this, reporting to George Washington, 'This Keeper of the Seals constantly communicated everything that passed in council to his coadjutors.'[11]

In the Versailles phase of Louis XVI's reign, the king had always presided over the committees which prepared the work of the council.[12] In the constitutional phase these committees met without the king, either in the residence of Duport du Tertre, or in a room in the Tuileries specially set aside for them. Furthermore, the king followed the advice of the committee. For example, Bertrand de Molleville wanted the king to act against an article in Brissot's *Patriote français* and sent Louis a letter on the subject. But Louis observed that the matter lay in the department of du Tertre as minister of justice and added, 'I shall await the determination of the committee.'[13] This procedure – (1) epistolary discussion between Marie-Antoinette and Barnave; (2) committee; and (3) transference by du Tertre to the council – was adopted over important decisions during this period: the formation of the king's constitutional guard and its uniform, and the Assembly's punitive legislation against the émigrés and refractory priests.

Pellenc analysed the modus operandi of what he called 'les Lameths'. The ministers, he said, were 'evidently and almost publicly' directed by them. They also directed the Feuillant Club. The result was that the king (who followed the ministers' 'impulsion'), the right wing of the Assembly and the triumvirs 'formed a single party, a single army'. Pellenc thought that the above analysis of the triumvirs' modus operandi was a 'given' which one needed to grasp in order to understand the political situation. Pellenc, however, observed that the right wing on which the triumvirs increasingly relied was a 'minority'.[14] They had to bring round the uncommitted to achieve anything against a more determined and better organised left wing.

AN EXAMPLE OF THE WORKING RELATIONSHIP BETWEEN BARNAVE AND MARIE-ANTOINETTE: THE ORGANISATION OF THE KING'S CONSTITUTIONAL GUARD

Barnave wanted the guard to be organised along patriotic lines, notably by getting the departmental directorates to nominate 500 or 600 out of the total of 1,800 from their local National Guard. The patronage would also weld the departmental administrations to the regime. Marie-Antoinette agreed, but was worried that if their choice of deputies to the legislative was anything to go by, the départements would send radicals for a body whose primary purpose was to afford the royal family protection against another 5 October rather than fraternising with the assailants.[15] She was proved right – the moderate départements sent moderate men, the radical départements sent *enragés*, who immediately joined the Jacobin Club and denounced the guard itself as counter-revolutionary.[16]

Another difficulty concerned the uniform of the new guard. Barnave thought that it should comprise the three national colours of the Revolution: red, white and blue. So if the body of the uniform were white, the collar and facings should be blue and red. Moreover, the blue should be dark blue, *bleu du roi*, after Louis's dark blue eyes, which also gave a new colour to the Sèvres porcelain palette. Sky blue would remind the people of foreign regiments. Marie-Antoinette did not like this idea and she came up with a compromise – why not choose the colours of the former grenadiers who had enjoyed an illustrious career? Surely, she said, 'that would be very French', and the main colour was indeed *bleu de roi*. 'The points made by *ces Messieurs* are fair and would have been incorporated. So it will be like the former grenadiers of France.' However, she omitted to say that the facings of this uniform would be yellow and Barnave observed that *ventre-de-biche*, doeskin, was used by the émigrés at Coblenz.

That may well be the case, replied Marie-Antoinette, but my facings will be daffodil yellow. She added that it was too late to change the order, which had already gone out to the suppliers. 'The inconvenience of sky blue having been avoided, no one could object to jonquil facings which everyone recognised as the colours of the grenadiers.' Also, her proposal would be cheaper. And the guard could wear the national cockade in their hats. But Barnave persisted: 'the three colours will unite the people against the Jacobins. Yellow will unite the people with the Jacobins against the king.' Marie-Antoinette caved in, even thanking Barnave for his 'persistence'. She would try to change the order without arousing suspicion that the change had been dictated by secret advisers, 'this matter having been already definitively settled'. But it was too late to change the order and Barnave sulked: 'Since the matter has been settled there is no point discussing it.'[17]

Trivial perhaps, the gradations between sky blue and *bleu de roi* – Marie-Antoinette and Barnave were not artists, when all was said and done, though in fact she was the patronne of Vigéele Brun and he had studied painting as a boy.[18] And the stomach of a roe deer bore scant resemblance to a daffodil. But these were symbols in an age of symbolism. After all, did not Artois's grandson (Henri V to his adherents) turn down the offer of the crown because he would not surrender the white flag for the tricolour? As Barnave told the queen, 'the French can be led by ribbons'. This heated haggling over colours, replicated over more important matters, is perhaps the best indication of Marie-Antoinette's sincerity in her dealing with Barnave: would she have argued the toss over a constitutional uniform if she had been banking on a foreign intervention to restore the insignia of old France?

More important than the uniform was to have good relations between the king's bodyguard and the Parisian National Guard. Marie-Antoinette had got off to a bad start by having the king appoint the duc de Cossé-Brissac as the commander of his guard. Barnave told her that everyone was retailing the story that when interviewing recruits, he had asked them if they were patriots. When they inevitably said yes, the commander had replied, 'in that case your place is at the front; the king has no need of patriots in his guard'. Marie-Antoinette replied that if he had used these words, it was indeed blameworthy, but it was unlikely that he had been so stupid.[19] Indeed.

On 1 October the Legislative Assembly finally opened. The new boys had been arriving for weeks, nervous, excited, hoping to live up to their famous predecessors, ready to take some risks to do so and to make an immediate impression, perhaps by demeaning the king. Call him 'Monsieur' not 'Sire', ventured Couthon, soon – with the beautiful, ear-ringed Saint-Just and the old boy Robespierre – to be a member of a new triumvirate. The king refused to open Parliament on those terms and won a minor victory. The first of few. To mark the opening of the new Assembly, Madame de Staël gave what she was pleased to call 'a coalition dinner'. However, all the guests who Morris lists belonged not to the new Assembly but the old: 'Beaumetz, the Bishop of Autun, Alexandre Lameth, the prince de Broglie etc. Malouet comes in and also the comte de La Marck who converses with Madame.'[20]

Madame de Staël's guest list symbolised the contempt for their successors felt by those members of the Constituent Assembly still lingering in Paris. And their determination to cling to power though the new constitution barred them from office. As a coalition it represented various tendencies within the old Assembly. Though they had come together after the king's flight, they still retained their separate identities.

⚜

The new Assembly was more radical than its predecessor, despite the stiff property qualification for the electoral colleges. The aristocratic right wing entirely disappeared, many to join the princes at Coblenz, and there were only about twenty nobles in the entire Assembly. The new right was made up of the constitutional monarchists, whether followers of Lafayette or of the triumvirs: 264 deputies joined the Feuillant Club, out of 743 deputies (the total reduced by the absence of the noblesse and clergy as separate orders); 124 joined the Jacobins, mostly running over their membership of their local club but, finding the mother society too radical, many left, leaving a hard core of 52.

Hard core is the operative term because though the left wing was numerically inferior, they tended to include the more forceful as well as the most eloquent speakers, notably a group of lawyers from the Département of the Gironde headed by Vergniaud; they were allied with Brissot and (outside the Assembly now) the ex-Constituents Pétion and Buzot. Barnave said bluntly that Brissot 'only wanted to become a deputy the better to destroy the constitution' – exactly the point Marie-Antoinette had made.[21] Some were republicans, all wanted to capture the ministry. Though the triumvirs were out of Parliament, Théodore de Lameth, the fourth of the brothers and Mathieu Dumas, of the post-Varennes 'inner committee', had been elected.

C.J. Mitchel has proposed a new method for classifying voting patterns depending on whether deputies voted 'yes' or 'no' on radical measures on the seven occasions on which individual votes were recorded. He found a consistency in the way individual deputies voted. In fact, his division between '*oui*' and '*non*' voters approximates to the conventional left and right which we will continue to use, but Mitchel's schema by definition excludes those of naturally centrist tendencies who on these seven occasions were forced to make up their minds. Vaublanc, who unofficially led the right-wing Feuillant grouping and who had close contact with Barnave, considered that the call for an *appel nominal* was a left-wing tactic to shame monarchists into voting for radical measures. He observes that if the trial of the king by the National Convention had been conducted under the usual rules, he would have been acquitted by a large majority. He called these centrists *ventrus* – from the word *ventre* (stomach). Caring more for their stomach than the burning issues of the day, they sloped off for their dinner in the afternoon, abandoning the field to the radicals. This was symbolic of the half-heartedness of the moderates, to which Barnave attributes the setbacks experienced by his party.

Barnave himself produces the best analysis of the overall working of the Legislative Assembly: 'It is a remarkable fact that hitherto [March 1792] there has never been a majority in this legislature.' In the Constituent Assembly, the Monarchiens aligned with the right so there was in effect a two-party system in which the left had a permanent majority. The right 'watched, criticised and resisted while the other party decreed'. In the Legislative Assembly, however, neither side had an inbuilt majority for 'the Independents [Vaublanc's 'stomach'] often made the majority fluctuate'. Barnave, with his medical preoccupations, compared the result to a sick man with two doctors offering opposing treatments; even if they were 'men of genius' – 'angels', he corrects – 'they would kill the patient'.[22]

The triumvirs' attitude towards the new Assembly was ambivalent, if not hostile, as can be seen from a letter of Charles de Lameth to his mother, who had now emigrated: 'The Legislative Assembly is . . . badly composed but even this is a good thing because if its proceedings are bad, it will lose its credit by the day and soon you will learn that we have been recalled, yes us the Constituents to support and perfect our work.'[23] This is redolent of the dangerous flirtation with a *politique du pire* pursued by the right in the previous Assembly and, like them, aimed at an impossible return to former days – in their case, a recall to front-line politics. Barnave took the same line in his letter to the queen of 30 October: 'The more serious the faults [of the Assembly] the sooner it will grow up and the sooner the need for a [strong] government will be felt.'[24] This remained his view in the summer of 1792: the Assembly 'by their very faults have hastened the period of maturity and reason, so one must not be unduly upset'.[25]

If Barnave took the new Assembly for granted, he was soon in for a shock. On 28 September he told the queen that the triumvirs were 'working on the king's speech for the opening [of the Assembly]. We will get it to the queen in enough time to allow her to examine it and let us know her opinion.' She stressed that the new Assembly was 'an ordinary legislature and not a Constituent body'.[26] The king delivered his speech on the 7th setting out the agenda for the session, as in an English speech from the throne – fleshing out the skeletal initiative in legislation that Barnave had obtained for him. The Assembly was to work on the budget deficit, army discipline, balance between liberty and order, public education, employment and poor relief. Louis added, 'if the laws are insufficient, I will let you know what measures I think are appropriate and the legislative body will need to enact'. Only when he came to national defence did he gain his first applause – and when he said he wanted to create an environment in which the émigrés felt safe to return.[27] In the course of October and November, the only part of the king's speech to which the Assembly responded was its own interpretation of the last sections: introducing savage legislation against the émigrés and refractory priests designed to make the king incur unpopularity by exercising his veto.

On 29 October Duportail, the war minister, was manhandled in the Assembly for the state of the frontier fortresses.[28] Marie-Antoinette blamed Barnave for his poor management of the Assembly: 'It is certain that if those with intelligence and resources do not get a grip on the Assembly very soon neither the ministers nor the king himself will be able to do anything. If *ces Messieurs* want a good outcome they must seriously concentrate on this matter.'

Barnave blustered that a distinction should be made between the government and the king and queen: 'In our opinion, the path of government and the personal course of the king and queen are two different things. Each must be pursued as well as possible; but when the steps of the government falter, it is more than ever important that the personal side should hold good, so that they [the king and queen] are not charged with the shortcoming of the government.'[29] Barnave blustered again when Roederer was elected *procureur syndic* of the département, which, according to Marie-Antoinette, 'proved how much the republican party was gaining'.

When Pétion was elected mayor of Paris – a major defeat for the triumvirs – Barnave riposted unfairly: 'If the people gives its preference to MM Pétion and Roederer and the king gives his to those who share the opinions of Coblenz, the constitutional party, which is today much the more powerful, will no longer be able to stand.' Pétion and Roederer had been part of the small knot of republicans of whom Barnave had complained in the last months of the Constituent. Both would play a major role in the fall of the monarchy. Pellenc was scathing. Barnave's group had made the mistake of calculating 'that the sections voted like an electoral assembly', whereas the republicans had gone out into the highways and byways to bring out their vote. 'It was no way to run a revolution.'[30]

However, on 9 November the Assembly's punitive decree against the émigrés indeed forced '*ces Messieurs*' 'to concentrate seriously on this matter'. The decree ordered all émigrés to return to France within two months, upon pain of being deemed 'conspirators', having their lands confiscated and being punished by death. On 29 November another decree declared that priests not taking an oath to the constitution within eight days were to be 'considered in revolt against the law and of evil intentions towards the *patrie*'. They were to be stripped of their pensions and held responsible for all religious disturbances in their neighbourhood.

In order to make the king's veto acceptable, Marie-Antoinette decided that the émigrés must be dealt with. She sought to dissuade them from raising a loan of 40 million on their estates to pay for the Counter-Revolution or from invading France on their own, which would ruin both themselves and the king. This was a key point for both the queen and Barnave. Both of them wanted the émigrés in general and the king's brother 'Monsieur' in particular to return. Marie-Antoinette told Fersen that Monsieur should have returned from Belgium the moment he heard of the king's recapture and that life within the Tuileries was 'hell' because Elizabeth was forever siding with her émigré brothers.[31] They stayed put, but Marie-Antoinette did persuade Madame de Lamballe to return and, again on Barnave's advice, they went to the opera together. Lamballe even resumed her salon, which had been eclipsed by that of Madame de Polignac.

The return of the émigrés would both remove the principle stick the republicans used to beat the monarchy and swell the ranks of the royalist party. Indeed, Pellenc thought that the main objective of the decree against the émigrés was to put them on their honour *not* to return. He told La Marck that the decree was not one of those spontaneous outbursts which characterised the Revolution but had been 'carefully prepared in the committees' of the Assembly, which were frightened that the returning nobles, joining forces with the refractory clergy in the countryside, 'would give greater force to an embarrassing resistance'.[32] The queen made the same point to Barnave.

The following fortnight saw a daily flurry of letters between Barnave and the queen, who agreed that the veto must be accompanied by an order to the king's brothers to return. To organise this, Barnave would get the ministers to ask the king for an emergency cabinet that night. It was followed by a ministerial committee to iron out the details. In the margin of a 'bullet point' note by the foreign secretary, the king wrote: 'agenda for a ministerial committee concerted with MM Alexandre Lameth and Barnave'. The agenda is: king's veto; further letter to the king's brothers, which must be 'fraternal and royal'; further proclamation to the émigrés and a new letter to the foreign courts not to shelter émigrés.[33] The discovery of this note would later incriminate everyone involved.

On 12 November the king vetoed the decree against the émigrés but the Assembly would not let du Tertre read the king's letter explaining that he would have accepted some of its provisions and the measures he was himself taking against the émigrés. Louis wrote on Duport du Tertre's projected speech: 'They did not want to hear it.'[34] The Assembly then asked Bertrand de Molleville to address the question of the emigration of naval officers but after the treatment du Tertre had received, he simply left the chamber and on the 14th published a letter in the *Moniteur* saying some officers had left their post because of indiscipline in the ranks but that they were all in contact with him and ready to resume their duties.[35]

Both Barnave and the queen thought these ministers had been spineless. At 5 p.m. on 12 November Barnave told the queen: 'the ministers did not communicate anything [to the Assembly] and yet they had the right to. If the Assembly was led astray, it was solely the result of the ministers' feebleness.' Marie-Antoinette was more expansive: 'The timidity of the ministers did harm in the session before yesterday and if they do not know how to cope with circumstances as they arise, how can the government have force let alone public confidence? . . . We need courageous ministers who instead of trying to please everyone concentrate exclusively on what is to the advantage of government.'

She concluded: 'If it is thought that the suggestions of *ces Messieurs* for the composition of the ministry can restore its vigour and fulfil this object without which nothing can proceed, they must be adopted.' With this sentence Marie-Antoinette seems to accept that if Barnave is to be responsible for the success of his strategy, he must be able to influence the principal agents of execution, though she does qualify this: 'Therefore, I ask for their opinion once again and we will consider it on our part.'[36] Barnave had written: 'I still think that the choice of M. de Lessart for foreign affairs, M. Garnier for the interior and M. de Narbonne at the war office will put everyone in his right slot and will form a perfectly unified ministry and one as strong as can be hoped for in the present circumstances.'[37] For a month Barnave and Marie-Antoinette had been haggling over the renewal of the ministry on Montmorin's pending retirement – it occurred on 31 October.

The queen had asked du Moustier to succeed Montmorin but Barnave objected on the grounds that he was lukewarm about the Revolution and his appointment would suggest repugnance on the king's part also. 'We deserve to be believed in this particular', he explained, 'because far from bearing any ill-will towards him we have had dealings with him and think that . . . once things have settled down . . . he can usefully be employed in the highest positions.'[38]

Barnave had indeed had dealings with du Moustier, who on 5 November 1790 wrote asking for the return of some papers, 'on the assumption that they are no longer of any use'. 'If he had managed to catch him at home, he would have been delighted to retrieve them himself.' Or, even better, invite him for dinner but he feared that would be 'indiscrete'. Meanwhile he wished success 'for operations tending to the *gloire* of our country on which you have influence and to judge by your zeal and means can bring about directly'. For his part all du Moustier could do was 'raise his eyes and arms to heaven and not allow myself to despair'.[39] Dinner would have been 'indiscrete' because, as Barnave tells the queen, he was viewed with suspicion by ultra patriots. There is a suggestion that Barnave's views were less radical than he wished people to believe – and that Barnave shared du Moustier's struggle with despair.

Instead, Barnave suggested Bigot de Saint-Croix to the queen. Du Tertre also pressed Bigot's case 'in the name of all the ministers'.[40] In seeking ministerial unity, du Tertre was acting as a prime minister in the English style. Moustier told Morris that du Tertre 'keeps the king in constant alarm and governs him by his fears, so that M. de Montmorin has little influence left'.[41] Marie-Antoinette objected to Bigot: apart from his lack of diplomatic experience

> there is a major obstacle in his family connections. I am astonished that I did not raise the matter at the outset. One can be certain that with M. Talon for a brother-in-law and M. de Sainte-Foix for an uncle, the entire funds of the foreign office will soon vanish and will never be enough. No one is in a better position to know the facts than us [the king and queen]. He must no longer be considered for this place.

Talon and Saint-Foix had been agents in Mirabeau's corruption machine, using funds provided by the king from the civil list. Montmorin, who had thought that the money was not being efficiently applied, also raised 'pecuniary' objections to Bigot.[42] But there is another possibility.

Barnave was to employ Bigot for a diplomatic initiative in December. But it is not impossible that already Barnave, or more likely Alexandre, was himself using some of the civil list money in an attempt to control the popular movement. Madam Campan relates that

> one day Barnave told M. de J[arjayes], 'we still [*sic*] hold the purse-strings that move this popular mass', showing him a fat volume in which were inscribed the names of all the people that could be mobilised by the sole power of gold. It was a matter of paying a large number of people to cheer loudly when the king and queen started going to the theatre after the king's acceptance of the constitution.[43]

We have seen that Marie-Antoinette was aware that the applause was 'bought'. Had Barnave told her who was buying it? Talon was Mirabeau's agent for disbursing this money. Moreover, we have seen that Talon believed that the triumvirs had offered him the justice ministry in 1789.

Barnave and the queen then settled on a candidate for the foreign office that was acceptable to them both: the comte de Ségur, ambassador to Prussia, and their original choice to be the coordinating minister. He accepted on the 29th but, as his wife told Morris, resigned on the morning of the 30th because of the way Duportail had been attacked in the Assembly the day before.[44] They then settled on de Lessart. He was a capable and loyal man who before becoming foreign secretary had been finance minister under Necker and was now minister of the interior. We have seen him find posts for two of Barnave's relatives.[45] Barnave proposed to replace de Lessart at the interior with Cahier de Gerville. He was at heart a republican and affected to be insulted when the king gave him 'permission' to read a report. Marie-Antoinette called him 'a small-time lawyer earning only 700 livres a year'.[46] Barnave had taught her the gradations of bourgeois society. Nevertheless, he was appointed on 17 November.

There were now three bourgeois ministers. Throughout the *ancien régime* there had only been one – Necker. In July 1792 Barnave incorporated this fact into his general theory: 'the people served as the prince's auxiliaries against the nobles until they felt themselves strong enough to rival [erased] enter the government itself.'[47]

The king and queen chose Bertrand de Molleville as minister of the marine. Unlike his predecessors in the job, he was an ex-intendant, a *noblesse de robe* functionary rather than a military aristocrat. Rightly believing that he gave only technical allegiance to the constitution, Barnave advised the queen against his appointment. But Marie-Antoinette told him that 'the most important thing at the moment is to have a minister who . . . can speak to the new Assembly with authority and enforce the legitimate rights of the king.'[48] In pursuance of this, Bertrand persuaded the ministers to deal directly with the Assembly, bypassing the committees which shadowed their own ministries – an informal and dangerous institution, he observed, and one not mentioned in the constitution.[49]

However, such an approach concealed a weakness: 'the ministry, by turns haughty and timid, could do nothing better than dig itself in behind some of the formal provisions of the new constitution, refraining from seeing the deputies or setting a foot in the committees and claiming that it should only communicate with the Assembly by proposing decrees or appearing at the tribune where it was powerless.'[50]

In short, it abandoned any attempt to manage the Assembly, a wooden correctness which suited the king. The ministers did not engage with the Assembly, although Barnave had worked hard during the Revision to ensure that they had opportunities to do so – opportunities which he hoped and his enemies feared might evolve into the initiative in legislation. The quotation is from the memoirs of Villemain, an admirer of the man who was to change the passive system, engaging with all parties and living daily in the pockets of the committees – the brilliant comte Louis de Narbonne-Lara, the lover of Madame de Staël.

After initial misgivings on both sides, Barnave and Marie-Antoinette chose Narbonne to replace the harried Duportail, who resigned as war minister on 3 December. These misgivings would be justified for Narbonne's appointment led to the breakup of their system. Narbonne was persona grata with both the Girondins and the Talleyrand-Beaumetz-d'André-Chapelier group. He knew everyone through the salon of Madame de Staël. Villemain listed the gamut of those with whom Narbonne was 'intimate': 'Talleyrand, his childhood friend, Barnave younger than he by several years, Adrien Duport, Thouret, the marquis de Ferrières, the three Lameth brothers, Cazalès, Lally-Tollendal and Mounier.'[51]

Narbonne, one of Louis XV's many natural children, had the advantage, Barnave told the queen, of being 'a man of quality in the *ancien régime*' whose appointment would 'perfectly balance' the bourgeois ministers.[52] He was also, as Marie-Antoinette told Fersen, being 'frantically plugged' by Madame de Staël. Barnave and Marie-Antoinette also joked about her: Madame de Staël, Barnave said, was even better at publicity than her father Necker; indeed 'thousand-tongued fame was not her equal'. But, he added, 'however unsuited M. de Narbonne may appear for the post he desires, the queen will see, no doubt', that he must be humoured to avoid causing resentment in his circle 'at this critical time when it is necessary to gain over anyone who has a finger in the popular pie'.

Later Barnave would class Narbonne among the 'ministers who pretended to be patriots and destroyed everything'.[53] The queen must also say nothing of the reconciliation with Lafayette (which Barnave had urged on her) because Narbonne's circle hated Lafayette's. He added: 'M. de Lafayette is the only man in France who could get into the saddle and find himself at the head of a party against the king.'[54] In the end Marie-Antoinette concluded: 'If M. de Narbonne must be appointed minister of war, it should be done swiftly.' She added: 'It is important to have a safe pair of hands [*sic!*] in that post.'[55]

In Pellenc's insider analysis of the ministerial factions, Narbonne was allied with Talleyrand, Beaumetz and Le Chapelier, and he concluded that Barnave's party 'has little influence on the conduct of M. de Narbonne'.[56] Pellenc presents a picture of a divided cabinet with different alliances, rather than the unified ministry Barnave claimed. Molleville was on his own and was the only one the king and queen trusted. However, Marie-Antoinette told Fersen that Narbonne 'seems to me to want to ally with M. Bertrand in the council and he is right for he is the only one who is worth anything'.[57] Duport du Tertre 'worked with' the triumvirs but 'he was not entirely dependent on them and received other counsels on the right and on the left'. Narbonne 'takes his advice principally from the Bishop of Autun, Beaumetz and Le Chapelier. He does not work in concert with M. de Lessart', who 'worked sometimes with Beaumetz and Le Chapelier but more often with the Lameths and Duport'. Le Chapelier 'resigned his post in the Court of Appeal, though he needed the money to live on. It is said that he wants to remove the obstacle barring a career in the ministry or diplomatic service.'[58]

Beaumetz quipped: 'If the émigrés do not bring about the Counter-Revolution, they will be doing us a disservice for we will have to bring it about ourselves'; and Pellenc recounts a move by the ex-Mirabeau group in the Feuillants to try to close down the Jacobins, a move also favoured by Narbonne:

> The same disunity [as in the ministry] prevails outside. Beaumetz and Le Chapelier were the authors of the address that the Feuillants were to have presented. It was strong but it renewed the personal quarrels of the former deputies with the Jacobins. It was to have been signed by 10,000 people and presented [to the king? to the Assembly?] by ten national guards. In a second session the Lameths, Duport and Barnave had it rejected. These people are not always in step.

The fragmentation of the constitutional party was a necessary ingredient in the move towards war.

The Feuillant Club, having pursued a desultory course since September, was refounded at this time.[59] Pellenc notes: 'The Lameths turn up but with no éclat.' Barnave's own account is also lukewarm:

> [A] fairly substantial number of deputies and other persons which did not include me tried to re-establish the club in December. . . . I was urged to go to the Feuillants; it was even borne upon me and my friends that by refusing to go we would cast doubt on the durability of our opinions and on our political character. So, I went and spoke twice on the colonies. In less than a fortnight this club acquired such solidity that it already numbered over 300 deputies [364 to be precise]. The Jacobins were terrified by these numbers, they thought their reign was going to end.[60]

Soon afterwards, under popular pressure, the Feuillant Club closed. Barnave regretted that his party had been identified with it 'because many people thought the party had fallen with it'. Besides it was the role of Revolutionary clubs 'to change the existing order of things but a *conservative* club on *the defensive* is unnatural. It must either be untrue to the purpose of its institution or die of inanition.'[61]

THE DRIFT TOWARDS WAR

On 14 December the king made a major speech on the émigré formations along the Rhine. He was accompanied to the Assembly by Narbonne, who had written the speech after other drafts, including one by Duport, had been rejected.[62] The background to this seminal speech, a milestone on the road to war, is complicated. We begin with an extract from the memoirs of the comte de Vaublanc: 'I employed the only way of saving the king: it was to follow the advice given by Barnave to the king to seize the pretext of the émigré formations to form an army on the frontiers.' This advice was contained in 'one of the notes which since the king's arrest at Varennes Barnave was constantly giving the ministers to forward to the king . . . it said that he saw no other remedy than to have an army'.[63] As leader of the constitutional monarchists in the Assembly, there is no reason to doubt Vaublanc's reference to Barnave, given almost en passant.

Barnave showed this note to Vaublanc and they came up with the idea of a message from the Assembly to the king urging him to take steps to disperse the émigré formations. Vaublanc couched his proposed message 'in the declamatory language of the time'. One had to: 'even the king did' – it was the only way to succeed; and it did, 'beyond my wildest expectations'. The Assembly deputed Vaublanc to deliver the message to the king. This contained passages such as: 'The nation expects to hear energetic declarations from you to the Circles of the Upper and Lower Rhine, the Electors of Trier, Mainz and other German princes. Let the hordes of émigrés be instantly dispersed. Prescribe a date beyond which no dilatory response will be entertained. Let your declaration be accompanied by movements of the troops which have been entrusted to you.'[64] 'Supported by the ministers', Vaublanc continues, 'we had this army. It was royalist and demanded to march against the Jacobin Club at Paris . . . but unfortunately the command was given to Lafayette, who was incapable of vigorous action.'

The Assembly's message was delivered to the king on 29 November. Two days afterwards, that is, on 1 December, Marie-Antoinette reminded Barnave, 'I asked *ces Messieurs* to work on the [king's] reply and on every single occasion I wrote to them subsequently I pressed the matter.'[65] Marie-Antoinette was not interested in the king's reply per se but because it would smooth the way for the king to veto the punitive measures against the refractory clergy.

Barnave, however, was reluctant to see the king exercise his veto on behalf of the nonjuring priests and was supported by a majority in the council of ministers. The king, however, who normally 'let himself be dragged along', said, 'surely I do what everyone wants enough times to be able to get my own way just once'. He was backed up by Bertrand de Molleville, who wrote 'begging to inform him that yesterday he had a long conference with MM. Beaumetz, Le Chapelier and the Bishop of Autun [Talleyrand]'. They 'unanimously' agreed that it was 'of the utmost urgency' that the king go to the Assembly to announce steps against the émigré concentrations and neighbouring powers.' In their minds and the queen's the speech was related to the veto, in Narbonne's to a military parade through the minor German states to reinforce the monarchy and perhaps close down the Jacobin Club. War ministers tend to want war.[66]

With Barnave dragging his heals over the speech as preparing the way for the veto, on 14 December the king gave the speech which Narbonne had written and Louis had corrected. He told the Assembly that he would summon the Elector of Trier to disperse the émigré formations in his territories before 15 January 1792 on pain of war and, to reinforce this ultimatum, Narbonne announced the formation of three armies, under Luckner, Rochambeau and Lafayette, who had relinquished his command of the National Guard to run as mayor.

Duport finally came up with a draft speech and Michon thought that the king actually delivered it, and that Barnave's scathing reference in the *Introduction à la Révolution française* marks a cooling between the friends. In fact, Barnave chided Marie-Antoinette for *not* using Duport's draft. Michon would have avoided this serious error had he accepted the authenticity of the Barnave–Marie-Antoinette correspondence.[67] For, as Marie-Antoinette explained to Barnave, de Lessart had only received the Lameth–Duport draft 'at 5 p.m. and he had given it to the king only five minutes before the council was due to open', leaving him no time to read it.

Barnave chided Marie-Antoinette for the speech, 'which was put into the king's mouth', and argued in his *Introduction à la Révolution française* that before the speech, Brissot and the Girondins 'scarcely even dared to speak openly of war', but the king's ultimatum 'seemed to announce war to the nation and seemed to push public opinion in that direction'.[68] In fact, Duport's and Narbonne's versions are equally belligerent – the speech talked of 'war' and Duport's draft 'force of arms'.

Moreover, only two paragraphs of Barnave's long letter to the queen refer to the king's speech and he did not criticise it so much for its belligerence as for pandering to the populace: 'This speech was applauded because it was more than popular. But it degrades the king's character. It authorises doubts as to his sincerity [as the circular letter of 23 April]. It places him on his knees before the people and the Assembly. It will appeal to the multitude. It will make a very bad impression on the enlightened class which forms the true king's party.' On 2 February he wrote of 'the mistrust engendered by seeking an artificial popularity'.[69]

But the aggressive tone towards the German princes and the patriotic rhetoric of the king's speech was matched with an attack on the Jacobins: the executive and the legislative were 'distinct but not enemies'.

If the troublemakers continued to slander him, he 'would not stoop to bandy words with them'. The speech could be seen as preparing the way for Lafayette's army crushing the forces of the puny German princelings and then turning it on the Jacobins back home. Is this what Barnave was really objecting to? Is this the context for the Feuillant Club address of Beaumetz and Le Chapelier which the triumvirs had rejected? On this reading, Barnave blamed the speech for artificially feeding the war frenzy in order to ease the closing of the Jacobins, which Le Chapelier had always wanted – his fellow founder Barnave was reluctant.

And there was a residue of pique. Barnave told the queen: 'If we are exposed to see our carefully pondered ideas submitted to other counsels, our zeal will be useless and we will no longer be in a situation consonant with the purity of our opinions and our conviction that we alone understand the state of affairs and have the means to restore them.' But he and Alexandre wanted 'to learn from the queen herself whether these recent incidents were the result of a lack of confidence in us or a misunderstanding'.[70]

Perhaps this 'misunderstanding' should be viewed as a failure of procedure. In the system devised by Barnave, he would have drafted a king's speech and given it to the queen for her comments – she kept asking Barnave for his draft. Barnave would then incorporate her comments and give the revised draft to du Tertre to put to the cabinet committee, and thence to the council for the king's formal approval. This time de Lessart gave his incomplete draft to the king and he made his own corrections. Because there was no time with the king due to go to the Assembly that night, the committee stage was bypassed and the document went straight to the council. In a sense this was a return to normal government. The king wanted to be involved 'just for once' because the veto that the declaration facilitated was a matter of his personal conscience, not his constitutional prerogative. If Barnave had got Duport's draft to the queen earlier, then the normal procedure could have perhaps been observed. But he dragged his feet.

✤

Bigot de Saint-Croix, de Lessart's envoy recommended by Barnave, arrived at Coblenz on 27 December and saw the Elector on the 29th;

the émigrés were dispersed by the 11th. He had an easy task – the Elector himself wanted to be rid of the émigrés for, as Bigot told de Lessart, 'the French émigrés are now the masters of the Electorate'.[71]

That should have ended the matter; but on 17 December the Austrian chancellor, Kaunitz, handed the French ambassador a gratuitously provocative note to the effect that if France attacked the Elector's territories, the emperor would defend them with his own troops. Barnave told the queen that the king himself should take the sting out of the note by disclosing it himself to the Assembly and making a 'patriotic' speech. He and his friends would write the speech and give it to de Lessart to give the council. It must be delivered unchanged. But at 8 a.m. the next day (31 December) Barnave told the queen that 'at four in the morning *ces messieurs* wrote to me to tell the queen at the moment of her *levée* that a message from the king to the Assembly would better serve than his going there in person'.[72] The letter was read, unchanged, by Duport du Tertre. Marie-Antoinette usually referred to Barnave and his friends as *ces Messieurs*; now he does the same. The king's letter made little difference.

Mercy said 'the emperor . . . has at last changed systems',[73] and Marie-Antoinette used the same phrase in a letter to Barnave. But in view of Leopold's 'profound silence', she had to speculate why. Her interpretation was that the emperor had believed that 'having signed the constitution, the king would have been allowed to govern in accordance with the rights it gave him'. When he saw that this was not the case, 'how could he not change his language and his system? Not for the interests of the émigrés but the thing in itself, the wounded dignity of every crowned head.'[74] Hitherto Leopold had found it convenient to take Louis's acceptance of the new constitution at face value and Kaunitz had been even more pacific than Leopold: he observed that the new constitution rendered France less of a danger than previously, and that 'if it was bad, it was bad only for France'.[75] Now Austria announced that she would order 'proportionate' mobilisations to the French ones.

There were other issues apart from 'wounded dignity'. Kaunitz had also raised the question of the *princes possessionés*, which Barnave believed was 'the root' of the whole problem. Barnave believed that 'the diplomatic committee which wanted war' was deliberately allowing this issue to fester. Whether it was resolved or not he thought would determine which 'direction' France took: towards a republic or towards a reinvigorated monarchy.

Barnave in his *Introduction à la Révolution française* gives a deeper explanation of why the emperor changed systems. Before the Revolution Leopold and Joseph, like Louis XVI, had seen the aristocracy as the enemy. Now, however, that the Girondins were 'proselytising' – propagating international revolution – they forged a guarded alliance with their former foes. The other European rulers adopted the same stance and seeing 'democracy' as the common enemy they also dropped their inter-state rivalry and became 'allies in their terror'.[76] So the emperor was not the only one who, stung by the reckless wrecking tactics of the Girondins, had 'changed systems': all of Europe had – except England, where monarchy and aristocracy were already united.

However, the drift to war also arose from major misunderstanding, both on the Austrian and French sides. Leopold claimed (and apparently believed) that his aggressive response to French mobilisation, 'far from swelling the fanatical party [in France], would tend to constrain their fury' and aid the 'moderate' party. But he had completely misread the French situation. He believed that the bluff of Pillnitz had frightened the National Assembly into restoring Louis XVI and revising the constitution in his favour. He now believed that similar threats would see off the Girondins' incursions against Louis's restored throne.[77]

Barnave saw the danger of the emperor's threat. 'Leopold is destroying the king', he told Théodore de Lameth. 'Things which are well and good when said in cabinet overthrow everything when they are said for public consumption. Above all he will destroy the king.'[78] As well as thinking bullying language could cow the Girondins, Leopold – partly because his information was coming from Pellenc and Mercy – overestimated the strength of Barnave's party. He said that he wanted to open a channel of communications with 'the chiefs of the moderate party', that is, the triumvirs in Paris. Pellenc was suggested. Marie-Antoinette disagreed.[79]

Leopold's misjudgements may not have led to war had not the French understanding of the international situation been even more mistaken than the Austrian. For the key to an understanding of foreign affairs in 1792 – and one vouchsafed to few of the parties in France – is that Austria and Prussia, for fifty years mortal enemies, had come to a solid understanding, which was ratified by a treaty of alliance on 7 February 1792. Therefore, the Girondins' gamble of detaching Prussia and isolating Austria was a pipe dream. Barnave, however, knew that the Brissotins' hope of alliance with Prussia was illusory. Prussia's instincts had always been acquisitive and she concluded an alliance with her old enemy Austria in order to carve up France and/or Poland.[80]

Brissot, who dominated the Legislative Assembly's diplomatic committee, desired war with Austria in order to smoke out the presumed treason of Marie-Antoinette when confronted with war with her brother. As Brissot put it in December 1791, 'I have only one fear; it is that we won't be betrayed. We need great treasons; our salvation lies there, because there are still strong doses of poison in France and strong emetics are needed to expel them.'[81]

The Assembly's diplomatic committee could not in itself conclude treaties (or declare war), so they needed a Trojan horse within the ministry. Narbonne did not need much persuading to fulfil this role for, as Barnave had warned Marie-Antoinette (somewhat late in the day): 'M. de Narbonne needs to be watched . . . [he and] his friends seem to be allying themselves with a section of the republican party which has always favoured the English and Prussian alliance system.'[82] Barnave, on the other hand, based his whole system on alliance with Austria: 'When the 1756 treaty was ended [when France declared war on Austria in 1792], it would perhaps have been as desirable to maintain it as it would have been not to have concluded it in the first place.'[83]

In order to scupper the proposed English alliance, Adrien Duport went to the extraordinary length of writing a pamphlet attacking William Pitt.[84] Prussia and England spurned these overtures and these failures should have given the Girondins pause; instead, they pressed on and Kaunitz's bellicose statement enlarged the scope of the conflict and enabled the Girondins to persuade Narbonne to raise his sights from the Elector to the emperor himself. In the Assembly, Gensonné questioned whether the emperor's declaration was compatible with the 1756 alliance and on 25 January the Assembly asked Leopold to clarify this point before 1 March; otherwise, France would be obliged to go to war.

BARNAVE LEAVES PARIS

Barnave could only comment from the sidelines and at a distance on the steps towards a war which Pellenc said 'is going to decide the destiny of mankind',[85] the first European civil war; for on 5 January 1792, he set off back to Grenoble, arriving there two or three days later.[86] We do not really know why he left. On 5 January he sent the queen his last letter. On it Marie-Antoinette writes: 'End of the correspondence with 2:1 [Barnave] who left the same day. It is 4:15 [Duport] who will carry on the correspondence.'

As far as we know Duport did not 'carry on the correspondence'. Barnave later realised that the system he had operated with Marie-Antoinette had ended with his departure when he wrote 'all might have been well if the ministers having decided these [salutary] measures amongst themselves, had sent a résumé of them to the king, bolstered by the opinion of the [remaining] two former deputies', Lameth and Duport – a variant on the mechanism by which he and Marie-Antoinette had governed.[87]

However, in his last letter he seemed to envisage something different, urging Marie-Antoinette in effect to emerge into the open and act like a prime minister. She must conceal her dislikes in order 'by such painful accommodations' to acquire 'popularity and public confidence'. But popularity was useless unless it was converted into power. 'It would give her the means of governing, of appointing and dismissing her ministers rather than being dominated by those who having been appointed by the king, try to make themselves an independent force and sometimes one opposed to him.' On 15 December she had told Barnave that she never saw the ministers. That must change. She must give the ministers backbone. 'They need to be invigorated and supported. The queen can achieve a lot if from time to time she has discussions with the different ministers. She will give them courage and confidence.' He repeated: she must 'often see the ministers herself to impress upon them the force of her decisions and the solidity of her character'. And through them word would get out to the public and the Assembly that she was a force to be reckoned with.[88] They must, in short, 'faire règner la reine'.

Marie-Antoinette told Barnave on 28 December, 'I know that M. Barnave is leaving any day and the powerful reasons which have made for his departure. I trust he will never forget the end of our last conversation.'[89] We do not know what the 'powerful reasons were': in his absence his uncle Antoine's will was being contested, but was the need to sort it out – which he did – a sufficiently powerful reason to leave the queen in the lurch? Alexandre wrote that he saw her 'at the moment of his departure for Dauphiné', which gives credence to Madame Campan's account of a final meeting.

Barnave urged her not to give up on the constitutional monarchists: their 'flag was tattered, but the word "constitution" on it was still legible'. And people would rally to it if the king would give it his backing; then the authors of the constitution, 'recognising their own errors', would make the necessary changes. Theirs was the only national party – all the others, the princes, the foreign powers, would dismember France. Barnave told the queen that staying in Paris hoping to be rescued by an invading army would be hopeless: 'You are too far from help; you would be lost before it reached you. I sincerely hope that my gloomy prediction is wrong; but I am convinced that I will pay with my head for the interest that your misfortune awoke in me and the services which I have wanted to perform for you. All I ask for in recompense is to be able to kiss your hand.' The queen granted this favour, her eyes bathed in tears. And she kept the most favourable judgement of the high and noble sentiments of this deputy. Madame Elizabeth shared it, and the two princesses often talked of Barnave with lively interest.[90]

It may seem that Barnave was deserting Marie-Antoinette in what he called in his last letter to her 'a moment of crisis'. But he explains: 'The whole point of my voyage is to augment my means of furthering the public interest with which the king has completely united his own resources. The duration of my absence will be guided by the same principles. I will always recall that in our last conversation the queen assured me that her confidence was sincere and her intentions unwavering. This memory will be the rule of my opinions and the principle of all my public conduct.'[91] Barnave specifically talks of a '*voyage*' rather than a '*retour*'.

There is in Barnave's papers a draft letter which may also have been intended for the queen. It ends, 'I am the one whom you sought out through your attraction to men of talent. But above all [I am] unswerving [in my support] of those in whom I find character and fidelity.' There is a postscript: 'I want us to be in agreement on principles and that you may make them prevail but without your giving any publicity to this letter.'

It was the queen who 'sought out' Barnave by renewing their acquaintance after the return from Varennes. And there are key words from their correspondence: 'character', 'fidelity', 'principles'. Earlier in the letter there is the forced optimism which suffuses the rest of his correspondence with the queen. The other possibility is Lafayette. He had 'sought out' Barnave in the summer of 1790 in the hopes of a reconciliation between the 89 and the Jacobin clubs. And Barnave had insisted that on certain fundamental principles he could not compromise. At the end of 1791 Lafayette and Narbonne were flirting with a limited war against the Elector and Barnave may have been interested. But, above all, he may have been urging a united front against the Brissotins. A few months later Barnave would view Lafayette as the main hope of saving the monarchy.[92]

A month after Barnave's departure, Fersen, his rival in affection and policy, made a secret visit to the Tuileries. Before he left, Marie-Antoinette gave him her correspondence with Barnave with the enigmatic comment, 'you shall judge of it yourself, for I am keeping it all for you'. She had told him earlier that she was 'keeping a very interesting volume of correspondence for when we meet in happier times; it is all the more interesting because one must give their due to those who have taken part in it. No one suspects it.'[93]

— FOURTEEN —

THE RETURN OF THE NATIVE

JANUARY–AUGUST 1792

Barnave reached Grenoble around 7 January 1792 and after three years' absence with scant communications between them joined his mother and sisters at their (now his) château at Saint-Robert. He wrote, probably to Charles de Lameth's wife, 'I have just found my Grenoble family again and I have just left my Paris one.' He was ill and said that his journey had made him worse. It must have been sheer nervous exhaustion, for he told Madame de Lameth: 'Hardly had I left that whirlpool of noise and corruption where one thinks and acts at speed and doesn't have time to feel than I rediscovered my soul quite intact just as I had left it; and looking back I found that I had all the elements of a delicious existence within me; and that I had not realised just how much I regretted people and how easy it was to detach myself from material things.'[1]

He told Madame de Lameth that he had met with a mixed 'reception, though a better one than I had expected . . . most of the people who greeted me most warmly on my arrival had been censuring me a week before and I saw this as a new proof of their fickleness.' The inhabitants of the tiny hamlet of Saint-Egrève gave him an enthusiastic reception and the neighbouring communes sent delegations to welcome him back. Even the *Journal patriotique* of Grenoble, which had recently published a critical article in a Paris journal, joined in the welcome.[2]

Barnave told his friend that human fickleness had not made him cynical; it was just that 'it was very rewarding to start a revolution but being obliged to end one was a heavy burden.' He then explained his personal and political philosophy: 'I have always despised those philanthropists who sacrifice the happiness of their country for chimerical theories about the happiness of humanity. But now I am even more perfectly willing to disapprove of those who extend their solicitude and affection beyond a tight circle of friends.' An example would be the Girondin-inspired decree offering 'fraternity and help' to all oppressed peoples. Barnave concluded: 'It is a rare and happy thing that in a revolution where it can be said that vice and corruption have been the leading players rather than patriotism and purity, a circle of friends placed at the very centre of affairs could preserve intact . . . the most delightful society which has ever existed.'

But Barnave then progresses to a more controversial idea: 'We must serve men for their own sakes and not for ours but if happiness does not lie at their gates and they do not know how to enjoy it, we must therefore devote our lives to struggling to teach them how.' This sentiment borders on the Rousseauesque 'forcing to be free' and seems to inhabit the realm of the second revolution Barnave had striven to prevent. As if realising this, he hastens to qualify this darkish thought: 'Ah! If we knew the full extent of such an undertaking before we began . . .'. But 'madame', he jokes, 'scrub these thoughts from your mind – a Jacobin would be shocked to hear them'. Then he continues more seriously, it is just that 'for these last three years I have not allowed myself to frame such a thought' – self-censorship, the darkest tyranny of all. His correspondent replied that she loved him more than all the Jacobin 'clubbists put together'.

But these dark thoughts were not his abiding memory. For the short time remaining to him his years in Paris would glow in the same way that university does for some alumni. The revolution was in a sense his university – the farce at Orange scarcely counted, apart from being the first time he had left the home to which he was now returning: 'It is painful to cut oneself off from an intimate society one has known for two years.' For these years had formed his character, given that they

> fleeted by in the midst of the most lively agitation when such events have enabled one to judge oneself better than in an entire lifetime; the affections formed then engrave themselves as deeply as the first feelings of childhood and one finds oneself so completely integrated that it is hard to imagine that one has not always known these years which passed so rapidly while one was experiencing them – in

retrospect they seem like centuries because of the impressions they have left and the connections that have been formed.

Reading this, one wonders whether the rest of his life would not have been an anti-climax.

It was hard for Barnave to recreate even a semblance of the society he had known in Paris because *le tout Grenoble* had emigrated. 'I have been here for twenty-four hours' – Barnave spent a few weeks recuperating at Saint-Robert before coming to Grenoble – he told his friend, 'and I find my native town almost deserted. All my former acquaintances, save five or six persons, are aristocrats; the majority have emigrated, even those who were not noble. Of those who began the Revolution I find that I am the only one who is not its enemy – the others have followed Mounier or were connected with the Parlement.'

Barnave's Paris family missed him as much as he did them. Taking up the conceit of a family of friends, Madame de Lameth begs Barnave to call her 'sister' rather than 'Madame'. Another of the group tells Barnave on 11 January that 'since Alexandre no longer has you, he has become melancholy, he is more indifferent to politics, he only seeks solitude'. They wanted him back once he had recuperated physically and mentally. He himself talked of 'donning his breastplate' and rejoining the '*mêlé*' – he even flattered himself that he would be re-elected to the next Parliament[3].

⚜

Meanwhile the revolutionary carriage hurtled on. But we now witness the march towards war and the final agony of the monarchy, as we saw the origins of the Revolution through the eyes of Barnave as analyst rather than participant. His political views were now diverging from those of the friends he had left behind and he complained of the paucity of their letters.

Narbonne, in alliance with Brissot, quarrelled with his ministerial colleagues. Duport and Lameth, who now regretted Narbonne's appointment, since their system was based on alliance not war with Leopold, persuaded the king to dismiss him.[4] But Barnave thought that the 'brusque' dismissal of Narbonne on 9 March 'smacked of vertigo'.

He told Théodore de Lameth that Narbonne 'was the only one who had worked to create a [ministerial] party in the Assembly, that is to say to trace a path for the ministers in the new regime'. For 'with a majority', he told Riccé, Narbonne 'would necessarily try to govern' – as in England. He could forgive Narbonne's coalition with Lafayette's group, 'provided it led to a consolidation of the constitution'. Narbonne 'was in the process of separating his new friends [the Girondin leaders] from their sectaries and his dismissal would throw them back into their arms'.[5]

The Girondins threw their weight behind Narbonne and, though he was not reinstated, they were able to bring down the Feuillant ministry by impeaching de Lessart and having him sent before the national High Court at Orléans to stand trial for the crime of *lèse-nation*. Terrified, the remaining Feuillant ministers – Duport du Tertre, Tarbé and Cahier – all gave in their resignations between the 15th and the 20th of March, leaving the field to the Girondins and the war party.[6] Alexandre de Lameth noted: 'The king has abandoned de Lessart and appointed Dumouriez. If he knows his history of England [which he knew Louis did], he would not have sacrificed his minister' – a reference to Charles I's allowing the execution of Strafford, the prelude to the English Civil War. He advised his correspondent to sell his *assignats*, which would depreciate by 30 per cent.[7]

Du Tertre took up the lucrative post of public prosecutor of the central criminal court, which Robespierre vacated on 10 April. Their tenures were equally brief: for du Tertre, the court was too radical; for Robespierre, not radical enough. Barnave asked Théodore de Lameth to lobby for du Tertre's appointment as governor to the dauphin – an important role as there was increasing talk of the king's abdication or dethronement. But du Tertre sought safety in retirement, making the same mistake as Barnave and later Danton did of believing that it was possible to retire from the Revolution. Its pension was death.

But whereas Charles I, shortly after sacrificing Strafford,[8] left London to raise an army against those who had forced his hand, Louis XVI appointed a Girondin ministry in the certain knowledge that it would advise him to declare war on the emperor. Barnave saw the logic in this: 'If we have war, it is necessary that the nation be engaged in it by the Jacobins and extricated from it gloriously by men of character and virtue.'[9]

There were other equally compelling reasons for what has always seemed a puzzling and fatal appointment. The very day that Louis replaced de Lessart as foreign minister with Dumouriez, Pétion, the Girondin mayor, withdrew his opposition to the formation of the king's constitutional guard and it was immediately activated. Pellenc considered that this would cover the departure of the court to Fontainebleau. At the same time, Brissot's journal scotched the idea that Marie-Antoinette was going to be put on trial, which had seemed a real possibility; there had been talk of denouncing Alexandre de Lameth together with the queen.[10] The baying hounds were temporarily called off.

At the same time, however, Louis informed the Assembly that the former ministers had 'earned the respect of public opinion for their honourable conduct', while their replacements were only 'accredited by popular opinion', a neat distinction. Barnave thought that by sending this message, which he suspected had been written by 'the former ministers' themselves, the king had played into the hands of those who wanted to drive a wedge between him and the nation. He thought that the Girondins were mainly interested in 'money and ambition'. Since the king had not the power to prevent their appointment, he should allow them to discredit themselves by displaying their venality. They were the only ones with the energy to govern and it could be channelled into defence of a constitution the Feuillants no longer had the strength to save.[11]

What the king should do, Barnave cynically observed, was 'stuff the pockets of the abbé Siéyès with gold and give Guadet and Vergniaud carriages' – the equivalent of today's ministerial car. 'If Vergniaud, who has denounced the queen, were to praise her even in private conversation, the Revolution would be finished.'[12] Vergniaud had told the Assembly: 'All the inhabitants [of the Tuileries] should be aware that only the person of the king is inviolable.'

Barnave had a mixed view of the new administration. The choice of Clavière as the new finance minister was 'excellent', but that of Dumouriez 'execrable'. He noted the continuing influence of Narbonne's old allies Talleyrand and Biron. And it was the replacement of Rochambeau by Biron as commander of the Army of the North that led him to conclude that though 'he viewed the changes in the administration with pleasure, it was not the same with the armies'. Biron, like Dumouriez, was an 'adventurer'. However, Barnave liked Biron's superior, the war minister de Graves, and asked him to find places for his protégés. He had asked this of Narbonne, hoping for some gratitude for Barnave's role in his appointment. Delay d'Agier, a noble deputy for Dauphiné, now head of a bureau in the war department, assured Barnave that he would give Narbonne 'the list of your protégés' to be made 'sub-lieutenants'. Narbonne was under enormous pressure from the 'personal promises' he had contracted, but Delay knew that he was 'extremely desirous of gratifying you'.

Not, however, desirous enough: Narbonne had filled some places before he fell but not Barnave's recommendations. So Delay urged Barnave to lose no time applying to de Graves. As for Delay himself, he was giving up his place at the war office and retiring to his fastness in Lorraine since he preferred 'horses to certain men', as did Barnave.[13] Graves told Barnave that though he would not be able to accommodate all his recommendations to fill the vacant posts of sub-lieutenant, he would 'do his best to place those he specially recommended'.

Barnave's conciliatory line was not adopted by his friends. Within a day of the appointment of the Jacobin ministry, Duport, the Lameth brothers and Méréville met Lafayette and his friends at Duport's house to discuss radical changes to the constitution. Both sides agreed that there should be a second chamber, but Duport wanted a hereditary peerage, which was a red line for Lafayette. Duport, the Lameth brothers and Dumas wanted the Legislative Assembly to be dissolved prematurely. Lafayette accused them of being 'counter-revolutionaries'; the whole meeting broke up and 'those who had proposed it lost face'. Pellenc concludes, smugly, 'Some regret was shown that I wasn't invited. I would have refused.'[14]

This report is important since it shows that both wings of the constitutional monarchists contemplated radical changes to the constitution earlier than is usually supposed and this in direct response to the formation of a Jacobin ministry which Barnave was ready to tolerate, telling Théodore: 'Don't force men to be villains who ask nothing better than to be knaves. That is the key right now. . . . I ask nothing better than that they form a party among themselves strong enough to make the government work. I only fear them when they are in opposition and they won't oppose as long as they flatter themselves that they can stay in power for a while.'[15]

He also noted the widening split in the Jacobins between Robespierristes and Girondins over war and peace. Robespierre was urging the affiliated societies to petition the Assembly for peace. He thought war was playing into the hands of 'the queen, who was the moving force behind the [European] powers.'[16] Robespierre's ostensible enemies, the Feuillants, also wanted peace, whereas his erstwhile allies, the Girondins, the Mensheviks, wanted war. Most of the generals, usually the beneficiaries of war, wanted peace because they feared insubordination in their troops. But Lafayette wanted war to restore his waning influence. Louis spent all day asking for divine guidance: 'Aware of the dangers surrounding me, I submit my fate to the Sovereign Master of the Universe.'[17] As for Marie-Antoinette, her attitude was '*vous l'avez voulu Georges Dandin*'. You asked for it, in other words.

And got it: on 20 April, as prescribed by the constitution, the king went to the Assembly to propose war on the king of Bohemia and Hungary, Francis II, son of the Emperor Leopold, who had died suddenly and mysteriously in March. The king's proposals were ecstatically accepted, with only seven dissenters, which included Théodore de Lameth and Dumas. Louis was pale and stammered; there were tears in his eyes; he delivered his speech in a monotone, 'in the same tone of voice as if he had been proposing the most insignificant decree in the world' – as if to distance himself from his words, as in a modern speech from the throne.

Barnave gave Théodore a prediction about the war which ranks in scope with Pellenc's about the 'destiny of mankind':

> If we have war its beginnings will be baleful and disastrous; without officers, without discipline, without trained troops, we will be fighting against the best armies in the world. Our original generals will see their glory eclipsed and perhaps even lose their jobs. But those who follow them will rally troops which have been taken by surprise rather than discouraged, and profit from their misfortune to impose discipline and, having . . . continued to hope when the nation despaired, they will have sufficient public support to see off the enemy and save France from her shame. The public will give them their whole confidence and theirs will be the dominant influence on the final outcome of the Revolution.[18]

The last sentence offers an uncanny prediction of the rise of Bonaparte.

⚜

For Barnave, the saving grace of the new ministry was the presence of de Graves, an orthodox constitutional monarchist. But on 8 May, following French defeats at Quiévrain and Tournai, he resigned. Barnave wrote that the resignation of de Graves almost persuaded him that individuals could play a part in the historical process. For Graves's presence had removed the venom from the Jacobins ministry, while allowing it to exploit its majority in the Assembly in order to govern. He considered that 'the constitutional party should have taken every imaginable step to prevent his resignation'.[19] For he 'was esteemed by all the parties and was strongly attached to the constitutional cause. The troop movements of the monarchy and the appointment of generals were solely at his disposal. He could have had more influence than any of his colleagues on the course of the Revolution. . . . France would have been saved by generals attached to the constitutional party.' Barnave constantly reminded Alexandre that he should dedicate himself to the army, eschewing drink and sex for the duration and winning the hearts of his troops with simple discourse.[20] When it was all over, the surviving generals would have the last word.

Barnave and Mirabeau were wrong in thinking that a Jacobin in the ministry was not the same thing as a Jacobin minister. The Girondins acted as an opposition party in power,[21] and continued to devise decrees which would embarrass the king. Between 27 May and 8 June Louis was asked to sanction a decree abolishing his constitutional bodyguard, which had only been set up on 16 March, a second one placing him thus unarmed at the mercy of a new camp of 20,000 *fédérés*, provincial national guards, near Paris, and a third ordering the deportation of refractory priests. Louis wanted to veto the decree abolishing his constitutional guard but since none of his ministers was prepared to countersign his veto, he was obliged to give his sanction.[22]

Thus disarmed, however, he did not intend to deliver himself up to the mercies of the *fédérés*; nor had he any intention of sanctioning the deportation of what he regarded as the only Catholic clergy in France. Exploiting a split which had developed within the ministry, on 12 June he dismissed the most intransigent, Roland (interior), Servan (war) and Clavière (finance), retaining Dumouriez, Duranthon, the keeper of the seals, and Lacoste at the marine. Dumouriez may have suggested this manoeuvre – he had not been informed about the camp of *fédérés* and drew his sword on Servan in the council. But when Dumouriez himself pressed the king to sanction the decrees, Louis dismissed him too on 16 June – Louis's diary specifically refers to a '*renvoi*'. Dumouriez was shocked – he did not know Louis had it in him, but the king said, "don't imagine you can frighten me with threats, I have made up my mind" '.[23] Dumouriez left to take up a command at the front. With difficulty Louis assembled a Feuillant ministry.

Barnave considered that the king was as 'weak' in appointing the Girondin ministry as 'imprudent' in dismissing it. 'In less than nine months three or four ministries have already appeared and disappeared like Chinese shadows; that the [Feuillant one] which has just been formed is perhaps the worst in the circumstances for this sort of anti-Jacobin revolution exists in the council but it does not exist in the nation, nor in the force of things, nor in the Assembly. Where will the council find support?'[24]

Did Barnave know that the man behind 'the administration which had just been formed' was none other than his ally Adrien Duport? Mercy, getting his information from Pellenc, who hoped to be made its cabinet secretary,[25] told Kaunitz: 'the present ministry has been formed entirely through the influence of M. Duport, formerly of the Constituent Assembly and who was, with the Lameths and Barnave one of the leaders of the Feuillant party. This Duport has maintained a correspondence with the king and was able to advise him on the choice of new ministers.'[26] This is confirmed by Bertrand de Molleville, who was reminded by Montmorin that the king 'as you know, reposes some confidence in' Duport.[27] It would seem that, instead of corresponding with the queen, as she and Barnave had expected, Duport was writing to the king instead. This would have consequences.

Despite hoping to be made cabinet secretary, Pellenc took the same view as Barnave on the dismissal of the Girondin ministry: they should have been retained as a lightning conductor. The dismissal, amid a growing conviction that the king was planning to seize control of Paris before the arrival of émigré or allied troops, provoked a reaction similar to that caused by the dismissal of Necker in 1789. A petition was due to be presented to the king asking him to withdraw his veto to the two decrees on 20 June, the double anniversary of the tennis court oath and the flight to Varennes. The orderly presentation of a petition degenerated into the occupation of the Tuileries for five hours by a mob drawn from the radical sections. The authorities – Pétion, the mayor, and Santerre of the National Guard – let it go on for hours. Arriving on the scene, Pétion said: 'Sire, I have just this minute learned of the situation you are in.' 'That is very surprising', the king replied, 'this has been going on for two hours.' The crowd finally left at 8 p.m.[28]

In a piece he called 'On the 20th June, its causes and effects', Barnave says: 'What a remarkable thing . . . that the French court [by creating martyrs] should have given the award of great men to three individuals [Clavière, Servan and Roland], two of whom would never have claimed it.' And he concluded: 'This *journée* has given such an accurate measure of the forces in play that today practically the only hope of salvaging the constitution lies in the divisions and timidity of those who are attacking it.' 'Divisions and timidity' there were aplenty: the Girondin leaders kept their fingers on the trigger but were reluctant to pull it, while Robespierre hid during the final assault on the monarchy.

Barnave then wrote a section entitled 'After the *journée* of 20 June'. He envisaged three scenarios: bankruptcy, the outcome of a war whose outcome depended on 'the quirks of fate' and 'an attack on the Tuileries by the people'. 'As for the last . . . if the principal personages [the king and queen] perish in it, all that can be expected is anarchy and Counter-Revolution.'[29]'

Louis's passive courage temporarily rekindled support for the monarchy. Petitions expressing outrage flowed in from provincial authorities, including that of Varennes. A petition condemning the *journée* was signed by 20,000 Parisians, each of whom would fall foul of the Law of Suspects in 1793. On 28 June having sent a letter signed by senior officer Lafayette appeared before the Assembly to denounce the *journée* of 20 June. Next day he attempted to close down the Jacobin Club, but received no adequate response, either from the National Guard or (apparently) from the queen. Barnave commented: 'Lafayette has raised his standard so openly that if he does not carry his army with him, he is lost; but if he is sure of it, he will decide the fate of France because if he can guarantee a central force, a mass of men and money will flow to him.'[30]

Still, he thought, at least this would lead to a resolution: 'All the parties want a crisis.' 'In our position it is absolutely certain', he wrote in his notebook, 'that the war must be fortunate, otherwise the constitution is lost because the king by dismissing his ministers and M. de Lf [Lafayette] by the steps he took have assumed all the responsibility for whatever happens, and if we meet with reverses both of them are lost and the republicans will become the centre of confidence and hope.'[31]

Barnave was not the only ex-Constituent to be following these events from Grenoble. Dubois-Crancé, who had attacked Barnave both in the Assembly and in print and would re-enter his life in 1793, had resumed the military career he had been forced to abandon in his youth and was lodging with a Mme de Vaux, presumably a relative of the old marshal who had been sent to crush anti-government resistance in 1788. On 23 June,

> M. Dubois de Crancé presided over an assembly where it was decided that the nation should arise as one man, that the decree of 20,000 men [the *fédérés*] should be regarded as having been sanctioned since it conformed with the wishes of the sovereign people. It was decided to send twenty men to Paris at Grenoble's expense. Réal gave 100 livres a month, M. Dubois de Crancé five livres, etc.[32]

The military 'reverses' Barnave feared came thick and fast. And as Marie-Antoinette said, 'the *journée* of 20 June forebodes another'.[33] To break the deadlock between the executive and the legislative in early July, an orchestrated campaign began for Louis's dethronement (*déchéance*): the Assembly was flooded with petitions from clubs, sections, from town and country. Vergniaud explored the constitutional possibility of overriding the royal veto if 'the *patrie* was in danger', which it was proclaimed to be on 11 July when Pétion's suspension was lifted.

In protest the Feuillant administrators of the département resigned en masse. Feuillant deputies also asked for leave of absence from the Assembly and passports – over 160, according to the *Patriote français*.

Barnave was appalled at such spinelessness. At the beginning of August, he wrote to Théodore:

> How comes it that in such a situation some of the most important members of your party either take *congés* or resign or withdraw from the committees? Everyone seems to think of himself and withdraw from the fray. You cannot hope to keep up public morale by such means. . . . Allowing the most extravagant notions to take hold without a fight. Nevertheless, I hope your Assembly will think long and hard before decreeing *déchéance*.[34]

That is Barnave's last letter before the dénouement, so we must guess what his response might have been to the actions of his friends who, far from 'withdrawing from the fray', embarked on a bold and desperate last-ditch attempt to save the monarchy. As Théodore de Lameth relates, 'Lafayette, who proceeded openly driven by a single desire, Adrien Duport, d'Abancourt, minister of war, and my brothers, were the first [*sic*] to hit on the idea of taking the king to Compiègne, surrounded by sufficient forces.' Marie-Antoinette told Fersen: 'The king is disposed to lend himself to this project; the queen is against it. The outcome of this great venture which I am far from approving is still in doubt.' Informed of her resistance, 'Adrien Duport . . . ran to the queen . . . and threw himself at her feet', begging her to accept the plan. 'All to no avail.' She had been dissuaded by men (such as Fersen) 'who were prepared to sacrifice the individual fates of the royal family if that was the price to be paid for the restoration of the *ancien régime*'.[35] Duport and Marie-Antoinette disliked each other. The unanswerable question is whether Barnave could have brought her round by persuading her that Lafayette was a necessary evil.

⚜

With no news from his friends in Paris, Barnave learned of the fall of the monarchy on 10 August from the newspapers. The palace was in a far better state of defence than it had been on 20 June for there had been ample warning: the Assembly had been told that unless they abolished the monarchy there would be a rising on the 10th. The thousand Swiss Guards, absolutely loyal, had been brought back from their barracks at

Rueil and Courbevoie and there were a thousand mounted police and two thousand national guards.

These forces, Reinhard considers, were 'enough to contain the insurrection, perhaps to 'crush it'. The king had been told that 20,000 men were surrounding the palace, whereas the numbers of the two forces were numerically equal. But all depended on the attitude of the National Guard, Parisian and provincial – the *fédérés* who were going via Paris to a camp at Soissons whose formation Louis had allowed. In prospect was an internecine struggle within the National Guard, one battalion turning out for the king, one against him and within a single battalion – the grenadiers maybe for the king and the gunners against. But the balance was tipped during the night by the replacement of the municipality, from which the National Guard took its orders, by an 'insurrectionary Commune' comprising delegates from the sections, which gave the orders to march on the Tuileries next day. Mandat, the loyal commander of the National Guard, having been summoned to confer with the old municipality, was murdered by the new one.

Roederer, the only member of the Département of Paris who had not resigned, advised that resistance was impossible and that the royal family should take refuge in the Assembly. On leaving the palace, Louis had omitted to countermand the orders to defend it. This the Swiss Guards did, killing or seriously wounding about 300 insurgents. When Louis, at about 10 a.m., finally gave orders to the Swiss to stop firing, they were butchered almost to a man.

The rising was as much against the Assembly as against the king, and it did as much for the king as it dared under mob pressure. Louis was suspended from his functions, not deposed: his fate was to be decided by a new Assembly, a National Convention, voted by manhood suffrage. Vergniaud even proposed that the dauphin's governor, M. de Fleurieu, be replaced, from which Louis took some negative comfort.

Barnave was full of contempt for the Assembly 'whose despicable feebleness had given a fistful of men the audacity to subjugate it and make a great revolution in the state by means of a popular riot'.[36] This 'great revolution in the state' was the 'second Revolution' he had striven to prevent.

⚜

Barnave spent July settling his affairs, though he could not know it would be his last month of freedom. On the 7th he paid Messrs. Charles Durand and son, perhaps M. Perier's agent, 1,400 livres 'on account' and on the 18th 1,597 livres, also 'on account'. In June there had been further attempts to mend the dyke on his property bordering the Isère but the river was too high to get at the foundations.[37]

— FIFTEEN —

A LONG INCARCERATION

On 19 August, Barnave was asleep in the country residence at Saint-Robert. Perhaps despite the disturbing news – it was a week to the day after news of the fall of the Tuileries had reached Grenoble – he was sleeping soundly for he rode his horse for miles every day, galloping down the steep wooded escarpments to the Isère, which marked the boundary of the estate and gave its name to the new départe-ment. In the morning, as its captain, he was due to review the National Guard of his parish, Saint-Egrève. Fearing resistance, the captain of the local gendarmerie, two junior officers and forty-five gendarmes sent to arrest him arrived at four in the morning.

His papers were sealed with the seal of the département and Barnave's own seal, A.B. (in capitals). Barnave himself was carted off to the citadel of Grenoble. According to Achard de Germane, there had been an attempt to string him up from a lamppost and a variant of his notorious words had been thrown in his face: 'Is this blood so pure that we dare not shed it?'[1] His flat at Grenoble had already been locked and the next day Barnave's mother, who had been allowed to accompany her son to Grenoble, showed them round. Nothing of interest was found. Barnave would spend the next seventeen months in prison.

His arrest must have come as a complete surprise to him. The king and queen had been protective of Barnave. Marie-Antoinette had given a copy of their correspondence to Fersen for safe-keeping, risking his jealousy; but when the Tuileries was sacked, a piece of paper was found in one of the drawers of the king's bureau. On 15 August 1792, it was read out to the Legislative Assembly and an order issued for Barnave's arrest. Since this was the only documentary evidence produced against him, it merits some discussion.

The paper (which we have used to show how government was conducted) was in the hand of de Lessart, the foreign secretary, and titled in the king's: '*Projet du comité des ministres concerté avec MM. Alexandre Lameth et Barnave*.' It concerned steps to mitigate any adverse reaction to the king's veto of the decree against the émigrés of 9 November 1791. The steps were: (1) 'refuse the sanction'; (2) 'write a new letter to the princes in a fraternal and royal tone'; (3) 'new proclamation on émigrés'; (4) 'requirement to the powers' not to suffer émigré formations on their territories; (5) steps to deal with army desertions; the ministers of justice, foreign affairs, war and the interior to tell the Assembly what measures they are taking.

Finally, 'It is thought that next it would be very expedient to ask each *département* to supply a certain number of men to be placed in the king's guard,' which Barnave advised the queen to do.

After the reading of this paper, Cambon 'demanded that the accusation of the two ex-Constituents be decreed. This document will convince even the most incredulous of the existence of a den of conspiracy known as the Austrian Committee.' The abbé Fauchet thought that the Assembly should arrest all the members of this 'counter-revolutionary committee' – the ministers du Tertre, Duportail, Montmorin, Tarbé and Bertrand de Molleville. Their arrest was also decreed to maintain the Assembly's reputation for impartiality.[2] Lameth was saved by Lafayette, who escorted him to the Army of the North. A warrant for his arrest, issued by the Paris Commune on 22 November, notes, 'He is no longer in France; he is in England.' On the same day the Commune issued a warrant for du Tertre.[3] Molleville, Duportail and Tarbé escaped; Montmorin was assassinated; du Tertre went into hiding.

Even the ultra-radical Marat wondered what all the fuss was about. 'It was not said what there was in the project to merit a decree of accusation against the Lameths. Nothing . . . that the most honest patriot nor most faithful friend of the constitution could not acknowledge.' Marat thought all 'this fuss about nothing' was part of a Girondin plot 'to deceive the people and give the king advance exculpation for having worked against the constitution.'[4] It is an idea to retain. The Girondins, including Brissot, were in the saddle – in the Assembly, if not in Paris – and they were Barnave's determined enemies.

The inspiration for the meeting of the committee which drafted this document came from Barnave. On 10 November 1791 he had told Marie-Antoinette that the exercise of the veto must be accompanied by pressure on the émigrés and princes, adding: 'I am going to see some of the ministers to persuade them of the need for this and to ask the king for an extraordinary meeting of the council tonight to propose the necessary measures.'

He told two colleagues in the Constituent, Alquier and Boissy d'Anglas, who had promised to intercede for him in the National Convention, to which both had been elected, that he was a long-standing friend of du Tertre and had kept up contact after the end of the Constituent Assembly. He had seen him maybe six times. One day he and Lameth had dropped in when the king's veto was being discussed. There were two or three ministers present and some others he would not mention for fear of incriminating them. Barnave told them that the veto was 'indivisible' and the king could not choose which parts to accept. Whether du Tertre then told the king that the proposals had been 'concerted' with Lameth and himself, two men who had saved the king's throne, he did not know; but 'no one knew better than this minister that we did not have any private relations with the king'.[5]

This is what du Tertre said at his own trial.

> The piece of paper in question was only the project for a message [of the king to the Assembly]. It is perfectly true that a part of its contents was implemented, such for example as the letter to the princes, and so on. Those who were familiar with the working practices of the former king know that he disliked long discussions. He would give in note form the matters he wanted to be discussed in the council of ministers with the order to convey the conclusions to him.

In other words, the numbered bullet items at the start of the document were the king's and the fuller recommendations the ministers'. The first half was an agenda or 'project'; the second half was the ministers' recommendations, some but not all of which were implemented.

Hermann, the formidable president of the Revolutionary Tribunal, chose to misunderstand du Tertre's words: 'It would appear from what you have said that your conclusions were transmitted by Capet [the king] to the manipulators of the Assembly, who did their level best to have them executed.' In other words, the king bypassed his ministers and communicated directly with men such as Vaublanc. Rattled by such malevolent ignorance, du Tertre blustered: 'I know absolutely nothing of this. In truth the former king's request for these notes raised my suspicions.' Hermann said in that case he should have reported his suspicions to the Commune. Du Tertre: 'I admit I was wrong in not doing so.'[6]

The upshot of all this evidence is that though Barnave certainly did not attend the *Conseil d'etat* and probably not any formal session of the ministerial committee (though this often met in du Tertre's house), the incriminating document was not only 'concerted with' but concerted *by* Barnave, who asked the queen for 'an extraordinary meeting of the council tonight'. It should not be necessary but (given the climate of French historiography until recently) one must say that Barnave had committed no real crime.

Achard de Germane believed that Barnave had been arrested because he was 'compromised by the discovery of a correspondence with the queen'.[7] If Barnave picked up this rumour, his blood would have run cold. For until he learned of the reason for his arrest, he must have feared that his correspondence with the queen had been discovered. He had no idea what had happened to the correspondence. When he had left Paris, it was intact.

⚜

Barnave did not stay long in the citadel: on 24 August he was in the Conciergerie, the prison attached to the former Parlement where he and his father had pleaded. On that date he received a letter from d'Aiguillon, now serving under Biron in the Army of the North. Barnave was not meant to receive letters or visitors, but his mother, disguised as the servant who brought his meals, smuggled the letter in. It was later confiscated and extracts published in the *Moniteur* of 1 September. It began: 'It is time my dear Barnave, in the midst of the horrors surrounding us, to break a long silence. What has become of you? Are you still at Grenoble? Do you still plan to remain in this land of desolation or are you going to leave it for more peaceable climes?'

He ended: 'Do me the pleasure, my dear Barnave, of giving my declaration [protest against the king's suspension] maximum publicity and of having it reprinted as well as Broglie's. Adieu my friend, who knows when we will meet again? But this I can say for certain: I will never cease to esteem and love you.'[8] This very personal but also very incriminating letter was read out in the Assembly on 30 August and Barnave regretted the part this played in d'Aiguillon's decision to emigrate.[9] It also kept Barnave's case on the boil.

D'Aiguillon did not know that Barnave was in prison and could not know what was about to happen in Paris. De Lessart had been sent for trial before the High Court at Orléans, which had also been seized of Barnave's case,[10] but on 17 August a new tribunal, proposed and briefly presided over by Robespierre, was set up to judge cases relating to 10 August. De Lessart and fifty-two prisoners were sent back to Paris to be judged by the new tribunal, but when they stopped off at Versailles their escort murdered forty-four of them.

On 1 September news reached Paris that Verdun, the last fortress between the invading Prussians and Paris, would not be able to hold out. On 2 September began the September Massacres. They lasted until the 6th, by which time some 1,300 prisoners had been murdered, including Montmorin, who had been incarcerated in the Abbaye prison. The massacres were directed by the Commune's surveillance committee on which Robespierre sat. Robespierre's purpose was twofold: to maximise the chances of his party (the Montagnards) in the elections to the Convention; and to have the Girondin leaders murdered. He was successful in Paris, where his colleagues swept the board, but not in the provinces, where his Girondin opponents made substantial gains.

On the night of 2 September, the surveillance committee ordered the arrest of Brissot, Roland and up to thirty leading Girondins (accounts vary). If the order had been carried out, they would all have perished. But it was countermanded by Danton, now minister of justice and working alongside the reinstated Girondin ministers. The political backdrop to the rest of Barnave's life centred on the internecine struggle between the Girondins and Montagnards. Beginning with a quarrel over peace or war, it continued over the king's fate and remained one between Paris and country, leading to a desultory civil war in the summer of 1793.

At all events Barnave counted himself fortunate to have been down on the Swiss border when all this was going on: 'The High Court [at Orléans] having been abolished I thank my lucky stars that I escaped the massacres of Paris and Versailles.' The new tribunal had been inaugurated on 17 August after pressure by the Robespierrist Commune on a reluctant Legislative Assembly led by Brissot. Robespierre was briefly the tribunal's president and his influence continued to be dominant.

Barnave felt he would stand no chance with 'such a tribunal with the accusatory zeal of the audience for whom my head would be scant but just compensation for the escape of Lafayette, Lameth etc. and the very likely preservation of the life of Louis'.[11] Barnave was writing this in mid-January 1793, when the outcome of the king's trial still seemed in the balance. He thought of offering the king his services but, on reflection, thought that would be counter-productive – Bérenger found a draft defence of the king in Barnave's papers.[12]

The king's trial lasted from 14 to 20 January. After the inevitable guilty verdict, a vote was held as to his punishment – death, banishment, imprisonment or exile. Out of 721 voters, only 361 voted unconditionally for death – a majority of one. The king was executed on the 21st. The execution of the king marked the turning point in the struggle between Girondins and Montagnards. The Girondins had wanted to avert the trial but not enough of them had the guts to vote to save his life. But the Girondins, though doomed, were not defeated yet for their strength lay in the provinces.

Thinking the king's life might yet be preserved, Barnave thought he could detect a move towards leniency in Paris and also that it might be possible to exploit the tension between Montagnards and Girondins to his advantage. He had 'read in the papers that the decree against Duquesnoy had been rescinded'. He was outraged: '[Y]ou must agree, dear Alquier, that it is a sign of the times that this individual, who it is common knowledge has been the vile servitor and perhaps the pimp of all the ministers, was no sooner accused than set free while I against whom there is only one piece of evidence, which even if authentic tends to my justification, have languished in prison these five months.'

Likewise, Talleyrand, whose association with Duquesnoy we have noted, was left alone. But Talleyrand 'is the secret friend of the men of the moment [the Girondins] and I am their public enemy'.

Commissioners of a Montagnard complexion had been sent to investigate General Montesquiou, a friend of Barnave's on the Swiss border. Barnave writes that the commissioners 'told our [Grenoble] administrators very frankly that it was expedient to keep me in prison for some time yet until the situation was more stable; that I should probably be against all current policies etc.'[13] – for Barnave did not disguise his disapproval of the rising of 10 August and the king's trial and execution. However, the commissioners had also told the Grenoble administration that they had done well to stop Barnave being sent to Paris and hinted that the decree against him had been '*une affaire de circumstance*' due to the malevolence of the Girondins, who were then in the driving seat.

He concluded that the commissioners

> were probably favourable to me; now it seems to me that this influence comes from the Mountain [the Left Wing of the Assembly sitting where the seats banked up steeply] and that is a quarter where it is good to have friends. Although the conduct of this party seems thoroughly disorderly, I confess that I don't find them wicked and infinitely less hypocritical than certain parties who paraded their virtue. Of the Paris deputation [to the Convention] I only know Legendre and Danton, and I have not had any dealings with them for nearly two years and none I would blush to acknowledge. I don't think they would do me any disservice.[14]

As we saw just before the Massacre of the Champ de Mars, Alexandre had warned Legendre to tell Danton and Desmoulins 'to get out of Paris today; dine in the countryside'. Nor, in the prevailing climate, would Barnave have 'blushed' to acknowledge his earlier links through Danton with the popular movement. Danton more than repaid the favour to Adrien Duport. The Commune's surveillance committee (the one whose tender mercies Barnave dreaded) had ordered that Duport be arrested at his country estate and sent back to Paris. Théodore Lameth sent a note to Danton begging him to intervene, which he did, first telling the local authorities not to send Adrien back to Paris (Danton knew the massacres were about to start) and then ordering his release. Danton told him to lie low – he went to England – to save him embarrassment: letters found on him concerning negotiations with Mercy-Argenteau had been published in Marat's *Ami du Peuple* on 13 September, which 'likewise asked: what has happened to Barnave incarcerated in Grenoble?'[15]

Danton was a cuckoo in the Girondin ministerial nest. Its guiding spirit was Roland, now back as minister of the interior, and *his* guiding spirit was the formidable Madame Roland, who wrote at the time of the September Massacres, 'Robespierre has a knife at our throats.' Roland told the Grenoble authorities to inventory Barnave's papers and send anything incriminating or suspicious to him. Barnave said this was illegal: a prisoner's papers should accompany him to the place of his trial – currently Orléans. He got his way. He said he needed his papers 'to carry a great case before the tribunal of public opinion when the time has come'.[16] In saving his other papers, Marie-Antoinette had a similar thing in mind.

In February 1793 Barnave learned that some of his expatriate friends had returned to Paris: Théodore, Dumas, the wives of Charles de Lameth and Victor Broglie – all of them his correspondents. Charles had been arrested at Rouen on his way to England. After six weeks' imprisonment, he emerged from captivity, though 'barely recognisable', through the good offices of Danton. They settled in Hackney but Madame Charles returned to France to prevent her vast estates – at Bayonne as well as Saint-Domingue – from being confiscated. She was imprisoned for a period and then lay low at Osney, hiding their silver, eating off wooden platters and watching their avenue of poplars being cut down to make trees of liberty.[17]

Barnave apologised for not letting them know his whereabouts, explaining 'I have perhaps only escaped from those who hate me by silence and being forgotten', though luckily 'the principles of 2 September' did not rule in Grenoble. He had written to Théodore a few days before, giving him his mother's address, to which he had replied with the news of his friends' return. But he was also anxious about the fate of Madame de la Châtre and d'Aiguillon, who (he believed) had been forced to emigrate because his letter to Barnave had been intercepted. He was right to have been concerned about Madame de la Châtre – she had been incarcerated in the Abbaye prison, a centre for the September Massacres, but had been freed in time through the influence of Talleyrand and Madame de Staël. She then emigrated, returning to France in 1799. Curiously, he signs this letter 'Barnave, *f*[*ils*]' in the middle of an uncompleted sentence.[18]

Renewed contact with his close friends cheered him but, as he told another ex-Constituent friend, probably Baillot, in late February/ March, his affairs were suffering by his imprisonment. Some of his farms in the Drôme département had narrowly escaped being burned down. So he turned again to the state of his captivity. His paradoxical position was that he was detained by 'a kind of *lettre de cachet*' – imprisonment without trial, as in the *ancien régime* – and yet he did not want to stand trial, at least in Paris, though the Revolutionary Tribunal had been abolished on 1 December. Political cases were being tried by the criminal court in Paris with more observance of the normal rules of justice. To his amazement, two of the king's political agents, Saint-Léon and Sainte-Foix, had been acquitted on 22 and 27 February respectively. But he thought the public mood was too 'variable' and Parisian hostility towards himself too constant to risk it: 'So I want to be given another tribunal – the choice is immaterial so long as it is in a tolerably peaceful town where I can have a fair trial.'[19]

However, on 10 March a second Revolutionary Tribunal was established at Paris for political crimes. It was proposed by Danton in order to prevent a recurrence of the September Massacres: 'We must be terrible to prevent the people being terrible.' Blood must flow along official channels. But though Danton had made the prospect of a trial even more perilous, Barnave's friends entertained hope from that quarter. On his election to the Convention, Danton had had to resign from the ministry but on 5 April he had set up the Committee of Public Safety (CPS), which was in effect the government. He dominated this first CPS – the second or 'great' CPS was dominated by Robespierre, who entered it on 27 July. The CPS had been created in response to defeat abroad and the royalist rising in the Vendée at home, which at one point threatened Paris.

Barnave's friends also sought help from Danton's ally Basire, who sat on the Convention's police committee, the Committee of General

Security (CGS), together with Legendre. Basire had displayed appreciation for Barnave well before his aid was enlisted. On 3 March Basire and Legendre were sent on a mission to Lyon, which was already exhibiting signs of resistance to the Convention, resistance that erupted into full scale revolt on 29 May. Robespierre's younger brother Augustin, also a deputy and on mission in the Midi, thought that Basire and Legendre were too soft on Lyon.

With these contacts Barnave 'addressed the Convention's Committee of General Security – this committee where all the denunciations are made and where all the proofs are deposited and I obtained its assurance that it had received no denunciation either oral or written against me'.[20] It was the police committee which ordered arrests and releases and it may have been on this occasion that Danton made the first of his two attempts to save Barnave. But he told Théodore that Barnave had made too many enemies by his reference to 'men [like Brissot] who grow fat on public misfortunes like insects on dung', which had not been forgiven.

Théodore approached Danton again, working in conjunction with Boissy d'Anglas, and 'soon' had good news: 'All the leaders were agreed – even the most resistant had been won over and Barnave would be restored to liberty.' He simply had to write to the Convention requesting it. Barnave was tempted and encouraged by his friends drafted such an appeal. But it was by no means a humble petition. He had, he said, been held for ten months without charge 'or even interrogation', 'enveloped in the destruction of a work I had helped to build', honoured 'to be among those who had to be struck down when the constitution of my country was being toppled'. He then sought to refute the only evidence against him along the lines we have examined. Finally, he briefly surveyed his activity in the Constituent Assembly. Revision: 'reconciling liberty with the need for strong government'. Diplomatic committee: 'avoiding war with dignity'. Colonies: 'I wanted to preserve them for France.'[21]

But the appeal was never sent. Barnave wrote to Théodore thanking him for his efforts but told him: 'to ask them for justice would be to recognise the justice of their previous acts and they have killed the king'! He concluded, 'No, my friend, I would rather suffer and die than lose one scintilla of my moral and political character.' He would rather be condemned than condemn his life's work. So, Théodore concluded, 'he suffered and he died'.[22]

⚜

We know why Barnave was arrested – he had fallen foul of the Girondins who controlled the Legislative Assembly in its dying days – but why after fourteen months of detention he was suddenly brought to trial needs some explaining. And for this we must look at the general crisis of spring/summer, as reflected in relations between Paris and the départements. On 5 April Dumouriez was defeated by the Austrians at the Battle of Neerwinden in Belgium. He negotiated a truce to allow him to march on Paris and proclaim the dauphin king as Louis XVII. His troops refused to follow him and he crossed to the Austrian lines with his entire general staff. The creation of the CPS and the Revolutionary Tribunal was a response to this crisis. The *assignats* had depreciated by 50 per cent and there had been food riots in Paris on 24/5 February in which d'André's grocery stores were looted. Between 10 and 15 March the département of the Vendée in the Catholic west rose for throne and altar. A contributory factor in the revolt had been the decree of 24 February ordering the conscription of about 300,000 men; each French département was to supply a quota of recruits.

To aid the recruitment the Convention sent out representatives-on-mission to the départements. To improve their position in the Convention the Girondins voted to send Montagnards on a mission and on 23 April two of them, Amar and Merino, arrived in Grenoble. Amar was a local man. Born in 1755 he had, like Barnave, been an advocate attached to the Parlement of Grenoble and in 1788 had bought an office conferring nobility. He now reported back that he 'had found nothing but *parlementaire* pride and regret at the death of the tyrant'. He must have known the Barnaves well, though no evidence of contacts has survived. None of the Barnave family were included in the 'long list' he drafted 'of the cruellest enemies of the Revolution strongly suspected of intelligence with the external [Piedemontese] enemy'. Amar was deputy for the département of Isère (*chef lieu* Grenoble) and would have local scores to settle and favours to bestow. In the *ancien régime* the kings had been careful not to appoint intendants to their own locality for this reason.

At the end of his long report back to the CPS on 9 May, Amar writes: 'Barnave often instigates agitation which is on the point of irrupting into popular explosions. We have the intimate conviction that he conducts a correspondence and dangerous intrigues seconded by his family's comings and goings [to his prison]. We think that it would be expedient to transfer him to Paris.'[23] On13 September following a further leftward lurch of the Revolution, Amar was voted on to the CGS.

No action was taken on Amar's suggestion. The next representative on mission to arrive at Grenoble was another enemy with local connections, Dubois-Crancé. He was one of four such representatives sent by the CPS on 30 April to bolster the army of General Kellermann, which was fighting the Piedemontese in Savoy. But the commissioners' remit extended beyond the military situation to cover the whole Rhône valley, where allegiance to the Convention was frail. Dubois-Crancé arrived at Grenoble on 2 June and 'soon afterwards' gave orders for Barnave to be transferred from Grenoble to Fort Barraux in the mountains bordering Savoy. Crancé did, however, allow the faithful David to continue to stay with Barnave in prison. Saying he was a fool, he added: 'Well then! Go young man; the commandant of the fort will receive you.'[24]

The day Dubois-Crancé arrived in Grenoble a central committee of the Parisian sections had forced the Convention to order the arrest of twenty-two Girondin leaders and some of them had broken house arrest to raise the flag of rebellion. The whole of the Rhône valley sided with the rebels, save only Valence, which, as we have seen, had a vendetta against Grenoble and was guided by Claude Payan, soon to be Robespierre's right-hand man. Not sure what would happen, Dubois-Crancé tried to humour the Grenoble authorities by releasing some of the nobles Amar had ordered to be imprisoned. The departmental authorities suspected a trap. A shadow Convention was in prospect. Lyon had risen against the Convention on 20 May – before the coup d'état against the Girondins. Barnave had predicted that if a republic were proclaimed in a large country such as France, it would inevitably become a federal one. But there are no prizes in politics for being right.

Crancé moved on to his central objective, the siege of Lyon. He favoured a siege rather than the frontal attack which Robespierre favoured; so he was recalled and replaced by Robespierre's ally in the CPS, Georges Couthon, who bombarded the city into submission on 9 October. Couthon would have liked to raze the rebel city to the ground, plant trees of liberty and resettle those inhabitants not executed by firing grapeshot (*les mitraillades*) in scattered communities throughout France. A column was to be raised with the inscription, 'Lyon made war on liberty: Lyon is no more'! In the event, on grounds of expense, only fifty houses were destroyed, but the city was re-named Ville-Affranchie ('liberated city').

Dubois-Crancé's subsequent career may be of interest. In March 1794 Robespierre drew up a proscription list which included Crancé; he survived, but in July Robespierre drew up a more select list of only six, on which Crancé figures. After Lyon he had been sent to Brittany but had been again recalled – this time for being too severe. Robespierre divided his opponents into those who were too severe (the *ultras*) and those who did not go far enough (the *citras*). Poor Crancé had been both: *citra* (towards Lyon) – hence his appearance on the March proscription list together with Danton; and *ultra* (towards the Vendée rebels – 250,000 had already been killed, perhaps enough) – hence his re-appearance on the July list. On hearing that he had been recalled Crancé, or Dubois de Crancé, as Robespierre persisted in calling him, galloped back from Rennes and without changing went straight to the CPS on 7 Thermidor and denounced Robespierre who had absented himself in a sulk. The CPS refused Couthon's demand that Crancé be arrested; instead, the Convention brought Robespierre, Saint-Just, Payan and the whole Robespierrist regime down on the 9th.[25] Crancé went on to be war minister for a brief month before Bonaparte's coup in 1799.

⚜

It would seem that Barnave was given every opportunity to escape from Fort Barraux, up in the mountains to the northeast of Grenoble. It was right on the border with Savoy and the lower-ground windows of Barnave's cell were left unbarred. David recounts that Barnave even woke a sentry sleeping at his post with the warning that he would be in trouble if he escaped. But Barnave would not heed 'the ardent pleas of his friends' to avail himself of such opportunities: 'I could in all conscience have emigrated in present circumstances if I had played no part in public affairs,' he said, which Théodore called 'an exaggeration of generosity'.[26] He would have offended against his personal conception of '*gloire*'.

It was apparently also while Barnave was in Fort Barraux that Danton said that he would be freed if he appealed to the Convention. But Danton was no longer the same power in the land. He had played little part in affairs since leaving the CPS; he was ill and on 12 October asked for leave to retire to his home at Arcis-sur-Aube to convalesce. 'Leave of absence of this kind was quite exceptional,' notes his biographer. And he may have wanted to avoid the harrowing spectacles of the show trials of Marie-Antoinette and the Girondins. And Basire had been replaced in the CGS by Amar – a friend in high places exchanged for an enemy. The appointment of Amar was a consequence of the popular *journée* of 5 September, when the Revolution reached its climacteric and the Convention was forced to introduce price controls and pass the Law of Suspects. The climacteric, that is, of popular pressure on Parliament; thereafter, the CPS, the embodiment of '*gouvernement révolutionnaire*' – provisional dictatorship – when terror was officially 'the order of the day', began to exert its grip.

Early in September Barnave was moved from Fort Barraux to Saint-Marcelin, some 20 miles east of Grenoble. Why? Because, we are told, of the approach of the Piedemontese army. Would it have mattered if he had been captured? It may be of significance that Amar, in his recommendation that Barnave be moved to Paris, had also commented that, unlike Grenoble, Saint-Marcelin was one of the country towns that 'breathed the pure air of . . . republicanism'.[27] No one to turn a blind eye to escape there. There was now a new proconsul on the scene, Petijean, more doctrinaire than his predecessors. He boasted to the CPS that he had held an 'auto-da-fe' in Grenoble, a public bonfire of the royalist vanities: ancient tapestries hanging in the *ci-devant* Parlement with the arms of the kings and the old dauphins as well as those of popes, bishops, seigneurs. What particularly annoyed him was the multiplicity of fleurs-de-lys: 'I believe that their very multiplicity prevents the patriots from seeing them. . . . They even penetrate the very sittings of the popular society, placed behind and in front of the president.'[28]

But at least the president was up to speed: 'Citizen Chépy, the political agent of the executive power animates and excites them to put themselves forward. During this evening's session they decided to open a voluntary subscription for the war against the English' – on 27 August the naval base of Toulon had been handed over to an English fleet. We last met Chépy presiding over the Jacobin Club at the time of the flight to Varennes.

Pierre-Colandre Chépy had been in the diplomatic service since late March 1792. He had been appointed under the auspices of the Girondins and corresponded with their foreign secretary, Lebrun. He also had a close relationship with the editor of the *Patriote français*, Girey-Duprey. So when the Gironde fell and on 4 June Lebrun was arrested, Chépy covered his tracks by adopting an ultra-revolutionary stance – hence his moves against Barnave. His mission, which the new minister, Desforges, continued, was to watch over General Kellermann's army in the Midi and report on the patriotism of the general and his staff officers; and additionally, to assure the Republic of Geneva that France had no present plans to annex the city. But he also, off his own bat, decided to make Grenoble his base and use its popular society to try keep the département of Isère from joining the federalist rebels.

On 20 October Chépy told the foreign minister: 'Barnave who the representative of the people Gaultier had transferred to Barraux and who was moved at the time of the Piedemontese invasion is today at Tullins. The département of Isère would very much like to be rid of him. Bring this to the attention of the Committee of Public Safety; he should be sent before the tribunals [*sic*].' It is unlikely that the département did want to be rid of Barnave, at least on ideological grounds, for in another dispatch Chépy wrote: 'the directorate of the Département is *feeble, very feeble* . . . it is necessary to *revolutionise* the Isère'.[29] It is curious also that Chépy says that Barnave is at Tullins rather than Saint-Marcellin. Tullins was 14 miles from Saint-Marcellin but equally patriotic, according to Amar.

Chépy's subsequent dispatch, dated 29 October, ends: 'P. S. My thanks for having Barnave sent on his way to Paris.' It was actually the minister of justice, Gohier, rather than Desforges, the foreign minister, who on 22 October sent orders to the département of Isère to transfer Barnave; on the 29th they bundled up his papers and gave them to Millet, a gendarme lieutenant who was to escort Barnave to Paris.

Barnave set off for Paris on 3 November in a closed carriage with Millet and escorted by a cavalry detachment. They went via Burgundy – we are told to avoid demonstrations in Barnave's favour; they travelled in small stages and did not reach Paris until the 18th. From the first stop, Bourgoin, Barnave wrote to Boissy on the 4th. He starts his letter brightly, 'I don't know . . . if you have learned that I am coming to Paris.' He then recommended his mother to him. Boissy was 'a mere acquaintance' who had not sought him out in his 'blazing prosperity' but had become 'the friend of his misfortunes'. His mother would be travelling up separately and though she had not yet set out, she should arrive first. Julie, at twenty-seven the younger of Barnave's sisters, would accompany her; Adélaide, aged twenty-nine, would remain at Saint-Robert. Barnave had told his mother to call on Boissy and seek out his friendship if this could be done without compromising him. 'If things turned out against her wishes', he wrote, 'she would be in extreme need of consolation.'

He had no illusions as to how things *would* 'turn out' – 'I regard the outcome as pretty well predetermined.' But he would fight with all his strength for his reputation. There was nothing compromising in his confiscated papers, Barnave said, but 'what once counted as patriotism is almost a crime today'. He asked Boissy to write 'to my friend' – Basire he could not say in case the letter was intercepted – in the hope that he would be able to get the Convention to stop the trial, though 'he didn't think there was any more that could be done.'[30]

Basire told Boissy,

> sorrowfully, I am grieved by what you tell me, but I can do nothing more for your friend; I have less influence than you as you will soon see . . . [he was arrested on 17 November and guillotined on 5 April 1794, together with Danton]. I am touched by the interest you take in a young man I like and by your confidence in me. I want to show you how much I appreciate it by giving you good advice. Don't repeat the request you have made to me to anyone else; you are sure to destroy yourself and you will not save him.[31]

This mirrors closely what Basire's friend Danton replied when Théodore asked him to try to influence the king's trial: 'I will expose myself if I see any chance of success but if I lose all hope, I will be among those who condemn . . . [the king], since I don't want my head to fall with his.'[32]

Madame Barnave and Julie, escorted by young David in his uniform of a National Guard lieutenant, caught up with Barnave's party at Beaune on the 10th and Millet let them stay in the same *hôtel*. Likewise at Dijon, the next stop the following day. Then the ladies travelled on ahead, the cavalry escort was dismissed and Barnave continued on to Paris with two guards. From Dijon Barnave wrote his last letter to Adélaide, dated 13 November:

> I parted with my mother and Julie yesterday; they will arrive the day after tomorrow, that is, two or three days before me because I will be making the rest of my journey by coach. No doubt you will hear from them before this letter reaches you and you will learn how things stand with me better than I could explain in a letter. I still hope but as it is best in my situation to prepare for the worst, I am going to give you the reflections I could not say to their face without distressing them too much; and in any case I would rather give you my thoughts in writing.
>
> My dear love, I am perhaps going to be separated from you forever. The moment is cruel; but let us not make too much of it; and instead of giving ourselves over to the sad thoughts it causes, let us rather try to derive what consolations it may afford.
>
> I am still in my youth and yet already I have known and experienced all the good and evil which make up human life. Endowed with a lively imagination, I have for long believed in chimeras; but I am now disabused and at the moment when I see myself about to quit this life, the only things I shall miss are friendship (none more than I can claim to have savoured its charms) and the cultivation of the mind – a habit which has often filled my days with delight.
>
> But, truth to tell, my mind has been too active; there is a powerful spring within me which will not allow me to regard these unadulterated blessings as sufficient. I have acquired enough philosophy and reflection to be able to reject false lights but my mental ardour is too strong to allow me to appreciate the true ones and I feel that this almost ungovernable tendency will always stand between me and true happiness.

> Death is nothing. The more I have had time to contemplate it, the more I am convinced of this not only by reflection but by sentiment. Today it is my habitual thought and I live with it as calmly and serenely as if, like with other men, it was only a distant prospect. *One second, one indivisible moment of pain followed by complete disappearance [*évanouissement complet*]; an indivisible moment beyond which there is no more pain, no more regret, nor memories is easier to bear than those to which one attaches the least importance in the course of life.*
>
> So, my good friends, totally separate the grief that my fate will cause you (and I certainly hope it will not be the one I expect), separate I repeat any feelings to do with my own pain and consider only your own for it will be real enough and allow it all the consolations to which a loss, however great, is always susceptible when it concerns only yourself and you do not allow feelings of compassion for the person one loves.

When Bérenger published this letter, he omitted the italicised passage lest its nihilism offend the religious sensibilities of the day. This was Barnave's settled view, though, and one which he did not hide from his family. Earlier he had scribbled on a piece of paper above the profile of a naked woman and the words '*monsieur*' and '*papier*': '*Post mortem nihil est, mors ipsa que nihil*' ('there is nothing after death and death itself is nothing'). Originally used by Seneca in his play *Troades* ('Trojan women'), the idea was taken up by Voltaire in connection with religious toleration and the persecution of Jean Calas. Beneath it Barnave writes another quotation from Voltaire: '*Demeure . . . il faut choisir et passer à l'instant de la morte à la vie et de l'être au néant*'. This again is from Voltaire: his translation of Hamlet's soliloquy 'To be or not to be'.[33]

Voltaire prided himself on his free translation,[34] and one can respect that. However, there are limits and he transgressed them by projecting the views of the afterlife of an eighteenth-century sceptic on to those of a sixteenth-century dramatist. The whole point of Hamlet's soliloquy is fear of what might happen in the afterlife – bad dreams. What Hamlet wanted and what Shakespeare wanted for himself was 'quiet consummation' and a 'renownèd grave'. Barnave just wanted the 'renownèd grave'.

Barnave continues his letter:

The law has just returned to you what you are owed by natural justice by dividing among the three of you what my father left. You will be comfortably well-off and certainly the settlement which my stormy and uncertain life has delayed may be speedier and more advantageous for you. That is my dearest, sweetest wish and I take pleasure in dwelling on it.

My poor mother has raised two sons and turned them into men distinguished both in mind and heart. Perhaps when you read this, she will have lost both of them in the flower of their age. Our misfortune, my good friend, is as nothing compared to hers. But I hope she may soon be comforted and perhaps it can only be done by you. We need new children to whom to attach the hopes of their namesakes. They will grow up to be inspired by a name which can only be honourable and they will receive an education from you all which will make them worthy of it. Above all, only marry men whose conduct and character accords with ours. It matters little if they have no fortune and provided they make up for it with a standing or a capacity for work that should not be an obstacle. You must be able to think and feel together and form one family such as ours was: that is the basis for happiness. If both of you do not remain with my mother, Julie will stay and you will be as near as possible as it is to my mother, who will raise your sons. She will endue them with that courageous and open manner which makes men and which for my brother and myself was worth the rest of our education put together. Provided her feelings are engaged, she will keep her strength for a long time and by working for the good of your children she will taste any remaining happiness or at least consolation.

I still have precious friends that I leave behind. Treasure them. Make new ones from those who have taken an interest in my fate. Honourable and distinguished friends are one of the greatest assets in life. That virtuous man [Boissy d'Anglas] who has never ceased to take an interest in me and who my mother will see in Paris is also among those you should try to make a friend; and you may be sure that soon his name will be loved and honoured and will bring you goodwill and respect.

My good friends, the hope that you will find a happy life will brighten my last moments and fill my heart. If this sentiment survives beyond life, if one can recall what one has left behind, this idea would be the sweetest for me. May my idea gradually become tender rather than sad. Think that I am making a prolonged journey, that I do not suffer, that if I could feel I would be happy and content so long as you were.

Adélaide, Julie, I adopt each of your first-borns. I adopt them legally. Let each bear my name. Let the youngest be called Dugua. Let them be bound together by every tie; let them belong to all three of us. Let them give back her two sons to my mother, sons worthy of a better fate.

Adieu my good friend.

Barnave *f*[*ils*][35]

I have some paper and time left and I take up my pen again. Continue to cultivate your mind. It is one of the sweetest things in life. Those who regard my memory as a recommendation will want to be associated with you, especially if your conversation provides an additional attraction. Do not be cast down or languid because of my absence. Rather, by touching you let it stir your soul anew.

I have nothing of importance to say to you about business matters. You will easily find more informed advice than mine. If my share is not swiftly detached and sold [that is, confiscated by the state], it will remain with you. Because if, against my expectation, in these intemperate times, I experience a striking injustice, reparation will soon be at hand.

Adieu, my love.[36]

— SIXTEEN —

TRIAL AND DEATH

Paris had not forgotten Barnave. His arrival was eagerly anticipated – too eagerly: on 9 November, when he was still in transit, the *Moniteur* and the *Journal de Paris* reported that he had been taken to the Abbaye prison. Still, a pleasure deferred is a pleasure enhanced, and on the evening of the 18th Barnave was safely ensconced in the Conciergerie, the antechamber of the guillotine, no halfway house like the Abbaye. It was getting late but Gohier, who had ordered Barnave's transfer, 'hastened to inform the Convention that Barnave, ex-deputy in the Constituent Assembly has just been transferred to the Conciergerie'.[1]

Barnave must have been both comforted and saddened to find that his friend and secret governmental colleague Duport du Tertre was already there and that they were to stand trial together. Du Tertre had been in the Conciergerie since 18 October, narrowly missing Marie-Antoinette, who had left the Conciergerie on the 16th on her way to the scaffold. Du Tertre must have wondered whether she would 'crack' under interrogation – after all, she knew things about him and Barnave which would have made public prosecutor Fouquier-Tinville's lank hair stand on end. But she remained steady under fire, as Barnave knew she would.

In their desperation to link Marie-Antoinette with the Girondins the prosecution made a schoolboy error. They put it to her that 'despite the lively objections of Duranthon, at the time minister of justice, she had determined Louis Capet to veto' the decrees against the émigrés and refractory priests. Marie-Antoinette replied 'that in the month of November, Duranthon was not a minister'. She did not say that the minister in question had been Duport du Tertre.[2]

Another ex-minister sharing the prison was l'Averdy, finance minister from 1763 to 1768 and now aged seventy. His case may serve to illustrate just what Barnave was up against. L'Averdy's 'crime' – bizarre even for the times – was that some wheat (instead of oats) had been found in a large water trough on his estates. The witness did not see the old man placing the corn there but he was still to blame. Today this is called 'strict liability'. It was even stricter then.

L'Averdy was accused of placing the offending substance there as part of a 'generally acknowledged plot to deliver up the republic to the horrors of famine by letting the wheat necessary for the subsistence of the people go rotten . . . in order [to drive the people to despair and thus] bring about the Counter-Revolution and civil war . . .'. However ludicrous the charges, the supporting evidence was always punctilious. Hermann, the president of the Tribunal, asked l'Averdy, 'What is the diameter and depth of the water trough in question?' L'Averdy, entering fully into the spirit of the game, answered, 'It is twenty-five foot in diameter and 2¼ foot deep.' He was guillotined on 24 November.[3]

Another prisoner in the Conciergerie was the parliamentary journalist C.F. Beaulieu, who survived to write 'souvenirs' of his experience in 1797 and the six-volume *Essais historiques* 1801–3. He claimed to have had 'frequent conversations with Barnave', 'this amazing young man', which he summarised as follows:

> After he left the National Assembly and especially during his years in prison in Grenoble he studied prodigiously and the most profound and just reflections were bound to flow from a brain so well organised as his. He had examined the principal laws of all the governments of Europe and rendered them with exact precision and had concluded that considering the difficulties they had to overcome and the present inclinations of men, a unified strong constitutional monarchy was the only way to secure them peace and a little liberty.

Barnave confessed that his 'opinion on the royal sanction [that is, against the absolute veto] was one of those he most regretted'. 'Standing as he did at the gates of death, he defended the . . . [king's use of the veto], which served as the pretext for his own conviction; he advanced it quite openly with no fear of the reports of the spies (*moutons* in prison language) which were placed everywhere, even in our cells.' As he surveyed dukes and beggars thrown together pell-mell in the over-crowded prison, 'Barnave said to me one day, "when you consider these high mightinesses, these philosophers, these legislators, these miserable wretches all thrown together, does not that infernal stream of legend come to mind, from whose bourne no man returns?" '[4]

Étienne Baillot, ex-Constituent and now an appeal court judge and using what influence he had to help prisoners, was shocked to see a change in his friend: 'Knowing Barnave's strength of character he was surprised to see signs of enfeeblement in the features and voice of his unfortunate friend. Barnave noticed it and said: "No! No! My generous friend my spirit is equal to the challenge. But not content with depriving me of my life they want to deprive me of an honourable death. They are starving me and I shall succumb for lack of food." ' Baillot rushed in food and Barnave's 'strength quickly returned. Barnave thanked him profusely, adding, "what a service you have done me: I can now die as I should".'[5]

Treatment of prisoners was not uniform. Those with money could pay for better commons. The Commune allowed Madame Duport du Tertre to see her husband every day during his unusually long month's stay in prison – presumably waiting for his co-accused Barnave to make up the party. The correct word though was not party but *fournée* – a uniform baker's batch to go in the oven. Madame Barnave, however, was only able to see her son twice; Julie was able to see him once. When, as his trial was approaching, they asked to see him one last time, they were themselves thrown in prison for forty-eight hours, only hearing of its outcome from a sentry.[6]

The prosecution of Barnave was in two stages: the preliminary examination or *interrogatoire* was conducted in the Palais de Justice on 19 November, the day after his arrival; the trial proper, a week later. On both occasions the key players (with the exception of Fouquier-Tinville, the public prosecutor) were Robespierristes who figured on his lists 'of patriots with more or less talent' suitable for public appointments. For Barnave's trial Robespierristes included Hermann, the president, the vice-president Dumas, Lanne, a judge, and jurors Renaudin, Fauvetty and Desboissieux. Barnave's *interrogatoire* was conducted by Renée-François Dumas and Fouquier-Tinville. Some more can be said about these men. Armand-Martial Hermann, a year younger than Robespierre, had known him from boyhood and they had both practised law on the Artois circuit. Hermann heads Robespierre's list of patriots, where he is described as 'an enlightened and honest man capable of the highest employment' – he went on to be head of the home civil service during Robespierre's red summer of 1794, when he was succeeded by Dumas. Robespierre described Dumas as 'energetic', a slightly disturbing epithet in view of his formidable functions. Marie-Joseph-Emmanuel Lanne, the judge who was later Hermann's deputy at the interior ministry, was fond of using '*au courant*', a favourite code word with Robespierristes to signify being abreast with the latest twists of orthodoxy.[7]

Antoine-Quentin Fouquier-Tinville, the only one of the panel to figure in popular mythology about the French Revolution, was not a Robespierrist. He was no less revolutionary but was a stickler for correct procedure and stood for what passed then as the independence of the judiciary. Take the l'Averdy case. Fouquier had no doubt that feeding grain to a horse was an attempt to bring about the Counter-Revolution by wearying the people of the Revolution, but he needed to know that the horse trough in question was large enough to contain enough grain to bring about the desired result. So he asked l'Averdy for the exact dimensions. Robespierre, on the other hand, thought that without sticking to legal niceties – what he called '*arguties du palais* [*de justice*]' – they must have a nose for treason; it was more an art than a science. What made the Revolutionary Tribunal revolutionary was the personal character of its officials.

Barnave's *interrogatoire*, then, was conducted under the auspices of the 'energetic' Dumas, who was president of the Tribunal during the Great Terror under the law of 22 Prairial, which denied the accused counsel. Present at Robespierre's last stand at the Commune on 9 Thermidor, he was guillotined with him the next day. It was put to Barnave that the flight to Varennes had been 'a plot whose objective in part had been to revise the constitution and that he had participated in the plot'. Barnave replied that he had not participated in the plot and 'only knew the motives for the flight'. None of the participants thought that the king planned to leave the country. The hearing assumed that 'Lafayette, Bailly and the Lameths' had 'organised the flight'. They then turned to the heart of the indictment – the paper found in the king's bureau – and Barnave answered along the lines we have indicated. The hearing qualified the king's steps to neutralise the émigrés as 'feigning apparent activity'.[8]

On 27 November du Tertre and Barnave were arraigned before the Tribunal. Full details of trials were given in the *Bulletin du Tribunal Révolutionnaire*, but with so many show trials to report, it had fallen badly behind. In March 1794 it was just getting round to the trials of Barnave and du Tertre when those of the *ultras* (too hard) – the Hébertistes – followed (for balance) by that of the *citras* (too soft) – the Dantonistes – caused the *Bulletin* to drop the account of Barnave's trial, by now stale news. By then they had only got as far as du Tertre. This included his interesting take on the ministerial 'project' we have discussed, which, as Duport reminded Hermann, was the only thing for which he had been indicted. But evidence of character was included. Witnesses said he carried two pistols, which he did not deny; he had been overheard saying he would use them on his enemies if they were arraigned before the High Court at Orléans. 'I was referring to the Brissot faction', he explained.

Most of the discussion centred on du Tertre's opposition to the festival to celebrate the release of the Châteauvieux soldiers who had been imprisoned after the Nancy mutiny. He admitted that he 'was very much against this festival', while denying that he had been overheard in a restaurant saying that these soldiers should be 'exterminated'. Once he had criticised the Châteauvieux festival, he was doomed because for Robespierre this was the litmus test of patriotism. As the Revolution proceeded on its way, it acquired a baggage of such litmus tests and curricula vitae were constructed round them. Barnave privately wrote of the 'stupidity of the festival for the [Châteauvieux] soldiers'.[9]

Though the *Bulletin* did not publish the details of Barnave's trial, we do have the account of Barnave's defence taken down by his counsel Lépidor, either from notes or memory.[10] Fouquier spent little time on the original charge – the veto project – and Barnave spent as little time refuting it. He said that 'the project itself was not culpable' and made the point that its purpose was 'to avert the war with which France was threatened'. This was a clever point because Robespierre had been one of the few against the war and his quarrel with the Girondins dated from this issue. Barnave was hoping to undermine Fouquier's main line of attack: the illogical association of himself with Brissot and the Girondins, who were his enemies. Barnave reminded the court that it was the Girondin faction which had ordered his arrest and when he had heard of their fall on 31 May, he assumed he would be released.

However, in the Robespierrist mindset all conspirators were secretly united – in his colourful image, they were like bandits who met in a dark wood to concert their plans and then left in different directions to throw 'patriots' off the scent. The Girondins were the hate figures of the day. So Marie-Antoinette and Barnave had to be made to seem guilty by association.

An employee of the Tribunal's thought he had struck gold when he found a letter from Dumouriez to Barnave. Dated 8 October 1790 Dumouriez had advised him that a gathering in the Café des Tuileries was accusing him of being in hock to the planters in Saint-Domingue. Dumouriez signed his letter: 'Friend, though victim! Of the new constitution.' This letter was removed from Barnave's dossier as being 'worth further examination' but then put back. Fouquier-Tinville must have thought that using such flimsy evidence would bring the judicial system into disrepute.[11]

Barnave concentrated much of his defence in showing how the Girondin faction were his enemies – hoping that the enemies of his enemies would be his friends. He even managed the tour de force of defending his belief in monarchy as a way of preventing the Girondin federalist republic: 'Given the size of French territory, the diversity of its industry, the multiplicity of its diplomatic and commercial relations, I saw that the choice lay between a monarchy and a federal republic' – a view shared by Rousseau. Touring round his properties in June of the previous year, he had detected a natural split between the Midi and the North and ventured that if the North were conquered, the Midi would not fight to recapture it, but rather secede.[12] On colonial policy, Brissot's 'opinions were diametrically opposed to my own but he was condemned on these grounds'. Barnave thought colour 'prejudice was necessary' because it 'maintained slavery'.

It was the Brissotins, Barnave said, who had first created the myth of his volte-face by plastering the walls of Paris with the 'infamous cartoon' depicting him with two faces – the man of the people and the man of the court, with whom we began this book. Barnave observed that this cartoon dated not from the Revision but from the colonial debates which had caused the real volte-face: the reversal of his 'public idolatry'. Though this idolatry had been excessive, Barnave said at the outset of his defence that it had been rational and had only been reversed by 'revolutionary turmoil'.

He then proceeded to give his Revolutionary curriculum vitae which, he said, was de rigueur. It was his whole Revolutionary life that was now on trial – the advice on the veto had become a detail. And Barnave set out to show not only that he was a patriot but that he always had been one – from the age of twenty-one, when he had given his allocution on the separation of powers in the Parlement way back in 1783; a speech which he claimed with some exaggeration 'was regarded as a capital offence by the despotism of the day'. He then briefly alluded to his role in the Romans Assembly in 1788 and its adoption of double representation and voting by head. Then he fast-forwarded to 1791, where he remained for most of his defence. He alluded to the split within the patriot party symbolised by that between the Jacobins 'which I founded' and the 89 Club and the attacks on him by Mirabeau – now a hate figure thrown out of the Panthéon – and his acolyte Duquesnoy. He included a diatribe against Duquesnoy's *L'Ami des patriotes*, which was distributed free with government subsidy.

Then he turned to the main issue: the king's flight and the Revision. He denied, as he had in the *interrogatoire*, any involvement in the flight and any private discourse with the queen on the return trip. He had a useful witness here in Pétion who both in his memoirs and in the Jacobins at the time said that he never let Barnave out of his sight – never even dozed off. Fouquier also made what Barnave termed the 'puerile' accusation that he had paid the dauphin compliments in the carriage, though he did hold his chamber pot for him. He retorted: 'I have never sucked up to anyone, least of all a six-year-old boy'! As regards the Revision, Barnave was able to point out that on two of his main proposals, re-electability and standing in more than one constituency, his view had been adopted for the National Convention.

Taxed with his friendship with 'the Lameths and Adrien Duport', he said he was not so base as to deny his friends to save his life but he conceded that they were not perfect: 'They retained a trace of court manners. Incapable of humouring mediocrities ... They heaped buckets full of contempt on that crowd of pigmies who thought they were something in a great political movement.' Contrary to popular belief he had not been merely their mouthpiece but had always retained his 'independence'.

This assertion of his independence led on to his most vehement denial: 'You are accusing me', he said, 'an entirely free being and by nature independent, of entertaining secret relations with the château of the Tuileries, after the voyage to Varennes. I swear on my life that never, absolutely never did I conduct the slightest correspondence with the château. Never, absolutely never did I set foot in the château.' So if there was no correspondence and no visit – and an exhaustive trawl through the king's papers had shown neither – 'by what instruments, in what manner could I have been of utility to this court which I am accused of serving and *even directing*' (my emphasis). Just as in Marie-Antoinette's trial the tribunal did not have the evidence we have that she had sent French war plans to the enemy, and just as the tribunal did not have the evidence we have that Barnave had 'directed' the government, Robespierre and his allies had a sixth sense for conspiracy; they could, as one of them said, 'smell' (*flairer*) it and this for them was sufficient.

Bradby takes Barnave's denial at face value.[13] How could a man of his integrity swear on his head there was no communication with the court? To save his head, one might say. There is a special circle in Hell for those who deceive their biographers. Lefebvre in his introduction to Alma Soderjhelm's edition of his correspondence with the queen dismissed Bradby's 'pleading' as not so much special as 'sentimental'.[14] But one does wonder why Barnave made so specific a denial – no correspondence; not ever setting foot in the palace. He could simply have said the accusation was ridiculous. If Marie-Antoinette had been still living, his comprehensive lie could be explained as a desire to protect her. And if he still thought there was a chance that he could save his own life – as du Tertre apparently did – that would make sense too; but he did not entertain any such hope, telling the court: 'I shall conduct myself on the scaffold with the same calm you have seen me display during the trial.' And he had signed off his last letter to Julie '*adieu*', not '*au revoir*'.

He told Beaulieu that, faced with a duel with Cazalès, 'a crack shot and me never having fired a pistol in my life, I did not withdraw'. Hermann and his crew 'posed a higher order of danger than M. de

Cazalès. It will be a miracle if I escape from their clutches. Nevertheless, I shall defend myself not for my life but for my *gloire*.' Every schoolboy is taught that you do not just translate *gloire* as 'glory', though there was a trace of *vainglory* in Barnave. Advocated by Corneille in his plays about the brothers Horatii and El Cid, *gloire* connoted being true to yourself and your destiny as viewed by others. Barnave thought that Corneille had taken his inspiration from the 'high declamatory style' of such Latin authors as Seneca and Lucian, as 'transmitted' to him through 'Spaniards' such as Cervantes.[15]

Corneille's *Horace* – about defending Republican Rome from the Curatii – had a resonance in France and was performed several times during the Revolution. As a curtain raiser David (now an ardent Robespierrist and one of his few adherents in the CGS) had produced his Oath of the Horatii in 1784. It is clear from Barnave's correspondence in 1792/3 that he was fervent in his desire to save France from her enemies and we have noted even an (inherited?) militaristic streak. But it was more than patriotism. The Horatii and El Cid sacrificed themselves not just for their country but for an idealised conception of themselves. Barnave may have been shaken by Brissot's warning at the start of his *Lettre à M. Barnave*: 'You who are jealous of your gloire / Tremble lest it cease *before* your hour.'[16]

Barnave, then, was not trying to save his life but, rather, a particular reputation. When he had taken elaborate, even excessive, steps not to be seen entering the palace; when he had rejected Marie-Antoinette's requests to see him more often because conducting government by letter was not ideal, he was protecting not just the project and their lives but this certain reputation. He knew what sort of a reputation Mirabeau had, even before the discovery of *his* correspondence with the queen. Contrast this with Marie-Antoinette, who smuggled their correspondence out of the Tuileries in order to preserve it so that one day her story could be told, or at least privately understood. Marie-Antoinette was becoming a historian: undeservedly unpopular, she wanted to be able to give an account of the Revolution from her point of view, an *apologia pro vita sua*.

Barnave, however, felt the kind of shame for his reputation that Bradby would have felt for him had she not blinded herself to the facts. But Mirabeau and Barnave had to operate clandestinely because of the 'fatal decree', so that the fault – if fault there were – lay in the system. However, secrecy was a cardinal sin in the Revolution because it was associated with conspiracy and was considered so by Barnave himself – hence, paradoxically, his own secrecy. Secrecy was necessary to maintain a reputation for openness. But we are not obliged to judge people by their own standards, let alone by those of the age in which they lived. We can say that Barnave and even Marie-Antoinette were engaged in a noble attempt to preserve the best of the Revolution for France and preserve her from the worst. In short, we peer into that 'exquisite sensibility' Barnave detected in himself in his personal epiphany resulting from Dugua's death and in his decision not to gallop over the frontier when he heard of the fall of the monarchy.

Beaulieu thought that Barnave's defence

> was perhaps the most perfect speech he pronounced. He even touched the spectators – those paid 40 sous a day to applaud the judicial assassinations which were being committed those days.[17] 'It is a great pity', they said, despite themselves, 'to cause the death of a young man with so much talent.' Barnave overheard it and when he got back from the tribunal, he recounted this detail. 'My dear Beaulieu', he said, 'if you ever get out of here alive, don't omit this anecdote' – by which he meant, publish it. I promised and now I keep my word.[18]

Boissy and Baillot even entertained the faint hope that Barnave might even be acquitted – it still happened before the law of 22 Prairial.

But Hermann, who once dared to blame the CPS for commuting one of his death sentences to banishment, told the jurors in a summing up as harsh as Fouquier's to get a grip on themselves and do their duty. This they managed to do, retiring for the briefest period and returning with their guilty verdict. Hermann ordered that both the accused be executed the next day – for the night was well advanced. The *Glaive vengeur* ('avenging sword') noted that Barnave,

> still a young man and already famous both for his great talents and for his great crimes was, at the dawn of the Revolution, one of its most ardent apostles and strongest supports. He became the idol of Paris and of the whole of France. But his dealings with a perfidious

> court soon corrupted him. So, the people outraged at having been duped by the eloquence of a perfidious mandatory, applauded his death sentence today with the same warmth as it had his most illustrious speeches.[19]

But their boos drowned out a final show of Barnave's famous eloquence. Instead, it was his co-defendant, du Tertre, who held the stage when he told the Revolutionary Tribunal: 'You are going to kill me, Posterity will try me.' The version of the *Glaive vengeur* runs: 'You kill me today, that is the result of the Revolution; posterity will judge between us.'[20] Mirabeau had called du Tertre 'Cassandra' – a woman fated to predict the future but not be believed – yet some in the audience must have believed du Tertre now. And as ex-minister of justice he knew whereof he spoke. 'The result of the Revolution' – were such travesties intrinsic from its very beginning? Or were these the result merely of the 'second revolution' that he and Barnave had striven to prevent?

Outside, despite the late hour and the biting cold, a crowd was still gathered. It was pitch black but Barnave noticed the sensitive face of Camille Desmoulins lit up by the flaming torches. 'Goodbye Camille', he said and held out his hand. Desmoulins grasped it and is reported to have replied: 'You are certainly guilty but no matter; Brutus said farewell to his son. So, goodbye, Barnave.' This does not ring true. Desmoulins stammered and it is unlikely his words would have come out so pat – particularly in what must have been an emotional moment for them both.

It is in his number III of *Le Vieux Cordelier* that we find an authentic record of Desmoulins's verdict on Barnave. He called his satirical journal *Le Vieux Cordelier* to distinguish himself from Hébert, who had taken over the Cordelier Club that he and Danton had founded. It was through this club, as we have seen, that Barnave made his sorties into the popular movement. And so he had felt obliged to warn Camille that he stood in danger of arrest at the time of the Massacre of the Champ de Mars. Up to that time Camille had always written approvingly of Barnave in his *Révolutions de France et de Brabant*. He changed his tune at the time of the Revision. All this complicated history is summed up in his number III.

Desmoulins, of course, is defending himself from attacks from the left (the Hébertistes) and trying to persuade Robespierre that his policy of 'clemency' will not tip over into victory for the Counter-Revolution. He contrasts himself with the Johnny-come-lately 'patriots of 10 August' who had never had to sacrifice to their country the deep friendships he himself had formed with his fellow founders of the Revolution. Have these newcomers, he asked,

> been put to a sterner test than renouncing the friendship of Barnave and the Lameths and from prizing myself from Mirabeau, whom I loved to the point of idolatry, like a mistress? . . . Have they been obliged to condemn so many of their friends with whom they began the Revolution . . . from the moment they changed sides? The fact is that I have been more faithful to my *patrie* than to friendship. It is that the love of the republic had triumphed over my personal affections. And it was necessary that they be condemned before I could hold out my hand, as I did to Barnave.[21]

All we know of Barnave's last night on earth is that the faithful Baillot managed to enter the Conciergerie to shake his hand. Miraculously, the bachelor-bibliophile survived, 'protected by Heaven', as Bérenger says, and retired to his native département, refusing Napoleon's offer to make him its prefect.[22] The sun disdained to smile on the little party as it set off in the tumbril at 10.30 a.m. in near-freezing conditions for its journey of an hour and a half. There were five passengers: Barnave and Duport, an elderly priest and his sister, and a clockmaker – an assortment such as had prompted Barnave to compare his motley fellow prisoners – no carefully arranged *fournée* here – to men gathering on the edge of the Styx. They were joined in the tumbril by the ferryman in the shape of the executioner to give himself time to familiarise himself with his customers in case they had any special needs – the clockmaker was dying and would need help to climb the steps to the guillotine. They were steep and even brave victims such as the king had stumbled. Barnave wore his hair short so there was no need to shear it. The executioner was in high spirits, having just been awarded a pay rise. Barnave's trial had been halted at 2 p.m. on the second day to make this announcement, followed by the long lunch break traditional in France. The trial had not been resumed until 5 p.m. – hence the late finish.

There are several accounts of Barnave's death at about 12.30 p.m., but the most likely is that of the *Glaive vengeur*, cruel as ever but fair (it had even noted that Marie-Antoinette 'mounted the scaffold courageously'): 'Barnave bore a firm and tranquil countenance to the scaffold. He did not say anything to the people and chatted with Duport du Tertre . . . [who] mounted the scaffold if not with an imposing firmness, at least with a composure which seemed natural. During the journey two or three quips escaped his [Duport's] lips which did not seem forced.'[23] The *Glaive* must have got the tale from the executioner who, perforce, was the only one to survive to tell it. His witness countered the journal's natural bias since executioners are an impassive breed – they have to be – and something of a Vicar of Bray too: the grandfather of the man who executed Louis XVI, also called Samson, had broken Damiens on the wheel – the man who tried to assassinate Louis XV with a fruit knife. One version we can certainly reject is that of Fersen: 'Barnave died like a coward,' he wrote.[24] No one else, friend or foe, said he had died so and Fersen's quip was the product of sexual and political jealousy.

Chantal Thomas relates that in the Carnavalet Museum in Paris 'a fragment of embroidered silk is on display, from one of Marie-Antoinette's dresses, preserved by Barnave and found on him at his death.'[25] In the adjoining room is placed the marble bust of Barnave by Houdon depicting 'the fiery energy of his revolutionary zeal.' 'How can we reconcile,' Thomas asks, 'this amorous fetish with the preceding bust? Torn apart by his passion, Barnave found it impossible.' I like to think that the bit of silk *was* found on Barnave, but Thomas's calling Barnave 'the Girondin deputy' leads one to question her judgement. For those who have read this book will know that the Girondins were Barnave's deadly enemies; they undermined the chance that Barnave, through Marie-Antoinette's agency, could reconcile Europe to the Revolution by the establishment of a stable constitutional monarchy.

CONCLUSION

In March 1792 Barnave penned some bittersweet lines that were cited by Bérenger and Bradby, but they omit the heading suggesting that the page following these reflections is a continuation. The heading runs: 'On the Revolution: the presumed course of affairs & co'. The first page goes:

> What an immense space we have covered in these three years! Nor can we flatter ourselves that we have reached port. We have stirred the earth very deeply; we found a fertile and responsive soil. But how many corrupt exhalations arose from it.
>
> So much intelligence in individuals; so much courage in the mass of people; but how little real character, calm force and above all true virtue!
>
> Back amid my hearth and home, I ask myself, had it not been better never to have left it and I needed a moment's reflection to reply – so much had the first errors of the new Assembly deflated my hopes and energy.
>
> However, a moment's thought is enough to convince me that whatever befalls we shall remain free and that the main abuses we have abolished will never recur.

This last was incontrovertible. Absolute monarchy, the Parlements, financial and social privileges, occupations reserved in theory or practice to the nobility – all had been swept away, never to recur. Indeed, Barnave in his own person had smashed this glass ceiling, mixing with the very highest without the need for any legislation. Marie-Antoinette,

Madame Elizabeth and his aristocratic friends saw that he possessed the manners of a gentleman. A '*bourgeois gentilhomme*' if you will, but not in Molière's disparaging sense. For in a sense Barnave had always been a cuckoo in the bourgeois nest – despising the manners of his colleagues pleading before the local Parlement and those who staffed the *grand baillages*, and these were precisely the sort of people who became his new colleagues in the National Assembly.

The first page, then, of Barnave's retrospective ended on an optimistic note. But his gloom returns on the second: 'The Constituent Assembly precipitated its dénouement. They seemed to think one could end the Revolution with the wave of a wand! But for that a dominant and constant force would have been needed and it deprived itself of the means by the brusque termination of its session and by *non-rééligibilité*.' 'If the Constituent Assembly had continued in existence for a few months longer', all 'reasonable men' would have rallied to the Constitution and 'if our successors had tried to stir up the nation again, they would not have found it so easy'.[1]

This was a delusion. The idea that his party discredited in the country, as he seems to admit, could have finished the revolution on a harmonious chord was fanciful. Dubois-Crancé said it all: the men of the Constituent were superannuated – representing vanished constituencies and orders. Dauphiné itself had vanished. By his own admission, Barnave could only find fifteen to twenty people prepared to prolong the session.

By 'stir up the nation again', Barnave meant re-start the Revolution, as in 'Are we going to finish the Revolution or are we going to start it up again?'[2] Brissot's party in the Legislative Assembly was able to do this by warmongering. Specifically, Brissot wanted war with Austria in order to smoke out the presumed treason of the queen when faced with war with her brother. And it was this particular war that Barnave had to prevent because he was governing the country with the queen and because entente with Leopold was the international rock on which he had built the survival of the constitutional monarchy.

Back in Grenoble, he told Alexandre, sadly, 'If you expect men of goodwill to stabilise the Revolution, you will wait in vain.'[3] These comments stemmed from failure, and it has been claimed that Barnave stands in a line of failed politicians – writers stretching back through

Clarendon to Machiavelli.[4] But Barnave had worked out the main lines of his theories as early as his 1783 lecture and until war clouded the issue, his experiment in government had at least a sporting chance of success, having as it did the support of the king as well as the queen, control of the civil list, international support from Leopold and at least a paper majority in the Assembly. Barnave left Paris while the issue was still in doubt.

He planned to return. But with his friends moving to the right and the Assembly to the left, it is hard to imagine a context in which he could have operated effectively; could in short have prevented the fall of the monarchy he had given his whole heart and mind to preserve. Still, he thought he could have stiffened the resolve of the Assembly, 'whose despicable feebleness had given a fistful of men the audacity to subjugate it and make a great revolution in the state by means of a popular riot'.[5] This, the 'great revolution in the state,' was the 'second Revolution' he had striven to prevent.

⚜

It is often said that Barnave did not foresee 'the rise of the proletariat'. For him, the point where his class – the upper bourgeoisie – had gained power marked the end of history. He did not foresee that organised labour would wield power because they did not have, and still do not have, the necessary wealth and education which he regarded as a prerequisite. But he did foresee or rather fear something more germane to his theory: a levelling of fortunes. A note for his major speech of 13 July 1791 runs: 'On the conservative/preservative spirit which must succeed us – a step towards equality attacks property; a step towards liberty attacks the monarchy.'[6] And he meant the levelling of landed property – the *loi agraire*.

He travelled back to Paris in the closed carriage under guard at the high-water mark of the Revolution. The *journée* of 5 September 1793 turned out to be the zenith of the popular movement when, surrounded by sans-culottes, the National Convention was forced to institute price controls. But there was no attack on property – there never would be in France – and by the law of 14 Frimaire of the Year II (4 December 1793), the CPS asserted a control over France beyond the wildest imagining of

Louis XIV. Though more blood would flow, and different actors would fall through the trap-door – Camille who offered Barnave his hand, Danton who tried to save him, both killed like him for trying to finish the Revolution, finally Robespierre the presiding genius of the tribunal which condemned him – nevertheless, in institutional terms at least, the Revolution was indeed 'finished'.

⚜

In notes headed, 'Of the progress of governments' – from 'the individual man' to 'the family' to 'small societies' and finally to 'great federated empires' – Barnave predicted the rise and fall of a federal Europe. Barnave did not foresee a Napoleonic European empire created by wars of conquest but rather something akin to the European Union, brought about by revulsion from war and a determination to have no more of them. But, sadly, the memory of wars which had united the nations of Europe would fade and underlying tensions would reassert themselves: 'If the whole of Europe formed one empire, it would break up and the same events would recur. Union between all the parts of Europe is not possible because every alliance is simply founded on a danger stronger than rivalry and so when the danger no longer exists, rivalry determines conduct. The same applies to universal peace – enlightenment does not extinguish natural passions.' The only permanent way to prevent wars, he concludes, somewhat pessimistically, is 'a system based on the balance of power'.[7] 'Enlightenment does not extinguish natural passions' – this could also be the epitaph of the French Revolution.

⚜

The theoretical part of Barnave's *Introduction à la Révolution française* is concerned with how and why revolutions start. but he has less to say about how they end and how they end in the absence of his desired resolution – a stable constitutional monarchy. This is partly because the narrative portion of his work is too much *pro domo sua* but also, by definition, because he died before he or anyone could know what the end would be. Nevertheless, one can piece together from this and his scattered reflections a reasonable guess. For Barnave, there were three collective actors in the French Revolution: his class, the haute bourgeoisie, the peasants and the urban artisans, what we call the sans-culottes; and two collective victims: the nobility (both of the sword and, especially, of the robe) and the Church. The king stood outside his framework. The Revolution was a congeries of winners and losers, rather than a victory (or defeat) for mankind – Barnave scorned these abstractions and distrusted those who put humanity before individual friendship. He had the Brissotins in mind with their decree of 'fraternity and help' to mankind, though, ironically, they were as devoted to each other in friendship as Barnave's set were.

The haute bourgeoisie were the outright winners, gaining social recognition and political power: Barnave's career epitomised both. One of Barnave's best insights was the apparent paradox that the peasants were essentially the allies of the landed aristocracy and a conservative force. They played no part in the outbreak of the Revolution and in their looting of châteaux they saw no further (not even perhaps as far) as what Duport grandiloquently called 'the entire abolition of the feudal regime'. The other measures proclaimed on the night of 4 August had no logical connection with this abolition – they were merely an emotional overspill. The peasants were happy to see an end to tithes, but lamented the subsequent attack on the Church and the move to the implementation of the Civil Constitution and de-Christianisation.

Barnave, then, saw the peasantry as a reactionary force and one inherently opposed to the Revolution. Its natural supporters were the towns and centres of industry (although he always put industry first), especially commerce. Barnave lived to see peasants and nobles rise up in defence of throne and altar in the Vendèan rising. He argued (fallaciously) that the colonial regime had to be preserved because French commerce, and therefore the Revolution, depended on it.

Barnave had nothing against the nobility – or not the court nobility who formed his closest circle and many of whom, the Paris contingent, were his allies from the moment they entered the Estates-General. They hogged the best positions and this had to end, but they wielded no power. That belonged to the *noblesse de robe*, the *parlementaires*. Barnave's relationship with them changed dramatically in the period 1787–90. This, of course, was a general reaction for those who had been politically awake in 1787 – a sense of betrayal by the fathers of the people as many considered them to be. But, for Barnave, there was a particular resonance because both he and his father had pleaded before the Parlement of Grenoble and, in particular, he had experienced his first taste of celebrity when he delivered his allocution to them in 1783. We have charted this growing disillusionment through his private jottings. He also played a part in the downfall of the Parlements in 1789–90. He did not live to witness the mass execution of the Paris *parlementaires* in 1794. But he knew that their leading role could and should never be revived. This role existed in the absence of something – a representative assembly – not for any particular qualities or support base.

Barnave posed the question: how shall a nation be best represented? He answered: both by a king and a unicameral assembly in balance. With the king gone, France was ruled by one chamber – the National Convention – without a head of state. When Robespierre abolished the ministries in the spring of 1794 and staffed the Commissions which repleaded them with his supporters a possibly unique political experiment was completed – with the results we know.

⚜

Stephen Sondheim said something to the effect that ambiguity was an essential component of drama. That, perhaps, is why I have been drawn to write about characters who display this characteristic: Louis XVI, the conflicted anglophile, the *dévot-philosophe*; or Calonne, who tried to move to a safer ministry before the anticipated crisis, but yet was willing to be the sacrificial victim of his reform programme. Or Malesherbes, the *parlementaire* who saw through the patriotic smokescreen of his brethren. Or Robespierre, who proposed the abolition of capital punishment and then sent friend and foe alike to the guillotine. Or Marie-Antoinette, whose surface levity concealed an inner despair. And so to Barnave and the 'infamous caricature'. He *was* 'the man of the people' and 'the man of the court', but concurrently not consecutively. He served the one by serving the other. Barnave had always intellectually believed that France needed a monarchy and this became also emotional with his personal encounter with its fallen representatives in the coach.

He told Théodore that he would not appeal to the Convention because they 'killed the king'. He had definite notions about how to prolong his own life, buying a manual of that title. He fell for various quack cures based on 'hygiene', the correct consumption of water, whether fresh, acidulated, mixed with coffee or boiled with iron nails. The details are meticulous, prescriptive. But having taken all these measures he spurned to take the one that might, just might, have prolonged his life: begging for it.

ENDNOTES

INTRODUCTION

1. Stendhal, *Scarlet and Black*, trans. M. Shaw, 1953, pp. 127, 177, 428.
2. L. Emblard, 'Notes historiques sur Barnave', *Bull. Delph.*, vol. XXXII (1898), pp. 201–16, 204. Barnave, *Oeuvres*, ed. Bérenger de la Drôme, Paris, 1843, 4 vols, III, pp. 258–9 and 268.
3. E. Bradby, *The Life of Barnave*, Oxford, 1915, 2 vols. E. Bradby, 'Marie-Antoinette and the Constitutionalists; the Heidenstam papers', *The English Historical Review*, vol. 31, issue 122 (1916), pp. 238–55. Her book was reviewed in the same journal by J.H. Clapham (*E.H.R.*, vol. 30 (1915), pp. 733–6). G. Michon, *Adrien Duport et le parti feuillant*, Paris, 1924. The appendix has some of Barnave's correspondence in 1792.
4. Barnave to a 'cher confrère' in Grenoble, A.N. W 13, no. 32; J. de Beylié, *Lettres inédites de Barnave sur la prise de la Bastille*, Grenoble, 1906, pp. 12–17.
   Barnave, *Oeuvres*, II, p. 365; the draft of Barnave's lecture is given by J. Beylié, *Barnave avocat*, pp. 34–53.
5. A.N. W 15, Registre I, numbered by Barnave 1–2.
6. A. N. W 15, Registre I, pp. 117–18.
7. Barnave, *De la Révolution et de la Constitution*, ed. P. Gueniffey, Grenoble, 1988, p. 52.
8. Barnave, *De la Révolution et de la Constitution*, ed. P. Gueniffey, Grenoble, 1988.
9. Barnave, *Oeuvres*, II, pp. 205 and 222.
10. A.N. W 15, Registre, II, 75–6.
11. Barnave, *Introduction à la Révolution française*, ed. G. Rudé, Paris, 1960; Barnave, *Power, Property and History*, ed. E. Chill, New York and London, 1971.

1 RELUCTANT LAWYER

1. Barnave, *Oeuvres*, II, p. 364.
2. At least according to the right-wing pamphleteer: F.-L. Suleau, *Le Réveil de M. Suleau*, Paris, 1791, p. 8; *Letters from Paris during the Summer of 1791*, London, 1792, p. 248.
3. *Marie-Antoinette, Fersen et Barnave*, ed. O.-G. Heidenstam, 1913.
4. Richard Cobb to me in conversation.
5. The sources for Barnave's ancestry are: J. de Beylié, *La Famille Barnave, 1415–1854*, cited in R. Fonvieille, *Barnave et la Pré-Révolution: Dauphiné – 1788*, Grenoble, 1987; and J. Brun-Durand, *Dictionnaire biographique de la Drôme*, Paris, 1900, vol. 1, pp. 71–3.
6. J. Chevallier, 'L'église constitutionelle de la Drôme', *Bulletin de l'Académie delphinale*, 1916, pp. 297 ff., p. 298 n. 1.
7. J. de Beylié, 'Barnave, Pages inédites', *Bulletin de l'Académie delphinale*, 4th series, vol. 12 (1898), pp. 539–62, 558.
8. Barnave, *Oeuvres*, II, p. 141; A. Périer expressed the same views in *Histoire abrégée du Dauphiné de 1626 à 1826*, Grenoble, 1881, p. 18.
9. J. de Beylié, *Barnave avocat*, Grenoble, 1917, p. 10.

10. Brun-Durand, *Dictionnaire*, vol. 1, pp. 71–3.
11. A.N. W 13, nos. 100, 112 and 115; letters written to him in Paris in 1789, cited by Beylié, *Barnave avocat*, pp. 120–3.
12. R. Fonvieille, *Barnave et la Pré-Révolution Dauphine*, Grenoble, 1987, pp. 12–13 and 222, n. 18.
13. Fonvieille, *Pré-Révolution*, 222, n. 19.
14. Fonvieille, *Pré-Révolution*, p. 17 and n. 27 for a version of the song in standard French; *Dictionnaire de la Drôme*, p. 72; A. de Gallier, 'La vie de province au XVIIIe siècle', *Bull. Delph.*, vol. X (1876), pp. 369–86, 383 and 385.
15. Bibliothèque de Grenoble, R9814. Cited in Fonvieille, *Pré-Révolution*, p. 15.
16. *Sic* for military commandant – the governor was the duc d'Orléans, who never visited the province.
17. Cited by Fonvieille, *Pré-Révolution*, p. 17.
18. Barnave, *Oeuvres*, ed. Bérenger de la Drôme, Paris, 1843, 4 vols, I, pp. vi–vii.
19. J. Brun-Durand, *Dictionnaire*, vol. 1, p. 73.
20. A. de Gallier, 'La Vie de province au XVIIIe siècle', p. 241.
21. J. de Beylié, 'Barnave, Pages inédites', pp. 539–62, 546–9.
22. L. Emblard, 'Notes historiques sur Barnave', *Bull. Delph.*, vol. 32 (1898), pp. 201–16, 205.
23. Barnave, *Oeuvres*, IV, p. 313.
24. Fonvieille, *Pré-Révolution*, 1788, 21, 27; A.N. W 13, no number.
25. *Oeuvres*, I, v.
26. L. Emblard, 'Notes historiques sur Barnave', pp. 201–16, 202.
27. Duc de Lévis, *Souvenirs et portraits*, Paris, 1813, p. 220; A. N. W 13, no number, for the passport.
28. Cited in J. Egret, *Les derniers états de Dauphiné: Romans*, Grenoble, 1942, p. 14.
29. U 5216, 5th cahier, p. 142, cited in Fonvieille, *Pré-Révolution*, p. 27.
30. Bradby, *Barnave*, I, p. 30; Fonvieille, *Pré-Révolution*, p. 224, n. 44.
31. Brun-Durand, *Dictionnaire*, p. 73.
32. Barnave, *Oeuvres*, IV, pp. 328–9.
33. Barnave, *Oeuvres*, IV, pp. 326–7.
34. Barnave, *Oeuvres*, IV, pp. 320–1.
35. Barnave, *Oeuvres*, I, XI–XII.
36. Espinchal, comte de, *Journal*, ed. E. d'Hauterive, trans. R. Stawell, London, 1912, p. 128.
37. Fonvieille, *Pré-Révolution*, pp. 83–4; E. Campardon, *Le Tribunal révolutionnaire de Paris*, 1866, vol. I, p. 196, transcript of Barnave's *interrogatoire*.
38. Barnave, *Oeuvres*, I, XIV–XV; *Barnave, de la Révolution et de la Constitution*, ed. P. Gueniffey, Grenoble, 1988, p. 111.
39. Périer, *Histoire abrégée*, pp. 24–5.
40. J. de Beylié, *Barnave Avocat*, Grenoble, 1917, pp. 10–27.
41. Beylié, *Barnave Avocat*, pp. 77–107.
42. Gueniffey, *Barnave*, p. 111. The draft of Barnave's lecture is given in Beylié, *Barnave avocat*, pp. 34–53.
43. A.N. W 13, no. 7.

2 THE ORIGINS OF THE FRENCH REVOLUTION ACCORDING TO BARNAVE

1. Barnave, *De la Révolution et de la Constitution*, ed. P. Gueniffey, Grenoble, 1988, p. 111.
2. Ibid., p. 45.
3. Ibid., p. 54.
4. Ibid., p. 50.
5. Ibid., p. 94.
6. Barnave, *Oeuvres*, II, p. 85.

7. Barnave, *Oeuvres*, II, pp. 150–2.
8. Barnave, *De la Révolution*, p. 64.
9. A.N. W 15, Registre II, p. 6, published in Barnave, *Oeuvres*, II, p. 59.
10. Barnave, *Oeuvres*, II, p. 117.
11. Draft for his allocution to the Parlement of Grenoble, A.N. W 13, no. 7.
12. Barnave, *Oeuvres*, II, p. 92.
13. Ibid., II, p. 183.
14. Ibid., II, p. 179.
15. Ibid., p. 83; A.N. W 15, Registre I, no number.
16. Barnave, *Oeuvres*, II, p. 111.
17. A. Périer, *Histoire abrégée du Dauphiné de 1626 à 1826*, Grenoble, 1881, p. 37.
18. Barnave, *Oeuvres*, II, pp. 68–9.

3 POLITICAL AWAKENING: BARNAVE IN THE PRE-REVOLUTION, 1787–9

1. Barnave, *De la Révolution et de la Constitution*, ed. P. Gueniffey, Grenoble, 1988, p. 111.
2. A.N. W 12 (unnumbered), 'Etat des livres fournis à M. Barnave fils, avocat, par L.A. Girond, Imprimeur'.
3. Probably J.B. Pressavin, *L'art de prologer la vie et préserver la santé ou traité de hygiène* (1786).
4. Barnave to Rigaud de L'Isle, 25 September 1787, Sotheby's Paris, catalogue no. PF1303, 29 May 2013, lot 1.
5. Franque Giroud to Barnave A.N. W 12, p. 139.
6. A.N. W 15, Registre II, p. 50.
7. A.N. K164.4, 'Objections et réponses'.
8. Calonne to Lebrun 1786/7 in P.-D. Echouchard Lebrun, *Oeuvres*, 4 vols, Paris, 1811, vol. IV, pp. 273–9, cited in and translated by Michael Sonenscher, *Sans-Culottes: An Eighteenth-Century Emblem in the French Revolution*, Princeton, 2008.
9. Barnave's 1787 jottings, omitted from Bérenger's collection, have been published by F. Vermale, 'Barnave: fragments inédits', *Bulletin de la Société d'archéologie, d'histoire et de géographie de la Drôme*, vol. LXV, no. 266 (1935), pp. 46–9.
10. Barnave (attrib.) *Esprit des édits enregistrés militairement au parlement de Grenoble, le 10 mai 1788*, 24 pages, p. 4.
11. A. N. W 12, unnumbered, first page of 'Etat des livres'. For this he paid only 12 sous so presumably did not buy Baudeau's later editions.
12. N. Baudeau, *Idés d'un citoyen presque sexaganaire sur l'état actuel du royame de France*, Paris, 1787, pp. 19–21.
13. Calonne had paid off the debts of the king's brothers, his supporters the comte d'Artois and the comte de Provence, and lavished money on his faction, but all this was a drop in the ocean of royal indebtedness resulting from the war.
14. Barnave, *Esprit des édits*, pp. 6–7.
15. 'Discours prononcés par m. de Nicolaï, premier président de la cour des comptes et par M. de Barentin . . . 21 août 1787'. Barnave is billed 10 sous for this on 30 April but the only printed speech of Nicolai is as above.
16. Calonne's publications: *Requête au roi*, London, 1788; *Réponse de M. de Calonne à l'écrit de M. Necker*, London, 1788; *Lettre au Roi*, London, 1789; *Collection des mémoires présentées à l'Assemblée de Notables par M. de Calonne*, 1787; J. Necker, *Mémoire*, 6 March 1787.
17. Mirabeau, comte de, *Dénonciation de l'agiotage au Roi et à l'Assemblée des Notables*, March 1787.
18. Arsenal MS 3976, 948.
19. Archives de la Marine, *Journal de Castries*, MS 182/7964, 1–2, II, f. 344.
20. *Collection des mémoires présentées à l'Assemblée de Notables par M. de Calonne*, 1787.

21. J. Hardman, *Overture to Revolution: The 1787 Assembly of Notables and the Crisis of France's Old Regime*, Oxford and New York, 2010, p. 240.
22. Bibliothèque de Grenoble U5216, 11me Cahier, p. 70, published by R. Fonvieille, *Barnave et la Pré-Révolution Dauphine*, Grenoble, 1987, p. 52.
23. Stendhal, *Vie de Henry Brulard*, Chapter 5; Fonvieille, *Pré-Révolution*, p. 54.
24. J. Egret, *The French Pre-Revolution*, trans. W. Camp, London and Chicago, 1977, pp. 127–8.
25. Fonvieille, *Pré-Révolution*, p. 52.
26. These are contained in his pamphlet *Esprit des lois*, pp. 3–8.
27. Barnave, *Oeuvres*, 1843, vol. I, p. 83.
28. He lists them in the assembly at Romans; J. Egret, *Les derniers états de Dauphiné: Romans*, Grenoble, 1942, pp. 117–18.
29. Malesherbes, then a minister without portfolio, made the same point to the king. V. André, ed., *Malesherbes à Louis XVI ou les Avertissements de Cassandra, Mémoires inédits 1787–1788*, Paris, 2010, p. 147.
30. Hardman, *Overture to Revolution*, p. 123.
31. Letter of Marie-Antoinette to Joseph of 24 April 1788, *Marie-Antoinette, Correspondance*, ed. E. Lever, Paris, 2005, p. 459.
32. A.N. W 15, Registre II, pp. 34–5.
33. A.N. W 15, Registre II, p. 41.
34. Véri Cahiers 157 and 109, Archives Départementales de La Drôme (Valence), MSS Journal (unclassified).
35. A. N. W 15, Registre II, pp. 36–7.
36. M. Marion, *Le garde des sceaux Lamoignon*, Paris, 1905, passim.
37. Barnave, *Esprit des édits*, p. 13.
38. Pèrier, *Dauphiné*, pp. 50–3.
39. Fonvieille, *Pré-Révolution*, pp. 57–67.
40. Tocqueville, *L'Ancien Régime et la Révolution française*, Paris, 1951, 2 vols, II, 153.
41. Barnave, *Esprit des édits*, p. 2.
42. Marie-Antoinette, *Lettres*, ed. M. de La Rocheterie et le marquis de Beaucourt, Paris, 1895–6, 2 vols, vol. II, p. 109.
43. Barnave, *Esprit des édits*, p. 10.
44. Barnave, *Coup d'Oeuil sur la lettre de M. de Calonne*, 1789, p. 14.
45. J. Hardman, *The Life of Louis XVI*, New Haven and London, 2016, p. 277.
46. A.N. W 12, no. 75.
47. Egret, *The French Pre-Revolution*, p. 166.
48. *Jugement du Grand Baillage de Bourg-en-Bresse*, 1788, p. 5; Fonvieille, *Pré-Révolution*, p. 70.
49. J. Hardman, *Marie-Antoinette*, New Haven and London, 2019, p. 154.
50. Bourg-en-Bresse, pp. 7–8.
51. E. Maignien, *Bibliographie historique du Dauphiné pendant la Révolution*, Grenoble, 1891 gives seven editions of the *Esprit* and three for the *grand baillage*'s condemnation of it.
52. Hardman, *Overture to Revolution*, p. 123.
53. A copy is in A.N. W 13, no number.
54. *Profession de foi d'un militaire. Discours prononcé dans un Conseil militaire*, anon. (attributed to Barnave), 1788, eight pages.
55. Gueniffey, ed., *Barnave*, p. 112.
56. Tonnerre to Loménie de Brienne, 9 June 1788, published in Chaper, ed., *Documents relatifs a la journée des tuiles par un rèligieux*, 1881, pp. 89–90.
57. A manuscript with this title in Barnave's hand is in the Grenoble library (E. Maignien, *Dictionnaire des ouvrages anonymes et pseudonynyms*, no. 2511).
58. A. Périer, *Histoire abrégée du Dauphiné de 1626 à 1826*, Grenoble, 1881, p. 78.

59. A. Mailhet, *La Vallée de la Drôme*, Paris 1893, p. 243, n. 1.
60. Fonvieille, *Pré-Révolution*, p. 108.
61. J. Mounier, *Recherches sur les causes qui ont empeché les françois à devenir libres et sur les moyens qui leur restent pour acquérir la liberté*, 1789, 2 vols, vol. I, p. 234; cited in Fonvieille, *Pré-Révolution*, p. 108.
62. Bombelles, marquis de, *Journal*, ed. J. Grassion, F. Durif and J. Charon-Bordas, 4 vols, Geneva, 1978–98, vol. II, pp. 207, 227.
63. *Réflexions d'un Patriote Dauphinois*, cited in Périer, *Dauphiné*, p. 74; A.N. W 15, Registre II, p. 38.
64. *Lettre pastorale de Mgr. L'archevêque de Vienne aux curés de son diocèse*, 15 July 1788, ten pages.

4 THE ASSEMBLIES AT ROMANS: THE LAST ESTATES OF DAUPHINÉ

1. 'Etat des livres fournis à M. Barnave fils, avocat', A.N. W 12, no number.
2. Barnave, *Oeuvres*, II, 83.
3. A.N. W 15, Registre I, no number.
4. J. Egret, *Les derniers états de Dauphiné: Romans*, Grenoble, 1942, p. 9.
5. J. Egret, *La Pré-Révolution française, 1787–1788*, Paris, 1962, p. 372.
6. A.N. W 15, Registre II, p. 56.
7. H. Carré, *Le fin des Parlements (1788–1790)*, Paris, 1912, p. 113.
8. A.N. W 15, Registre II, pp. 38 and 41.
9. A. de Lameth, *Histoire de l'Assemblée Constituante*, Paris, 1828, 2 vols, vol. I, pp. 260–1.
10. Carré, *Fin des parlements*, pp. 242-3.
11. D. Wick, *A Conspiracy of Well-Intentioned Men: The Society of Thirty and the French Revolution*, New York, 1987.
12. *Lettre écrite au roi . . . le 14 Septembre 1788*; article 'Barnave' in A. Rochas, *Biographie du Dauphiné*, Paris, 1856, p. 76; Egret, *Romans*, p. 18. *Journal de J. Abel*, cited in X. Roux, *Mounier, sa vie et son œuvre*, 1888, p. 53.
13. Bibliothèque de Grenoble, N 920; Egret, *Romans*, pp. 59–60.
14. Viennois to des Andrets, 12 July 1788, cited in Egret, *Romans*, p. 23.
15. Louis XVI had abolished *mainmorte* on the crown lands and Turgot toyed with the idea of abolishing the feudal system altogether.
16. This is Mailhet's verdict on a letter no longer available.
17. Letters to Madame Barnave and Antoine Barnave, 2 and 1 November 1788, in A. Mailhet, *La Vallée de la Drôme*, Paris 1893, pp. 244–6.
18. A.N. Ba 74 (5) 22, cited in Egret, *Romans*, p. 21.
19. Egret, *Romans*, p. 26.
20. Caze de la Bove to Necker, 13 and 2 October 1788, A.N. Ba 74 (4) 13, and 74 (3) 9, cited in Egret, *Romans*, pp. 52–3.
21. Letter of the commissioners to their constituents, 30 October, Archives de Viennois, cited in Egret, *Romans*, pp. 62 and 63–5.
22. Egret, *Romans*, pp. 68–9.
23. Paul Filleul, *Le duc de Montmorency-Luxembourg*, Paris, 1939, p. 284.
24. A. Chérest, *La chute de l'Ancien Régime, 1787-9*, 1884–6, 3 vols, II, p. 221. The details of the discussion preceding the Résultat are to be found in Barentin, *Mémoire autographe*; and Necker, *De la Révolution Française*, Paris, 1797, pp. 87ff.
25. *Procès-verbal des Etats de Dauphiné assemblés a Romans dans le mois de Décembre 1788*, pp. 71–2.
26. *Procès-verbal*, p. 62.
27. Barnave to his father, 10 January 1789; A. Mailhet, *La Vallée de la Drôme*, Paris, 1893, pp. 246–7. The figures were supplied to Necker, A.N. H1 670 (174–75); Egret, *Romans*, p. 155. The list in the procès-verbal would seem to be in order of votes cast to decide who would go on the reserve list. *Procès-verbal*, p. 28.

28. Périer, *Dauphiné*, p. 98.
29. A.N. W 15, Registre II, pp. 55 and 58.
30. Embrun to Necker, 23 February 1789, A.N. H 1 870.
31. Egret, *Romans*, p. 158; Périer, *Dauphiné*, p. 99.
32. Egret, *Romans*, p. 161.
33. Egret, *Romans*, pp. 166–7.
34. *Procès-verbal*, pp. 68–9. This section can confidently be attributed to Barnave because he uses the same idea in his *Coup d'oeuil sur la lettre de M. Calonne* of 9 March 1789.
35. Barnave, *Coup d'oeil*, 19, pp. 11–12.
36. Calonne even claimed that academic distinction was the only kind he had desired; C.-A. de Calonne, *Réponse à l'écrit de M. Necker*, London, 1788, p. 185, note.
37. His father had been ennobled through judicial office.
38. *Procès-verbal*, p. 125.
39. T. Tackett, *Becoming a Revolutionary: The Deputies of the French National Assembly and the Emergence of a Revolutionary Culture (1789–1790)*, Pennsylvania, 2006; B. Shapiro, *Traumatic Politics: The Deputies and the King in the Early French Revolution*, Pennsylvania, 2009.
40. A.N. W 15, Registre I, pp. 40–1; see also Barnave, *Oeuvres*, II, p. 59, against Condorcet's plan for state education by the *philosophes*.
41. Barnave, *Oeuvres*, II, p. 148.

5 FROM ESTATES-GENERAL TO NATIONAL ASSEMBLY

1. Barnave to a 'cher confrère' in Grenoble, A.N. W 13, no. 32.
2. A.N. W 12 (unnumbered), cited and translated by Bradby, *Barnave*, I, p. 75, n. 2.
3. Bradby, *Barnave*, I, p. 67.
4. Barnave to Rigaud de L'Isle, April 1789 (day of the month unclear), Sotheby's Paris catalogue no. PF1303, 29 May 2013, lot 1.
5. There were two exceptions, Necker and Sartine. J. Hardman, *French Politics 1774–1789*, London, 1995, p. 43.
6. Published by Beylié, 'Barnave, Pages inédites', p. 558.
7. J. Hardman, *Overture to Revolution: The 1787 Assembly of Notables and the Crisis of France's Old Regime*, Oxford and New York, 2010, p. 232.
8. R. Fonvieille, *Barnave et la Révolution*, Grenoble, 1989, p. 14.
9. A.F. Bertrand de Molleville, *Last Year of the Reign of Louis XVI*, Boston, 1909, 2 vols, I, pp. 157–9.
10. A. Millin, *Antiquités*, fourth book, 1791, p. 179, cited in A. Aulard, *La Société des Jacobins*, Paris, 1889–97, XIII.
11. E.L.A. Dubois-Crancé (attrib.), *Analyse de la Révolution*, Paris, 1885, p. 49, cited in Aulard, *Jacobins*, I, XI.
12. Comte de la Galaissonière, 'Journal des Etats-généraux', *Arch. de la guerre*, A1 LVI, cited in Etats-Généraux, G. Lefebvre et al. (eds), *Recueil de documents relatifs aux Etats-Généraux de 1789*, Paris, 1953–70, 4 vols, I, p. 205, n. 2.
13. These have been published in *La Révolution française*, LVI (1909), pp. 193–8 and 318–29.
14. Louis XVI to Necker, *c.* 1 May 1789, J. Hardman, ed., *The French Revolution Sourcebook*, London, 1999, p. 91.
15. C.L.F. de Paule de Barentin, *Mémoire autographe sur les derniers Conseils du Roi Louis XVI*, ed. M. Champion, Paris, 1844, pp. 146–7.
16. Marquis de Bombelles, *Journal*, ed. J. Grassion, F. Durif and J. Charon-Bordas, 4 vols, Geneva, 1978–98, II, 293, entry for 4 April.
17. A. N. W 15, Registre I, pp. 100–1.
18. Mercy-Argenteau to Joseph II, 22 February 1789, *Marie-Antoinette, Correspondance*, ed. E. Lever, Paris, 2005, p. 478.

19. Archives Départementales de La Drôme (Valence), MSS Journal de l'abbé de Véri (unclassified), cahier 170.
20. F. Aulard, ed., *Récit des séances des députés des communes depuis le 5 mai 1789 Jusqu'au 12 juin suivant*, Paris, 1895, p. 29.
21. Adrien Duquesnoy, *Journal*, ed. R. de Crèvecoeur, Paris, 1894, 2 vols, I, p. 41.
22. F. Vermale, 'Barnave et les banquiers Laborde', *Annales historiques de la Révolution française*, 14e année, no. 79 (1937), pp. 48–64.
23. Barnave, *Oeuvres*, I, pp. 101–2.
24. Barnave to Rigaud de L'Isle, 15 May 1789, Sotheby's (Paris) catalogue no. PF1303, 29 May 2013, lot 1.
25. A. de Lameth, *Histoire de l'Assemblée Constituante*, Paris, 1828, 2 vols, I, 7.
26. Barnave to Rigaud de L'Isle, 8 May 1789, Sotheby's (Paris) catalogue no. PF1303, 29 May 2013, lot 1.
27. A.N. W 13, no. 82.
28. J.A. Creuzé de la Touche, *Journal des Etats-Généraux et du début de l'Assemblée nationale*, ed. J. Marchand, Paris, 1946.
29. *Journal des Etats-Généraux*, fo. 15.
30. Duquesnoy, *Journal*, I, pp. 40–1.
31. Conférence, 26, 'Barnave' scribbled on the printed page.
32. A.N. W 13, no number.
33. Duquesnoy, *Journal*, p. 55.
34. A. Lameth, *Assemblée Constituante*, I, p. 10. Lameth based his memoirs on notes taken at the time. His friend Barnave must have supplied him with transcripts of his speeches.
35. *Journal des Etats-Généraux*, pp. 32–3.
36. Duquesnoy, *Journal*, I, p. 89.
37. Duquesnoy, *Journal*, I, p. 57.
38. *Journal des Etats-Généraux*, 6 June.
39. Lameth, *Assemblée Constituente*, pp. 11–19.
40. *Journal des Etats-Généraux*, fo. 42.
41. Barentin to the king, 15 June 1789; Barentin, *Lettres et Bulletins à Louis XVI*, ed. A. Aulard, Paris, 1915, p. 32.
42. Arthur Young, *Travels in France*, London, 1909, I, p. 165.
43. Comte d'Angiviller, *Mémoires*, Copenhagen, 1939, p. 152.
44. Bombelles, *Journal*, II, p. 336.
45. *Journal des Etats-Généraux*, fo. 46; Barnave to Rigaud de L'Isle, 21 June 1789, Sotheby's (Paris) catalogue no. PF1303, 29 May 2013, lot 1.
46. Necker, *De la Révolution française*, I, p. 200.
47. Montmorin took a similar view. See A.N. K 679, nos. 86 and 87–88 for their memoranda for the king.
48. E. Dumont, *Souvenirs sur Mirabeau*, Paris, 1832, p. 86.
49. D'Angiviller, *Mémoires*, pp. 154–5.
50. Barentin to the king, 22 June, *Lettres et Bulletins*, 41–2.
51. Duquesnoy, *Journal*, p. 118.
52. Barentin to the king, 19 June 1789, *Lettres et Bulletins*, p. 39.
53. Cited in Aulard, *Jacobins*, I, p. xiii.
54. *Journal des Etats-Généraux*, fo. 49.
55. Barentin to the king, *Lettres et Bulletins*, 24 June, p. 44.
56. Duquesnoy, *Journal*, I, p. 129.
57. Barentin to the king, 25 June, *Lettres et Bulletins*, p. 45.
58. Young, *Travels*, I, pp. 178–79, entry for 25 June.
59. Letter to his mother, 4 July. J. Beylié, *Lettres inédites de Barnave sur la prise de la Bastille*, Grenoble, 1906, p. 9.

60. These letters are published by P. Caron in 'La Tentative de contre-rèvolution de Juin-Juillet 1789', *Revue d'Histoire moderne*, VIII (1906), pp. 25–30.
61. Barentin, *Lettres et Bulletins*, p. 50.
62. J. Gaultier de Biauzat, *Sa vie et sa correspondance*, ed., F. Mège, Clermont-Ferrand, 1890, 2 vols, I, p. 135 and 142.
63. Duquesnoy, *Journal*, p. 195.
64. Saint-Priest and Montmorin letters to the king, undated but *c.* 22 June. See A.N. K 679 nos. 86 and 87–8 for their memoranda for the king; Barnave to Rigaud de L'Isle, 11 July 1789, Sotheby's (Paris) catalogue no. PF1303, 29 May 2013, lot 1.
65. J. Hardman, *Marie-Antoinette*, New Haven and London, 2019, pp. 26–7.
66. Beylié, *Bastille*, pp. 12–17, Barnave's emphasis.
67. Duquesnoy, *Journal*, II, p. 223.
68. J. Hardman and M. Price (eds), *Louis XVI and the Comte de Vergennes: Correspondence, 1774–1787*, Oxford, 1998, p. 92.
69. A.N. W 13, no. 48 and p. 225.
70. Biauzat, *Correspondance*, I, p. 193.
71. *Journal des Etats-Généraux*, fols. 89v.–90. This diary also answers Bradby's question (II, p. 109) of whether Barnave's speech immediately followed Lally's. It did.
72. A.N. W 13, 251; Barnave to Rigaud de L'Isle, 23 July 1789, Sotheby's (Paris) catalogue no. PF1303, 29 May 2013, lot 1.
73. Barnave, *Oeuvres*, I, 'Introduction', Chapter 11, pp. 98–109. E. Burke, *Reflections on the Revolution in France*, ed., L. Mitchell, Oxford, 1993, pp. 74 and 76.

6 THE DECISIVE PHASE, 14 JULY–6 OCTOBER 1789

1. P.-V. Malouet, *Mémoires*, Paris, 1874, 2 vols, I, p. 250.
2. J. Hardman, *Robespierre*, London and New York, 1999, p. 22.
3. From the king's declaration on leaving Paris: J. Hardman, ed., *The French Revolution Sourcebook*, London and New York, 1998, p. 130, the king's emphasis.
4. Cited in P. and P. Girault de Coursac, *Sur la route de Varennes*, Paris, 1984, p. 228.
5. A.N. W 13, no. 71.
6. Arch. de la Marine, *Journal de Castries*, MS 182/7964, 1–2, II, pp. 363–6.
7. Barnave *Oeuvres*, I, 102. In 1789 he said old institutions were not obeyed because 'a people who wanted liberty' had no 'confidence' in unelected bodies, A.N. W 13, no 52.
8. A.N. W 13, no. 51.
9. Letter to Mounier cited in R. Fonvieille, *Barnave et la Révolution*, Grenoble, 1989, pp. 63–4; draft letter of Barnave, 5 September, A.N. W 13, p. 24.
10. A.N. W 13, no. 41.
11. A.N. W 13, no. 60.
12. A.N. W 12.
13. B. Shapiro, *Traumatic Politics: The Deputies and the King in the Early French Revolution*, Pennsylvania, 2009.
14. Barnave to a friend in Grenoble, undated but *c.* 25 July, A.N. W 13, p. 52; also cited in Bradby, *Barnave*, vol 1, p. 129.
15. A.N. W 13, nos. 20 and 35; I have borrowed from two drafts with the same title.
16. J. Gaultier de Biauzat, *Sa vie et sa correspondance*, ed., F. Mège, Clermont-Ferrand, 1890, 2 vols, II, p. 227.
17. MSS Journal des Etats-Généraux tenus en 1789, B.N. nouv. ac. fr. 12938, f. 107.
18. *Archives Parlementaires*, ix, pp. 28–31.
19. Cited in J.-C. Petitfils, *Louis XVI*, Paris, 2005, p. 712.
20. A. N. W 13, 24, cited by Bradby, *Barnave*, I, p. 134.
21. E. Dumont, *Souvenirs sur Mirabeau*, Paris, 1832, p. 146.
22. AP, VIII, p. 564.

23. Draft letter, 5 September 1789, A.N. W 13, p. 24.
24. *Moniteur* no. 131, p. 132.
25. A.N. W 13, no. 27, 'Objects for a declaration of rights'.
26. A.N. W 15, Registre II, p. 18.
27. M.A. de Bacourt, ed., *Mirabeau, Comte de, Correspondance entre le comte de Mirabeau et le comte de la Marck*, Paris, 1851, 3 vols, I, p. 157. Hereafter cited as La Marck, with volume number.
28. Gueniffey, ed., *Barnave*, pp. 169–70.
29. Barnave, *Coup d'oeil sur la lettre de M. Calonne*, 9 March 1789, p. 19.
30. Germaine de Staël, *Considerations on the Principal Events of the French Revolution*, Indianapolis, 2008, p. 213.
31. J. Mounier, *Exposé de la conduite de M. Mounier dans l'Assemblée nationale* . . . Paris, 1789.
32. A.N. W 12, p. 14 and unnumbered; *Lettre de M. Necker premier ministre des finances à M. Le Président de l'Assemblée Nationale*, etc., Versailles and Strasbourg, 1789.
33. J.F.X. Droz, *Histoire du Règne de Louis XVI*, Brussels, 1839, 2 vols, II, pp. 440–1.
34. In fashionable society, the main meal of the day, *diner*, was held in the early afternoon.
35. Staël, *Considerations*, p. 214.
36. E. Dumont, *Souvenirs sur Mirabeau*, Paris, 1832, p. 155.
37. Malouet says the 30th, but Mathiez disputes his chronology. See A. Mathiez, 'Etude critique sur les journées des 5 et 6 Octobre 1789' in *Revue Historique*, vol. 68 (1898), pp. 241–81, 271.
38. On 10 September Barnave wrote that 'the storm in Paris has completely subsided', interleaved with a love letter, A.N. W 13, p. 242.
39. Madame Barnave to her son, 6 October 1789, A.N. W 13, no 70.
40. A.N. W 13, no. 93, Barnave's correction of a report of part of his speech for publication.
41. A.N. W 12, no. 14; J. Beylié, *Lettres inédites de Barnave sur la prise de la Bastille*, Grenoble, 1906, pp. 20–2.
42. A.N. W 13, no number.
43. Bradby, *Barnave*, I, p. 131, n. 1.
44. A.N. W 12, p. 14; Beylié, *Bastille*, p. 21.
45. Marquis de Ferrières, *Mémoires*, eds. Berville and Barrière, Paris, 1822, 2 vols, II, p. 39.
46. *Les intrigues de Madame de Staël à l'occasion du départ de Mesdames de France*, Paris, 1791, pp. 20–1.
47. *Lettre de M. Necker premier ministres des finances à M. Le Président de l'Assemblée Nationale*, etc., Versailles and Strasbourg, 1789, pp. 7, 9, 17–22.
48. *Moniteur*, no. 50, cited in R. Fonvieille, *Barnave et la Révolution*, p. 95.
49. A.P. VIII, p. 569; De Visme (attrib.), Mss Journal des Etats-Généraux tenus en 1789, B.N. nouv. ac. fr. 12938, fo. 153.
50. *Dictionnaire des Constituents*, ed. E. Le May, Oxford, 1991, 2 vols, II, p. 955.
51. Barnave, *Esprit des édits*, 1788, 24, pp. 6–7.
52. Duquesnoy, *Journal*, I, p. 337.
53. 'Journal des Etats', fo. 156.
54. 'Journal des Etats', fo. 161, 18 September.
55. 'Journal des Etats' fo. 185, verso.
56. Printed in J.L.H. Campan, *Mémoires sur la vie privée de Marie-Antoinette*, 2 vols, 1823, II, pp. 296–7.
57. A.N. W 12, no. 15, published by A. Mathiez, 'Etude critique sur les journées des 5 et 6 Octobre 1789' in *Revue Historique*, vol. 68 (1898), pp. 241–81, 271–3.
58. Barnave, *Oeuvres*, I, pp. 116–19.
59. For example, his denial of any links to the court at his trial.
60. Bradby, *Barnave*, I, p. 144.

61. Marie-Antoinette, *Lettres*, ed. M. de La Rocheterie et le marquis de Beaucourt, Paris, 1895–6, 2 vols. II, p. 146.
62. A.N. C 31 (263), p. 6.
63. N. Hampson, *Prelude to Terror: The Constituent Assembly and the Failure of Consensus, 1789–1791*, Oxford, 1988, p. 78.
64. 'Journal des Etats', fo. 187.
65. J. Necker, *De la Révolution française*, 1797, II, pp. 77–9.
66. Necker, *Révolution*, II, p. 73.
67. Mallet du Pan, *Mémoires et Correspondance pour servir à l'histoire de la Révolution française*, ed. A. Sayous, 1851, 2 vols, I, p. 181, note.
68. J. Necker, *Sur l'Administration de M. Necker par lui- même*, 1791, p. 328.
69. E. Lever, *Louis XVI*, Paris, 1985, p. 534.
70. 'Journal des Etats', fo. 187.
71. Mathiez, 'Etude critique', p. 272.
72. Alexandre de Lameth, *Histoire de l'Assemblée Constituante*, Paris, 1828, 2 vols, p. 153.
73. Duquesnoy, *Journa*l, I, p. 406.
74. 'Journal des Etats', fo. 196.
75. Published in A. Mousset, *Un témoin ignoré de la Révolution, le Comte de Fernan Nunez*, 1924, p. 228.
76. A.N. W 13, p. 227.
77. Madame Barnave to her son, 14 October 1789, A.N. W 13, no. 74; A.N. W 12, p. 28 and W 13, scattered papers; *Lettre écrite à la commission intermédiare . . . des Etats de Dauphiné*, Paris, 1789; A.N. W 13, no. 46.
78. A.N. W 12, no number; and W 13, p. 238, Barnave to an unknown correspondent, 19 October 1789.
79. Letter of 24 November, A.N. W 12, p. 16.
80. A. Lameth, *Histoire*, p. 147.
81. Barnave, *Oeuvres*, I, p. 116.
82. M. Price, 'Lafayette, the Lameths and "Republican Monarchy", 1789–1791', forthcoming article, p. 5.
83. Barnave, *Oeuvres*, I, p. 85.
84. L. Lavallette to Barnave, 19 January 1792, A.N. W 13, p. 41.
85. Duquesnoy, *Journal*, II, pp. 466–9.
86. La Marck, I, pp. 219–20.
87. Dubois-Crancé (attrib.), *Supplément à la galérie de l'Assemblée nationale, October 1789*, pp. 24–5 and 46–7; and, *Véritable portrait de nos Législateurs*, p. 36.
88. *The Diary and Letters of Gouverneur Morris*, ed. Anne Morris, New York, 1888, p. 190, note.
89. F. Vermale, 'Barnave et les banquiers Laborde', *Annales historiques de la Révolution. française*, 14e année, no. 79, pp. 48–64, at 55–56; Marquis de Ferrières, *Mémoires*, eds. Berville and Barrière, Paris, 1822, 2 vols, II, p. 39.
90. Morris, *Diary*, p. 205.
91. A.N. W 13, no. 75.
92. Duquesnoy, *Journal*, I, pp. 368–9.
93. 'Journal des Etats', fo. 112.
94. 'Journal des Etats', 26 August.
95. 'Journal des Etats', fo. 173, verso.
96. 'Journal des Etats', 22 August.
97. A.N. W 13, p. 230.
98. A.N. W 13, no. 70.
99. A.N. W 13, no. 75, p. 398.
100. A.P. IX, 480–1.
101. Alexandre de Lameth, *Histoire de l'Assemblée Constituante*, Paris, 1828, 2 vols, I, pp. 180–6.

102. Staël to Gustavus III, 22 October 1789; Baron Staël-Holstein, *Correspondance diplomatique*, ed. Baron Brinkman, Paris, 1881, pp. 143–5.
103. Staël, *Correspondance*, p. 146.
104. Lafayette, *Mémoires*, II, p. 414; as usual, the correspondent is not named.
105. Talon to Lamarck, 20 October, La Marck, I, p. 274.
106. La Marck, I, p. 280.
107. Technically, Cicé could not be chancellor because that post in absentia was held by Maupeou who lived till 1792 and (at least according to the old rules) could not be dismissed, my emphasis.
108. On 18 October, Omer Talon tells La Marck, 'M. de Lafayette seems determined on M. de Ségur', La Marck, I, p. 268.
109. Barnave to the queen, 27 October 1791, *Marie-Antoinette et Barnave, Correspondance secrète*, ed. Alma Soderjhelm, Paris, 1934, p. 153.
110. Mirabeau to La Marck, I, p. 278.
111. Cited in J. Chaumié, *Le réseau d'Antraigues et la contre-révolution, 1791–1793*, Paris, 1965, p. 73; La Marck, II, p. 32.
112. Memorandum signed by all the ministers and published in A.P. IX, pp. 520–1.
113. Duquesnoy, *Journal*, II, pp. 19–20.
114. De Visme (attrib.), Mss Journal des États-Généraux tenus en 1789, B.N. nouv. ac. fr. 12938, fo. 229.
115. Duquesnoy, *Journal*, II, pp. 19–24.
116. 'Journal des Etats', p. 231.
117. La Marck, I, p. 80.
118. J. Hardman and J.M. Roberts, eds, *French Revolution Documents*, Oxford, 1966–73, 2 vols, I, p. 305.
119. A. de Lameth, *Histoire de L'Assemblée constituante*, II, pp. 52–3.
120. Gueniffey, ed., *Barnave*, p. 134, n. 88.
121. J.-P. Brissot, *Lettre à M. Barnave*, Paris, 1790, preface, no page; Duquesnoy, *Journal*, II, pp. 19–20.

7 THE YEAR 1790

1. I have here conflated two sections from the 'Introduction' in *De la Révolution et de la Constitution*, ed. P. Gueniffey, pp. 130 and 134.
2. Staël, *Correspondance*, p. 147, 12 November.
3. J.F.X. Droz, *Histoire du Règne de Louis XVI*, Brussels, 1839, 2 vols, II, p. 121.
4. A.N. W 13 no. 62.
5. Duchesse de Tourzel, *Mémoires*, ed. duc des Cars, Paris, 1904, 2 vols, I, p. 151; Tackett, *Becoming a Revolutionary*, pp. 291 and 431.
6. Desmoulins, C. Desmoulins, *Révolutions de France et de Brabant*, Paris, 1789–91, no. 28, p. 641.
7. Barnave, *Oeuvres*, I, pp. 180–3.
8. A.N. W 13, p. 199.
9. Cited in R. Fonvieille, *Barnave et la Révolution*, Grenoble, 1989, p. 196.
10. La Marck, I, p. 318.
11. La Marck, I, p. 321.
12. F. Régent, 'Slavery and the Colonies' in *A Companion to the French Revolution*, ed., P. McPhee, Oxford, 2013, pp. 397–418, at 400.
13. A.N. W 13 no. 4, undated but *c.* April 1790, my emphasis.
14. A.N. W 13, no number.
15. Brissot, *Lettre à M. Barnave*.
16. Brissot, *Lettre à M. Barnave*, p. 12.
17. Ibid., p. 84.
18. Brissot, *Lettre à M. Barnave*, p. 72.

19. A. Lameth, *Constituente*, I, pp. 445–6.
20. A.N. W 13, no. 65, *Moniteur*, no. 4, p. 676.
21. Barnave, *Oeuvres*, I, pp. 174–6.
22. Ferrières, II, pp. 153–4.
23. Tackett, *Becoming*, p. 289.
24. AP, XVI, p. 451.
25. There were some draft letters to the pope largely inspired by Archbishop Boisgelin found in the *armoire de fer*. These have been published in A.P. LIV, pp. 475–8.
26. N. Hampson, *Danton*, London, 1978, pp. 22–4.
27. A. Aulard, *La Société des Jacobins*, Paris, 1889–97, 6 vols, I, II–XVII.
28. Lameth, *Histoire*, I, p. 422.
29. Duquesnoy, *Journal*, II, p. 468.
30. Aulard, *Jacobins*, I, XVIII; Alexandre de Lameth, *Histoire de l'Assemblée Constituent*, I, p. 422; Bradby, *Barnave*, I, p. 213.
31. A.N. W 13, p. 217.
32. Aulard, *Jacobins*, I, XXX.
33. C. Desmoulins, *Révolutions de France et de Brabant*, Paris, 1789–91, no. 10, p. 438 (February 1790).
34. J. de Beylié, *Lettre de Barnave, du 30 juin 1790, à la société des amis de la constitution de Grenoble*, Paris, 1900, p. 411.
35. Hampson, *Danton*, p. 31.
36. Until the Hébertistes took it over.
37. Ferrières, *Mémoires*, I, pp. 367–9.
38. Beylié, *Lettre de Barnave*, p. 410; A.N. W 13, pp. 218–9, cited in Bradby, *Barnave*, I, p. 226.
39. Marquis de Bouillé, *Mémoires*, eds. S.A. Berville and J.F. Barrière, Paris, 1821, p. 208.
40. A.N. W 13, p. 236, 'the main parts' taken from Barnave's draft; and A.N. W 13, p. 204. Aulard, *Jacobins*, I, p. 153, meeting of 7 June 1790; Beylié, *Lettre de Barnave*, pp. 415–16.
41. A.N. W 13, pp. 218 and 219, undated draft and its continuation 13 June. A.N. W 13, 236, 'the main parts' taken from Barnave's draft; and A. N. W 13, p. 204.
42. A.N. W 13, pp. 228 and 229, draft letter of 13 June 1790.
43. Barnave to Mirabeau undated but June 1790; A.N. W 12, no. 28. The finished state of the letter seems to suggest that it is a copy rather than a draft, that is, the letter was actually sent.
44. Desmoulins, *Révolutions de France et Brabant*, no. 45, pp. 269–70.
45. Desmoulins, *Révolutions de France et Brabant*, no. 43, p. 177.
46. Mirabeau to the queen, 7 September 1790; La Marck, I, p. 407.
47. Lafayette to Bouillé, August 1790; Marquis de Lafayette, *Mémoires*, Paris and London, 1837, 6 vols, III, pp. 135–6.
48. Idem.
49. Lafayette, *Mémoires*, III, pp. 146–7.
50. A.N. W 13, no. 55.
51. Barnave to an unknown friend, Paris. 25 July 1790; A.N. W 13, no. 32; Beylié, *Grenoble*, p. 572.
52. Barnave to his mother, undated, A.N. W 12, no. 18.
53. J. de Beylié, 'Barnave maire de Grenoble', *Bulletin de l'Académie delphinale*, series 4, vol. 12 (1898), pp. 571–73.
54. Mirabeau's seventeenth note to the court, Saturday 14 August 1790; La Marck, I, p. 388.
55. Bouillé, *Mémoires*, p. 175, note.
56. Bouillé, *Mémoires*, p. 269.
57. Madame Elizabeth, *Correspondance*, ed. F. Feuillet de Conches, 1868, p. 290.
58. A.N. W 15, Registre I, p. 134.
59. Thirty-first and thirty-second notes for the court, 15 and 16 October 1790; La Marck, II, pp. 17–19.

60. La Marck to Mercy-Argenteau, 28 October; La Marck, II, p. 48.
61. Desmoulins, *Révolutions de France et Brabant*, no. 46, November 1790, pp. 417–19.
62. Desmoulins, *Révolutions de France et Brabant*, no. 46, pp. 420–1.
63. La Marck to Mercy-Argenteau, 9 November; La Marck, II, p. 55.
64. This has only survived for the period from June 1791.
65. Desmoulins, *Révolutions de France et Brabant*, no. 55, 119–20.
66. La Marck, II, p. 86.
67. La Marck, I, p. 229.

8 BARNAVE'S PRIVATE LIFE

1. A.N. W 15, Registre I, numbered by Barnave 1–2. See also his essay 'Des femmes', Barnave, *Oeuvres*, III, pp. 257–69.
2. A.N. W 15, Registre I, pp. 35–6.
3. Aulard, *Société des Jacobins*, I, p. 190, June 1790.
4. Barnave, *Oeuvres*, III, pp. 263–4; section entitled 'coquetterie'.
5. A.N. W 13, no. 32.
6. Mathurin François Adolphe de Lescure, ed., *Correspondance secrete sur Louis XVI . . . .*, 1866, 2 vols, II, p. 554, entry for 31 August 1791; *Galérie Historique des Contemporains*, Brussels, 1837, p. 323.
7. A.N. W 12, no. 16.
8. A.N. W. 13, no. 311, published in Michon, *Adrien Duport*, appendix, p. 511.
9. A.N. W 13, no. 90.
10. A.N. W 12, p. 37.
11. A.N. W 13, no number. To make sense of this, I have had to use portions that Barnave scratched out.
12. A.N. W 12, no. 38.
13. A.N. W 13, no. 110, published in Michon, *Adrien Duport*, appendix, p. 510.
14. A.N. W 12, no. 59; O. Blanc, 'Cercles politiques et "salons" du début de la Révolution (1789–1793)', *Annales historiques de la Révolution française* (2006), pp. 1–34 and 12–13; Comte de Espinchal, *Journal*, ed. E. d'Hauterive, trans. R. Stawell, London, 1912, pp. 224–5.
15. A.N. W 13, no. 73.
16. A.N. W 13, pp. 41 and 109, cited in Bradby, *Barnave*, I, pp. 126–7.
17. A.N. W 12, no. 75.
18. A.N. W 12, pp. 663, 665 and 666; de Lessart's reply dated 28 December 1790; de Lessart to Barnave, 8 May 1791, A.N. W 13, p. 122.
19. A.N. W 12, no. 37, 26 August.
20. Madame Barnave to her son, Grenoble, 6 August 1790, A.N. W 12, no. 37.
21. Madame Barnave to her son, 15 September 1791, A.N. W 13, no. 55.
22. A.N. W 13, no. 47.
23. A.N. W 15, Registre II, p. 8.
24. J de Beylié, 'Barnave maire de Grenoble', *Bulletin de l'Académie delphinale*, 4th series, vol. 12 (1898), pp. 562–93.
25. Madame Barnave to her son, 15 March 1791, A.N. W 13, no. 64. Joseph Pouchot (1720–92) was consecrated bishop of Isère on 3 April 1791. He died a year later (in his bed) on 7 September.
26. Madame Barnave to her son, 7 June 1791, A.N. W 13, no. 82.
27. Bills from Heux, Desreyeulx (who bills M. de Barnave) and Thomassin, A.N. W 13, nos. 25 and 39 and fo. 282.
28. Barnave, *Oeuvres*, II, pp. 388–9, from his defence.
29. E.L.A. Dubois-Crancé (attrib.), *Véritable portrait de nos Législateurs*, Paris, 1792; pp. 38 and 40.
30. A. Lamartine, *Histoire des Girondins*, Paris, 1847, 8 vols, I, p. 175. Cited in P. de Ségur, *Marie Antoinette*, London, 2015, p. 332.

31. Campardon, *Le Tribunal révolutionnaire de Paris*, Paris, 1866, 2 vols., I, p. 196; transcript of Barnave's *interrogatoire*.
32. A.N. W 13, no. 2.
33. A.N. W 13, no number.
34. A.N. W 13, no. 43.
35. Barnave to his mother, draft letter of 2 January 1789 [*sic* for '1790']; A.N. W 13, no. 12.
36. A.N. W 15, Registre I, p. 136; see also J.B. Pressavin, *L'art de prologer la vie et préserver la santé ou Traité de hygiène*, 1786, p. 26.
37. A.N. W 13, no. 34.
38. A.N. W 13, no number.
39. A.N. W 15, Registre I, p. 138.
40. J.C. Lavater, *Essai sur la physiognomie destiné à faire connaitre L'homme et le faire aimer*, The Hague, 1781–6, 3 vols; Barnave to Rigaud de L'Isle, 25 September 1787, Sotheby's Paris, catalogue no. PF1303, 29 May 2013, lot 1.

9 BARNAVE AND THE COURT BEFORE THE FLIGHT TO VARENNES

1. La Marck, II, p. 32.
2. La Marck, II, p. 334.
3. Mirabeau to La Marck, 15 October; La Marck, II, p. 231.
4. Barnave to Théodore de Lameth, April 1792; *Oeuvres*, IV, pp. 374–9. Barnave to Riccé, *c.* 20 March 1792; A.N. W 13 no. 15. La Marck to Mercy-Argenteau, La Marck, II, p. 49, 28 October.
5. They are in the *Troisième Recueil*, vol. II, nos. 199, 200, 239 and 280.
6. A.N. W 13, no number.
7. La Marck, I, p. 220.
8. La Marck, II, p. 387.
9. La Marck, II, pp. 414–504.
10. La Marck, II, pp. 468–71.
11. A.N. W 13, p. 222.
12. A. Duquesnoy, *L'Ami des patriotes*, 1791–92, I, pp. 172–4, 1 January 1791.
13. Mirabeau to the queen, 5 February 1791; La Marck, II, 119 and 217. Mirabeau to La Marck, 15 January, pp. 198–9.
14. La Marck, II, p. 201.
15. Duquesnoy's note for Mirabeau – one of several now lost; La Marck, II, p. 222.
16. For the debate see Duquesnoy, *L'Ami des patriotes*, I, pp. 401–6.
17. *Journal des débats*, no. 627, p. 15 (24 February); Duquesnoy, *L'Ami des patriotes*, I, pp. 404–5.
18. La Marck, II, p. 224.
19. 'Grande Motion faite à l'Assemblée Nationale etc.', in Aulard, *Jacobins*, II, pp. 141–4.
20. For the details, see Desmoulins, *Révolutions de France et de Brabant*, no. 67, pp. 61–91.
21. La Porte to the king, 16 April 1791, afternoon, AP 55, p. 651.
22. La Porte to the king, 20 April 1791, AP 55, p. 467.
23. Fersen to Taube; A. Fersen, *Diary and Correspondence*, ed. G. Fortescue, trans. K. Wormely, Boston, 1909, p. 93.
24. A. Caiani, *Louis XVI and the French Revolution 1789–1792*, Cambridge, 2012, p. 95.
25. Duport du Tertre to the king, night of 18/19 April 1791; *French Revolution Documents*, I, p. 295.
26. Note of Cabanis to the Court, 21 April, La Marck, II, pp. 274–5; this note is in the king's papers found in the *Armoire de fer, troisième recueil*, no. 191.
27. Duquesnoy to La Marck, 19 April 1791; La Marck, II, p. 264, my emphasis.
28. La Marck to the queen, 21 April; La Marck, II, p. 273.

29. Comte de Montlosier, *Mémoires sur la Révolution française etc.*, Paris, 1830, 2 vols, II, p. 129.
30. G. Michon, *Adrien Duport et le parti feuillant*, Paris, 1924, p. 180 et seq.
31. Bertrand de Molleville, *Histoire de la Révolution française*, IV, pp. 312–13.
32. Barnave to Marie-Antoinette, 19 October 1791; E. Lever (ed.), *Correspondance de Marie-Antoinette*, Paris, 2005, p. 641.
33. Montmorin's letters are in La Marck, II, pp. 276–78.
34. The queen to Mercy-Argenteau, 20 April 1791; Lever, *Correspondance de Marie-Antoinette*, p. 528.
35. La Marck, II, pp. 279–80.
36. B. Brémond was a pamphleteer who also wrote for the *Logographe* (a rival to the *Moniteur*) which the triumvirs bought in 1791. He became *premier commis* to Terrier de Monciel, an ally of Barnave's group and one of Louis XVI's last ministers. For the identity of Brémond, see Bradby, *Barnave*, II, p. 41, note.
37. *The Diary and Letters of Gouverneur Morris*, ed. Anne Morris, New York, 1888, p. 413; Michon, *Adrien Duport*, p. 184, states erroneously that 'this list was given to Brémond'.
38. Morris, *Diary*, p. 419.
39. Fontanges to La Marck, 21 June 1791; La Marck, II, p. 283.
40. Mercy-Argenteau to Maria-Theresa, 18 March 1777, Marie-Antoinette, *Correspondance secrète entre Marie-Thérèse et le comte de Mercy-Argenteau, A. d'Arneth and M. Geffroy*, eds., 2nd ed., Paris, 1875, 3 vols., 36.

10 BARNAVE ON THE DEFENSIVE

1. A.N. W 15, Registre I, p. 19.
2. Duquesnoy, *L'Ami des patriotes*, III, p. 436, n. 2.
3. J. Michelet, *Histoire de la Révolution française*, Paris, 1889, p. 397.
4. AP XXIV, p. 621, 7 April.
5. Mirabeau's forty-ninth letter for the court, 17 January 1791; La Marck, II, p. 201.
6. *Journal des débats*, no. 723, p. 19, 16 May.
7. Michelet, *Histoire*, p. 396.
8. Desmoulins, *Révolutions de France et de Brabant*, no. 86, p. 33.
9. Bradby, *Barnave*, II, p. 90.
10. *Discours d'Adrien Duport, député de Paris, sur la rééligibilité des membres du corps législatif prononcé à la Séance du 17 mai 1791.*
11. Barnave, *Oeuvres*, II, pp. 66–7.
12. A.N. W 15, Registre II, p. 78.
13. Duquesnoy, *L'Ami des patriotes*, III, p. 436, n. 2.
14. Duquesnoy, *Journal*, II, p. 272, note, citation on pp. 274–5.
15. *Journal des débats*, no. 715, 9 May, p. 7.
16. Michelet, *Histoire*, p. 399.
17. *Mercure Universelle*, III, pp. 293–7.
18. C. Kuhlmann, *Robespierre and Mirabeau at the Jacobins, December 6, 1790*, Lincoln (Nebraska), 1911, p. 353. I am indebted to Peter Campbell for sending me Kuhlmann's pioneering studies; *Mercure Universelle*, III, pp. 327–30.
19. Aulard, *Société des Jacobins*, II, pp. 189–92. A.N. W 13, nos. 5 and 6, p. 11 and 15 for drafts of Barnave's circular, and no. 40 for the fair copy dated by him 11 March 1791.
20. *Mercure Universelle*, III, pp. 486–8.

11 VARENNES AND ITS REPERCUSSIONS

1. Barnave to Marie-Antoinette, 28 August. E. Lever, ed., *Correspondance de Marie-Antoinette*, Paris, 2005, p. 587.

2. F. de Fontanges, *La Fuite du Roi*, Gallica, pp. 88–9.
3. F. de Fontanges, *L'arrestation de la famille royale à Varennes*, pp. 110–11.
4. Duc de Choiseul, *Relation du départ de Louis XVI le 20 juin 1791*, Paris, 1822, pp. 33–5.
5. F. Hue, *Dernières années du règne de Louis XVI*, 3rd ed., Paris, 1860, pp. 220–1.
6. Théodore de Lameth, *Notes et souvenirs*, ed. E. Welvert, Paris, 1913, pp. 224–5 and 388.
7. Madame Roland, *Lettres et correspondance*, ed. C. Perroud, Paris, 1900–2, 2 vols, II, p. 303.
8. Barnave, *De la Révolution et de la Constitution*, ed. P. Gueniffey, Grenoble, 1988, p. 138.
9. Théodore de Lameth, *Souvenirs*, p. 127, n. 1.
10. Barnave, *Oeuvres*, II, p. 325 – draft petition to the Legislative Assembly.
11. M. Robespierre, *Oeuvres*, ed. Société des études Robespierristes, 10 vols, Paris, 1912–67, VII, pp. 518–23 and VIII, p. 383.
12. Desmoulins, *Révolutions de France et de Brabant*, no. 82, pp. 162–173; Gueniffey, ed., *Barnave*, p. 139; *Oeuvres*, I, p. 129.
13. P.J.B. Buchez and P.C. Roux, *Histoire parlementaire de la Révolution française*, 1834–8, 40 vols, X, p. 289.
14. Bradby, *Barnave*, II, p. 105.
15. Kuhlmann, 'Conflict in the Jacobin Club', p. 249.
16. Aulard, *Jacobins*, II, pp. 541–2, where '*Chépy fils*' is misspelt '*Cherry fils*'.
17. A.N. W 13, pp. 203 and 212.
18. Duc de Choiseul, *Relation*, pp. 33–5; Hue, *Dernières années du règne de Louis XVI*, pp. 220–1.
19. F. de Fontanges, *L'arrestation de la famille royale à Varennes*, p. 111.
20. Pétion's account of the commissioners' journey is published in M. Mortimer-Ternaux, *Histoire de la Terreur*, Paris, 1862–81, 8 vols, I, pp. 353–71; this reference at pp. 353–4.
21. Barnave, *De la Révolution et de la Constitution*, ed. P. Gueniffey, Grenoble, 1988, p. 140.
22. A.N. W 13, no. 89.
23. Dumas, *Souvenirs*, I, p. 489.
24. The queen to Mercy-Argenteau, 6 May 1791; Marie-Antoinette, *Lettres*, ed. M. de La Rocheterie and le marquis de Beaucourt, Paris, 1895–6, 2 vols, II, p. 237.
25. M. Klinckowstrom, ed., *Le Comte de Fersen et la cour de France*, Paris, 1878, 2 vols, p. 8.
26. Hampson, *Prelude to Terror*, p. 174.
27. Barnave, *Oeuvres*, I, pp. 130–1.
28. Barnave to Marie Antoinette, 28 August 1791; Lever, ed., *Correspondance de Marie-Antoinette*, p. 589.
29. Le Nôtre, *Varennes*, pp. 233–4.
30. Michelet, *Histoire*, p. 455.
31. C.F. Beaulieu, *Essais historiques sur la Révolution de France*, Paris, 1801–3, 6 vols, II, p. 533.
32. E. Burke, *Reflections on the Revolution in France*, ed. L. Mitchell, Oxford, 1993, pp. 74 and 76.
33. J.L.H. Campan, *Mémoires sur la vie privée de Marie-Antoinette*, 2 vols, 1823, II, pp. 154–4.
34. F. de Fontanges, *L'arrestation de la famille royale à Varennes*, p. 116; A. Lamartine, *Histoire des Girondins*, Paris, 1847, 8 vols, I, p. 160.
35. Marquis de Clermont-Gallerande, *Mémoires*, Paris, 1826, 3 vols, III, pp. 132–3.
36. Marie-Antoinette, *Lettres*, II, p. 328.
37. Marquis de Ferrières, *Mémoires*, eds. Berville and Barrière, Paris, 1822, 2 vols, pp. 386–89.
38. Klinckowstrom, *Fersen*, I, p. 1.
39. Lafayette, *Mémoires*, London and Paris, 1837–8, 6 vols, III, p. 96, n. 1, and pp. 99–100.

40. Théodore de Lameth, *Notes et souvenirs*, Paris, 1914, pp. 100 and 231–3 ; *Pièces trouvées: Troisième recueil des pièces trouvées dans l'armoire de fer*, Paris, 1792, no. 133.
41. Marie-Antoinette's own account of how the correspondence was set up and the initial encounters is published in *Marie-Antoinette et Barnave, Correspondance secrète*, ed. Alma Soderjhelm, Paris, 1934, pp. 37–48. It has been republished in a more accessible volume in *Marie-Antoinette, Correspondance*, ed. E. Lever, Paris, 2005, pp. 550–3.
42. Barnave's position is laid out in letters to the queen of 10 and 21 July; *Marie-Antoinette Correspondance*, pp. 555–9.
43. Barnave, *Oeuvres*, I, p. 194.
44. For an excellent discussion on this, see T.C.W. Blanning, *The Origins of the French Revolutionary Wars*, New York, 1986, pp. 101–3.
45. Barnave, *Oeuvres*, I, pp. 189–95.
46. Soderjhelm, *Marie-Antoinette et Barnave*, p. 40.
47. *Marie-Antoinette Correspondance*, pp. 554–5.
48. *Louis XVI, Marie Antoinette et Mme Elizabeth, lettres et documents inédits*, ed., F. Feuillet de Conches, 1864–9, 6 vols, II, pp. 170–4.
49. Klinckowström, *Fersen*, p. 5.
50. *Armoire de fer, troisième recueil*, I, p. 240; Bradby, *Barnave*, II, pp. 169–70.
51. Gueniffey, ed., *Barnave*, pp. 142–4.
52. *Journal des débats*, 13 July, p. 12; A.N. 440 AP/1, decoded and translated by E. Farr, *I Love You Madly: Marie-Antoinette and Fersen: The Secret Letters*, London, 2016, p. 202 (Marie-Antoinette's emphasis).
53. Salle's speech is given in *Journal des débats*, no. 785 (14 July), pp. 6–19.
54. Barnave's speech in *idem*, pp. 10–13. The full version is given in *Oeuvres*, I, pp. 242–66.
55. A.N. W 13, no. 10.
56. Barnave, *Oeuvres*, I, p. 262.
57. A.N. W 13, no. 10.
58. Barnave, *Oeuvres*, I, p. 262.
59. O. Browning, ed., *The Dispatches of Earl Gower*, Cambridge, 1885, p. 293. In fact, Lafayette made a short speech in support.
60. Madame Roland, *Lettres et correspondance*, ed. C. Perroud, Paris, 1900–2, 2 vols, II, p. 328.
61. *Journal des débats*, 15 July, p. 5.
62. AP XXVIII, p. 261.
63. A.N. W 13, p. 157.
64. La Marck, II, p. 294.
65. Hampson, *Danton*, pp. 50 and 65.
66. Michon, *Adrien Duport*, pp. 261–3.
67. Hampson, *Danton*, p. 50.
68. The other was Durand, on the payroll of the civil list.
69. Sergent's recollection in *Révue rétrospective*, 1834, 1re série, v, pp. 278–85.
70. Desmoulins, *Révolutions de France et de Brabant*, no. 86, pp. 18–20.
71. Desmoulins, *Révolutions de France et de Brabant*, no. 86, pp. 14–15.
72. Desmoulins, *Révolutions de France et de Brabant*, no. 86, p. 31.
73. Dubois-Crancé (attrib.), *Le véritable portait de nos Législateurs*, Paris, 1791, p. 41.
74. AP XXVIII, pp. 402–3.
75. Barnave breaks off his narrative to give an account of the Feuillant Club. *Barnave de la Révolution et de la Constitution*, ed. P. Gueniffey, pp. 145–50.
76. A. de Lameth, *Histoire de l'Assemblée Constituente*, Paris, 1828, 2 vols, I, p. 431.
77. C.F. Beaulieu, *Essais historiques sur la Révolution de France*, Paris, 1801–3, 6 vols, II, pp. 545–56.
78. A. Challamel, *Les Clubs Contre-Révolutionnaire*, Paris, 1895, pp. 286–93.

12 THE REVISION OF THE CONSTITUTION

1. *Moniteur*, IX, p. 375.
2. E. Lemay, 'Les révelations d'un Dictionnaire: du nouveau sur la composition de l'Assemblée nationale constituante, 1789–1791', *Annales historiques de la Révolution française*, vol. 284 (1991), pp. 159–89, 161–2.
3. *Liste MM. les Députés de la majorité de l'Assemblée Nationale, vulgairement appelés le côté gauche ou les enragés se disant patriotes*, Paris, 1791, p. 19, 'the 33 columns of the Revolution'.
4. AP XXVIII, p. 91.
5. AP XXVIII, 13 July, p. 243, note.
6. P.-V. Malouet, *Mémoires*, Paris, 1874, 2 vols, II, p. 132.
7. Malouet, *Mémoires*, II, p. 132.
8. Marie-Antoinette, *Lettres*, ed. M. de La Rocheterie et le marquis de Beaucourt, Paris, 1895–6, 2 vols, II, p. 274.
9. Barnave to the queen, 12 and 17 August, *Marie-Antoinette Correspondance*, ed. E. Lever, Paris, 2005, pp. 578–9.
10. Duquesnoy, *L'Ami des patriotes*, III, p. 436, n. 2.
11. Gueniffey, ed., *Barnave*, p. 134, n. 88.
12. *Moniteur*, IX, p. 353.
13. *Journal des débats*, no. 828, 27 August, p. 2; *Moniteur*, IX, p. 504.
14. Michon, *Adrien Duport*, pp. 322–3.
15. Aulard, *Jacobins*, III, p. 111.
16. *Journal des débats*, 28 March, p. 6.
17. *Moniteur*, IX, pp. 363–4.
18. *Moniteur*, IX, pp. 374–9.
19. *Moniteur*, IX, p. 392.
20. *Moniteur*, IX, pp. 389–98; *Observation des Comités de Constitution et de revision à l'Assemblée Nationale*, cited in Bradby, *Barnave*, II, p. 222.
21. Gueniffey, ed., *Barnave*, pp. 151–2.
22. Gueniffey, ed., *Barnave*, p. 156.
23. *Moniteur*, IX, pp. 391–2.
24. *Moniteur*, IX, p. 396.
25. Michelet, *Révolution*, pp. 528–30.
26. Michelet, *Révolution*, p. 528.
27. O. Browning, ed., *The Dispatches of Earl Gower*, Cambridge, 1885, p. 120.
28. Comte de Montlosier, *Mémoires sur la Révolution française etc.*, Paris, 1830, 2 vols, II, pp. 212–13; Michelet, *Révolution*, 539–40.
29. Michelet, *Révolution*, p. 531.
30. E.L.A. Dubois-Crancé (attrib.), *Analyse de la Révolution*, Paris, 1885, pp. 71–2.
31. Michelet, *Histoire*, p. 534.
32. Marquis de Bouillé, *Mémoires*, eds. S.A. Berville and J.F. Barrière, Paris, 1821, p. 289; Michelet, *Révolution*, p. 531.
33. Montlosier, *Mémoires*, II, p. 255.
34. Staël to Gustavus III, 4 September; Baron Staël-Holstein, *Correspondance diplomatique*, ed. Baron Brinkman, Paris, 1881, p. 231.
35. *Actes des Apôtres*, no. 275, pp. 92–102.
36. *Courrier extraordinaire*, 2 September; *Actes des Apôtres*; *Bulletin des Journaux*, 5 September; *Correspondance secrete*, II, p. 545; Michon, *Adrien Duport*, p. 324.
37. La Marck to Mercy-Argenteau, 6 September 1791; La Marck, II, p. 302.
38. Barnave to Marie-Antoinette, 1 September; *Correspondance de Marie-Antoinette*, p. 594.
39. A.F. Bertrand de Molleville, *Histoire de la Révolution française*, Paris, 1801–3, 14 vols, V, pp. 221–2.

40. *Troisième Recueil*, I, pp. 310–5.
41. A.N. W 13, p. 232.
42. *Troisième Recueil*, I, pp. 310–15, at 314.
43. For the king's speech, *Moniteur*, IX, p. 655.
44. *Troisième Recueil*, I, pp. 299–302.
45. T.C.W. Blanning, *The Origins of the French Revolutionary Wars*, New York, 1986, pp. 86–7.
46. Bertrand de Molleville, *Révolution*, V, pp. 27–8.
47. Leopold II to Marie-Antoinette, 17 and 20 September; *Correspondance de Marie-Antoinette*, pp. 581–4.
48. Marie-Antoinette to Barnave, 31 August, and Barnave's reply, 1 September; *Correspondance de Marie-Antoinette*, pp. 592–4. See also J. Flammermont, 'La Correspondance de Pellenc avec les comtes de La Marck et Mercy', in *Revue de la Révolution française*, vol. 16 (1889), pp. 481–502.
49. J. Hardman and J.M. Roberts, eds, *French Revolution Documents*, Oxford, 1966–73, 2 vols, I, pp. 365–6, for the text of the constitution and Louis's speech.
50. R. Griffiths, *Le Centre Perdu, Malouet et les 'monarchiens'*, Grenoble, 1988, p. 104.
51. J.L.H. Campan, *Mémoires sur la vie privée de Marie-Antoinette*, 1823, 2 vols, II, p. 150.

13 GOVERNING IN SECRET

1. E. Campardon, *Le Tribunal de Paris*, Paris, 1866, 2 vols, I, pp. 195–6.
2. Marie-Antoinette to Barnave, 13 October 1791; E. Lever, ed., *Marie-Antoinette Correspondance*, p. 635.
3. Marie-Antoinette to Barnave, 20 October 1791; *Marie-Antoinette Correspondance*, p. 647.
4. Letter of 3 October; *Marie-Antoinette Correspondance*, p. 627; J.L.H. Campan, *Mémoires sur la vie privée de Marie-Antoinette*, 2 vols, II, 1823, p. 25.
5. Marie-Antoinette to Barnave, 7 August 1791; *Marie-Antoinette Correspondance*, p. 574.
6. Marie-Antoinette to Barnave, 2 October, and Barnave to Marie-Antoinette, 1 October; *Marie-Antoinette Correspondance*, pp. 625–6.
7. Alma Soderjhelm, ed., *Marie-Antoinette et Barnave, Correspondance secrète*, Paris, 1934, p. 137.
8. Marie-Antoinette to Barnave, 27 October; *Marie-Antoinette Correspondance*, p. 653, Barnave's emphasis.
9. Bertrand de Molleville, *Mémoires secrets pour servir à l'histoire de la dernière année du règne de Louis XVI, roi de France*, London, 1797, 3 vols, I, p. 359.
10. Molleville, *Mémoires secrets*, I, p. 346. This was due to his position as Keeper of the Seals – chancellor he could not be because through all the turmoil of the Revolution Maupeou refused to resign his post.
11. Morris to Washington, 4 February 1792; Anne Morris, ed., *The Diary and Letters of Gouverneur Morris*, New York, 1888, pp. 504–5.
12. J. Hardman, *French Politics 1774–1789*, London, 1995, pp. 170–5.
13. Molleville, *Mémoires secrets*, I, p. 312.
14. Pellenc to La Marck, 23 December 1791; La Marck, II, pp. 344–6.
15. Marie-Antoinette to Barnave, 14 November; *Marie-Antoinette Correspondance*, p. 673.
16. Bertrand de Molleville, *Mémoires particuliers pour servir à l'histoire de la fin du règne de Louis XVI*, Paris, 1816, 2 vols, I, p. 153.
17. For the question of the uniform, see O.-G. Heidenstam, ed., *Marie-Antoinette, Fersen et Barnave*, 1913, pp. 185–201.
18. Barnave, *Oeuvres*, I, p. v.
19. Barnave to Marie-Antoinette, 1 December, and her reply, 2 December; *Marie-Antoinette Correspondance*, pp. 715–17.
20. Morris, *Diary*, p. 461.

21. Barnave, *Oeuvres*, I, p. 141.
22. A.N. W 15, Registre II, pp. 17–18.
23. Comte d'Allonville, *Mémoires d'un homme d'état*, Brussels, 1839, 2 vols, I, p. 300.
24. *Marie-Antoinette Correspondance*, pp. 655–6.
25. Vermale, 'Barnave: fragments inédits', pp. 82 and 97.
26. *Marie-Antoinette Correspondance*, pp. 618 and 623.
27. *Moniteur*, X, p. 57.
28. Morris, *Diary*, p. 473, entry for 30 October.
29. Marie-Antoinette to Barnave, 30 October 9.30 a.m., with his reply, same date; *Marie-Antoinette Correspondance*, pp. 655–6.
30. The queen to Barnave, 11 November, and Barnave to the queen, 17 November; *Marie-Antoinette Correspondance*, pp. 670 and 676. In an ideal world Marie-Antoinette would have liked both mayoral candidates (Lafayette and Pétion) to lose. Pellenc to La Marck, 17 November; La Marck, II, p. 342.
31. The queen to Fersen, 31 October; *Marie-Antoinette Correspondance*, p. 656.
32. Pellenc to La Marck, 12 November; La Marck, II, p. 340.
33. *Archives Parlementaires*, XLVIII, pp. 482–3.
34. A.N. C221 160 (148), pièce 19, quoted in P. and P. Girault de Coursac, eds, *Louis XVI a la parole*, 1989, p. 276.
35. *Moniteur*, X, p. 390.
36. The queen to Barnave, 14 November; *Marie-Antoinette Correspondance*, p. 673.
37. Barnave to the queen, 13 November; *Marie-Antoinette Correspondance*, p. 672.
38. Barnave to Marie-Antoinette, 29 September 1791; *Marie-Antoinette Correspondance*, p. 625.
39. A.N. W 13 no. 12.
40. Morris, *Diary*, 22 October, p. 468.
41. Morris, *Diary*, p. 470, entry for 25 October.
42. Marie-Antoinette to Barnave, 10 October; *Marie-Antoinette Correspondance*, pp. 639–41.
43. Campan, *Mémoires*, II, p. 162.
44. Morris, *Diary*, p. 473, entry for 30 October.
45. A.N. W 12, pp. 663, 665 and 666; de Lessart's reply dated 28 December 1790; de Lessart to Barnave, 8 May 1791; A.N. W 13, p. 122.
46. M. Klinckowström, ed, *Le Comte de Fersen et la cour de France*, Paris, 1878, 2 vols, II, p. 7.
47. A.N. W 15, Registre I, p. 124.
48. Marie-Antoinette to Barnave, 29 September; *Marie-Antoinette Correspondance*, pp. 623-624.
49. Molleville, *Mémoires*, I, p. 218.
50. M. Villemain, *Souvenirs contemporains*, Paris, 1855, 2 vols, I, p. 31.
51. Villemain, *Souvenirs*, I, p. 18.
52. Barnave to the queen, 15 November; *Marie-Antoinette Correspondance*, p. 674.
53. Barnave, *Oeuvres*, II, pp. 92–3.
54. Barnave to Marie-Antoinette, 5 November; *Marie-Antoinette Correspondance*, pp. 664–6.
55. Marie-Antoinette to Barnave, 4 December; *Marie-Antoinette Correspondance*, p. 716.
56. Pellenc to La Marck, 3 January 1792; La Marck, II, pp. 351–2; Duc de Lauzun (Biron), *Correspondance intime, 1791–92*, ed. Comte de Serignan, Paris, 1906, passim.
57. Marie-Antoinette to Fersen, 7 December; *Marie-Antoinette Correspondance*, p. 724.
58. Pellenc to La Marck, 3 January 1792; La Marck, II, p. 347.
59. 'The reopening of the club appears to have occurred on 27 or 28 November 1791.' F. Dendena, 'A New Look at Feuillantism: The Triumvirate and the Movement for War in 1791', *French History*, vol. 26, no. 1 (2012), pp. 6–33, at 214.
60. Gueniffey, ed., *Barnave*, p. 149.

61. A.N. W 15, Registre II, p. 72.
62. Dendena, 'Feuillantism', p. 18, n. 60.
63. Vaublanc, *Mémoires*, ed. M.F. Barrière, Paris, 1857, p. 166; Bertrand de Molleville, *Histoire de la Révolution française*, I, p. 335.
64. *Moniteur*, X, 29 November.
65. Marie-Antoinette to Barnave, 15 December; *Marie-Antoinette Correspondance*, pp. 718 and 733.
66. An exception was Montbarey, who opposed entry into the American war.
67. Michon, *Adrien Duport*, pp. 356–7. Soderjhelm, in *Marie-Antoinette et Barnave*, pointed out Michon's error in an extended footnote to p. 210.
68. Barnave, *Oeuvres*, I, p. 212.
69. Barnave to unnamed 27 January and 2 February 1792; *Oeuvres*, IV, pp. 344 and 447.
70. Barnave to Marie-Antoinette, 14 December; *Marie-Antoinette Correspondance*, pp. 730–2. See also Dendena, 'Feuillantism' and Soderjhelm, *Marie-Antoinette et Barnave*, p. 210, n. 2.
71. A.A.E. Trèves, Sup. 4, f. 22, cited in P. and P. Girault de Coursac, *Enquête sur le procès du roi Louis XVI*, Paris, 1982, p. 338.
72. Barnave to Marie-Antoinette, 30 and 31 December; *Marie-Antoinette Correspondance*, pp. 746–7.
73. Klinckowstrom, *Fersen*, II, p. 12.
74. Marie-Antoinette to Barnave, 3 January 1792; *Marie-Antoinette Correspondance*, p. 751.
75. *Marie-Antoinette Correspondance*, p. 734, n. 1.
76. A.N. W 15, Registre I, p. 120; Barnave, *Oeuvres*, I, pp. 104–95.
77. T.C.W. Blanning, *The Origins of the French Revolutionary Wars*, New York, 1986, p. 89.
78. Barnave to Théodore de Lameth, 31 March 1792; *Oeuvres*, IV, pp. 355–6.
79. *Marie-Antoinette Correspondance*, pp. 868–9.
80. A.N. W 15, Registre II, pp. 128–9.
81. J. Hardman, ed., *The French Revolution Sourcebook*, London and New York, 1999, p. 141.
82. Barnave to the queen, 5 January 1792; *Marie-Antoinette Correspondance*; Gueniffey, ed., *Barnave*, pp. 195, 755.
83. Barnave, *Oeuvres*, II, pp. 151–3.
84. Morris, *Diary*, p. 498.
85. Pellenc to La Marck; H. Glagau, *Die Französiche Législative . . . 1791-92*, Berlin, 1896, appendix, p. 286.
86. Bradby, *Barnave*, II, p. 276.
87. Barnave, *Oeuvres*, I, p. 212.
88. Barnave to Marie-Antoinette, 5 January 1792; *Marie-Antoinette Correspondance*, pp. 753–6.
89. Barnave to the queen, 28 December; *Marie-Antoinette Correspondance*, p. 746.
90. J.L.H. Campan, *Mémoires sur la vie privée de Marie-Antoinette*, 1823, 2 vols, II, pp. 204–5.
91. Barnave to Marie-Antoinette, 5 January 1792; *Marie-Antoinette Correspondance*, p. 756.
92. Vermale, 'Barnave: fragments inédits', p. 49. Barnave to Marie-Antoinette, 5 January 1792; *Marie-Antoinette Correspondance*, p. 756.
93. P. de Ségur, *Marie-Antoinette*, London, 2015, p. 335.

14 THE RETURN OF THE NATIVE: JANUARY–AUGUST 1792

1. Barnave to a lady, probably Madame Charles de Lameth, January 1792, A.N. W 13, no. 24, published by Michon, in the appendix of *Adrien Duport et le parti feuillant*, Paris, 1924, pp. 512–14.
2. *Journal patriotique*, 1792, nos 142 and 143, cited in A. Prudhomme, *Histoire de Grenoble*, Grenoble, 1888, p. 627.

3. Madame de Lameth's reply, 30 January 1792, A.N. W 13 no. 25, Michon, appendix, pp. 514–15; a lady to Barnave, 11 January 1792, A.N. W 13, Michon, Appendix, p. 512.
4. R.M. Klinckowström, *Le Comte de Fersen et la cour de France*, Paris, 1878, 2 vols. II, p. 13; Fersen's diary entry for 13 March 1792.
5. Barnave to Théodore de Lameth, April 1792; *Oeuvres*, IV, pp. 374–9. Barnave to Riccé *c.* 20 March 1792, A.N. W 13, no. 15, published by Michon, in the appendix of *Adrien Duport*, pp. 485–7.
6. Bertrand de Molleville, *Mémoires secrets*, p. 363.
7. [Alexandre] de Lameth to Pellenc, undated, but *c.* 15 March, cited in H. Glagau, *Die Französische Legislative . . . 1791–1792*, Berlin, 1871, p. 301.
8. A.N. W 15, Registre II, p. 4, for Barnave's take on Strafford.
9. Barnave to Théodore de Lameth, 31 March; *Oeuvres*, IV, p. 359.
10. Pellenc to La Marck, 14 March 1792; Glagau, *Französische Legislative*, p. 297.
11. Michon, *Adrien Duport*, p. 493, letter to Duport, 4 March 1792, and to Théodore de Lameth, 12 May, p. 497.
12. Barnave to Théodore de Lameth, 31 March; *Oeuvres*, IV, pp. 356–7.
13. Delay to Barnave, 18 February and 10 March; Graves to Barnave, 31 March; Michon, *Adrien Duport*, appendix, pp. 483–4 and 488–9.
14. J. Flammermont, 'La Correspondance de Pellenc avec les comtes de La Marck et Mercy', in *Revue de la Révolution française*, vol. 16 (1889), pp. 481–502, at 400.
15. Barnave to Théodore de Lameth, April 1792; *Oeuvres*, IV, pp. 374–5.
16. Glagau, *Französische Legislative*, p. 312.
17. L.C. Bigot de Sainte-Croix, *Histoire de la conspiration du 10 août 1792*, London, 1793, pp. 95–6.
18. Barnave to Théodore de Lameth, 31 March; *Oeuvres*, IV, p. 359.
19. A.N. W 15, Registre I, p. 73; Barnave to Dumas; Michon, *Adrien Duport*, appendix, p. 502; Gueniffey ed., *Barnave*, p. 201.
20. Barnave to Alexandre de Lameth, 6 April, and to Théodore, 31 March; *Oeuvres*, IV, pp. 358 and 365–70.
21. Soulavie argued that this had been the case throughout the reign of Louis XVI, with such ministers as Turgot and Necker playing this role.
22. Bertrand de Molleville, *Mémoires particuliers pour servir à l'histoire de la fin du règne de Louis XVI*, Paris, 1797, 3 vols, II, p. 223.
23. Dumouriez, *Mémoires*, Paris, 1822–3, 4 vols, II, pp. 278–9 and 294–6.
24. Barnave to Dumas, undated but late June, A.N. W 13, no. 19; Michon, *Adrien Duport*, appendix, pp. 500–3.
25. Abbé Louis to Mercy, 26 June; Glagau, *Französische Legislative*, p. 342.
26. Mercy to Kaunitz, 27 June 1792; Glagau, *Französische Legislative*, p. 339.
27. *Annales patriotiques*, no. 115, vol. XI, pp. 511–12.
28. P.L. Roederer, *Chronique de cinquante jours*, Paris, 1832, pp. 50–3 and 76–8; Dumouriez, *Mémoires*, II, p. 153.
29. Barnave, *Oeuvres*, II, pp. 22–5.
30. Vermale, 'Barnave: fragments inédits', p. 94.
31. A.N W 13, Registre I, p. 73.
32. A. Prudhomme, *Histoire de Grenoble*, Grenoble, 1888, p. 630, citing a letter of Achard de Germane.
33. J. Arnaud-Bouteloup, *Le rôle politique de Marie-Antoinette*, Paris, 1924, p. 338.
34. Barnave to Théodore de Lameth, August 1792, A.N. W 13, no. 16, cited in Michon, *Adrien Duport*, appendix, p. 506.
35. The queen to Fersen, 11 July; *Marie-Antoinette Correspondance*, pp. 801–3; Théodore de Lameth, *Notes et souvenirs*, ed. E. Welvert, Paris, 1913, pp. 126–8.
36. Barnave, *Oeuvres*, I, p. 218.
37. A.N. W 13, no number (the receipt) and nos. 12 and 18; M. Martin to Barnave, Lyon, 21 March and 14 June.

15 A LONG INCARCERATION

1. A. Prudhomme, *Histoire de Grenoble*, Grenoble, 1888, p. 632.
2. *Moniteur*, XIII, p. 431.
3. A.N. W 12, no number.
4. Marat, *L'Ami du peuple*, 19 August 1792, p. 3; cited in Bradby, *Barnave*, II, p. 308.
5. Barnave to Alquier, January 1793, and to Boissy d'Anglas, same date; *Oeuvres*, II, pp. 316–25.
6. *Bulletin du Tribunal Révolutionnaire*, no. 11, pp. 43–4.
7. Prudhomme, *Grenoble*, p. 632, citing *Lettres adressées par Achard de Germane à M. de la Coste 1791–1793*, Valence, 1891, letter of 30 August 1792; Bradby, *Barnave*, II, p. 311, n. 3.
8. D'Aiguillon to Barnave, 17 August, A.N. W 13 *Moniteur*, XIII, p. 579.
9. Barnave to Madame de Broglie or Madame Théodore de Lameth, published as a facsimile in Barnave, *Oeuvres*, I.
10. *Registre de correspondance*, A.N. C, p. 170.
11. Barnave to Alquier, mid-January; Barnave, *Oeuvres*, II, pp. 316–8.
12. Barnave, *Oeuvres*, I, CXXV–VI.
13. Barnave, *Oeuvres*, I, facsimile.
14. Barnave to Alquier, mid-January; *Oeuvres*, II, pp. 326-328.
15. For a full account of Danton's intervention, see Michon, *Adrien Duport*, pp. 432–4. For Barnave, see *Journal de la République*, no. 1, p. 2.
16. Bradby, *Barnave*, II, p. 311.
17. Nicolaï, *Extraits des Mémoires inédits de Madame Nicolaï née de Lameth*, Pontoise, 1930, pp. 98–100.
18. Facsimile letter, placed at the end of Barnave, *Oeuvres*, I.
19. Letter probably to Baillot, late February and March; Barnave, *Oeuvres*, I, pp. 326–332.
20. Notes for an appeal to the Convention; Barnave, *Oeuvres*, II, p. 337.
21. Barnave, *Oeuvres*, II, pp. 332–8.
22. Théodore de Lameth, *Mémoires*, p. 95.
23. F.A. Aulard, ed., *Recueil des actes du Comité de Salut Public*, 1889–1911, 21 vols, IV, pp. 74–8.
24. Bradby, *Barnave*, II, p. 325. David's memoir is in Théodore de Lameth's manuscripts.
25. J. Hardman, *Robespierre*, London and New York, 1999, p. 194.
26. T. Lameth, *Mémoires*, pp. 93–4; Bérenger's introduction in Barnave, *Oeuvres*, I, p. cxxviii.
27. F.A. Aulard, ed., *Comité de Salut Public*, IV, p. 76.
28. F.A. Aulard, ed., *Comité de Salut Public*, VIII, pp. 71–2.
29. Chépy, *Correspondance*, XL and p. 279, Chépy's emphasis.
30. Barnave to Boissy d'Anglas, 4 November; Barnave, *Oeuvres*, II, pp. 339–40.
31. Barnave, *Oeuvres*, I, p. cxxxi.
32. Théodore de Lameth, *Mémoires*, ed. E. Welvert, Paris, 1913, p. 243.
33. A.N. W 13, no number; *Lettres écrites de Londres sur les Anglois et autres sujets*, Basel 1734, by M.D.V. (Voltaire), pp. 162–4. The Latin is usually written *ipsaque mors*.
34. Ibid., p. 164.
35. Bradby, *Barnave*, II, p. 333, misreads *f* for *J* – as in Joseph; but Barnave has a distinctive 'f' and always signs himself 'Barnave *fils*'.
36. Barnave, *Oeuvres*, IV, facsimile as appendix – the italicised portion is omitted from Bérenger's printed version; Barnave, *Oeuvres*, II, pp. 341–5.

16 TRIAL AND DEATH

1. *Moniteur*, XVIII, pp. 365 and 472; *Journal de Paris* for 12 November, p. 1271.
2. J. Hardman, *Marie-Antoinette*, New Haven and London, 2019, p. 301.

3. E. Campardon, *Le Tribunal révolutionnaire de Paris*, 1866, 2 vols, I, pp. 190–3.
4. C.F. Beaulieu, *Essais historiques sur la Révolution de France*, Paris, 1801–3, 6 vols, II, p. 140, n. 1.
5. Théodore de Lameth, *Mémoires*, p. 97.
6. C.F. Beaulieu, *Les souvenirs de l'Histoire ou le diurnal de la Révolution de France pour l'an de grace 1797*, p. 243; Barnave, *Oeuvres*, I, cxxxii.
7. J. Hardman, *Robespierre*, London and New York, 1999, pp. 108–9.
8. Campardon, *Tribunal révolutionnaire*, I, pp. 195–8.
9. Barnave, *Oeuvres*, II, p. 12, dated 23 March 1792. A.N. W 15 Registre.
10. Barnave, *Oeuvres*, II, pp. 362–99.
11. A.N. W 13, no. 42, Dumouriez's exclamation mark.
12. Vermale, 'Barnave: fragments inédits', pp. 89–90.
13. E. Bradby 'Marie-Antoinette and the Constitutionalists; the Heidenstam papers', *The English Historical Review*, vol. 31, issue 122 (1916), pp. 238–55.
14. Alma Soderjhelm, ed., *Marie-Antoinette et Barnave, Correspondance secrète*, Paris, 1934, preface, p. VII.
15. Barnave, *Oeuvres*, IV, pp. 161–2, numbers XXXVII and XXXVIII in a series of short literary criticisms.
16. Brissot, *Lettre à M. Barnave*, Paris, 1791, epigraph.
17. Beaulieu refers to the money paid since September to those attending the popular societies – in fact, an attempt to muzzle them by giving them a state salary.
18. Beaulieu, *Essais*, II, p. 141.
19. *Glaive vengeur de la République . . . ou galérie révolutionnaire*, Paris, Year II (1793), pp. 140–1.
20. *Glaive vengeur*, p. 141.
21. C. Desmoulins, *Le Vieux Cordelier*, no. III, pp. 83–4, reprinted, Paris, 1825.
22. Barnave, *Oeuvres*, I, p. cxxxviii.
23. *La Glaive vengeur de la République française* (Paris year II), pp. 137 and 141.
24. M. Price, *The Fall of the Monarchy, Louis XVI, Marie-Antoinette and the baron de Breteuil*, London, 2002, p. 345.
25. C. Thomas, trans. Julie Rosse, *The Wicked Queen: The Origins of the Myth of Marie-Antoinette*, New York, 2001, p. 105.

CONCLUSION

1. A.N. W 15, Registre II, numbered by Barnave first and second page; Barnave, *Oeuvres*, I, p. 220; Bradby, *Barnave*, II, p. 304.
2. *Discours d'Adrien Duport, député de Paris, sur la rééligibilité des membres du corps législatif Prononcé à la Séance du 17 mai 1791.*
3. Dendena, 'Feuillantism', p. 3.
4. Dendena, F., 'L'expérience de la défaite, la rencontre avec l'histoire: Barnave et ses écrits historiques', *La Révolution française*, vol. 10 (2016), pp. 1–13, at 5.
5. Barnave, *Oeuvres*, I, p. 218.
6. A.N. W 13, no. 10.
7. Barnave holograph, *c.* 1792, offered for sale on eBay in January 2002. I am indebted to Alan Peachment for pointing out this document.

BIBLIOGRAPHY

MANUSCRIPT SOURCES

Barnave's archive is in two places: Grenoble, where he was born and grew up and was arrested, and Paris, where he was killed. He was able to insist that the papers which the police confiscated should accompany him to his trial. However, his resourceful mother was able to hide many of his papers from the authorities. The bulk of these were published by Bérenger de la Drôme in 1843 at the wish of his surviving sister, Adélaïde Madame Sainte-Germaine, who also gave the manuscripts (twelve bound *cahiers*) to the Bibliothèque municipal de Grenoble, where they are classified Réserve U 5216 (1–12).

Bérenger's edition was criticised by Vermale in 1938 but defended by Gueniffey, who published a critical edition of his most influential work, which Bérenger called *Introduction à le Revolution française* and he called *De la Révolution et de la Constitution* (see my Introduction)[1]. Bérenger published the rest of the archive with minor omissions influenced partly by the political and religious climate under Louis-Philippe – for example, Barnave's attacks on the Girondins, were back in favour at the time. A series of fine local historians over the past hundred years, notably J. de Beylié, F. Vermale and, most recently, R. Fonvieille have combed through the archive and published omissions and corrections.

The Paris archive A.N. W 12–15 is at once more chaotic and, perhaps for that reason, has been less exploited. W 15 is a bound exercise book and has normal pages but the rest is chaotic: the numbering is haywire, in no order either chronological or thematic. The references I give sound conventional, for example, W 12, no. 15 or p. 12, but 15 does not follow 14, nor is it succeeded by 16, which may not exist. On 10 September Barnave wrote that 'the storm in Paris has completely subsided', interleaved with a love letter.[2]

The Tribunal officials only extracted '3 items, nos. 40, 41, 42 . . . as worth examining' – and restored no. 42,[3] so this does not explain the disorder, which is probably due to Barnave's habit of never throwing anything away. So the reader will have to trust that my references are accurate, though they refer to nothing intelligible. The only way they could be followed up would be if I put my PDF of the film I commissioned online and gave references to the page number it created. Otherwise, one would have to trek through seven boxes containing 2,787 pages, mostly of manuscript.

Sotheby's Paris catalogue no. PF1303, 29 May 2013, lot 1 contains seventy-six letters from Barnave to Rigaud de L'Isle, 29 November 1781–30 June 1790. This archive failed to meet its reserve price of 10,000 euros and Sotheby's Paris have not managed to trace its present whereabouts for me. The seven excerpts in the catalogue which I have used suggest the tip of an important iceberg.

The other archive I have relied on heavily is Mss Journal des Etats-Généraux tenus en 1789, B.N. nouv. ac. fr. 12938, attributed to the Third Estate deputy for Laon, de Vismes. Barnave himself briefly kept a diary – for the period 14–17 May 1789 on the conferences he attended trying to solve the dispute over voting with the nobility and clergy. No other record is so complete for this crucial, if doomed, attempt. It can be found (with difficulty) in A.N. W 13 (no number).

BIBLIOGRAPHY

PRINTED PRIMARY SOURCES

Actes des Apôtres, Les, 1789–91 (royalist journal).

Achard de Germane, *Lettres adressées par Achard de Germane à M. de la Coste 1791–1793*, Valence, 1891.

Allonville, comte d', *Mémoires d'un homme d'état*, Brussels, 1839, 2 vols.

André, V., ed., *Malesherbes à Louis XVI ou les Avertissements de Cassandra, Mémoires inédits 1787–1788*, Paris, 2010.

Angiviller, comte d', *Mémoires*, Copenhagen, 1939.

Aulard, F., ed., *Récit des séances des députés des communes depuis le 5 mai 1789 Jusqu'au 12 juin suivant*, Paris, 1895.

— ed., *Recueil des actes du Comité de Salut Public*, 1889–1911, 21 vols.

— *La Société des Jacobins*, Paris, 1889–97, 6 vols.

Barentin, C.L.F. de Paule de, *Lettres et Bulletins à Louis XVI*, ed. A. Aulard, Paris, 1915.

— *Mémoire autographe sur les derniers Conseils du Roi Louis XVI*, ed. M. Champion, Paris, 1844.

Barnave, A.P.J.M. (attrib.), *Avis aux Campagnes de Dauphiné*, n.p., 1788.

— *Coup d'Oeuil sur la lettre de M. de Calonne*, Dauphiné, 28 March 1789.

— *De la Révolution et de la Constitution*, ed. P. Gueniffey, Grenoble, 1988.

— *Esprit des édits enregistrés militairement au parlement de Grenoble, le 10 mai 1788*, Grenoble, n.p., 1788.

— *Introduction à la Révolution française*, ed. G. Rudé, Paris, 1960.

— *Lettre écrite à la commission intermédiare . . . des Etats de Dauphiné*, Paris, 1789.

— *Lettre de M. Barnave à M. Linguet*, Paris, 31 March 1791.

— *Lettre de M. Blanchard, magister du village du Moivieux à Monseigneur Georges Lefranc de Pompignan, L'archevêque de Vienne*, n.p. [1788].

— *Oeuvres*, ed. Bérenger de la Drôme, Paris, 1843, 4 vols.

— *Power, Property and History*, ed., E. Chill, New York and London, 1971.

— (attrib.), *Profession de foi d'un militaire. Discours prononcé dans un-Conseil militaire*, n.p., 1788.

Baudeau, N., *Idées d'un citoyen presque sexaganaire sur l'état actuel du royame de France*, Paris, 1787.

Beaulieu, C.F., *Essais historiques sur la Révolution de France*, Paris, 1801–3, 6 vols.

— *Les souvenirs de l'Histoire ou le diurnal de la Révolution de France pour l'an de grace 1797*, Paris, 1797.

Bertrand de Molleville, A. F., *Histoire de la Révolution française*, Paris, 1801–3, 14 vols.

— *Mémoires secrets pour servir à l'histoire de la dernière année du règne de Louis XVI, roi de France*, London, 1797, 3 vols.

Beylié, J. de, 'Barnave, Pages inédites', *Bulletin de l'Académie delphinale*, series 4, vol. 12 (1898), pp. 539–62.

— *Lettre de Barnave, du 30 juin 1790, à la société des amis de la constitution de Grenoble*, Paris, 1900.

— *Lettres inédites de Barnave sur la prise de la Bastille*, Grenoble, 1906.

Bigot de Sainte-Croix, L.C., *Histoire de la conspiration du 10 août 1792*, London, 1793.

Bombelles, marquis de, *Journal*, ed. J. Grassion, F. Durif and J. Charon-Bordas, Geneva, 1978–98, 4 vols.

Bouillé, marquis de, *Mémoires*, ed. S.A. Berville and J.F. Barrière, Paris, 1821.

Brissot, J., *Lettre à M. Barnave*, Paris, 1790.

Browning, O., ed., *The Dispatches of Earl Gower*, Cambridge, 1885.

Buchez, P.J.B. and Roux, P.C., *Histoire parlementaire de la Révolution française*, Paris, 1834–8, 40 vols.

Bulletin du Tribunal Révolutionnaire, Paris, 1793–4.

Burke, E., *Reflections on the Revolution in France*, ed. L. Mitchell, Oxford, 1993.

Calonne, C.A. de, *Collection des mémoires présentées à l'Assemblée de Notables par M. de Calonne*, Paris, 1787.
— *Lettre au roi*, London, 1789.
— *Réponse à l'écrit de M. Necker*, London, 1788.
Campan, J.L.H., *Mémoires sur la vie privée de Marie-Antoinette*, Paris, 1823, 2 vols.
Campardon, E., *Le Tribunal de Paris*, Paris, 1866, 2 vols.
Chépy, Pierre, *Correspondance avec le Ministre des Affaires Étrangères, 1793–1794*, ed. R. Delachenal, Grenoble, 1894.
Choiseul, duc de, *Relation du départ de Louis XVI le 20 juin 1791*, Paris, 1822.
Clermont-Gallerande, Marquis de, *Mémoires*, Paris, 1826, 3 vols.
Colomb, C., 'L'échec d'un serviteur du roi – Vidaud de la Tour, premier président du parlement de Maupeou à Grenoble', *Histoire, Economie et Society*, vol. 3 (2006), pp. 371–83.
Compte rendu par la société des gardes nationaux à l'armée Parisienne et aux 83 Départements de France, Paris, *c.* 11 December 1790, 30 pages.
Creuzé de la Touche, J.A., *Journal des Etats-Généraux et du début de l'Assemblée nationale*, ed. J. Marchand, Paris, 1946.
Desmoulins, C., *Le Vieux Cordelier*, no. III, 83–4, reprinted, Paris, 1825.
— *Révolutions de France et de Brabant*, Paris, 1789–91.
Dubois-Crancé, E.L.A. (attrib.), *Analyse de la Révolution*, Paris, 1885.
— *Supplément à la gallérie de l'Assemblée nationale*, n.p., October 1789.
— (attrib.), *Véritable portrait de nos Législateurs, Ou Galerie Des Tableaux. Exposés À La Vue Du Public Depuis Le 5 Mai 1789, Jusqu'au Premier Octobre 1791*, Paris, 1792.
Dumas, Mathieu, *Souvenirs*, Paris, 1839, 2 vols.
Dumont, E., *Souvenirs sur Mirabeau*, Paris, 1832.
Dumouriez, *Mémoires*, Paris, 1822–3, 4 vols.
Duport, A., *Discours d'Adrien Duport, député de Paris, sur la rééligibilité des membres du corps législatif Prononcé à la Séance du 17 mai 1791*, n.p.
Duquesnoy, Adrien, *L' Ami des patriotes*, 1791–2.
— *Journal*, ed. R. de Crèvecoeur, Paris, 1894, 2 vols.
Echouchard Lebrun, P.-D., Oeuvres, 4 vols, Paris, 1811.
Elizabeth, Madame, *Correspondance*, ed. F. Feuillet de Conches, Paris, 1868.
Emblard, L., 'Notes historiques sur Barnave', *Bull. Delph.*, vol. XXXII (1898), pp. 201–16.
Espinchal, comte de, *Journal*, ed. E. d'Hauterive, trans. R. Stawell, London, 1912.
Etats-Généraux, Lefebvre, G., et al. (eds), *Recueil de documents relatifs aux Etats-Généraux de 1789*, Paris, 1953–70, 4 vols.
Ferrières, marquis de, *Mémoires*, ed. Berville and Barrière, Paris, 1822.
Fersen, A., Klinckowstrom, M., (ed.), *Le Comte de Fersen et la cour de France*, Paris, 1878, 2 vols.
Fersen, A., *Diary and Correspondence*, ed. G. Fortescue, trans. K. Wormely, Boston, 1909.
Feuillet de Conches, F., ed., *Louis XVI, Marie Antoinette et Mme Elizabeth, lettres et documents inédits*, Paris, 1864–9, 6 vols.
Filleul, Paul, *Le duc de Montmorency-Luxembourg*, Paris, 1939.
Flammermont, J., 'La Correspondance de Pellenc avec les comtes de La Marck et Mercy', *Revue de la Révolution française*, vol. 16 (1889), pp. 481–502.
Fontanges, F. de, *L'arrestation de la famille royale à Varennes*, reissued by the weekly *Récits des grands jours d'histoire*, no. 44, Paris, n.d.
— *La Fuite du Roi*, reissued by the weekly *Récits des grands jours d'histoire*, no. 43, Paris, n.d.
Gallérie Historique des Contemporains, Brussels, 1837.
Gaultier de Biauzat, J., *Sa vie et sa correspondance*, ed., F. Mège, Clermont-Ferrand, 1890, 2 vols.
Glaive vengeur de la République . . . ou gallerie révolutionnaire, Paris, Year II [1793].
Gower, Earl, *Dispatches*, ed. O. Browning, Cambridge, 1885.

Jugement du Grand Baillage de Bourg-en-Bresse, n.p., [1788].
Lafayette, Marquis de, *Mémoires*, London and Paris, 1837–8, 6 vols.
Lameth, Alexandre de, *Histoire de l'Assemblée Constituante*, Paris, 1828, 2 vols.
Lameth, Théodore de, *Notes et souvenirs*, ed. E. Welvert, Paris, 1913.
Lauzun (Biron), duc de, *Correspondance intime, 1791–92*, ed. Comte de Serignan, Paris, 1906.
Lavater, J.C., *Essai sur la physiognomie destine à faire connaitre L'homme et le faire aimer*, The Hague, 1781–6, 3 vols.
Les intrigues de Madame de Staël à l'occasion du départ de Mesdames de France, Paris, 1791.
Lescure, Mathurin François Adolphe de, ed., *Correspondance secrète sur Louis XVI*, Paris, 1866, 2 vols.
Letters from Paris during the Summer of 1791, London, 1792.
Liste MM. les Députés de la majorité de l'Assemblée Nationale, vulgairement appelés le côté gauche ou les enragés se disant patriotes, Paris, 1791.
Mallet du Pan, *Mémoires et Correspondance pour servir à l'histoire de la Révolution française*, ed. A. Sayous, Paris, 1851, 2 vols.
Malouet, P.-V., *Mémoires*, Paris, 1874, 2 vols.
Marie-Antoinette, Correspondance, ed. E. Lever, Paris, 2005.
Marie-Antoinette: Correspondance secrète entre Marie-Thérèse et le comte de Mercy Argenteau, ed. A. d'Arneth and M. Geffroy, 2nd ed., Paris, 1875, 3 vols.
Marie-Antoinette et Barnave, Correspondance secrète, ed. Alma Soderjhelm, Paris, 1934.
Marie-Antoinette, Fersen et Barnave, ed. O.-G. Heidenstam, Paris, 1913.
Marie-Antoinette, Joseph II und Leopold II ihr Briefwechsel, ed. A. von Arneth, 2nd ed., Vienna, 1866.
Marie-Antoinette, *Lettres*, ed. M. de La Rocheterie and le marquis de Beaucourt, Paris, 1895–6, 2 vols.
Mercure Universelle, Paris, 1791–5.
Mirabeau, Comte de, *Correspondance entre le comte de Mirabeau et le comte de la Marck*, ed. M.A. de Bacourt, Paris, 1851, 3 vols.
— *Dénonciation de l'agiotage au Roi et à l'Assemblée des Notables*, Paris, March 1787.
— *Mémoires biographiques, littéraires et politiques*, Paris, 1835, 8 vols.
Montlosier, Comte de, *Mémoires sur la Révolution française etc.*, Paris, 1829, 2 vols.
Moreau, J.N., *Mes souvenirs*, Paris, 1898–1901, 2 vols.
Morris, Gouverneur, *The Diary and Letters of Gouverneur Morris*, ed. Anne Morris, New York, 1888.
Mortimer-Ternaux, M., *Histoire de la Terreur*, Paris, 1862–81, 8 vols. (Pétion's account of the commissioners' journey is published in vol. 1, pp. 353–71.)
Mounier, J., *Recherches sur les causes qui ont empeché les françois à devenir libres et sur les moyens qui leur restent pour acquérir la liberté*, Geneva, 1789, 2 vols.
Necker, J., *De la Révolution française*, Paris, 1797.
— *Lettre de M. Necker premier ministres des finances à M. Le Président de l'Assemblée Nationale etc.*, Versailles and Strasbourg, 1789.
— *Sur l'Administration de M. Necker par lui-même*, Paris, 1791.
Nicolaï, *Extraits des Mémoires inédits de Madame Nicolaï née de Lameth*, Pontoise, 1930.
Nouveau Dictionnaire françois, Paris 1793, 2 vols.
Périer, A., *Histoire abrégée du Dauphiné de 1626 à 1826*, Grenoble, 1881.
Pièces trouvées: Troisième recueil des pièces trouvées dans l'armoire de fer, Paris, 1792.
Pressavin, J.B., *L'art de prologer la vie et préserver la santé ou Traité de hygiène*, Paris, 1786.
Procès-verbal des Etats de Dauphiné assemblés a Romans dans le mois de Décembre 1788, Grenoble, 1788.
Procès-verbal des Conférences tenus dans la salle du Comité des États-Généraux, Paris, 1789.
Révue rétrospective, Paris, 1834, 1re série, v, pp. 278–85 (contains Sergent's recollection of the Massacre of the Champ de Mars).

Robespierre, M., *Oeuvres*, ed. Société des études Robespierristes, Paris, 1912–67, 10 vols.
Rochas, A., *Biographie de Dauphiné*, Paris, 1856.
Roederer, P.L., *Chronique de cinquante jours*, Paris, 1832.
Roland, Madame, *Lettres et correspondance*, ed. C. Perroud, Paris, 1900–2, 2 vols.
Saint-Priest, Comte de, *Mémoires*, ed. Baron de Barante, Paris, 1929.
Sallier-Chaumont de Laroche, G., *Annales françaises depuis le commencement du règne de Louis XVI jusqu'aux états-généraux, 1774–1789*, Paris, 1813.
Smith, Adam, *The Wealth of Nations*, London, 1776.
Staël, Germaine de, *Considerations on the Principal Events of the French Revolution*, Indianapolis, 2008.
Staël-Holstein, Baron, *Correspondance diplomatique*, ed. Baron Brinkman, Paris, 1881.
Stendhal, *Scarlet and Black*, trans. M. Shaw, London, 1953.
— *Vie de Henry Brulard*, Paris, 1961.
Suleau, F.-L., *Le Réveil de M. Suleau*, Paris, 1791.
Tourzel, Duchesse de, *Mémoires*, ed. duc des Cars, Paris, 1904, 2 vols.
Vaublanc, *Mémoires*, ed. M.F. Barrière, Paris, 1857.
Vienne, J.G., Le Franc de Pompignan, archbishop of, *Lettre pastorale de Mgr. L'archevêque de Vienne aux curés de son diocèse*, 15 July 1788, Vienne, 1788, 10 pages.
Villemain, M., *Souvenirs contemporains*, Paris, 1855, 2 vols.
Voltaire, F.M. Arouet, *Lettres écrites de Londres sur les Anglois et autres sujets*, Basel, 1734.
Wallon, H., *Histoire du tribunal révolutionnaire de Paris*, Paris, 1880–2, 8 vols.

PRINTED SECONDARY SOURCES

Acton, Baron, *Lectures on the French Revolution*, London, 1910.
Arnaud-Bouteloup, J., *Le rôle politique de Marie-Antoinette*, Paris, 1924.
Beylié, J. de, 'Barnave maire de Grenoble', *Bulletin de l'Académie delphinale*, series 4, vol. 12 (1898), pp. 562–93.
Beylié, J. de, *Barnave avocat*, Grenoble, 1917.
Blanc, L., *Histoire de la Révolution française*, Paris, 1847–63, 12 vols.
Blanc, O., 'Cercles politiques et "salons" du début de la Révolution (1789–1793)', *Annales historiques de la Révolution française* (2006), pp. 1–34.
Blanning, T.C.W., *The Origins of the French Revolutionary Wars*, London, 1986.
Bradby, E., *The Life of Barnave*, Oxford, 1915, 2 vols.
— 'Marie-Antoinette and the Constitutionalists; the Heidenstam papers', *The English Historical Review*, vol. 31, issue 122 (1916), pp. 238–55.
Brun-Durand, J., *Dictionnaire biographique de la Drôme*, Paris, 1900.
Caiani, A., *Louis XVI and the French Revolution, 1789–1792*, Cambridge, 2012.
Caron, P., 'La Tentative de contre-révolution de juin–juillet 1789', *Revue d'Histoire moderne*, vol. 8 (1906), pp. 5–34 and pp. 649–78.
Carré, H., *Le fin des Parlements (1788–1790)*, Paris, 1912.
Challamel, A., *Les Clubs Contre-Révolutionnaire*, Paris, 1895.
Chaper, E., ed., *Documents relatifs à la journée des tuiles par un réligieux*, Grenoble, 1881.
Chaumié, J., *Le réseau d'Antraigues et la contre-révolution, 1791–1793*, Paris, 1965.
Chérest, A., *La chute de l'Ancien Régime, 1787–9*, Paris, 1884–6, 3 vols.
Chevallier, J., 'L'église constitutionelle de la Drôme', *Bulletin de l'Académie delphinale*, 1916.
Coursac, P. and P., *Le secret de la reine*, Paris, 1996.
Debien, G., *Les colons de Saint-Domingue et la Révolution, essai sur le Club Massiac, août 1789-août 1792*, Paris, 1953.
Degachi, S., *Barnave, rapporteur du comité des colonies, 1789–1791*, Révolution Francaise. net., 2007.
Dendena, F., 'A New Look at Feuillantism: The Triumvirate and the Movement for War in 1791', *French History*, vol. 26, no. 1 (2012), pp. 6–33.

— 'L'expérience de la défaite, la rencontre avec l'histoire: Barnave et ses écrits historiques', *La Révolution française*, vol. 10 (2016), pp. 1–17.
Dictionnaire des Constituents, ed. E. Le May, Oxford, 1991, 2 vols.
Droz, J.F.X., *Histoire du Règne de Louis XVI*, Brussels, 1839, 2 vols.
Egret, J., *Les derniers états de Dauphiné: Romans*, Grenoble, 1942.
— *The French Pre-Revolution*, trans. W. Camp, London and Chicago, 1977, pp. 127–8.
— *La Pré-Révolution française, 1787–1788*, Paris, 1962.
Farr, E., *I Love You Madly: Marie-Antoinette and Fersen: The Secret Letters*, London, 2016.
Félix, J., *Louis XVI et Marie-Antoinette*, Paris, 2006.
Fitzsimmons, M., 'The Committee of the Constitution and the Remaking of France, 1787–1791', *French History*, vol. 4, no. 1 (1990), pp. 23–47.
— 'From the Estates-General to the National Assembly, May 5–August 4, 1789,' in P. Campbell, ed., *The Origins of the French Revolution*, Basingstoke, 2005, pp. 268–89.
Fonvieille, R., *Barnave et la Pré-Révolution: Dauphiné - 1788*, Grenoble, 1987.
— *Barnave et la Révolution*, Grenoble, 1989.
Gallier, A. de, 'La vie de province au XVIIIe siècle', *Bull. Delph.*, vol. X (1876).
Girault de Coursac, P. and P., *Sur la route de Varennes*, Paris, 1984.
Glagau, H., *Die Französiche Législative . . . 1791–92*, Berlin, 1896.
Griffiths, R., *Le Centre Perdu, Malouet et les 'monarchiens'*, Grenoble, 1988.
Hampson, N., *Danton*, London, 1978.
— *Prelude to Terror: The Constituent Assembly and the Failure of Consensus, 1789–1791*, Oxford, 1988.
Hardman, J., *French Politics 1774–1789*, London, 1995.
— *The French Revolution Sourcebook*, London, 1999.
— *The Life of Louis XVI*, New Haven and London, 2016.
— *Marie-Antoinette*, New Haven and London, 2019.
— *Overture to Revolution: The 1787 Assembly of Notables and the Crisis of France's Old Regime*, Oxford and New York, 2010.
— *Robespierre*, London and New York, 1999.
Hardman, J. and M. Price, eds, *Louis XVI and the Comte de Vergennes: Correspondence, 1774–1787*, Oxford, 1998.
Hardman, J. and J.M. Roberts, eds, *French Revolution Documents*, Oxford, 1966–73.
Hue, F., *Dernières années du règne de Louis XVI*, 3rd ed., Paris, 1860.
Kennedy, M., *The Jacobin Clubs in the French Revolution: The First Years*, Princeton, 1982.
Kuhlmann, C., *On the Conflict of Parties in the Jacobin Club (November, 1789–July 17, 1791)*, Lincoln, NE, 1905.
— *Robespierre and Mirabeau at the Jacobins, December 6, 1790*, Lincoln, NE, 1911.
Lamartine, A., *Histoire des Girondins*, Paris, 1847, 8 vols.
Lemay, E., 'Les révelations d'un Dictionnaire: du nouveau sur la composition de l'Assemblée nationale constituante, 1789–1791', *Annales historiques de la Révolution française*, vol. 284 (1991), pp. 159–89.
Maignien, E., *Bibliographie historique du Dauphiné pendant la Révolution*, Grenoble, 1891.
Mailhet, A., *La Vallée de la Drôme*, Paris, 1893.
Masson, F., *Le Département des affaires étrangères pendant la Révolution, 1787–1804*, Paris, 1877.
Mathiez, A. 'Etude critique sur les journées des 5 et 6 Octobre 1789', *Revue Historique*, vol. 68 (1898), pp. 241–81.
Michelet, J., *Histoire de la Révolution française*, 1899, Paris.
Michon, G., *Adrien Duport et le parti feuillant*, Paris, 1924. (The appendix has some of Barnave's correspondence from 1792.)
Mortimer-Ternaux, M., *Histoire de la Terreur*, Paris, 1862–81, 8 vols.
Mousset, A., *Un témoin ignoré de la Révolution, le Comte de Fernan Nunez*, Paris, 1924.

Petitfils, J.-C., *Louis XVI*, Paris, 2005.
Price, M., *The Fall of the Monarchy: Louis XVI, Marie-Antoinette and the Baron de Breteuil*, London, 2002.
— 'The "Ministry of the Hundred Hours": A Reappraisal', *French History*, vol. 4, no. 3 (1990), pp. 318–39.
— 'Mirabeau and the Court: Some New Evidence', *French Historical Studies*, vol. 29, no. 1 (2006), pp. 37–76.
— *Preserving the Monarchy: The Comte de Vergennes, 1774–1787*, Cambridge, 1995.
Prudhomme, A., *Histoire de Grenoble*, Grenoble, 1888.
Régent F., 'Slavery and the Colonies' in *A Companion to the French Revolution*, ed. P. McPhee, Oxford, 2013, pp. 397–418,
Roux, X., *Mounier, sa vie et son œuvre*, Paris, 1888.
Ségur, P. de, *Marie Antoinette*, London, 2015.
Seligman, A., *La Justice en France pendant la Révolution 1791-93*, Paris, 1913.
Shapiro, B., 'Revolutionary Justice in 1789–1790: The Comité des Recherches, the Châtelet, and the Fayettist Coalition', *French Historical Studies*, vol. 17, no. 3 (1992), pp. 656–69.
— *Revolutionary Justice in Paris, 1789–1790*, Cambridge, 1993.
— *Traumatic Politics: The Deputies and the King in the Early French Revolution*, Pennsylvania, 2009.
Sonenscher, M., *Sans-Culottes: An Eighteenth-Century Emblem in the French Revolution*, Princeton, 2008.
Stanhope, Earl, *Life of the Right Honourable William Pitt*, London, 1861, 2 vols.
Tackett, T., *Becoming a Revolutionary: The Deputies of the French National Assembly and the Emergence of a Revolutionary Culture (1789–1790)*, Pennsylvania, 2006.
Thomas, C., *The Wicked Queen: The Origins of the Myth of Marie-Antoinette*, trans. Julie Rosse, New York, 2001.
Tocqueville, A. de, *L'Ancien Régime et la Révolution française*, Paris, 1951, 2 vols.
— *The Ancien Régime and the French Revolution*, ed. H. Brogan, London, 1966.
Vermale, F., 'Barnave: fragments inédits', *Bulletin de la Société d'archéologie, d'histoire et de géographie de la Drôme*, vol. LXV, no. 266 (1935), pp. 81–98.
— 'Barnave et les banquiers Laborde', *Annales historiques de la Révolution française*, 14e année, no. 79 (1937), pp. 48–64.
— 'Manuscrits et éditions des oeuvres de Barnave,' *Annales historiques de la Révolution française*, vol. XV (1938), pp. 75–7.
Wallon, H., *Histoire du tribunal révolutionnaire de Paris*, Paris, 1880–2, 8 vols.
Wick, D., *A Conspiracy of Well-Intentioned Men: The Society of Thirty and the French Revolution*, New York, 1987.
Young, A., *Travels in France*, London, 1909.

INDEX

Abancourt, Charles-Xavier-Joseph de Franqueville d', minister of war, 313
Adelaide, Madame, daughter of Louis XV, 210–11
Aiguillon, Armand de Vignerot du Plessis, duc d', 120, 143–4, 146, 148, 157, 167, 203, 208, 240, 260; and Jacobins, 172, 176; last letter to Barnave, 319–20, 323
Aiguillon, Emmanuel Armand de Vignerot du Plessis, duc d', foreign secretary (1771–4) and minister for war (1774), father of above, 39, 143–4
Alquier, Charles-Jean Marie, deputy, 318
Amar, Jean-Baptiste-André, member of Committee of General Security, 326–7, 329, 330
André, Antoine d', deputy, related to Barnave, 72; links with Mirabeau and the Court, 157, 207, 211–17 passim; and Varennes aftermath, 229–33, 240–3, 251, 253, 255; and the Revision, 256, 257, 261, 262, 265, 266; and king's letter of acceptance, 269–72; attacked, 232–3, 268; post constituent, 221, 290, 326
Angiviller, Charles Claude de la Billarderie comte d', directeur des bâtiments du roi, 154
Artois, Charles Philippe, comte d', later Charles X, 49, 51, 68, 91, 101, 104, 107, 242
Aubert de Bayet, Jean-Baptiste Annibal, 106
Aumary, lemonade seller and Breton Club, 88–9
Autichamp, Jean-Louis de Beaumont, marquis d', 105

Baillot, Étienne-Catherine, deputy, 324, 338, 35, 347
Bailly, Jean Sylvain, deputy, Mayor of Paris, 86, 100, 175, 185, 251, 253, 339
Barentin, Charles de Paule de, keeper of the seals (1788–89) and *Résultat du Conseil,* 76; and Estates-General, 90, 91, 96; reports Barnave to the king, 98, 103; and July crisis, 106, 114; and séance royale, 101–2
Barère, Bertrand, deputy, 223, 260
Barnave, Antoine-Pierre-Joseph-Marie, deputy, as an *avocat*, 22–5; his 1783 lecture, 25–9; his theory of history, 3–5, 25–9, 56, 120, 310; political ideas, 31–40; his pamphlets, 56–61, 81–3; draws parallels with England, 8, 76, 115, 125–36, 131–2, 151, 162, 250, 261–2; on foreign policy, 5, 35, 122, 161–4, 243–4, 298; his book purchases, 42–5, 47; his hypochondria, 200–2; his love letters, 190–4; his religious beliefs, 333; self-analysis, 21, 332, 345; his sense of *gloire*, 17, 166, 221, 328–9, 343–5; and patronage, 4–5, 130–1, 181–2, 196–8, 268, 279, 307; *see also*, Brissot, Marie-Antoinette, Lafayette, Mirabeau, Necker
Barnave's ancestors, 6–7, 10
Barnave, Jean-Pierre, father, 7–17, 22, 23, 24, 55, 59; aware of relationship to Necker, 129; death, 106
Barnave, Jean-Pierre-César du Gua, 'Dugua,' younger brother, 12, 18–21, 23, 41, 195, 335
Barnave, Marie-Louise, née de Pré de Seigle de Presle, Barnave's mother, 17, 23; her influence on Barnave, 8–16, 52, 67; her concerns about status, 11–12, 13–15, 117; Barnave's letters to, 74, 85, 92, 94–5, 109, 200; mother and son, 195–8; during Barnave's imprisonment, 316, 319, 323; follows him to Paris, 331–2; her grief, 20, 334–45
Barnave, Julie, afterwards Mme Saint-Germain, sister, 13, 15, 17, 331

Barnave, Marie-Françoise-Adélaide, sister, 13, 380; Barnave's last letter to, 332–5
Barnave, Antoine, paternal uncle, 8, 10, 23, 63–4, 72, 199
Basire, Claude, deputy, tries to save Barnave, 324–5, 329–31
Bayez, N., 197–8
Beaumarchais, Pierre Caron de, playwright, 43–4
Beaumetz, Bon-Albert Briois de, deputy, 157, 180, 185, 268, 281; in d'André, Chapelier group, 210–22, 230, 233, 242, 291, 293, 295; new allies of Barnave, 256, 257, 260, 262
Beaumont, Christophe de, Archbishop of Paris, 170
Beauveau, Charles-Just, prince de, *ministre*, 133, 137
Bergasse, Nicolas, 132, 203
Berthier de Sauvigny, Louis Jean, Intendant of Paris, lynched, 109–11
Bertrand de Molleville, Antoine-François, minister for marine (1791–2), 216, 219, 279, 286, 289, 291, 293; secret adviser after resignation, 310, 317
Besenval, Pierre-Victor, (baron de, in July 1789), 105
Biauzat, Jean-François, Gaultier de, deputy, 105, 109
Bigot de Sainte-Croix, Claude, diplomat and foreign minister, and émigrés, 208, 295
Biron, Armand-Louis de Gontaut, duc de, 306, 319
Boissy d'Anglas, François-Antoine, deputy, tries to save Barnave, 318, 325, 331, 334, 345
Bombelles, Marc, comte de, diplomat, diarist, 64
Bossu, abbé, 18
Bouillé, François, marquis de, general, suppresses Nancy mutiny, 178–80, 182, 183; and 'Varennes', 244, 246, 250
Bouvard de Fourqueux, Michel, finance minister, 50
Breteuil, Louis-Charles le Tonnelier, baron de, minister for the Maison (1783–8), resigns, 69; second ministry, 106–7, 132; and Counter-Revolution, 154
Brienne, Étienne-Charles de Loménie de, Archbishop of Toulouse, during Assembly of Notables, 42, 48, 50; ministry, 62, 64–5, 66, 67, 270; Barnave's pamphlets against, 57–61; fall, 68, 70, 84
Brissot, Jean-Pierre, journalist, deputy, 58, 230, 253, 278, 320, 321; against Barnave, 164–7, 227–8, 233, 234, 317–18, 344; Barnave against, 262–4, 282, 294, 298, 301, 304, 306, 324, 340–1, 350, 353
Broglie, Victor François, maréchal-duc de, *generalissimo*, minister for war (1789), 104–6, 143
Broglie, Victor, prince de, 195, 268, 28, 320
Broglie, Sophie de, wife of above, 146, 323
Buzot, François-Nicolas, deputy, 180, 231, 246; stays in Jacobins, 254, 255; resists Barnave over the Revision, 256–64 passim, 282

Cahier de Gerville, Bonne-Claude, minister of interior, 289, 305
Calonne, Charles-Alexandre de, finance minister, 1783–7, appointment, 22, 27, 39; his reform programme, 31, 41, 42, 45–50, 51, 53, 60, 65, 72, 75, 80; anticipates the August decrees, 120–1; Barnave criticises, 28, 39, 45–7, 54, 70; Barnave attacks his *Lettre au Roi*, 81–4, 126; Duport demands his impeachment, 93, 144; Mirabeau and Talleyrand suspected of aiming to recall him, 154; other references, 26, 87, 99, 250, 354
Cambon, Jean-Louis-Augustin-Emmanuel, deputy, demands Barnave's arrest, 317
Campan, Jeanne-Louise-Henriette, 243, 274, 276, 288, 300
Carnot, Lazare, 7
Castries, Charles Gabriel de la Croix, marquis de, minister for marine (1780–7), 57, 115
Cazalès, Jacques-Antoine-Marie de, deputy, 207, 230, 234, 257, 290; wounded in duel with Barnave, 343–4
Caze de la Bove, Jean-Louis de, Intendant, 52, 53, 55
Charles I, king of England, 305
Charles IV, king of Spain, 113, 140
Choiseul, Étienne-François, duc de, minister, 14
Choiseul, duc de, Claude-Antoine-Gabriel, son of above, 230
Cicé, Jérôme Marie Champion de, Archbishop of Bordeaux, keeper of the seals, 132, 133, 152, 154, 186, 204

Clavière, Étienne, financier, minister, 306, 310, 311
Clermont-Tonnerre, Stanislas, deputy, thwarts Barnave's attack on the ministers, 180, 184–5; in Mirabeau's grand project, 206, 207; in constitutional committee, 257, 258; other refences, 128, 132
Clermont-Tonnerre, Jules-Charles-Henri, duc de, military commandant of Dauphiné, crosses Madame Barnave, 13, 14, 15; and Day of Tiles, 55, 61–3
Colbert, Jean-Baptiste, 53
Condorcet, Marie-Jean-Nicolas de Caritat, marquis de, deputy, mathematician, 361
Corroller du Moustoir, Louis-Jacques-Hippolyte, deputy, 255
Cossé-Brissac, Louis-Hercule, duc de, 281
Couthon, Georges, deputy, 281, 328

Damiens, François, would be assassin, 348
Danton, Georges-Jacques, deputy in Convention, minister of justice (1792), Barnave's link to the popular movement, 3, 171, 174–6, 178–9, 185; warned to leave Paris, 252–3; receiving money from Montmorin, 212, 214; saves Barnave's friends, 322–4; tries to save Barnave, 324–5, 329, 331–2, 352; other references, 10, 233, 320, 328, 340, 342, 346
Dauphin, Louis-Ferdinand, father of Louis XVI, 37
Dauphin, Louis-Charles, the 'second', (Louis XVII), 134, 161, 261, 271–2, 305, 326; captivates Barnave, 236, 238, 342
Dauphin, Louis-Joseph, the 'first', son of Louis XVI, death of, 174–5
David, Barnave's servant, 206, 327, 328, 332
David, Jean-Louis, painter, member of CGS, 34
Démeunier, Jean-Nicolas, deputy, 233, 246, 257, 266, 312, 327
Desmoulins, Lucie-Simplice-Camille, journalist, supports Barnave, 174, 178, 184, 185; turns against him, 211, 223, 246, 253; warned to leave Paris, 252, 322; shakes Barnave's hand, 346–7; against Assembly's committees, 18
Dubois-Crancé, Edmond-Louis-Alexis, his hatred of Barnave, 145, 199, 212–13, 234, 253, 257; subsequent career, 328, other reference, 163
Dumas, Mathieu, deputy, 235, 236, 243, 282, 307, 308, 323
Dumas, René-Francois, vice-president of Revolutionary Tribunal, 338–9
Dumouriez, Charles, foreign minister (1792), general, 305, 306, 310, 326, 341
Dupont de Nemours, Pierre-Samuel, deputy, economist, 134, 242
Duport du Tertre, Marguerite-Louis-François, minister of justice, appointment through Barnave's influence, 185–6; ministerial conduit for Barnave's policy, 278–9, 286, 291, 296; resigns, 305; arrest and trial, 336, 340, 346–7
Duport, Adrien, deputy, 3; in committee of thirty, 72, 93; as 'triumvir' 113, 115, 121, 126, 127, 144, 145, 148, 182, 209, 211, 215, 236, 245, 252, 253, 257, 268, 342; and Revision, 259, 260, 262, 265, 291; and ministry, 150–7, 203–5, 208, 220, 269; in Jacobins, 157; reconciliation with Lafayette(?), 177–80, 235, 307; supper party, 194; prophetic speeches, 220–5; against king's dethronement, 247, 249; takes king's statement, 240–1; last-ditch attempts to save monarchy, 310, 313; saved by Danton, 32
Duportail, Louis Lebègue, minister of war, 185–7, 284, 289–90, 317
Duquesnoy, Adrien-Cyprien, deputy, journalist, dislikes Barnave, 93, 95, 97, 103, 133, 156, 176, 208, 209, 210, 225–6; on need for a quick constitution, 114; against committees, 158; on October Days, 139, 140; linchpin of Mirabeau's plan, 207, 211, 212; advises queen after Mirabeau's death, 213, 215, 216, 255; Barnave criticises, 321–2, 342; other references, 101, 110, 111, 125, 133–4, 144, 154, 257, 259
Duranthon, Antoine, keeper of the seals (1792), 309, 336

Élizabeth, Madame, sister to Louis XVI, warms to Barnave, 183, 236, 238, 300, 349; on Necker's resignation, 285
Emmery, Jean-Louis-Claude, deputy, 154, 196, 207, 215, 243, 255; in Mirabeau's plan, 211

Fauchet, Claude, bishop of Calvados, 317
Ferrières, Charles-Elie, marquis de, deputy, chronicler, 169, 175, 241, 290
Fersen, Axel von, queen's lover, 147, 193, 214, 236, 237, 247; political relations with her, 241, 245, 285, 290, 291, 313; rivalry with Barnave, 237, 238, 246, 301, 316, 348
Fontanges, François de, Archbishop of Toulouse, adviser and chronicler of Marie-Antoinette, 213, 215, 217–19, 230, 236
Foulon, Joseph- François, conseiller *d'état*, minister in the Breteuil cabinet, 106; lynched, 109, 110, 112
Fouquier-Tinville, Antoine-Quentin, public prosecutor in Revolutionary Tribunal, 336, 338–42, 345
Francis II, Emperor, 308
Frederick II, king of Prussia, 84
Fréteau de Saint-Just, Emmanuel, deputy, 163, 184, 211, 225, 257, 261

Gagnon, Henri, the Barnaves' family doctor, 52
Garnier, Louis-Antoine, ministerial candidate, 287
Gensonné, Armand, deputy, 298
George Ill, king of England, 108
Gohier, Louis-Jérôme, minister of justice, orders Barnave's trial, 330, 336
Goupil de Prefelne, deputy, 260, 262
Gower, Earl, 250, 265
Grave, Pierre-Marie, chevalier de, minister, admired by Barnave, 307, 309
Grégoire, Henri, abbé, deputy, 262

Hermann, Armand-Martial, president of the Revolutionary Tribunal, 319, 338, 339, 340, 343, 345
Humbert II, last dauphin of Dauphiné, 73
Hume, David, philosopher, influence on Barnave, 8, 43

James II, king of England, 115
Jansen, Cornelius, 24
Jarjayes, François-Augustin Regnier de, go-between for Barnave and Marie-Antoinette, 242–3, 277
Joly de Fleury, Jean-François, finance minister (1781–3), 40, 48
Joseph II, Holy Roman Emperor (1765–90), 245, 287

Kaunitz, Anton, prince von, Austrian Chancellor; cynicism about French Revolution, 244, 272, 296, 310
Kersaint, Armand, deputy, 255

L'Averdy, Clément-Charles-François, ex-finance minister, ludicrous charge against, 337
La Châtre, Marie-Charlotte-Louise-Perrette-Aglaé Bontemps, comtesse de, friend of Barnave, 146, 194–5, 323
La Luzerne, César-Henri, comte de, naval minister (1787–90), 137, 184
La Mark, August-Marie-Antoine-Raymond, comte de, his assessment of Barnave, 144–5, 239; Mirabeau and Marie-Antoinette want him to be a minister, 153–4; coins phrase 'fatal decree', 157; his political assessments, 163, 184, 185, 186, 187; Barnave's special role in Mirabeau's project, 205; after Mirabeau's death, 213, 255, 281; and Easter crisis, 215–19
La Porte, Arnaud de, Intendant of the Civil List, 214, 229
La Rochefoucauld, François de, epigrammist, 1, 188
La Rochefoucauld, Louis-Alexandre, duc de, deputy, 144, 153, 154
La Tour du Pin, Jean Frédéric de, war minister, 151, 183, 185
La Tour-Maubourg, Charles-César de Fay, comte de, deputy, 127, 150; and return from Varennes, 235–6, 239, 243
Laborde de Méréville, François-Louis-Jean-Joseph, 'quadrumvir', 93, 105, 143, 144, 146, 148, 151, 153, 154, 167, 176, 260
Laborde, Jean-Joseph, banker, father of above, 236, 245
Lacoste de Maucune, 8, 9
Lacoste, Benjamin, Eléonor-Louis Frotier, marquis de, 148, 243
Lacoste, Élie, minister for the marine, 310
Lafayette, Marie- Jean- Paul Motier, marquis de, calls for Estates-General, 49–50; commander of National Guard, 71, 120; deputy, 148, 243; tries to broker deal with Mounier, 127–36; and October Days, 136–9; and plans to topple Necker, 150–9 passim; and abolition of nobility, 169; attempted reconciliation with Barnave in 1790,

175–180; and Nancy mutiny, 182–3; and replacement of Necker ministry, 183–6, 203, 204; and 'Saint-Cloud departure', 214–15; and flight to Varennes, 229–35; flirts with republicanism, 241–2; but works with Barnave to absolve king, 242, 243, 245 251, 253, 255, 267; as general, 290, 294–5, 308; Barnave sees him as saviour of the monarchy, 301; attempted deal with Duport, Lameth and Méréville, 307; last ditch attempt to save monarchy, 311–13; emigrates with Lameth, 317, 321

Lally-Tollendal, Trophine-Gérard, marquis de, deputy, prompts Barnave's 'pure blood' quip, 110, 116; in first constitutional committee, 128, 132; ex-deputy, 290

Lamballe, Marie-Thérèse Louise de Savoie Carignan, princesse de, returns to France, 285

Lameth, Alexandre de, deputy, 'triumvir', 'buries parlements', 71; praises Calonne, 82; 'triumvir' 96, 113–15, 144, 220, 223; and autumn 1789 crisis, 127, 134, 142; social life, 143, 146, 304; against Necker, 150–1, 156; in committees, 157–8, 209, 260, 264; and foreign policy, 161, 163; and abolition of nobility, 167–8; and Jacobin club, 172–3, 178, 233, 254; against Lafayette, 176–7; on revision committee, 180, 257; and the court, 204, 208, 216, 229, 242–3, 277, 286, 288, 295, 300, 313, 317; quarrels with Mirabeau, 209–12; narrows franchise, 227; and Desmoulins, 252–53; satirised, 268; opposes Girondins, 304, 305, 306; Barnave writes to, 309, 350

Lameth, Théodore, deputy in Legislative Assembly, 282, 305, 307, 308; social life, 195; despair of, 223; asks Danton to help: Duport, 322–3, and Barnave, 326 and the king 331–2; Barnave will not petition Convention, 328–9, 335

Lamoignon, Chrétien-François de, marquis de Bâville, Keeper of the Seals, (1787–8), 50, 54–5, 76, 102; Barnave against, 58–66, passim, 121

Lanne, Emmanuel-Joseph, judge in Revolutionary Tribunal, 338

Launay, Bernard-René-Jordan, marquis de, governor of Bastille, 109, 110, 113

Laurent, abbé, Barnave's tutor, 16, 41, 197

Law, John, 10

Le Chapelier, Isaac-René, deputy, early radicalism, 90, 94, 95, 100, 104, 111; founds Jacobin Club with Barnave, 15, 172; attacks same club, 226, 233, 254, 259, 295; against Necker, 148, 153–6; on constitutional committee, 132, 135, 157, 211, 230, 242, 246, 257, 268; links with ministry, 163, 206, 207, 211–13; 215, 217, 230, 293; other references, 167, 212, 222, 290, 291, 303

Lebrun, Echouchard, poet, 46

Lebrun, Girondin Foreign secretary, 330

Legendre, Louis, deputy, 252, 322, 325

Leopold II, Holy Roman Emperor, Robespierre on, 232; linchpin of Barnave's strategy, 239, 243, 244–5; 246, 272, 304; changes stance, 296–8

Lépidor, Jean, Barnave's counsel, 340

Lessart, Antoine de Valdec de, minister, 196, 269, 278, 287, 289, 291, 294–96, 317; impeached, 305–6; murdered, 320

Louis XIV, king of France, Barnave on, 27, 32–6, 46, 314

Louis XV, king of France, 109, 142, 348; Barnave on, 33, 36, 37, 39, 46, 51, 92, 83

Louis XVI, king of France, as reformer, 8, 27, 31; Barnave on, 46, 66, 247; moves to Paris, 139–41; and Easter crisis, 213–18; his manifesto, 140, 158, 219, 232, 239, 260, 273; flight and recapture, 29–54; suspended but not dethroned, 246–50; accepts the constitution, 269–74; fall of the monarchy, 313–14

Luckner, Nicolas, baron de, general, 294

Luther, Martin, 34

Mably, Gabriel-Bonnot abbé, 8, 52

Malesherbes, Chrétien Guillaume de Lamoignon de, minister, his political analyses, 35, 54, 58, 78, 99, 154, 187, 270, 354

Malouet, Pierre-Victor, deputy, 95, 97, 113, 114, 160; included in coalition building, 152–3

Marat, Jean, 253, 317

Marie-Antoinette, queen of France, her major role in the Pre-Revolution, 50–1, 53–57, 58, 68; supports third estate, 76; volte face in 1789, 91–2, 101; and Mirabeau, 179, 182, 205; and Easter

crisis, 215, 218–29; negotiates with Barnave, 229, 239, 242–6, 272; governs with Barnave, 275–97; bids him au revoir, 299–301; dissuades king from going to Compiègne, 313
Marx, Karl, 4, 38
Maupeou, René Charles Augustin de, Chancellor of France (1768–92), his coup d'etat, 14, 27–28, 36, 37–39, 46, 53, 70, 88, 144
Menou, Jacques-François, deputy, 144–5, 148, 182, 211, on committees, 157, 163, 184–5; first president of Jacobins, 172, 176; and Montmorin, 186, 205–6
Mercy-Argenteau, Florimond, comte de, ambassador, Marie-Antoinette's mentor, 92, 258; as go-between, 154, 185, 245–6, 323
Millet, N, lieutenant of gendarmes, 330–332
Mirabeau, Honoré-Gabriel Riquetti, comte de, deputy, resists pressure on king, 137, 140; links to Calonne, 47, 49, 83; against Necker, 149–156; advises the court, 157, 163, 179, 182, 184, 203, 222, 344; Barnave buys his 1787 publications, 49, but won't let him publish his own speech, 93; assignats, 148–50; foreign policy debate, 161–3; Barnave invites to dinner, 177–8; Barnave his heir?, 134, 203, 205, 212–13; and fatal decree, 155–7, 222; his 'propaganda machine' 205–7, 211–12, 288; quarrels with Alexandre Lameth, 208–11, 212; death, 212–13; other references, 90, 95, 103, 122, 128, 118, 123, 141, 145, 146, 148
Miromesnil, Armand Thomas Hue de, Keeper of the Seals (1774–87), 50, 54
Monciel, Terrier de, Antoine-Marie-René, minister of interior, 218
Montesquieu, Charles de Secondat, baron de, 26, 52; Barnave's critique of, 33–4
Monteynard, Louis-François, marquis de, 33–4
Montlosier, Reynaud de, deputy, 216, 265, 268
Montmorin, Armand-Marc de Montmorin de Saint-Hérem, comte de, Foreign Secretary (1787–91), contact with individual deputies, 127, 151, 186, 207, 211, 215, 216; and the Assembly, 161–4, 185–6; plans to pension him off, 153–4; secret relations with Barnave, 171, 186, 204–6, 216, and with Danton, 171, 179, 212, 213; not under triumvirs' thumb, 208; and circular letter, 216–17; and king's flight, 229, 231, 232; and king's letter of acceptance, 270, 271; and Kaunitz, 272; waning influence, 288; resigns, 276; arrested and murdered, 317, 330
Morris, Gouverneur, American chargé d'affaires, 146–7, 278
Mounier, Jean-Joseph, deputy, in Pre-Revolution, 22, 62–4, 72, 73; and estates of Dauphiné, 77–9; in Estates-General, 90, 93, 95, 97; and Tennis Court Oath, 102; begs Necker to resign, 104; and the constitution, 114, 119–36 passim; and rural unrest, 116–17, 122; and October Days, 136–8; secedes, 141–2, 394; considered as royal librarian, 153; made prefect by Napoleon, 142

Napoleon Bonaparte, 18, 47, 82–3, 142, 347
Narbonne-Lara, Louis, comte de, minister for war (1791–2), 287; flirts with war, 290–4, 298, 301; dismissed 304–5; lover of Madame de Staël, 193, 290; Barnave seeks his patronage, 307
Necker, Jacques, finance minister (1776–81 and 1788–90), related to Barnave, 10, 21–2, 86; Barnave and his Dauphiné network, 21–2, 107; Barnave's scathing verdict on, 39, 73, 147–50; *Compte rendu* and resignation, 39–40, 48–9; recalled, 68–70; and Romans assemblies, 73, 75, 77, 79; and *résultat du conseil*, 76–7, 81; refuses Bretons' offer, 89; opening speech to estates, 90–1; Marie-Antoinette turns against, 92; and séance royale, 100–1, 104; dismissed, 106, 311; recalled 107–8; and veto, 127–33; attempts to topple, 133–4, 136, 150–9; and speech of 4 February, 160; and abolition of nobility, 169; final resignation, 182–84
Necker, Suzanne Curchod, Mme, 10, 39, 147
Nicolaï, Armand-Charles-Marie, 48, 51
Noailles, Louis-Marie, vicomte de, 106, 120, 121, 240, 260; Barnave challenges to a duel, 163

Noailles, Philipe duc de, 139
North, Frederick, Lord, English premier, 108

Orléans, Louis-Philippe, later king of the French, 246
Orléans, Louis-Philippe-Joseph, duc d', (Égalité), 102, 127–8, 148; supposed links with Barnave, 141–2, 190, 199
Ormesson, Henri François-de-Paule Lefevre d', finance minister (1783), 40–1

Payan, Claude, *agent nationale*, 327, 328
Pellenc, Jean-Joachim, Mirabeau's secretary, analyst, and participant, 187, 213, 216, 269, 272, 279, 285, 291–2, 297, 299, 306–7, 310
Pétion, Jérôme, deputy, 113, 157, 177, 215, 231, 253, 282; and return from Varennes, 235–40, 246, 342; stays in Jacobins, 254, 255, 256–7, 261, 262; on constitutional committee, 180; resists the Revision, 256–60; as mayor of Paris, 264, 284–5, 306, 311–12
Pitt, William, (the Younger) English Prime Minister, 108, 298
Pius VI, Pope, 122, 171
Polignac, Yolande, duchesse de, queen's favourite, and her circle, 68, 107 153–4, 285
Presle, Marie-Anne de Pré de Seigle de, née d'André, Barnave's maternal grandmother, 9–11, 12
Provence, Louis-Stanislas-Xavier, comte de, 'Monsieur', 75, 91, 143, 209–10, 285, Barnave wants him to return, 179
Puységur, Pierre-Louis de Chastenet, comte de, minister for war (1788–90), 104, 106

Rabaud de Saint-Étienne, Jean-Paul, deputy, 95–6, 104, 132
Radix de Saint-Foix, Claude Pierre, political agent, 288
Revol, Pierre, deputy, Barnave's flat mate, 85
Rewbel, Jean-Francois, deputy, 157, 231, 254; resists the Revision, 258, 260–1
Riccé, N., officer, 35
Richelieu, Armand-Jean du Plessis, Cardinal de, Barnave sees him as architect of Bourbon despotism, 33, 47, 132
Rigaud de l'Isle, Louis-Michel, Barnave's letters to, 93, 94, 100, 106–11, 202
Robespierre, Maximilien, deputy, 3, 10, 91, 114, 220, 305, 311, 354; Barnave on, 224; Declaration of Rights the bedrock, 113, 123; and self-denying ordinance, 161, 221–4; and Jacobins, 172, 173, 226–8, 232, 233, 251, 254–5, 258, 261, 267, 308; and 'Varennes', 219, 229, 231, 232, 246, 250; quarrels with Barnave over the franchise, 227; and over the Revision, 260, 261, 262, 264–6, 269; and September massacres, 320, 323; in CPS, 324, 327, 328; influence on Revolutionary Tribunal that condemns Barnave, 320–1, 339, 340, 343, 352
Rochambeau, Jean-Baptiste-Donatien comte de, general, 294, 306
Roederer, Pierre-Louis, deputy, 255, 260, 261, 262; verbal duel with Barnave, 263–4; procureur of Département, 284–5, 314
Rohan, Louis, Cardinal de, 86
Roland de la Platière, Jean-Marie, minister, 310, 311, 320, 323
Roland, Jeanne, Madame, 15, 231, 250, 258
Rousseau, Jean-Jacques, 8, 221–2, 341
Royale, Marie-Thérèse-Charlotte, Madame, Louis XVI's daughter, in coach with Barnave, 236

Saint-Foix, Maximilien Radix de, political agent, 288
Saint-Just, Louis-Antoine, deputy, 84, 281, 328
Saint-Priest, François-Emmanuel Guignard, comte de, minister for the Maison du Roi, 101, 106, 137, 186; refuses Barnave's request to withdraw the Flanders regiment, 134
Santerre, Antoine-Joseph, brewer, commander of the National Guard, 311
Ségur, Louis-Philippe, comte de, diplomat, considered as foreign secretary, 153, 278, 289
Ségur, Philippe-Henri, marquis de, minister for war (1780–87), his Ordonnance, 30, 42, 61
Servan, Joseph, minister of war, 310, 311
Siéyès, Emmanuel-Joseph, abbé, deputy, 120, 132, 153, 154, 176, 215, 246, 257, 306; early radicalism, 89, 96–102, passim, 104, 111, 114; Marie-Antoinette

wants him in charge of 'public education', 153
Smith, Adam, economist, 2, 149
Staël-Holstein, Erik Magnus, baron, Swedish ambassador, 151, 159, 268
Staël-Holstein, Germaine baronne de (Madame de Staël), Barnave's cousin and correspondent, 86, 109, 125, 126, 193, 194, 324; negotiates veto with Barnave, 127–31; her salon, 146–7, 281, 290; and appointment of Narbonne qv, 324
Stendhal (Marie-Henri Beyle), 2, 51
Strafford, Thomas Wentworth, earl of, 305

Talleyrand-Périgord, Charles-Maurice, later prince de, 22, 47, 132, 134, 157, 257, 268; links with ministers, 206, 207, 213, 293, 322, 324; and church lands, 148; considered for minister, 153–64; links with Narbonne, 268, 290–1, 306
Talon, Jean-Omer, political agent, 151–2, 213; Marie-Antoinette on, 288
Target, Guy-Jean, *avocat,* deputy, 86, 95, 96, 98, 99, 104, 172; considered for mayor of Paris, 153–4; on constitutional committee, 132, 257
Terray, Jean-Marie, abbé, finance minister (1769–74), 39, 144
Thouret, Jacques-Guillaume, deputy, 153, 154, 215, 290; links with ministers, 206–7, 211, 215–17; on constitutional committee, Barnave's main ally in Revision, 222–3, 246, 257, 258, 260–3, 268
Tocqueville, Alexis de, 4, 38, 56, 224
Tourzel, Louise-Elizabeth, duchesse de, *Gouvernante des Enfants de France*, and flight to Varennes, 235–6

Vadier, Marc-Guillaume Alexis, deputy, 260
Vergennes, Charles Gravier, comte de, foreign secretary (1774–87), 244
Vergniaud, Pierre-Victornien, deputy, 282, 306, 312, 314
Véri, Joseph Alphonse, abbé de, diarist, 92
Victoire, Madame, daughter of Louis XV, 209
Vidaud de la Tour, Jean-Jacques de, premier président of Parlement of Grenoble, 88; *conseiller d'état,* and Séance royale, 101
Virieu, François-Henri, comte, deputy, 52, 141
Voltaire, François Marie Arouet de, 34, 36, 333

Washington, George, 278